MISSION ACCOMPLISHED
on Founding Constitutional Adjudication in Central Europe

MISSION ACCOMPLISHED

on Founding Constitutional Adjudication in Central Europe

by

RADOSLAV PROCHÁZKA

CEU PRESS

Central European University Press
Budapest New York

Published in 2002 by
Central European University Press

An imprint of the
Central European University Share Company
Nádor utca 11, H-1015 Budapest, Hungary
Tel: +36-1-327-3138 or 327-3000
Fax: +36-1-327-3183
E-mail: ceupress@ceu.hu
Website: www.ceupress.com

400 West 59th Street, New York NY 10019, USA
Tel: +1-212-547-6932
Fax: +1-212-548-4607
E-mail: mgreenwald@sorosny.org

ISBN 963 9241 51 2 cloth

Library of Congress Cataloging-in-Publication Data

Procházka, Radoslav.
MISSION ACCOMPLISHED: on Founding Constitutional Adjudication in Central Europe/by Radoslav Procházka.
p. cm.
Includes bibliographical references and index.
ISBN
1. Constitutional courts--Europe, Eastern. 2. Constitutional law--Europe, Eastern. 3. Judicial review--Europe, Eastern. 4. Political questions and judicial power--Europe, Eastern. 5. Post-communism--Europe, Eastern. I. Title.
KJC5456. P76 2002
347.47´012//dc21

2002007930
Printed in Hungary by Akaprint

To my parents,
Daniela Procházková and Rudolf Procházka

CONTENTS

PREFACE

This book offers a description of the establishment and the formative years of constitutional adjudication in Poland, Hungary, the Czech Republic, and Slovakia, the core countries of what is commonly denoted as Central Europe or, more specifically, the Visegrád Four. It attempts to explain the rise and functioning of the Central European constitutional judiciary by identifying factors of decisive relevance to both the similarities and the country-specifics emerging within the given geopolitical space—factors having to do with the respective polities' legal, political, cultural, social psychological, and institutional development. I therefore discuss transitional constitutional adjudication within a broader, and a more loose, framework than comparative constitutional law, approaching the practice of constitutional review in ways that also relate to the fields of comparative political science, legal history, and sociology of law, without, however, aspiring to offer on the basis of such disciplines an exhaustive account of the region's recent developments.

The book provides a relatively comprehensive account of both the role that constitutional adjudication played in founding the respective regimes as *Rechtsstaat* democracies and the more general context of transitional Central European constitutional politics. The findings presented herein thus may be of use both to students of comparative constitutional law and to students of democratic transitions, especially those with an interest in what role law in general, and constitutional adjudication in particular, can play in shaping transition scenarios and agendas. A few important provisos are warranted, however. First, I do not engage in transitology, that is, I do not discuss the region's post-1989 transformation in much detail. The emphasis lies on phenomena that I find relevant to the establishment and the conceptualisation of constitutional adjudication. Secondly, I do not pretend to have accounted for all the aspects of the respective constitutional courts' jurisprudence, and focus on those that have in one way or another proved relevant to the shape and the nature of the emergent *Rechtsstaat* regimes. Again, this is a book that aims 'only' at shedding light on the region's place in the wider European constitutional space, and thus analyses, and suggests which of the various endogenous and exogenous environments impacting the polities' development have facilitated and may in the future continue to facilitate their becoming full members of Community Europe.

The review offered is up to date on case law (published either in print or on the respective courts' official websites) as of autumn/winter 2001, my take on the Polish and the Hungarian constitutional jurisprudence being slightly less fresh than that on the Czech and Slovak courts. All translations from Czech, French, German, Polish, and Slovak are mine, unless otherwise noted.

The book draws on research I conducted as a doctoral candidate at the Yale Law School in 1999-2001. I would like to thank the Yale Law School Administration, and the many people who have acted on its behalf, for the financial and other support which has made my research possible. I would also like to thank Judge Guido Calabresi and Professors Mirjan Damaška and Paul Kahn for their availability and academic assistance throughout my stay at Yale. The support I received from Chief Justice Ján Mazák and Justice Daniel Šváby of the Slovak Constitutional Court was generous, and vital to my completing the book.

I am indebted to Kirsten Edwards, Alexander Patsaouras, and Ralf Sauer for their struggling through earlier versions of my manuscript to offer valuable comments. I cannot overestimate Professor Bruce Ackerman's contribution to this book. His readiness to devote time and effort both to suggest improvements to the manuscript and to offer encouragement proved crucial to my ability to complete this project and was a form of academic collegiality that I do not dare to hope to come across in the future. Needless to say, all flaws in this book are mine and mine only.

Finally, I will remain forever indebted to my parents without whose support in all ways imaginable neither this book nor anything else on my part would ever have come about.

LIST OF ABBREVIATIONS

AFD	Alliance of Free Democrats (Hungary)
CACC	Czech Act on the Constitutional Court
CCC	Czech Constitutional Court
CSAC	Czechoslovak Supreme Administrative Court of 1918
CSCC	Czecho-Slovak Constitutional Court of 1991-92
DU	Democratic Union (Slovakia)
ECHR	European Court of Human Rights
ECHRFF	1950 Convention on the Protection of Human Rights and Fundamental Freedoms
EKA	Opposition Round Table (Hungary)
EU	European Union
FIDESZ	Association of Young Democrats (Hungary)
HACC	Hungarian Act on the Constitutional Court
HCC	Hungarian Constitutional Court
HDF	Hungarian Democratic Forum
IC	Imperial Court of Austria of 1867
ICCESR	International Covenant on Cultural, Economic, and Social Rights
ICCPR	International Covenant on Civic and Political Rights
ILO	International Labour Organisation
MDS	Movement for Democratic Slovakia
NATO	North Atlantic Treaty Organisation
OECD	Organisation for Economic Cooperation and Development
OSN	Orzecznictwo Sadu Najwyszego (Jurisprudence of the Polish Supreme Court)
OTK	Orzecznictwo Trybunalu Konstytucyjnego (Jurisprudence of the Polish Constitutional Tribunal)

PACT	Polish Act on the Constitutional Tribunal of 1997
PCT	Polish Constitutional Tribunal
PCTA	Polish Constitutional Tribunal Act of 1985
PSAC	Polish Supreme Administrative Court
PSC	Polish Supreme Court
RT	Round Table
SAC	Supreme Administrative Court of Poland
SACC	Slovak Act on the Constitutional Court
SCC	Slovak Constitutional Court
V4	Visegrád Four

LIST OF TABLES

LIST OF FIGURES

INTRODUCTION

Constitutional review is one of the defining features of the Central European post-revolutionary institutional and political environment,[1] and is as vivid a part of the region's legal topography as it is of that of Germany, Spain, or Italy. After only a decade, the Central European constitutional courts more or less equal their counterparts elsewhere in the Western world in terms of political relevance, jurisprudential sophistication, and interpretive creativity. My book describes how this has happened and explains why.

CONCEPT

I describe the rise and functioning of constitutional review in Central Europe as a helix at the beginning of which exigencies of the region's return to Europe combined with the need to establish governments responsive to both legitimacy- and efficiency considerations.[2] The indigenous legal psyches thereby became exposed to, and were consequently conditioned by, phenomena emanating from the context of post-revolutionary transition. Then followed the country-specific elaboration of the general institutional choices, reflecting the logic of the respective polities' legal, social-psychological, and institutional development. This process resulted in specific institutional designs combining the countries' traditional political economies with their transition-informed updates. The designs and the texts that this logic produced translated into constitutional jurisprudence, subject to acculturation by the traditional local codes of institutional behaviour.

My theme is not completely alien to an English-speaking audience. Scholarly analyses of the different aspects of the respective constitutional courts' jurisprudence, especially those of Poland and Hungary, have appeared in American and Western European law journals on a fairly regular basis. A few books have also been published recently.[3] My book, however, aspires to a more comprehensive framework.

First, it is comparative in method. It points out and explains differences and similarities in how different countries have responded to the same questions; how governments were to be fashioned, how constitutional review was to be conceptualised, what role jurisprudence was to play in social development, and to what extent law should frame solutions to transition-related moral dilemmas. In this respect, my review is different from the accounts of Brzezinski, Garlicki and Brunner, and Sólyom and Brunner. Brzezinski's book is an excellent, comprehensive source on Poland's constitutional development, but does not—and does not purport to—address the question of how this development is related to that of the region as a whole. Sólyom's and Brunner's book is narrower in approach, offering an introduction to the world of Hungarian constitutional justice. It discusses in detail the operational features of the Hungarian Constitutional Court (HCC) and provides valuable insights into its case law, but it is not concerned with anything beyond that. The book by Brunner and Garlicki on the Polish Constitutional Tribunal (PCT) employs the same approach and has the same strengths and limitations. In addition, a parallel book on the Czech Constitutional Court (CCC) was published very recently.[4] The overview it offers is both extensive and well structured, although it shares the basic methodological coordinates of its Polish and Hungarian predecessors. The Slovak contribution offers a complex review of both the constitutional and the statutory regulation of the Slovak Constitutional Court (SCC), but the analysis of the jurisprudence it provides is limited, even sketchy.

Secondly, I am as concerned with historical and cultural factors as I am with political, institutional, and textual ones. My discussion of the respective courts' emergence and operation takes into account the long-entrenched social mores and codes of judicial behaviour, in addition to more immediately accessible, more contemporary, and more exogenous factors. In this and other respects my work is different from Professor Schwartz's analysis.

I exclude from my scrutiny some of the courts that Schwartz does include, and include one—a very important one, I believe—that he omits, namely the Czech Constitutional Court. I am thus concerned only with the constitutional courts of Poland, Hungary, the Czech Republic, and Slovakia. I have three reasons for this approach: (i) the Visegrád courts are at the forefront of constitutional development in the region and their jurisprudential achievements bear comparison with those of the more prominent Western European constitutional courts;[5] (ii) there is a place on Europe's spiritual (as well as political) map called Central Europe, which has for me and many others come to be embodied by the Visegrád Four (V4).

It would be wrong to press the claims of the region's exceptionality too far, but I do assert the uniqueness and the autonomy of the cultural, social-psychological, and intellectual experience of the Visegrád nations;[6] and (iii) the Visegrád Four as a distinct geopolitical entity has recently witnessed a strong revival.[7] The surge in intra-regional cooperation in economic, diplomatic, cultural, and other areas makes the Visegrád's alleged clinical death an unfortunate *intermezzo* in the collective emancipation of Europe's semi-periphery. If things go well, the region is bound to become as relevant to the face and the psyche of the European Union as the Benelux countries and Scandinavia.

I also draw from those local sources of legal and political commentary that are considerably less enthusiastic than me or Schwartz's local sources about what has happened in the realm of constitutional law in Central Europe in the past decade. Most importantly, I understand the region's transitional constitutional jurisprudence not as a struggle for some pure form of constitutional justice, but rather as a struggle for a particular path of social and legal development within which the constitutional judiciary has often proved as ideologically coloured and manipulative as the respective legislatures and administrations. I explain both the courts' establishment and their jurisprudence as a function of a series of contexts: historical, cultural, socio-psychological, political, and institutional. In my account, the scenarios that these multi-faceted environments produced did not involve a party that struggled for constitutional justice against another party that kept obstructing it. I portray the events that have constituted and affected the founding as a process in which the polities' social-psychological undercurrents were exposed to, and became conditioned by, the challenges of modern-day political development and then were translated into policy outcomes and legal and social practices. I take the constitutional judiciary to have been as much a captive of this process as any other institution engaged in the mission of founding.

I do not aim to deal with every aspect of the respective courts' jurisprudence or to praise the courts for their various achievements. I will leave a significant portion of the courts' jurisprudence unattended, either because it only reaffirms tendencies that I will point out, or because it deals with the most ordinary and universally uncontested aspects of constitutional adjudication, or because it is unrelated to my core arguments. Instead of providing an in-a-nutshell account of case law, I will point out those features of constitutional review that are illustrative of the courts' interpretive approaches and offer an insight into the extent and the nature of the justices' self-understanding as founders. The ensuing review thus attempts to find a middle ground between a detailed analysis of all the particular issues of constitutional adjudication and a more superficial approach limiting itself to taking note of the milestone decisions of the respective courts. Similarly, instances in which the respective courts' case law echoes—directly or less so, explicitly or not—the jurisprudence of their more seasoned Western counterparts, especially the German one, are pointed out only when relevant either to the very nature of the given interpretive technique or to some other key argument pursued.

STRUCTURE

The strategies and processes of societal redefinition and their effect on institutional design in transitional Central Europe are examined in the first chapter. The ambition is not to engage in a comprehensive interpretation of the transition, as various insightful and competent accounts have been offered in the past decade,[8] and many will certainly follow. The aim is to illustrate the decisive impact of 'the end of history' in the late 1980s on the path of institutional reform. I argue that the well-tested concept of liberal-democratic government, the prospect of European integration, and the effect of informational and reputational cascades[9] led the new Central European regimes unequivocally to adhere to the notion of a government rooted in popular sovereignty, implementing a free-market economy, and offering its citizens institutional protection of their rights.

In Chapter Two, country-specific versions of legal culture,[10] transitional political economy,[11] and the distribution of transitional leadership roles are explored to account for the different designs, functions, and powers of the respective courts. I argue that the conceptualisation of constitutional review was inextricably bound to both historical and contemporary features of the development and consolidation of authority in the realm of public governance. In other words, indigenous legal traditions, and the way they translated into the countries' political economies, shaped the respective constitutional courts. True, the historically documented undertakings of the Visegrád polities lack an over-arching set of traits that could account for the contemporary reality of constitutional review. The patterns of inter-subjective as well as institutional interaction emerge and then fade away, many without leaving an imprint on a nation's soul. But many stay, subject to gradual deepening, conditioning, and modification. Those that did stay affected the conceptualisation of constitutional review. It was by the intermingling of the general constraints and the country-specific ones, by the delicate colloquy between local constitutional traditions and the challenges of global development that these courts came to be fashioned as well as to operate quite differently from each other.

The variations in the communal understanding of how public authority in general and justice in particular should be administered and how law should be made, structured, approached, implemented, and understood translated into corresponding differences in the conceptualisation of constitutional review. When the social, cultural, and political legacies combined with the demands of systemic transformation and the attendant 'Euro-conformity urge', the varying modes of constitutional review in Central Europe emerged not as mere historical contingencies but rather as stages of organic evolution. Many of the fits and starts that helped the evolution of constitutional review in Central Europe might have been accidental. This is, after all, the tone of any institutional development. More importantly, the ways in which the respective courts were fashioned and have come to operate largely corresponded both to the logic of their communities' legal development and to the expectations that these courts have come to internalise as guideposts for their activity.

In Poland, for instance, the tradition of oscillating between an authoritative leader at the helm of the executive branch and a powerful but inefficient legislature, and the emergence of a similar conflict in the wake of the change of regime, served both to marginalise the Constitutional Tribunal in the interim institutional reform and to conceptualise it as an assistant to, rather than a supervisor of, the legislature. The Hungarian tradition of the judiciary's active participation in policy making and the local obsession with being at the forefront of progressive tendencies in the realm of constitutionalism proved conducive to providing the Constitutional Court with adjudicative equipment with extremely broad scope. The vivid presence of the Kelsenian version of constitutional review in the Czechs' and Slovaks' legal consciousness allowed their drafters to draw from available local experience and subscribe to the continental standard of constitutional review. Even though the immediate political environment in Czechoslovakia's successor states was unfavourable to building an overly powerful constitutional judiciary, the gravitational pull of tradition—which included a long chain of institutions akin to constitutional adjudication—was potent enough to impact post-revolutionary institutional reform.

The basic formula that I employ in accounting for the emergence of constitutional review will also serve to explain its operation. By this formula I mean the institutional designers' self-conscious exposure to exogenous constraints and the subsequent conditioning of the exogenous factors by an 'inner universe' of cognitions and layers of self-understanding rooted in the indigenous legal consciousness. Accordingly, in discussing in the third chapter the effect on jurisprudence of the differences in the conceptualisation of the Visegrád courts' authority I argue that this effect has been modified by the specifics of the political environment and the local legal culture, which gave rise to variations in the justices' self-understanding as constitutional adjudicators and as agents of social change. Similarly, in discussing in the fourth chapter the courts' interpretive approaches, I locate the decisive factor in the extent and the authority of the respective constitutional texts, but simultaneously point out the impact of the legal, political, and moral philosophies of the justices.

The country-specific combination of these factors translated into a variety of jurisprudential concepts, adjudicative approaches, and interpretive techniques, and into significant differences in the courts' handling of two major transitional dilemmas common to the region as a whole. Both of these dilemmas stemmed from the tension between a legitimate and an efficient pursuit of the transitional policy agenda. Perfect legitimacy and unconstrained efficiency were the transitional Scylla and Charybdis, the points between which the courts—and the governments themselves—were to operate, and between which a middle ground was to be found. The first dilemma reflected the courts' awareness of the need to instil legitimacy into the emergent regimes by grounding them firmly in Western standards of democratic participation and protection of rights, and their simultaneous awareness of the need for urgent and efficient implementation of transformation policies. The different ways in which the respective courts dealt with this dilemma translated into a dichotomy of permissive/prohibitive modes of constitutional adjudication. Where the political economy emphasised the efficiency element of the transitional equation, the respective courts proved ready to exhibit a particular kind of self-restraint, one that they would most often justify as reflecting so-called transitional peculiarities. Where the constitutional courts deemed the transitional equation to be lacking in legitimacy, constitutional review proved more prohibitive to unrestrained pursuit of legislative agendas.

The second dilemma stemmed from the tension between the exigencies of incomplete constitutional reform and the courts' limited authority. The different ways of dealing with this tension translated into a dichotomy of constructivist/preservationist modes of constitutional interpretation. Here, the effect on judicial activism of the preference for legitimacy/efficiency was the opposite. Where the foundational arrangements were provisional and required extensive elaboration and specification, the courts proved ready to disregard constraints attendant on their authority as negative legislators. Where the relevant texts were deemed to provide a sufficient guideline, the courts were less willing to create rules of law in addition to, or even in spite of, the available texts.

Thus two dividing lines emerge within Visegrád constitutional jurisprudence, each giving rise to two relatively distinct groups. The first dividing line has to do with a constitutional court's tendency to adhere to, or oppose, the legislature's policy choices, mostly but not only with respect to transitional agendas. For different reasons and in different fashions the Hungarian and Slovak constitutional courts appear to have been more willing in the past decade to challenge the substantive policy dossier of their respective parliaments than the Polish and Czech constitutional courts. This particular dichotomy does not concern indicators such as the overall number of statutes held to be unconstitutional. These numbers do not capture the essence of the different adjudicative agendas—either that of assisting the implementation of key legislative policies or that of obstructing them. Indeed, while the PCT is a more active constitutional court than the Slovak one, it identified to a greater extent with the transformation enterprise of the Parliament than did the latter court, not least because it did not have to confront as ruthless a parliamentary majority as the SCC did. Similarly, there is no way of putting the SCC on a par with the HCC in terms of judicial activism. Yet even though they vary in their degree of assertiveness, it is the SCC and the Hungarian Court that have, within the framework of negative legislation, proved to be more of a counter-majoritarian force than have the Polish and Czech courts. But while the PCT and the CCC have in general subscribed to the ideologies fostered by post-revolutionary leaders, they have been more active than the HCC and the Slovak Court in communicating with, and imposing their notions of constitutionalism upon, the ordinary courts. Again, this has nothing to do with the absolute number of judicial decisions invalidated by means of constitutional review. After all, the PCT has no such competence. The difference lies in the attitude of the court. The Slovak Court had at its disposal more comprehensive instruments for policing the ordinary courts but it regularly declined to employ them. The Polish Tribunal lacked concrete review equipment but was creative in trying to find ways of getting its message across to the ordinary courts.

The other dividing line concerns the provisionality of foundational texts. The HCC and the PCT reached outside the patchwork of constitutional amendments with such vigour and confidence that the respective texts appeared as mere orientational guidelines rather than strict imperatives. The CCC and the SCC were more or less happy working with what was available *expressis verbis*. True, the Czech Court launched its interpretive enterprise by attributing a very specific and very rich value content to the text of the constitution, and appears to feel bound more by the text's purpose than its letter. But when it has preferred teleological or functional interpretation to a literalist one it has usually done so in order to preserve the constitutional or legislative solution rather than either provide for a missing rule, as the PCT would do, or substitute the existing one with its own, as at times the HCC would do.

The differences in the courts' handling of the two dilemmas were not accidental. They reflected the diversity of traditions, political realities, adjudicative powers, and texts upon which the Central European constitutional courts were to work. Indeed, factors affecting constitutional adjudication in Central Europe are multi-faceted and, as John Stuart Mill might have put it, inextricably interwoven with one another. The jurisprudence of the respective courts proved to be a function of variables as contingent, intangible, resistant to unambiguous classification, and difficult to assess as was the multi-layered logic of consequentiality affecting the very emergence of constitutional adjudication. In order to give the discussion an intelligible structure whilst preventing a simplification that would blur the relevant differences, I identify four principal factors as having affected that part of the founding that the constitutional courts were to service.

The first factor I denote as 'design'. It comprises the structure and the extent of a court's adjudicative authority and is concerned with the effect on jurisprudence of both the framework within which constitutional adjudication was to operate and the inter-institutional colloquy that that framework facilitated. The second factor is denoted as 'text' and relates to the courts' approaches to, and their handling of, textual materials available for interpretation. The vertical axis based on the text-related features of the environment illustrates the nature of judicial activism and gives rise to the continuum of constructivist/preservationist attitudes. The horizontal axis based on the design-related features of the environment reflects the subtleties of interaction between the different government authorities in their quest for transitional leadership. It illustrates the degree of judicial activism and as a reflection of the level of the courts' confidence in advancing their own jurisprudential agendas gives rise to the continuum of permissive/prohibitive attitudes (Figure 1).

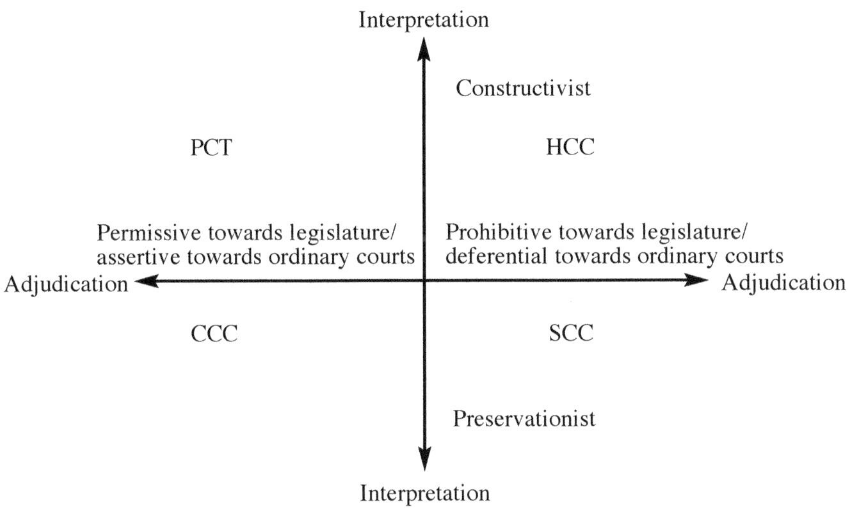

Figure 1. Patterns of constitutional adjudication/interpretation

The amorphous shape of the four boxes emerging upon the above axes acquires more precise contours only after the specifics of political environment and legal culture are accounted for. These are the vectors that mostly have to do with the courts' self-conceptualisation as institutions and as agents of social change. They reflect not only the courts' awareness of transitional exigencies but also the extent to which they internalised, or were trying to surpass, the legacies of local legal-historical development.

The pool of factors by means of which we can account for the relevant differences in the courts' case law thus includes the institutional framework within which constitutional adjudication was to operate, the texts made available for constitutional interpretation, the specifics of political environment, and the courts' 'DNA' informed by decades—or rather centuries—of local legal development. The varying intensity and quality of judicial activism demonstrates the interdependence of these basic variables. The instruments used by the respective courts to assert both themselves and that which they believed was necessary for the successful establishment of the *nouveau regime* were significantly affected by the courts' black-letter-law authority and the texts they were to elaborate upon. Factors transcending both the design and the text, however, proved equally important. The one lesson that constitutional review in transitional Central Europe offers in unequivocal terms is that inter-institutional colloquy not only is affected by the framework within which it takes place, but also reciprocally models this framework so that it accommodates the subtleties and the contingencies of this colloquy as they become relevant. These cognitions, beliefs, intuitions, behavioural patterns, and all that constitutes one's consciousness as an institutional agent are unaccounted for by law, but are as capable of reducing the impact on institutional and social development of design- and text-related features of the given environment as they are of enhancing it. The decade of transitional constitutional adjudication in Central Europe reaffirmed the notion that not only those who make it, but also those who implement it tend to harness law to particular social and political agendas. In other words, the normative significance of law is subject to, and a function of, the peculiarities of interaction between the institutions that make, implement, and interpret it. Of course, this is not a novel claim, but the performance of Central European constitutional review has more often vindicated its validity than one might expect.

PART I

CHAPTER 1

ESTABLISHING CONSTITUTIONAL REVIEW

In this chapter, I discuss in ascending order of specificity the circumstances relevant to the region's extrication from communism and examine their impact on post-revolutionary institutional design making in general, and the incorporation of constitutional review in particular. At the bottom of the pyramid lies the Euro-Atlantic concept of state and law, based on universal political enfranchisement and the inviolability of individual rights. The next layer is associated with the prospects of membership of the European Union (EU), requiring a more specific elaboration of institutional choices rooted in the above Western paradigm. I then focus on the striving for regional prominence among the Visegrád countries, which led the new establishments to adhere to concepts capable of enhancing their integrative ambitions (Figure 2). Constitutional review was deemed one such concept. Its emergence throughout the region reflected the spirit of the times and the bandwagon effect of institutional reform in the post-communist world, and to some extent was a function of the insurgents' desire to document by means of institutional similarity the 'European' pedigree of their public governance models. Indeed, the closer one moves from the basic paradigm of liberal democracy to the regional competition for foreign political recognition, the more prescriptive become the connotations attributed by constitutional designers to the exigencies of an integration-friendly reform, and the more favourable to the inclusion of constitutional review.

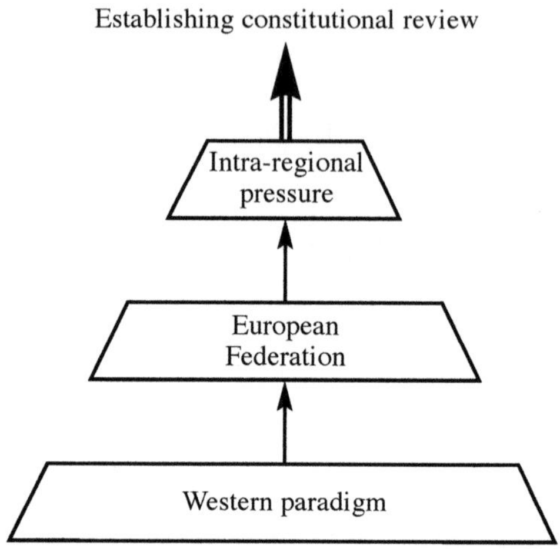

Figure 2. Establishing constitutional review in Central Europe

FRAMEWORK

Mircea Eliade, in his work on the history of religious ideas, locates the origins of religion in the moment of the Palaeolithic person's rise to stand upon two legs.[1] It was at the moment of substituting the previous exclusively horizontal experience with a multi-dimensional one that the need for both reflection and explanation of the surrounding world emerged in the minds of ancient people. Space was to be structured along axes of cognition that were not epistemologically relevant before the erection was complete. Eliade denotes this process of identifying a focal point of self-definition as *'orientatio'*.[2]

The post-communist transformation was in many ways similar. The region's citizenry did not have immediate experience with any societal arrangement other than a totalitarian/authoritarian regime,[3] preceded by a short period of relative freedom after the end of the Second World War and briefly interrupted by a few failed attempts at resurrecting that freedom. The experiential *instrumentarium* acquired during the strictly organized life in the past was inadequate for the challenges posed by the new era. The values perceived as perpetual were officially declared obsolete. The chains were lost but so was the comforting (or *dis*comforting, for the very few) predictability of one's place in society, one's life as a social being. This was a time of profound confusion, in both personal and collective terms. An immediate location of a reference point for the *orientatio* process became a question of survival.

None of the region's polities was a *tabula rasa,* however. A host of familiar candidates for the new religion submitted their offers immediately after the tender was announced. There were the gods of the pre-Soviet era, some of them 200 years old. The younger ghosts of the brighter moments of the socialist experiment were waiting for a second chance. The unholy warriors of the Second World War puppet regimes were declared by some to be saints. Even the bearded archdukes of blasphemy were roaming above the site of the temple as shamelessly as before.

The non-virgin citizen formerly known as *Homo sovieticus* thus had more cognitive luggage to carry than the open sky above and the emerging sense of 'standing upright' within. Related to the humiliating fact of life-long subordination were inferiority complexes that just would not go away. And then there was the catchall exculpation device for all sins—we the people of Central Europe were robbed of our inner worth by the big players around us and it has always been so. The evil was forcibly imported. The idols to which we bowed for four decades were alien.[4] An emphasis on restoring the age of innocence was naturally the card to be played. As the former Hungarian President Árpád Göncz once put it, we wished to make the past a future. The theme of transition has become one of return-return to Europe. The golden calf was to be renounced and replaced by the one true god we used to worship before, namely democracy.

But to which past and to which Europe were we to return? To the mythical 1791 Constitution of Poland, which failed to save Poles from themselves? Or rather to the Pilsudski era?[5] To post-Trianon Europe, which saw Hungary lose one-third of its historical lands? To the party democracy of Czechoslovakia with its imperative parliamentary mandate and, to put it mildly, failed minority policies? To the Slovak puppet regime sponsored by Germany during the Second World War? The pre-communist period either was tainted by its own inherent deficiencies and thus was not really 'European', as was the case to a great extent with Hungary and also post-1926 Poland, or, as in the case of Czechoslovakia (dubbed the only democracy east of the Rhine in the 1930s), became obsolete. The golden eras were too distant to serve as real guides and were golden only when seen from a distance of decades or even centuries. This lack of reliable experience prevented introspection from becoming the main orientating technique and induced the returnees to opt for a future that 'was not based on a model drawn from the past, nor conceived as a locally-born program. The design of the future was imported.'[6]

On this very note, Whitehead argues that in Central Europe, '"democratisation" has acquired unusually prescriptive connotations... incubated in Eastern Europe by forty years of bitter experience'.[7] The following sections explore the nature of these connotations. Before discussing in Chapter Two the country-specific factors, I will now attend to three levels of constraint common to the entire region: (i) constraints emanating from adherence to the Western paradigm, (ii) those related to the prospects of membership of a European federation, and (iii) those stemming from the region's quest for political recognition.

TRANSITIONAL CONNOTATIONS

Western Paradigm

In 1989 history ended. And it ended by proving the model of liberal democracy to be worthier than any other. It was partly the self-congratulatory demeanour of the Cold War victors,[8] but mostly the self-imposed perception of the transition agents as to what was right and what was wrong that left virtually no room for any other ideological inclination on the part of the returnees than that towards the West.[9] For the Central European followers of Fukuyama, 'right' has come to mean a free-market economy, democratic government, and geo-political alliance with the North Atlantic community; 'wrong' was more or less everything apart from that.

Anything but a close following of the Western paradigm was destined to fail also because of the region's devastating experience with experiments. Throughout its history, *Zwischeneuropa* has been a laboratory for testing out social and political theories. But Central Europeans have grown sick and tired of their 'extremely concentrated history',[10] and their fatigue worked in favour of the one model that did not need much testing upon import. Moreover, the loss of a predictable environment required that the *orientatio* process accelerates—this served to narrow the scope of choices acceptable for deliberation, so as not to delay accommodation to the new framework.

The institutional ramifications of the region's adherence to the Western paradigm, however, were limited to the minimum concept of democracy, which includes political competition, political participation, and a set of basic rights.[11] This or other versions[12] of the democratic minimum did not prescribe a single specific institutional design, and the prescriptive connotations concerned 'functions rather than specific institutional implementations of functions'.[13]

After all, the West itself offered too many varying and at times contradictory examples of societal organization to operate as a model to be bought wholesale. True, it gave the newcomers three rules to operate their polities by: (i) rule by the people instead of rule by the working class, (ii) the rule of law instead of rule by the Party, and (iii) the rule of supply and demand instead of the command of a central planning committee. But when looking for a context conducive to the enormous growth of constitutional review in Central Europe, we have to break down the Western paradigm a bit further, for it includes Westminster in addition to Karlsruhe.

European Federation

It was on the European level that the quest for particular constitutional arrangements became truly constrained. This was so because of the historical affiliation between the Central European and the continental constitutional traditions,[14] the active engagement of the European Communities (EC)[15] in the new democracies' development, and the logic of geographical proximity. What deserves special attention, however, is what Ackerman denotes as the 'dynamics of prospective federation',[16] precluding the new political elites from ignoring the effect their choices might have on the prospects of a country's integration in the EU. Ackerman discusses these dynamics mostly with respect to judicial review. The EU membership perspective, however, impacted also the process of constitution making as a whole. In fact, it became the principal legitimising feature of political action as such.

Shortly after the liberation, things looked less clear than they were later to become. In the initial euphoria, fed by the Western acknowledgment of the moral credit of the dissidents-become-presidents, the insurgent leaders might have believed that this was the time to join forces in the building of a new world order; that a pan-European *civitas* could emerge from the ashes of the burnt-down Yalta cage. The idea of a mutual convergence of the two parts of Europe which one could detect in Havel's proposal to substitute NATO with a new all-European defence and security mechanism or in his and Hungarian ex-President Göncz's recurring appeals for gradual humanization, by means of intellectual and ethical endeavours, of the technocratic 'Brusselian' mode of politics,[17] soon proved illusory and void of any political viability.

Victors are unlikely to make concessions. If political establishments act rationally and instrumentally, it is difficult to conceive of any incentives that the EC/EU might have had for a large-scale institutional reform of Eastern inspiration. In fact, the internal reform of the Community, taking place more or less simultaneously with Central Europe's transition, served to delay rather than to bring about a more complex and more immediate interaction between the two parts of the continent. If the EU wanted to get involved with Central and Eastern Europe at all, it was rational for it to export its model, not to expose it to any tampering—in other words, to expand eastwards rather than to merge with the East.

Accordingly, Visegrád's return to Europe was the return of the prodigal son. The European governments set forth certain yardstick-criteria against which any relevant progress was to be measured: 'identification marks' for all those that wished to be deemed 'European'. Simply, 'Europe expect[ed], and... certainly demand[ed], a definite minimum commitment to such democratic requirements'.[18] The returnees' policies and institutions were not to inform any reform of the EC/EU but were to be adjusted to its policies and institutions as well as to those of the member states. After all, setting the integration agenda as one of assimilation rather than convergence was a ritualistic finale to the inter-systemic conflict in which the West doubtlessly emerged as victorious.[19]

The choice as then perceived in Central Europe was either to buy the ready-made stock or to be denied access to the store, possibly forever. Even more so, substantial credit was to be extended to those who would not hesitate to sign up for an exclusivity arrangement with the store itself. The Community mastered the necessary political and economic resources for the reconstruction of Europe while the returnees lacked both the confidence and the willingness to compete with the West, be it in the realm of foundational values and norms or their institutional implementation.

The Euro-constraints also were rapidly institutionalised. Czechoslovakia, Hungary, and Poland signed their agreements on association with the EC and the member states (the so-called European Agreements) in December 1991. Shortly after the division of their country, the Czechs and the Slovaks signed new agreements in 1993.[20] The main purpose of the European Agreements was to establish a legal ground for the candidates' future accession to the EU by making sure that their legal and economic orders became compatible with those of the member states. It was with these agreements in mind that a Polish author remarked that the inclusion of European standards 'in domestic law [was] the Polish constitutional legislator's duty and not an option to be accepted at his own discretion'.[21]

However, this is not to argue that the European powers have imposed their own normative ideals. The returnees' new establishments themselves exhibited a strong urge to conform to 'normality' and came to see the path of assimilation as completely logical. In reaction to a dramatic reconfiguration of political and economic power on a continent-wide scale, an integration as rapid and complete as possible became the order of the day for each of the Cold War losers positioned in the orbit of Western influence. The need for European backing became especially acute in the fearsome days following the unsuccessful *coup d'état* in the USSR in 1991.[22] The integration tendency also reflected deeper currents of the collective psyche of the Central European polities—it is in the inner logic of small nations to strive only for so much autonomy as can be guaranteed by a powerful ally.[23] There is a deeply rooted—and very natural—need to have a tutor in a region where neighbours have been at each other's throats for centuries, and where national freedom is but a correlate of (inter)national security.

The institutional similarity, being at once the necessary precondition for Central Europe's settling in the continent politically and the effect of the dynamics of prospective federation, seemed able to kill two birds with one stone: on the one hand, it served to support the integrative ambitions of the returnees towards Western Europe; on the other, the success story of the West was sold to ordinary folk at home in order to legitimise the new path of social development.[24] In the end, not only was adherence to the 'European' criteria warranted by the transition agents' instrumental considerations; it also proved attractive to, and was supported by, the Central European citizenry as the proper *orientatio* strategy.[25]

The institutional dynamics of the European perspective thus supplemented the minimal concept of democracy with more particular arrangements. Schmitter introduces the notion of 'a partial regime', which is but a component of democracy, is assigned specific tasks, and operates within a hierarchical structure composed of other partial regimes.[26] Although not fully corresponding to the notion of a partial regime as Schmitter understands it, these specific arrangements included, inter alia, the office of ombudsman or concentrated constitutional review, phenomena of an exclusively European origin. Naturally, these were not the only areas in which Western Europe affirmed its historically proven ability to penetrate the Central European region with its concepts and institutions. There was more to the continental legacy and some of it will surface in the country-specific discussion. Here it suffices to note that as much as the Western paradigm served to constrain the general political and economic orientation of Central Europe, the prospect of membership of the European federation proved capable of inducing the compatibility of the returnees with the EC/EU member states on the level of constitutional particularities. In other words, on the axis of institutional evolution the move from the Western paradigm to the perspective of European Federation was a move from liberal democracy to its more particular version, a *Rechtsstaat.*

Intra-Regional Pressure

The Euro-Atlantic governance paradigms affected the deliberative enterprise of the Visegrád polities through both informational and reputational cascades. While the informational cascades have to do mostly with the norm transmission facilitated predominantly by the Helsinki Accords, the reputational cascades concern the competition among the Visegrád countries for recognition by Western Europe and the attendant rhetorical entrapment of major transition agencies.

Norm transmission. The rise of constitutional jurisdiction in the second half of the twentieth century, especially the telling examples of Germany and Italy in the aftermath of the Second World War or Spain in the 1970s, indicates that it became a device intended to demonstrate a democratic transition, if not an almost automatic reaction to the fall of an authoritarian/totalitarian regime. Cappelletti, for instance, suggested with great foresight in 1985,

> it seems as though no country in Europe, emerging from some form of undemocratic regime or serious domestic strife, could find a better answer to the exigency of reacting against, and possibly preventing the return of, past evils, than to introduce constitutional justice into its new system of government.[27]

Zupančič elaborated on the theme after the wave of liberal revolutions in 1989, arguing that constitutional review might be warranted as an anti-totalitarian device, especially in countries lacking a democratic tradition.[28] One way or the other, with growing emphasis on the protection of personal and/or collective rights and liberties, often at the expense of the principle of national sovereignty, the late twentieth century indeed proved a fertile soil for balancing the relationship between regulatory power and its addressee in favour of the latter.

But the *Zeitgeist* factor has more to it, and to interpret the emergence of constitutional review as the ultimate anti-totalitarian device would be simplistic. The efforts to incorporate human rights into constitutional texts were already widely spread in the inter-war period, and what the success of their insulation from majoritarian assaults in the last few decades mostly reflects is the growing importance of the transnationalisation of law. The available evidence includes the proliferation of international and transnational organizations—many of them of a judicial or quasi-judicial nature—aimed at providing safeguards for personal as well as collective safety, in addition to the safeguards provided by national governments, including those offered by constitutional courts. The transnational remedy-providers, after all, tend to correct failures and omissions of not only legislative and executive bodies, but also of judicial bodies of national pedigree.[29] In the realm of constitutional politics, the story of the second half of the twentieth century—particularly, but not only, in Europe—is as much a story of a transnational colloquy between and among national governments and international or supranational organizations as it is a story of constitutional review. Even though constitutional review has come to be seen as an important, if not necessary, feature of any post-totalitarian regime aspiring to be ruled by law, it has never become sufficient to legitimise a system lacking acceptance by international organizations run under the auspices of Western governments.

The process of the internationalisation of both law and politics served to infuse specific concepts into national discourses. It is indeed the notion of norm transmission by means of dialogue and interaction that helps us to understand the readiness of some of the Central European establishments to open themselves to concepts requiring a shift of emphasis in their understanding of legality, legitimacy, statehood, or civil society even before the Berlin Wall came down. This shift was evidenced by, for instance, the introduction of a constitutional court and an ombudsman in the late years of Poland's socialist dark ages, or by attempts to strengthen citizens' protection against administrative abuse in Hungary during the 1980s. Not that these measures could have undone the undemocratic core of the respective regimes, but the active involvement of the Soviet camp in various international organizations—mostly those operating within the framework of the United Nations—has, despite contrary efforts by the then socialist establishments, provided ground for cross-fertilization of legal and socio-cultural experiences between the two blocs. Casper points out, 'ironically, the very steps that formally stabilized the political map of post-war Europe (the West German *Ostpolitik* dating from around 1970 and the Helsinki Accords of 1975) probably expedited disintegration by facilitating interaction',[30] and gave rise to the growing feeling of historical inevitability of some degree of convergence between the two political *Weltanschauungs*.

The intra-European conditioning of the socialist bloc through *détente* in general and the Helsinki Accords in particular played a prime role in the norm transmission process. In Central and Eastern Europe, which was actively involved in the drafting of the 1975 Helsinki Final Act, the emphasis was put on the principle of non-interference with the governments' internal affairs and the principle of international peace and security. The socialist establishments thus used the era's single most important all-European rights instrument to insulate themselves against rights-abuse accusations by Western Europe. Yet the very fact of adherence to the Helsinki Accords had far-reaching implications. There were tenets of the Accords available other than those relied upon by the communist authorities in their efforts to insulate themselves against international criticism, and these were the very norms that those who were persecuted because of their alleged attempts to subvert the socialist order would regularly invoke. The role of *détente* in bringing the communist regimes down is indisputable, if only for the fact that without the Helsinki Accords—which were both a consequence of the *détente* and the cause of its carefully managed deepening—'opposition in Eastern Europe would have been weaker, less coherent, easier to suppress, and slower to foster the development of civil liberties in Eastern Europe in preparation for the transition to democracy when the opportunity finally came'.[31] Even more importantly, the continental standards of rights protection were slowly penetrating local discourses and the process of gradual norm transmission 'paved the way for a smoother transition to democracy when the old regimes crumbled because it had fostered alternative structures and authorities to take their place'.[32]

The norm transmission facilitated by the Helsinki Accords and, on the extra-European level, by the International Covenant on Civic and Political Rights (ICCPR) and the International Covenant on Cultural, Economic, and Social Rights (ICCESR) also had some more immediate implications. Even though the application by the communist governments of supranational human rights treaties was overly selective and the rights commitments remained largely unobserved before 1990, they were there and waiting to be answered. After 1990, adherence to international rights-protection mechanisms combined with the new regimes' willingness to make the attendant obligations directly enforceable domestically. Both the domestic constitutions and the international agreements came to be understood as normative rather than merely declaratory documents, and as such were in need of institutional protection. An important part of the Central and Eastern European countries' answer to the invitation to become full, law-abiding members of the international community therefore was to provide for mechanisms designed to enforce the existing, and the newly arising, human rights commitments.[33]

Moreover, the new elite replacing the outgoing leadership had a strong affiliation to the international human rights movement. Most of the former dissidents were relatively familiar with the development of the rights protection scheme in the West, had internalised its model, and as such were true believers in the rule of law, the institutional protection of rights, and other concepts organically linked to the idea of limited government and, less directly, constitutional adjudication. After all, constitutional review was born in larger Central Europe and orbited on the periphery of local legal theory even during times that were hostile to its emergence. The concept of institutional protection of rights could not have re-entered the post-communist polities' consciousness at a better time than in the late 1990s. Not only was it well tested by many a nation in Western Europe and believed to be historically inevitable; it also was deemed capable of offering a unique and irreplaceable contribution to dealing with the legacies of a totalitarian regime and preventing the possibility of its re-emergence. In addition, the new establishments that came to power after the Round Table talks found themselves morally committed to the very instruments they were advocating and relying upon in their dissident capacity.

Competition for recognition. Less noble motivations were also under way, which brings onto the scene the factor of regional competition for a 'market niche' in the process of the EU's eastward expansion. It became clear very soon in the process of the old continent's integration that there was only so much of the European pie and that its incumbent holders might be reluctant to share. Ackerman, for instance, pointed out in 1997 that the EU was 'looking for excuses to defer the heavy economic costs that admission of the East entail[ed]'.[34] The regional competition became stiff. To gain recognition from the West, especially the EC/EU, and to use that recognition to advance one's regional interests, became the principal foreign-policy imperative in Central Europe. The strategy was twofold: deferential towards the European pie-holders, assertive *vis-à-vis* the pie-competitors.

One of the ways of competing for foreign-policy leverage was to strive to achieve as much similarity as possible, for upon achieving such similarity—both substantive and institutional—the grounds for reticence on the part of the EC/EU as regards the respective country's full integration would be substantially diminished. On the domestic scene, the proponents of that strategy often argued that first it was necessary to abide firmly by whichever guidelines were coming from Brussels because only upon admission would any political empowerment be possible and new bargaining power gained.[35] A certain degree of autonomy was to be sacrificed for the sake of more autonomy in the future.

The need to assert oneself as worthier of political acknowledgment than others induced a passionate desire among the Central (and Eastern) European establishments to be distinguished from their counterparts especially—but not only—those to the east. The entire region arrived at the door of the club at more or less the same time but each party insisted it was not 'with the group'. Here the issue of institutional similarity, particularly with regard to constitutional review, creates a puzzle. Neither the Western paradigm nor the European federation perspective has exhibited so rigorous a normative structure as to require a specific institutional design, for example, rendering incorporation of constitutional review a political imperative, a *sine qua non* of integration. Estonia, a country lacking a specialized constitutional tribunal but ranking among the forerunners in the integration race, is an illustrative case in point. The transitional environment was devoid of any 'entrenched transformative interests',[36] and of embedded cognitions and values setting a standard of legitimacy from which it would be difficult to deviate without a considerable loss of credibility. The initial fluidity of normative responses to the *orientatio* inquiry on the level of particularities prevented an indisputable predetermination of certain institutional outcomes at the expense of others. Although strongly prescriptive in terms of the general political orientation, the extrication context was not bound by connotations that would, by a mere urge to conformity, lead inevitably to incorporation of constitutional review. Moreover, jumping on the bandwagon of constitutional jurisdiction[37] served to blur the lines between the club applicants rather than provide them with distinctive credentials.

On the other hand, the almost universal adherence to constitutional review (although in different variations—in the already mentioned Estonia, for instance, it is the Supreme Court as the highest ordinary adjudication instance that performs a kind of constitutional review) indicates that the connotations attributed to Europeanisation are widely shared among the post-communist polities and that they might have been quasi-prescriptive in terms of inclusion of some sort of constitutional review. The answer to the puzzle is to be found in a simple cost-benefit analysis.

Although there was no comparative advantage to be gained by embracing the concept of constitutional review at the expense of other club-membership-seekers, the inclusion of certain gimmicks of constitutional government was certainly a plus that would not—or so the relevant actors might have thought—go unnoticed in the power circles of Community Europe. The former Chief Justice of the HCC argued, for instance, that constitutional review became 'a kind of symbol of the rule of law, an internationally approved trade-mark'.[38] On a similar note, Sajó suggested, 'the new political mechanism and the emerging power elite share[d] their interest in legalism. The new governments hope[d] to achieve internal and external [international] legitimisation by making their actions more legalistic and basing their legalism on attractive formal criteria.'[39] By failing to adhere to the institution of constitutional protection of human rights a valuable legitimacy bonus could have been lost. At this stage, this is mere speculation but from the point of view of the then actors, who had to decide from behind a scarcely pierced veil of ignorance, it seemed rational to do all that might prevent any comparative disadvantage. Simply, although no net gain was incurred by subscription to constitutional adjudication, net loss was avoided.

Related to the above calculation was the displacement of national economies. The post-1989 trade-off between Central and Eastern Europe and the European Community was in a way similar to the deal underlying late *détente*—the provision of Western credits for the promise of democratisation. The Central European establishments were by and large aware that without structural assistance from the West, especially from the EC/EU, their economies were destined to fail. In order to induce Western Europe to provide help the Central and Eastern European establishments were trying to sell peace and stability in their corner of the world for the promise of political and economic integration.

As Pinder points out, however, the EC paid significantly more attention to the economic aspects of the transformation than it did to the establishment in Central and Eastern Europe of 'institutions and skills required for effective constitutional democracy and civil society'.[40] It is difficult to assess whether the Central European elites were consciously manipulating their Western counterparts to make them acknowledge the progress achieved in the realm of immaterial values rather than on the economic front, or whether they sincerely believed that constitutional advancement was a precondition of any economic interaction with the West.[41] One way or the other, the new Central European regimes felt more confident in their ability to tame the undemocratic elements of their polities and thus become more compatible with Western Europe in terms of political liberalism than in their ability to perform on equal terms with the West in the economic arena. It was therefore natural for the post-communist leaders to emphasize, at least initially, their achievements in the area of rights protection or public law reform and try to downplay the importance of GDP per capita or fiscal efficiency for their belonging to the family of European nations. The transition agents were working on the assumption that a sustained flow of financial aid from the EC/EU depended on the returnees' adherence to the founding values of Community Europe and to the accession criteria, including the stabilization of institutions guaranteeing democracy, the rule of law, human rights, and respect for, and protection of, minorities. Regardless of whether that assumption was self-imposed or induced by the Western European powers, the above criteria were implicitly asking for subscription to the concept of (some form of) constitutional review.

The displacement of the economy worked to strengthen the non-material aspects of transition on two fronts. Not only did it induce uncompromising adherence to the ideals professed by Western Europe after the Second World War, but it also played a role in communicating with the citizenry. As Batt points out, given the strong likelihood of an immediate decline in the material standard of living the transitional leaders had every incentive to emphasize non-material aspects of *orientatio,* reflected in concepts such as limited government, protection of rights, unrestrained mobility, freedoms of expression and association, and so on, even if only for tactical reasons.[42] Linz and Stepan argue in a similar vein that the political economy of legitimacy tends to insulate democratic regimes from overthrow in the case of economic malperformance more than it does non-democratic ones.[43] It is a trivial but none the less relevant observation that system-stability-enhancing features of institutional re-designing were also features fit to serve the region's urge to conformity; or vice versa, concepts serving integrative ambitions were generally deemed desirable for their own sake, for example, their fitness to support the emerging regimes and immunize them from collapse.

By stressing the politico-moral and philosophico-moral aspects of *orientatio,* and by presenting their mandate as a mandate to lead the polity into the community of liberal values rather than a commitment to bring about rapid and universal prosperity, the transition agents were at once trying to divert public attention away from the perspective of economic decline and looking for ways to insulate their legitimacy claims. Accordingly, the inclusion of a rights-protection device was a way of compensating the citizen for material hardship, being exactly the opposite of the previous 'deal' when a social safety net was put in place in order to compensate for a dramatic lack of individual autonomy.

Rhetorical entrapment. Checkel distinguishes between agents of change as either strategic calculators or cognitive puzzlers.[44] The former are knowledgeable policy entrepreneurs exploiting policy windows to promote their agendas; the latter learn preferences via interaction with a policy window rather than know how to exploit it.

The dynamics of transitional deliberation combined both the cognitive-puzzle and the strategic-calculation aspects. As for the former, it was difficult to foresee whether the relevant inter-subjective cognitions within the polity would work in favour of certain institutional arrangements and thus validate them as legitimate or not. Throughout the region, however, the cognitive puzzle concerned issues not directly related to the idea of constitutional review. In Poland, and partly also in Hungary, the emphasis was on the relationship between the legislature and the executive—the puzzle was to figure out how the anticipated holders of the respective offices would behave when elected or appointed and how to prevent their undesirable aggrandizement. In Czechoslovakia, the local leaders themselves were surprised by the sweeping effect on political and institutional choices of the issue of federalism.

Moreover, institutional dynamics in a transitional period—and especially their rhetorical base—have a tendency to take on a life of their own and become a self-sustaining process partly outside the control of those who initiated it. In other words, rhetorical patterns have a way of sustaining themselves.[45] As soon as the idea of constitutional review surfaced in the deliberation over constitutional frameworks, it became part of the transition mantra. The political actors would excessively invoke the rule of law, human rights, and their constitutional protection. Terms such as 'democracy', 'human rights', 'free market', and 'constitutional court' simply sounded right. Although the local leaders of the time did not have at their disposal vocabulary-producing machines as elaborate as politicians in mature democracies,[46] they instinctively felt the impossibility of overemphasizing what seemed to resonate well with the public. The combination of this unreflective attitude to the mantra and the focus on politically more delicate issues prevented any substantial public debate on constitutional review—at least until the first controversial decisions were handed down—and the cognitive puzzle was, superficially of course, solved on the level of rhetorical action.

Taking adequate account of strategic calculation may seem more complex. One possible solution would include accepting the proposition that the incorporation of constitutional review followed the logic of consequentiality according to which institutional choices are a result of instrumental consideration of rational actors seeking to advance their own interests. Plasser, Ulram, and Waldrauch, for instance, argue, 'decisions as to the type and character of political institutions to be formed as part of transition are based on the current or anticipated power relationships'.[47] Elster, too, ranks group interest and institutional interest among the most prominent factors shaping a constitution-making process.[48] In other words, agents of change seek to entrench a structure of power distribution that would be in their best interest. At first sight, especially if one tries to look at Central European constitution making only through the lens of methodological individualism, this seems implausible. Most of the transition leaders planned to become members of the executive or the legislature and had no immediate interest in providing for a strong constitutional court.[49] Even non-personal institutional interest should have clearly been working against it since the legislatures worked as constituent bodies, too.

It would be unduly restrictive, however, to confine the issue of instrumentality to rational choice. Indeed, strategic calculation has in many instances anchored quite peculiar elements having to do more with immediate gratification of personal ambition than with a long-term calculation aimed at reserving for oneself a favourable structural basis for political undertakings. In a world where yesterday's window-cleaners become today's state officials (and rightly so), and where the procedure for adopting political decisions with far-reaching consequences is, speaking euphemistically, very informal, one can never underestimate the effects that personal aggrandizement may have on institutional choices. Cynical as it sounds, one sure way of being quoted by a leading Western newspaper in the few months following the fall of the Berlin Wall was to endorse any institution or instrument in use by Western societies, regardless of whether it was organic to the speaker's environment. This must have been—and understandably so—a source of profound personal satisfaction for many of the former dissidents deprived of serious professional growth opportunities. One even sympathizes with their vanity. After all, this was the time of making dreams come true, not of seeing them vanish because of detached rationality.

In addition, there were powerful constraints limiting the self-interested action of the transition agents or, more euphemistically, their strategic calculation. The insurgents, while in their dissident capacity, communicated to the public through a human rights dossier, which, when elaborated upon and brought to consistency with the continental model, has come to include institutional protection of individual freedoms. Many of the new leaders made a name for themselves by vigorously supporting freedom of association, assembly, and speech, or the due process of law. To deviate from the core of their dissident agenda would necessarily have undermined their claims to be the messengers of true change. To subscribe to the idea of institutional protection of rights was thus a way for the insurgents to distinguish themselves clearly and firmly from the previous regime.[50]

A hint of structural considerations also can be found in the conceptualisation of constitutional review as a decommunisation tool. It stemmed from the fear that a popular mandate arrived at in the future via majoritarian democratic means could be used to subvert the new order by way of sophisticated substantive devolution rather than obvious institutional deconstruction. One of the anticipated roles of constitutional courts was to preserve the achievements of the post-1989 *orientatio* against possible attacks by local adversaries of the new developments and/or to serve as a counter-balance against the possibly too expansive attitudes of elected officials.[51] It was, however, an ambiguous strategy. The practical effect of constitutional review was an unknown variable, a double-edged sword from the point of view of self-interested political rationality. It was, for instance, quite obvious to the lawmakers that their efforts to punish the impersonators of the *ancien régime* would be challenged at the constitutional level. The outcome of any such litigation was far from being a foregone conclusion and it could have undermined the insurgents' legitimacy claims. After all, the retribution laws have withstood constitutional challenge in the Czech Republic, but were rejected in Hungary, became obsolete in Slovakia, and were partially constrained in Poland. And in Hungary, the new establishment had to experience its share of unpleasant surprises when it realized that the consensus-enhancing devices with which it packed the post-1989 constitutional amendments, including constitutional review, were working against it. Those keen on providing as many checks and balances as possible have by virtue of electoral victory come to see their policy choices—implemented through legislative and administrative means—frustrated by the very arrangements they supported.[52] These risks, however, were either not fully acknowledged initially or seemed less worrying than the prospect of revolutionary and post-revolutionary accomplishments being eroded.

Moreover, the typical strategy with which to win recognition was to be more papist than the pope himself. Although it is difficult to see how the benefit of instantaneous self-saturation could be greater than the cost of failing to insulate oneself against structural challenges,[53] the strategy was not irrational by definition. As Elster argues, self-interest was disqualified from arguments on transitional policies,[54] and so alternative ways of strategic manipulation had to be found. Further, progressivism served to increase the visibility of the respective government in the West. The beneficiaries of outside recognition then used it in the local political struggle to portray themselves as capable of gaining respect in the West and thus of guaranteeing its support, whether financial or political or, most often, both.

According to Professor Sunstein: 'But sometimes people support a law not because of its effects on norms, but because it is believed intrinsically valuable for the relevant "statement" to be made.'[55] This intrinsic value can sometimes be that of reputational utility.[56] And when combined with the constraint of rhetorical consistency, it can be miraculously progressive. Indeed, the logic of appropriateness stemming from reputational considerations appears to have been a more influential factor than the logic of consequentiality based on considerations of structural utility, namely the fit of constitutional review with the larger institutional framework. Thus, even though institutional interest might have been working against the incorporation of constitutional review, it was politically correct to support it. These dynamics proved of particular relevance to the rise of the Hungarian Court.

Overall, the larger-than-life supporters of 'progress' have played a positive role. Their competition for a 'European' image translated into rhetorical entrapment, as it became difficult for them to renounce prior public endorsements of a particular institution without damaging their own credibility. A gradual domestication of concepts endorsed by the respective transition agencies for whatever personal or other reasons has thereby become the principal consequence of their rhetorical exercise in Europeanism.[57] After a short period of uncritical reception, any proposed instrument of societal organization became subject to substantive scrutiny and played a role in the civic education of the respective populations.

The selection was becoming wider and the social learning more informed and more immediate. As a consequence, the polities' cognitive background was enriched and provided further grounds for the internalisation by the public of values and norms underlying the novel instruments of checking and balancing the government's action, be it constitutional review, an ombudsman, or direct applicability of transnational human rights instruments or other such tools. The citizens have thereby adopted 'into their own repertoire of cognitions and behaviours that which originally was intended either to boost one's political correctness and/or to diffuse the looming frustration with the economic outlook.'[58]

CHAPTER 2

DESIGNING CONSTITUTIONAL REVIEW

In Chapter 1, I examined the ways in which the major aspects of the Central European polities' extrication from communism translated into the vehement emergence of constitutional review. I suggested that the context in which post-communist Europe was searching for basic orientational devices proved overwhelmingly conducive to its adherence in general terms to the institutional designs, political ideals, and macroeconomic arrangements of the geographically, historically, and ideologically closest hegemon, Western Europe. In the meantime, however, the connotations that the transiting polities attributed to their return to Europe were not so prescriptive as to require the implementation of one definite set of institutional arrangements with no room for deviation or variance. Even less did those constraints require a particular concept of constitutional review.

In this chapter, I discuss the context in which the region's constitutional judiciaries were built. I explore on a country-by-country basis what roles were assigned to the respective constitutional courts, and why. My account focuses on three sets of variables: (i) legal culture, documenting the historical development of local notions of law and government; (ii) the contextualisation of legal culture by the political economy of transition; and (iii) the distribution within the polities of transitional leadership roles (Figure 3).

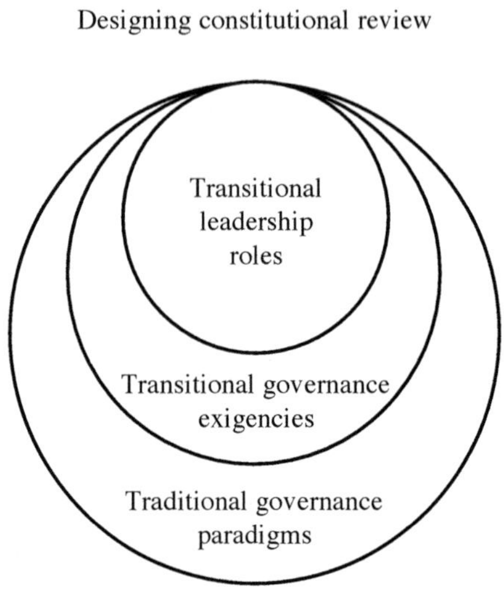

Figure 3. Designing constitutional review in Central Europe

FRAMEWORK

Elster explains the selection of a specific institutional design in a society transforming from a totalitarian into a democratic one as a function of a 'triple past', comprising the communist period, the more remote precommunist period, and the very immediate period of extrication from the communist regime.[1] My tendency instinctively to dismiss the relevance of the communist past to the present is a function of my immediate personal experience with the perversities of the era. True, as the former Hungarian President Göncz argued, the four decades of dictatorship 'continue[d] to determine the Central European citizen's contemporary reactions, behaviour and... forms of transformation of the country.'[2] But in terms of the structural rather than the cultural aspects of the communist legacy,[3] I concur with Elster in understanding this legacy mostly as a negative referent and a basis for a 'reactive institution building'.[4]

The extent and the relevance of communist-era systemic obstacles to institutional reform varied among the Visegrád countries. The Polish Tribunal, for instance, was complexly regulated at times when, as Brzezinski puts it, substantive and procedural limitations were imposed upon its functioning for political reasons, making it unable to overstep politically acceptable boundaries, let alone attempt to modify the totalitarian framework of power.[5] The then Chief Justice anchored the same theme when he remarked that the Tribunal was victimised by having been complexly regulated prior to post-revolutionary constitutional deliberation.[6] The PCT also was bound to work with an outdated charter of rights transplanted from the communist into the new era with almost no change.

In Hungary, the circumstances were more favourable than elsewhere in the region for the elimination of communism-originated systemic obstacles to institutional reform. The communist hard-liners either gave up the hard line or were marginalised. The local juristic elites harboured more 'Western' attitudes than did, for instance, their Czech or Slovak colleagues. Varga argues that lawyers managed to preserve some level of personal integrity—with varying degrees of success—even during the communist and Nazi eras,[7] a claim in which Örkény and Scheppele concur.[8] Similarly, Sajó argues that the judiciary "appeared independent under Hungarian state socialism"[9] and that 'in the last two decades the judiciary was rarely employed as a means of open political repression'.[10] Moreover, those judges who were responsible for the repressive political justice administration in the late 1950s retired on the basis of a 'gentlemen's agreement' and the 'judiciary leaders ...quickly adapted to the emerging new regime'.[11] Further, the constitutional amendments aiming at the democratic reconstruction of Hungary were more sweeping than those adopted in pre-1997 Poland or pre-1993 Czechoslovakia. Unlike the Polish Constitutional Tribunal (PCT), which had to work with an outdated charter of rights, the Hungarian Constitutional Court (HCC) had at its disposal an elaborate catalogue of rights.

One important way in which constitutional arrangements dating back to the communist era affected transitional reform in the former Czechoslovakia concerned the impasse-inducing scheme of federal law making, dubbed 'an authentic federation', which prevented coherent policy making on a federal level, unearthed the incompatibility of the political development of the two republics, and contributed to the split of the country. It also induced the federal legislature to leave certain matters in a state of interpretive ambiguity and, consequently, provided part of the rationale for constitutional review.

The relevance to the process of framing constitutional adjudication of the other two components of the triple-past varied, but each deserves and will be given due attention. Therefore, even though I will concern myself mostly with events that were in one way or another linked to the extrication period, at times phenomena of a *durée plus longue que ça* and the way they translate into present reality will force themselves upon the discussion.

To the examination of the pre-communist era, various approaches may apply. The Braudelian *longue-durée* perspective correctly forces us to look at particular institutions in their evolution over decades, even centuries. Sartori, on the other hand, finds it unnecessary to locate the origins of constitutionalism too far in the past, for example, in Ancient Greece and Rome.[12] History does seem to provide conflicting accounts. Oakeshott goes so far as to declare, 'in it events have no over-all pattern or purpose, lead nowhere, point to no favoured condition of the world and support no practical conclusions'.[13] Such a verdict on history's normative relevance, however, may be a bit too dismissive. Indeed, the logic of Central Europe's institutional reforms reflected not only the exogenous aspects of the *orientatio* process but was also heavily informed by implications of indigenous legal development. Factors of local particularity, such as the traditional understanding of law, authority, justice administration, and other cognitive undercurrents of the culture of law and public governance proved as prescriptive with regard to the specification of general institutional choices as the connotations attendant on the Western liberal democratic paradigm and the European federation perspective did with respect to the overall post-revolutionary orientation. The local patterns of institutional interaction stemming from a reservoir of collective cognitions served extensively to customise the 'imported product' and emerged as determinative of the concrete designs and modes of operation of the respective constitutional courts, and governments in general. In exploring the historical development of the respective legal cultures, I will focus on those patterns that were of most relevance to the country-specific conceptualisation of a constitutional court's authority.

As far as the process of extrication itself is concerned, it has throughout the region shared some important similarities, especially as regards the mode of transition and the overall goals of reform. Nonetheless, both the specific circumstances informing the Round Table talks and the institutional choices arrived at during, or as a consequence of, the changeover negotiations varied among the Visegrád countries. Poland, for instance, had a strong opposition movement with a clear mandate to become the principal transition agency. In Hungary, opposition to the regime was considerably weaker, and the dissident groups in Czechoslovakia, especially in Slovakia, were as inexperienced and lacking in confidence as they could possibly be. The intensity and the scope of the insurgents' initial mandate for transitional leadership, however, translated into constitutional reform in a less than straightforward way. Poland did not manage to enact a new post-communist constitution until 1997 and the Hungarian constitution is still, almost 13 years after the country became a democratic republic, only a patchwork of numerous amendments. The failure to adopt a new constitution became fatal to Czechoslovakia but both successor countries had their democratic constitutions implemented in 1993. I will therefore assess the implications for the process of constitutional reform in general, and the designing of constitutional review in particular, of both the strong/weak insurgency dichotomy and the reform finality/provisionality dichotomy.

COUNTRY SPECIFICS

Poland

Overview

In March 1982, the 1952 Constitution of Poland was amended with article 33a, which established constitutional review. Three years later, a statute enacting the Tribunal was promulgated,[14] and in January 1986 constitutional review began to operate. Some of the previously discussed *orientatio* constraints therefore may seem inapplicable to Poland. Time-wise and context-wise, however, the late 1980s were not as distinct from the *annus mirabilis* of 1989 as to render inapplicable factors such as *Zeitgeist* or the norm transmission effect. One, a kind of reform pressure was becoming more and more of a noticeable reality, especially in Poland and Hungary. Brzezinski argues, for instance, that the Tribunal's establishment was the government's 'reaction to the growing public pressure',[15] although one that tried to disguise rather than reform the nature of the regime and was part of a carrot-and-stick strategy. The willingness to concede some of its power clearly did not mean that the Party would be keen on 'excluding certain elements of the state machinery from its political influence'.[16] Nevertheless, several first-hand accounts of the era point out that the communist leadership had to, and did, take note of the growing involvement of Polish civil society in public life.[17] Also, everywhere in the region, and even more so in Poland, the years following the adoption and ratification of the UN Covenants (ICCPR, ICCESR) and the Helsinki Accords brought about a gradual shift in the understanding of the constitution as an enforceable document. As Lech Garlicki wrote in 1987, one could detect in Polish legal and political life the sign of the times, the *Verrechtlichung der Verfassung*.[18]

Pursuant to the constitution and the 1985 Constitutional Tribunal Act (PCTA), the PCT's role was to assess the conformity to the constitution of legislative acts and the constitutionality or legality of sub-statutory acts. While a decision on unconstitutionality or illegality of sub-statutory acts was to be final and binding *erga omnes*, the PCT's findings of statutes' lack of conformity to the constitution were subject to examination by the Sejm, which could overturn them by a two-thirds majority of the quorum.[19]

In 1989, after the Round Table talks and the ensuing change of regime, the powers of the PCT were enhanced by means of both constitutional and statutory amendments.[20] The PCT was granted the power to formulate universally binding interpretation of statutes,[21] as well as to carry out *ex ante* scrutiny of bills upon a motion submitted to it by the President.[22] The Tribunal itself, taking advantage of changes in the political climate, began to assert its authority in a more activist manner, increasing the number of statutes ruled unconstitutional from one in 1986–1988 to 13 in 1989–1991, and 20 in 1993 alone.[23]

The PCT, however, remained unable to adjudicate upon conformity of domestic legislation to international agreements, as well as to hear constitutional complaints of individual citizens. The notion of parliamentary supremacy over constitutional review remained firmly in place, too. In 1992, the Little Constitution was enacted but the deficiencies of constitutional review remained, once again, without a relevant remedy. It was not until 1997 that the Tribunal was put on a par with constitutional courts elsewhere in the region.

The provisional nature of Poland's pre-1997 constitutional order had a decisive effect on the conceptualisation by lawmakers of the Tribunal. Kurczewski's remark that the PCT's constitutional interpretation under the 'watchful eyes of the legislature [may be] more applaudable in a time of transition'[24] illustrates the Polish approach. He goes on to ask: 'After all, can you have a Constitutional Court when there is no final constitution, and the legislatures are at the same time supposed to be constitutional assemblies?'[25] The PCT itself stated it thus in an activity report:

> Introducing the principle of trilateral separation of powers into the Little Constitution and at the same time leaving in force the provisions of Chapter IV of the Constitution of the Republic of Poland [on judicial power] results in a situation in which all organs the status of which is regulated by Chapter IV are given specific characteristics, and their position may be finally decided upon only in the new Constitution.[26]

Despite the general agreement of those at the forefront of Poland's constitutional renewal that the PCT was in need of reform,[27] it was also agreed that the reform would have to wait until the adoption of the new constitution. The interim nature of the Little Constitution thus served to delay the PCT's appointment as the constitution's ultimate interpreter to the time following adoption of the 'real' document.

The provisionality effect extended also to the more specific aspects of the Tribunal's authority. First, the ambiguous constitutional regulation of domestic applicability of international law prevented the PCT's appointment as a supervisor of the conformity of national to supranational law. The yardstick of scrutiny that the Tribunal was to apply in assessing legislation thus excluded international agreements.[28] Secondly, among the provisions of the communist constitution that the Little Constitution has kept almost intact was Chapter VIII regulating rights and liberties. Frankowski argues, '[t]he democratically elected Parliament decided to retain the chapter pending completion of comprehensive constitutional reform culminating in the adoption of an entirely new constitution.'[29] This unavailability of a modern, or at least somewhat contextualised, catalogue of rights provided part of the rationale for limiting the Tribunal's authority in the realm of incidental protection of rights.

The question then is, however, how, if at all, did the prescriptive connotations attendant on the return to Europe inform the Polish constitution makers' deliberations.

Legal Culture

I have argued that the international context from which those connotations stemmed was not so rigid as to require a particular mode of constitutional review. It certainly was not so rigid as to erase those layers of Poland's tradition by virtue of which 'constitutionalism was not usually understood as a limitation of democratic and parliamentary authority'.[30] The country 'lacked the traditions and mechanisms of submitting parliamentary acts to constitutional review'[31] and in its culture of law and governance 'the traditions of administrative and constitutional courts were just as weak'.[32]

The 1791 Constitution of Poland is undoubtedly the most revered legal document in Polish history. Although it lived as law only for a year, both the public and scholarship have never tired of referring to it in debates on where the country should be heading and how it should be governed. It is also with the May Constitution in mind that Czeszejko-Sochacki argues that the 'roots of what later became known as constitutional review are found rather early in the Polish political tradition.'[33] Indeed, he claims that the May Constitution 'contains a number of significant provisions in the area of constitutional review'.[34] This, however, seems to be stretching things a little too far. Although the document did state that any subsequent statutes of the Diet were fully to adhere to the constitution, the drafters left the constitution's protection at that. No guarantees were provided for observance by the lawmakers of the constitution. And naturally so, given the context in which the May Constitution came about. If there was in Europe a fashionable constitutional idea at the end of the eighteenth century, it was the notion of popular and, by extension, parliamentary sovereignty. Czeszejko-Sochacki himself points out the imposing influence that Rousseau's political doctrine had on the substance of the May Constitution.

Given the gap between 1794 and 1918 in Poland's legal and political development, one can understand the readiness of Poles proud of their heritage to find elements in the May Constitution that either were never there or were not as central as they claimed. Constitutional review is one such example. Another is portraying the May Constitution as a hallmark of progressive liberalism, a fountain of personal rights and liberties, and a depository of a mature political culture.[35] Cole is right to point out, however, that in many respects the May Constitution was regressive rather than progressive and that its achievements in the realm of protection of rights tend to be over-estimated, to say the least.[36] This highly regarded charter, for instance, signalled a deviation from the sixteenth-century guarantees of religious tolerance in Poland by incorporating the infamous Cities Act sanctioning anti-Semitism—about the current displays of which in Polish politics Brzezinski rightly complains[37]—and disfranchised a large part of the nobility. The May Constitution is certainly indicative of Poland's prominent place in the history of European constitutionalism, of its intellectual capital, and of the richness of its legal history. The way in which it informed post-communist constitutional reform, especially with respect to constitutional review, was nonetheless very indirect.

During the very period in which both the Hungarians and the Czechs attempted to instil new concepts in their self-understanding as modern nations—the attempts of the former to transplant these efforts into political reality being much more successful than those of the latter—and during which Slovaks for the first time in their history presented a coherent claim for an autonomous place on Europe's map, Poland did not exist as a unified state. During the 125 years of partition, various primary legal systems operated in combination with provincial jurisdictions on Poland's territory. It therefore serves no immediate purpose to take that era into account in identifying patterns of legal development that could serve as an orientational device in evaluating Polish constitutional politics in the twentieth century. Unlike the very fact of partition, which resonates in the collective consciousness of the nation up to the present, the impact of the dark ages of 1794–1918 on Poland's indigenous constitutional culture is marginal.

Indeed, it was the negative referential status of the period of Poland's partition that impacted local conceptualisation of constitutional review. What merits special attention here is the Poles' traditional search for a middle ground between emphasis on the protection of autonomy and the need for effective government.[38] This is a trivial truth endemic to any modern state but it seems especially acute in the history of Polish constitutionalism torn between liberty and its perversion, anarchy, on one side and effectiveness and its perversion, autocracy, on the other. The traumatic experience that the Poles had with the *liberum veto*,[39] which contributed to the disappearance of their country in the eighteenth century, not only translated into the 1926 coup of Pilsudski and the autocratic Constitution of 1935, but also affected the post-communist constitution making. When one looks at constitutional enterprise in inter-war Poland, one sees that the Poles' reaction to the fragmentation of the political scene was, and naturally so, the strengthening of the central power rather than its further restriction. Brzezinski notes that Polish constitutional history 'reveals a cyclical pattern oscillating between a populist but ineffective government closely guarding individual freedoms, and a strong central power working to secure a unified Polish state'.[40] Osiatynski argues that even the more recent constitutional discussions in Poland were usually concerned with the choice between the parliamentarism of France's Third Republic and the presidential supremacy of its Fifth Republic.[41] The very same tensions were to re-emerge as strong as ever during the country's transition to democracy.

The PCT's authority could have been strengthened in various ways during the interim period. The PCT's standpoints on the unconstitutionality of statutes, for instance, could have been attributed finality and the Sejm stripped of its ability to overrule them. The Tribunal's authority to issue binding interpretations of ordinary laws could have been extended so as to cover constitutional laws, too. This, however, would require not only overcoming the provisionality factor and the attendant inertia in constitutional reform, but also Poland's pulling itself from the grasp of domestic constitutional tradition. Czeszejko-Sochacki, after all, described the pre-1997 model as 'a logical consequence of the nation's historical evolution'[42] and as 'deeply rooted in traditions indigenous to Poland'.[43] Two years into the operation of the PCT, Garlicki argued, 'the protection of individual rights and liberties from the administration seem[ed] to be more important and necessary than protection against parliamentary legislation'.[44] Six years and one revolution later, Kurczewski, albeit on a more descriptive note, was bound to observe that 'the present situation of the Constitutional Court... is akin to a quasi-law chamber that performs the role that in some other contexts is left to the Lords of Justice, being not outside of Parliament but part of it'.[45] As Brzezinski argues, 'this framework corresponded well with the model assumption articulated in 1988 by Leszek Garlicki'[46] in which the PCT was to help the Parliament maintain its position as the country's supreme legislator rather than to supervise it.

Transitional Political Economy

Poland's negotiated transition took place under a double-unity of political authority, with the relatively unified communist front facing the relatively unified Solidarity. The robustness of the negotiating parties created the illusion of a strong agreement on the basis of which the transition could take place. The structural unity brought about by elite settlement[47] thus seemed enough of a guarantee that the Round Table agreement would be observed.[48] This created an environment in which no special institutions or mechanisms were sought by the decision-makers to elaborate upon and supervise the execution of the agreement other than those that were to allow the opposition to compete for political power and pursue the choices arrived at the Round Table talks. And when the cohesion of the new establishment did prove illusory, both the traditional and the transitional modes of political economy served to emphasise the leadership role of the executive rather than that of constitutional review.

Indeed, the context of transition served to reinforce the traditional tendencies rather than to modify them. It did not offer reasons compelling enough to induce modification of the status quo with respect to the major aspects of the Tribunal's positioning, especially the lack of conceptual finality of a specific category of its judgments and the lack of standing for individual petitioners. Kolarska-Bobinska observed, for instance, that the Polish 'deputies to the Parliament frequently comment[ed] on how burdensome [was] the incessant need to amend or change the law'[49] and went on to argue that because of the need for speedy and efficient policy-making 'the point of gravity tend[ed] to shift from legislative to executive authority'.[50] To give the PCT the powers effectively to obstruct legislative measures would be a move in the opposite direction and it must have been seen by the deputies of the Sejm as establishing just another obstacle to coherent policy-making, the need for which seemed as urgent as ever. It might have been a regime-legitimating device but it certainly could turn out to be a frustrating one, too. The circumstances simply forced agencies across the political spectrum to stress efficiency and emphasise the need to find a workable arrangement between the cabinet's assertive pursuit of particular policies and the protection of legislative decisions against abuse by the executive.

After all, what could be more indicative of the traditional oscillation between legislature-centred and a strong hands-on politics than the confession of a prominent figure in contemporary Polish constitutionalism and politics, Bronislaw Geremek, who, in his own words, went from being 'programmed with an aversion and mistrust of authority' to a staunch supporter of a strong chancellor-centred executive power in just five years?[51] An even more striking—and more illustrative of Poland's transitional context—confession comes from a former high-ranking official in Suchocka's cabinet:

> The conception of law as a guarantor of individual rights was strongly present in my thinking until the moment when I came into contact, in reality, with the process of making law in the Sejm in 1989. In these new circumstances, I found myself in a situation where my youthful convictions about the rule of law had—under pressure of reality—to undergo a complete change. Since a more important goal, much more important from my point of view, was the effectiveness of the reform in Poland.[52]

Hence the fear of constitutional paralysis[53]; hence the anti-legal culture that Skapska finds prevailing in Poland's post-communist transition, as she argues that the country lacked 'a legalistic culture, consisting in the high prestige of existing law, and the subordination to it of political interests'.[54]

The public sentiment, too, favoured a strong state 'making order out of chaos'.[55] In 1992, 16 percent of Poles were willing to say that dictatorship was possibly better than democracy and two years later, even more people concurred.[56] Thirty-six percent of them believed that the country needed a strong man as opposed to 19 percent with the same belief in

Slovakia and 22 percent in the Czech Republic.[57] This has in some ways affected not only the PCT's manoeuvrability in the scrutiny of legislation, but also its capacity as a protector of rights.

It is in state-centred political economies—where the state has significant welfare-providing duties—that abstract review is preferred and constitutional courts are to work 'as a sort of adviser and/or policeman to the other two branches' instead of following the judicial paradigm by 'merely' deciding cases and controversies.[58] Poland fits the description perfectly. Moreover, its pre-1989 dissent centred around Solidarity and the Catholic Church. Accordingly, participation in subverting the regime was taking place on a collective rather than an individual level, through organisations that were better equipped to challenge power than were isolated individuals or even small groups.[59] The synergic effect of these oppositional attitudes made Poland the most sovietisation-proof society in the region and the fastest one to get on the track of systemic change. The syndicalist nature of the pre-1989 dissent and the legacy of a strong unified opposition that claimed to represent civil society, however, affected both the extent of the PCT's jurisdiction and its standing rules. According to the PCTA, a motion for abstract review of laws could have been submitted, in addition to organs of mostly political pedigree,[60] by

> communal or regional councils and local self-government appellate tribunals, the appropriately entitled principal bodies of national trade union organisations, inter-union organisations and associations of trade unions, cooperative organisations, social and professional organisations of individual farmers, and other trade organisations, as well as the Council for Social Insurance of Farmers, if the legislative act or other normative act subject to question relates to matters that fall within their jurisdiction as defined by provisions of law.[61]

Clearly, this made government policies more exposed to rights-based challenges than if access to constitutional review had been limited to bodies of an exclusively political nature.

Yet by channelling individual claims through institutional mediators the then existing model also required integration of personal interests into a socially coherent and community-friendly value system. Under such a model, different personal interests are scrutinised for their compatibility with collective interests before they can be meaningfully voiced let alone satisfactorily settled. Such a model also suggests a context which lacks a 'tough citizen, one who is willing to run significant risks deliberately in order to vindicate his rights, not one who waits for the paternalistic arms of the state to take care of him'.[62] It is telling that even Polish legal scholarship tended to interpret measures limiting access to constitutional review to different public bodies as creating the space necessary for citizens' participation in constitutional discourse. Patrźalek claimed, for instance, that while the ombudsman represented the citizens 'in an institutional and professional way', the public organisations did so 'more naturally, immanently and coherently'.[63] He also argued that since the relevant public corporations were functioning on democratic principles and were representative of their constituents' interests, they allowed citizens to exert influence, even though indirectly, on the administration of constitutional review.[64] Dzialocha added that the democratic nature of a state ruled by law stemmed from 'the procedurally guaranteed means of influencing the decisions of state authorities open to acknowledged civil associations (organisations) by way of public opinion'.[65] Here, even the semantics demonstrate the degree to which public opinion would be identified with that of 'acknowledged civil associations'.[66]

Both the provisionality of constitutional provisions regulating rights and the state-centric political economy worked against reformulating the PCT's rights protection competence. What also added to the context was, paradoxically, the rising importance of rights. Several layers of institutional protection against rights infringements were available at the time of drafting of the Little Constitution or were to become available upon its promulgation. In December 1992, President Wałesa signed the Law on the Ratification of the European Convention on Human Rights and Fundamental Freedoms (ECHRFF), and in March 1993, the Polish government declared its adherence to the jurisdiction of the European Commission/Court of Human Rights (ECHR), giving citizens the right to complain to the ECHR of a breach by the government of their rights. To deprive the national high court of hearing individual complaints and yet to provide for the possibility to file such complaints with a transnational body could be dismissed as a pitiful inconsistency. Again, however, the focus in the local arena was on President–Sejm–Cabinet cooperation, and the adherence to the jurisdiction of the ECHR was legitimising enough *vis-à-vis* Europe. The lack of a veritable rights jurisdiction for the PCT was not so much of a political liability as to overcome the inertia confining constitutional amendments to the few issues that were deemed of utmost urgency and practical importance.

The impact on constitutional review of the success story of the Commissioner for Citizen's Rights (ombudsman) cannot be ignored either. Indeed, it might have been the assertive approach of the first female ombudsman (Ewa Letowska) in Poland that made the need for the establishment of another mechanism of protection of individual rights seem less urgent than it might have seemed had she not been so persistent. The ombudsman was, and remains, entitled to file a motion with the PCT alleging unconstitutionality or illegality of a normative act, and would often do so upon consideration of submissions received from citizens.[67] In fact, Letowska as the first female ombudsman served in several cases as the mediator of quasi-complaints to the PCT and was the most active among authorities competent to initiate proceedings at the Tribunal. One of the more practicable ways of producing a rights case law thus was to adjudicate upon the ombudsmen's petitions.

After all, the PCT's *Rechtsstaat* and equal protection jurisprudence[68] blossomed in spite of structural limitations on its adjudicative competence, as 'the Tribunal has shown itself willing to develop normative principles on the basis of the limited language of the constitution'.[69] Various unenumerated rights were protected through the *Rechtsstaat* and equality clauses or the PCT's doctrine of vested rights. When the inertia combined with a seemingly sufficient level of protection of individual rights, the *status quo* in the realm of constitutional review, even though far from perfect, seemed sustainable enough to warrant waiting for the new constitution.

Transitional Leadership

Two other aspects of Poland's transitional politics served to marginalise constitutional review within the debate on institutional reform: one related to the country's favourable position on Europe's political map, the other had to do with the preoccupation of the public with President Wałesa's larger-than-life persona.

As for the regional contest for Western or European recognition, Poland had assets to offer for the lack of which countries such as Hungary or Czechoslovakia had to compensate. If only for the sheer size of the country and its geopolitical significance, and the moral credit of Polish civil society's resistance to sovietisation,[70] Poland had a comparative advantage in the regional race for political recognition. That any enlargement of the EU is unthinkable without Poland being one of the first-round new members, no matter how much more ready the rest of the region might be, is undisputed by the commentators of the integration agenda and is semi-officially acknowledged by all the relevant EU circles, too.[71] Even if not strikingly pretty, the shop was important enough not to require too much window dressing. More specifically, the insulation from constitutional review of legislation was, in the particular context of Poland's transition, deemed a system stability-enhancing feature and at once one not necessarily threatening the country's integrative ambitions. The very same factor which provided a significant rationale for the emergence of the Hungarian Court as the country's principal 'public relations' asset *vis-à-vis* the West was therefore much less important in Poland.

What did not happen in Poland, however, was the Weberian translation of personal charisma into institutional consolidation of authority. Soon after being elected to the highest office in the state Wałesa engaged in quarrels with other public officials, polarized the political scene, and, most importantly, reinforced rather than alleviated the culture of anti-legalism that Skapska finds typical of post-communist Poland. Despite the fact that he presented the Sejm with an impressive draft of a rights charter and although he never delivered on his promises to introduce enlightened dictatorship, Brzezinski points out that Wałesa's rhetoric was 'damaging to the development of a constitutional culture'.[72] Some students of Polish politics may find this treatment too harsh. But the way that the conflict over Poland's 1995 budget was solved offers a telling story. Wałesa as the then President refused to sign the budget and some budget-related statutes, and called on the PCT to declare their unconstitutionality. When the PCT did otherwise with respect to one of the issues presented to it, Wałesa still refused to promulgate the law and did so only after his and Prime Minister Oleksy's fist waving was brought to a halt by mutual concessions. Based on his deal with Oleksy, Wałesa, despite his contrary initial position, did not wait before signing the respective regulation for the PCT's other ruling, which, paradoxically, validated the President's challenge.[73] The adverse consequences of such and similar practices for law's centrality in political life are obvious. Either way, it would be difficult to deny that Wałesa failed to employ his charisma in the service of a thorough institutional reform, one that would go beyond the strengthening of presidential authority.

Both the interim constitutional reform and the wider political dialogue focused on providing for meaningful ways of cooperation between the President and the cabinet, as well as between the two executive branches and the legislature. Brzezinski describes the context in the following way: '[D]iscussion of the constitutional options centred on the persona of President Wałesa himself, with his supporters... pushing for a "French-style presidency"... and his opponents leaning toward a classical parliamentary democracy'.[74] No reputational bonus could have been gained by embracing the concept of aggrandisement of constitutional review, as the discourse was preoccupied with the role of the President *vis-à-vis* the Sejm and the cabinet. In the realm of institutional rather than substantive policies these were the lines along which both society at large and the political elite were divided.[75] These were the issues on the basis of which loyalty was professed. In a colloquy focused in this way, constitutional review is far from being a priority.

True, the Polish lawmakers believed this state of affairs to have fitted the particular needs and challenges of the transitory period during which the PCT was to operate under the watchful eyes of the legislature. In a way, the issue of the PCT's positioning within the institutional environment was merely deferred rather than decidedly solved against constitutional review. Yet even after the completion of constitutional reform the Sejm had kept for two more years the authority to reconsider those of the Tribunal's unconstitutionality findings that were related to statutes adopted prior to the coming into force of the new constitution. This suggests—if it does not prove—that the PCT's conceptualisation combined the traditional with the transitional modalities of the country's political economy. Placing the constitutional court on the same side of the field as the legislator rather than making it an umpire of the whole ballpark simply fitted both the context of transition and the traditional local understanding of the proper frame of a constitutional democracy.

Nevertheless, upon the adoption of the Constitution of the Republic of Poland in 1997 the PCT was put on an equal footing with constitutional courts elsewhere in the region. Its powers were expanded so as to include, inter alia, international agreements as a subject matter of conformity adjudication,[76] and the right to file a constitutional complaint in the case of infringements of individual rights.[77] The judgments of the PCT, including unconstitutionality findings with regard to statutes, are now of universally binding application and final.[78]

Listed among the factors that contributed to the bringing about of an almost full-fledged constitutional review should be, first of all, the fact that the adoption of the 1997 Constitution did away with the powerful provisionality constraints. It was the elevation of the constitutional order from a transitional to a definite one that provided the decisive rationale for the gradual insulation of constitutional case law from parliamentary reconsideration. Moreover, the PCT was throughout the *provisorium* trying hard to overcome its structural limitations by stepping outside its realm of competence and asserting itself as a player in the process of transition. These efforts increased the Tribunal's visibility in, and relevance to, Poland's public life and prevented its marginalisation by lawmakers in the course of deliberation over the 1997 Constitution.

The current delineation of the PCT's powers is also rooted in a consensus the origins of which can be traced to a time well before the enactment of the new Constitution. Before the promulgation of the Little Constitution, two constitutional drafts were produced both of which 'asserted the supremacy... of the decisions of the Constitutional Tribunal over ordinary legislation'.[79] According to Brzezinski, the need for a thorough reform of the PCT's jurisdictional design was generally accepted even in the immediate wake of the promulgation of the Little Constitution.[80] That the PCT's rulings as to the unconstitutionality of statutes had to be made final and that a mechanism allowing for constitutional complaints had to be provided for were the two principally uncontested cornerstones of the future delineation of the PCT's authority. Even though Brzezinski's claim that 'there was virtual unanimity on the future powers of the Tribunal'[81] seems to be going too far,[82] it is true that throughout the highly polarised discussion of the 1997 Constitution it was generally accepted that constitutional review as an institution was ready for a significant expansion of its authority.

Hungary

Overview

Hungary had its first written charter-like constitution promulgated by the dictatorial Revolutionary Governing Council in 1919, following an almost thousand-year-long development of the historical unwritten constitution.[83] After a few months, the revolutionary constitution was worth only the paper on which it was printed and Hungary went back to a monarchical form of government, which it retained until 1946.[84] Statute I of 1946, operating as the constitutional basis for Hungary's transition from monarchy to republic, was replaced in 1949 by Act XX, also known as the 'Stalinist constitution'. Forty years later another regime change subjected the 1949 Constitution to various systemic amendments, which continue to operate as the supreme law of the land. Notwithstanding the post-1989 patchwork, Hungary is still waiting to promulgate its first democratic charter-like constitution.

But while in Poland the wish to start anew by producing a democratic constitution did not offer enough of a rationale for providing a major role for the PCT in the interim constitution, in Hungary the effect on the conceptualisation of constitutional review of the provisionality constraint was radically different. The idea of adopting a new constitution, although never given up completely, was less of an issue: Arato claims, for instance, that in Poland the limitations and structural problems affecting constitutional amendments were more severe, and the need to produce a new constitution greater than they were in Hungary.[85] Both the elite and the public were gradually getting used to the idea that the constitutional achievements might be for a long time to come limited to the post-1989 patchwork and its elaboration by the HCC, which attitude was at once a consequence of the failure to adopt a single-body constitution and a cause for further inertia. Moreover, the idea of having a constitution that rests on a series of fundamental laws is far from being a novelty in Hungarian constitutionalism.[86]

The constitutional amendments adopted in the wake of the 1989 Round Table talks included Act XXXII on the Constitutional Court (HACC). The HACC provided the Court with an extremely broad adjudicative instrumentarium. The only major adjudicative tool missing from the Court's equipment is the review of petitions alleging rights infringements by administrative and judicial decisions. In the meantime, the HACC left the organisational aspects of the HCC's operation to be elaborated by the justices themselves.

Sólyom argues that in Central and Eastern Europe, "the Constitutional Courts did not emerge from the domestic organic development of law but were imported products."[87] It is also claimed that the 'Constitutional Court and the idea of judicial review itself were unknown in the Hungarian Constitutional tradition'.[88] How then did the 'most powerful constitutional court in the world'[89] come into being in a country in the tradition of which the 'respect for a written constitution is not deeply rooted'?[90]

Legal Culture

First of all, the country's legal tradition had been based on a diversity of law making authorities for too long for traces not to have been left in current practice. Throughout its centuries-long development, Hungarian law tended to resist the supremacy of codified law,[91] and the judiciary relied on an extensive body of customary law. The single most important body of medieval Hungarian law, the *Opus Tripartitum*, failed to be promulgated as law and became binding only by virtue of being adhered to by the courts.[92] The *Corpus Iuris Hungarici* followed a similar path, being produced by private parties and later becoming officially binding as a collection of statutes, decrees, and customary rules.[93] Even the Restatement ('Interim Legal Provisions')—produced by the *Iudex Curia* Conference in the aftermath of the re-establishment by the 1860 October Diploma of the continuity of the Hungarian legal order—has not been officially promulgated and became binding by virtue of being observed by courts and, consequently, by becoming customary law.[94]

True, following the Austro-Hungarian settlement in 1867, various realms of law underwent a solid codifying enterprise and the belated bureaucratic revolution was taking place at a fervent pace. Yet the paradigm of fluidity of the law making authority did not vanish and transplanted itself into the twentieth century. Based on Act 54/1912, special senates of *Curia Regis* were allowed to issue so-called *decisiae* as generally binding norms, which could be altered only by statute or by a nation-wide customary rule.[95] The civil law was solidified by codification only in 1959. Although the above sketch is somewhat selective,[96] it shows that courts in Hungary were used to relying on the safety net of customary law and that this has come to be expected of them. Varga argues that it is in the country's tradition for the actual message of law to be revealed through precedents elaborated by judicial practice.[97] Under traditions such as these, case law represents, as Weber would have put it, the real embodiment of law. Indeed, it was in Hungary that the tradition of the 'living voice of the law', the *lag saga*, caught the strongest hold.[98] The HCC strove to update this tradition, assisted especially by the Italian Constitutional Court.[99]

Moreover, in contrast to the Weberian approach to legal rationality, which rejects the expectations of law's addressees as irrelevant to the logic of a legal argument,[100] the practice of reflecting through adjudication the public's normative ideals and expectations, and its notions of justice, is not alien to Hungary's culture of law. This practice has affected not only certain aspects of the HCC's design, especially the posterior abstract review standing rules, but in a way also its adjudicative philosophy. Let us listen, for instance, to what a local scholar has to say of judicial application of the 1875 Commercial Code of Hungary: 'Court practice mitigated, however, the harshness of commercial rules when people inexperienced in business matters would have faced unexpected results.'[101] The following quote comes from a holding of the HCC exactly 120 years later: '[T]he constitutional requirement flowing from the principle of legal certainty and pertaining to the shift to the new system is to guarantee a period of preparation for those concerned necessary for adjustment to the amended provisions and for the organisation of the finances of the family in accordance with the new conditions.'[102] In Hungary, the court is your friend through thick and thin.

It was by conceptualising the constitutional court as a policy maker and, subsequently, by the Court's ingenious reinvention of the invisible constitution that Hungary reaffirmed its paradigm of polycentric law making. Not only does the safety net of the invisible constitution allow for an extensive interpretive discretion, but it also gives the Court the possibility of understanding its own precedents as a source of law superior to the written constitution. The HCC came to understand the suprapositive background as being informed more by pan-European standards than by national customs, that is, more by the universal source than by the tribal source, to use Bergson's dichotomy. The concept is the same, however: it is one of a plurality of sources of law. In Hungary, the rule of reason—a legacy of Enlightenment in general and of the Josephinian era in particular—did translate into legal scholarship as much as it did in the Czech lands. However, it did not serve to confine the sources of legal rationality to legislative or bureaucratic knowledge, and thus to erase the notion of judicial lawmaking from the country's legal topography. The active involvement of the HCC in shaping the living law merely updates Hungary's tradition of attributing a significant role of governance to the judiciary. By frequently identifying sources of normativity outside legal texts, the HCC builds on, rather than works against, the absence of a tradition of a written constitution.

Transitional Political Economy

It is often argued that the delineation of the Court's powers did not follow a thorough and complex analysis, and that the birth of 'the most powerful court in the world' was rather haphazard. The deliberation over the Court's role is said to have been both hasty and limited. In fact, those who are familiar with the situation claim that the 'idea for a constitutional court came up... on a Friday afternoon when the Parliament was supposed to vote on the Constitution on Monday'.[103] Sólyom concedes, "in the midst of political changes, the legislators who enacted the Court had but a vague cenception of the functions of a constitutional court" and describes the drafting of the respective provisions as a "hurried technical preparation."[104] One way to cope with the incorporation of an almost omnipotent constitutional court thus would be to subscribe to the 'they had no idea what they were doing' explanation.

True enough, the available evidence suggests that the birth of the HCC was not based on some elaborate exercise in political science. But to dismiss any rational considerations in bringing about constitutional review seems similarly implausible. It is hard to believe that no attention would be paid to a body that was radically to limit the manoeuvring space of both legislative and executive branches. Indeed, several months of intense negotiations preceded the draft of the first post-revolutionary constitutional act. Páczolay informs us that issues related to the operation of the HCC were 'discussed extensively during the Opposition Round Table talks',[105] and that 'the rules relating to a future Constitutional Court became a central issue in the negotiations among political groups during the summer of 1989'.[106] Sajó points out that even though "very little effort was devoted to placing the court in the context of a balanced arrangement of powers", during the RT talks "agreement was reached on the role and importance of the Constitutional Court."[107]

The constitutional and statutory delineation of the HCC's powers appears to be a function of both the accidental, 'veil of ignorance' aspects, and factors which, if judged separately rather than in combination, may seem of minor importance but which were not without consequence for the making of institutional choices during the Round Table talks. First, Hungary's dissident groups and even their umbrella forum, the Opposition Round Table (EKA), were weaker than Polish Solidarity. According to Arato, the Hungarian participants at the Round Table talks were, unlike their Polish counterparts, 'obsessed by their lack of legitimacy'.[108] In the meantime, distinct and distinguishable entities participated in negotiations with the communist incumbents, and were communicating their particular agendas to the public. The plurality of political inclinations was already in place at the time of the Round Table talks, during which the basis for a future deal between the insurgents themselves was debated. In short, while in Poland the debate on democratisation pitted two relatively strongly unified political groups against each other, in Hungary the tension extended to both the then establishment—internally divided into communist conservatives and reformers—and the opposition trying to reconcile conflicting interests emerging within it at an early stage. The arrangement between the negotiators thus was less of an elite settlement than it was in Poland in that the environment in which it was taking place was more confrontational.[109] The focus was on setting the stage for electoral competition rather than, as was the case in Poland, on outlining elaborate contours of social development by the two forces that seemed able directly to affect it.

Therefore, neither the incumbents nor the insurgents had particularly strong incentives to stick to the formula adhered to during the transition's initial phase. There was no reason to believe that the Round Table deal would outlive the first elections,[110] which in turn served to simplify it by making it focus on procedural guarantees for unfettered competition for political power and a few related areas: for example, criminal code, right to assembly, constitutional review. This was in contrast to the Polish experience where the Round Table agreement included sketches of reform to be undertaken in specific areas of public administration and was more laden with content than it was in Hungary. Consequently, both the uncertainty as to whether all the parties involved would observe the foundational agreement and the narrow scope of the agreement created a need for a mechanism that would at once supervise the agreement's execution, not be hostage to it, and yet be able to elaborate upon it as might be required. Thus, a 'guardian of the revolution by the rule of law' was brought about,[111] a body to preserve the *ruptura pactada*.

In addition, the incumbents' wish to evidence their divorce with the past led them to support novel institutions. Not only Sólyom, representing the opposition, but also Kulcsár, participating in the RT talks, on behalf of the incumbents, supported a strong constitutional court. Sajó says that Kulcsár, the Minister of Justice in Hungary's last communist cabinet, vigorously supported the concept of the rule of law and constitutional review already in 1988 when he came forth with a prosposal to establish a constitutional court.[112] Many of the communist reformers taking part in the negotiations believed that they would be able to distance themselves from the Kádár clique, and thus reserve for themselves some public appreciation, by subscribing to progressive ideas of Western provenance. Former President Göncz went as far as claiming that this attitude of the reform communists reflected their inner transformation from believers in the system into its opponents.[113] To stand behind ideas such as constitutional review, or at least not to oppose them vigorously, was therefore an understandable move for the incumbents, too.

It also appears from the delineation of the HCC's powers, especially with respect to the scope of its preliminary review, that providing for an active role of constitutional review in the legislative process was, in a way, compensating for the lack of a second parliamentary chamber. Indeed, it is in the Court's conceptualisation as an enforcer of abstract constitutionality that the specific elements of local political economy are most apparent.

On the one hand, the distinguishing features of the civil-law mode of constitutional review—namely its abstract and political nature—translated into the HCC's broad authority in the realms of policy-making and resolution of disputes between agencies of political pedigree. On the other hand, there were in place also the more common law-like features. The continental mode of constitutional adjudication usually limits abstract review standing to actors traditionally deemed competent to carry out public functions and influence the shape of public life. The direct accessibility of abstract constitutional review is confined to political agents, for example, a parliamentary faction, the Attorney General, the President—which with some variations is the case in both the Czech Republic and Slovakia—or, as in Poland, it extends to bodies of a corporate nature, such as the national offices of trade unions or farmers' organisations. In short, the emphasis lies on those with the institutional capacity to make a difference. A society accustomed to polycentric law making and thus to the plurality of sources of law learns to appreciate the jurisgenerative aspects of justice administration to a greater extent. This Hungarian society certainly has learned, as abstract review standing extended to virtually everyone.

Yet making abstract review accessible to individual petitioners did not by any means serve to undo the traditional elements of the local legal culture and the abstract nature underlying the Hungarian version of constitutional review. Sajó points out, for instance, the lack in Hungary of a culture that would encourage personal efforts to vindicate individual rights.[114] Accordingly, no personal interest was required for submission by citizens of abstract-review petitions, and no constitutional complaint provided to redress individual grievances. The tradition of an active involvement of the Hungarian judiciary in the contextualisation of both the content and the framework of governance therefore helped the HCC to rise to the very centre of constitutional politics. Yet its envelopment in the state-centred political economy—which tends to make constitutional courts part of the state machinery to a much greater extent than is the case in market-centred political economies, such as the United States—at once made the abstract non-adversarial mode of adjudication the Court's principal enterprise.

Transitional Leadership

With sizeable minorities living outside its territory and by being something of an ethno-lingual enclave surrounded by Slavic, Latin, and German elements, Hungary is very wary of the image it enjoys outside its borders. It knows it needs foreign support in order to advance its regional agenda,[115] and goes to great lengths to foster its relationship with the West. Batt says that in Hungarian foreign policy 'being "first" or at the forefront in developing new links with Western and European institutions appears to be an important psychological undercurrent'.[116] Schimmelfennig points out the Hungarians' insistence on their 'pioneering role in the changes in Central and Eastern Europe'.[117] And Klingsberg goes as far as speaking of 'Hungary's general fascination with the West'.[118]

When the Constitutional Court began to assert its power in a way that could not have gone unnoticed either in Hungary or by its students elsewhere, the country was working on its admission to the Council of Europe and was in the midst of negotiating the association agreement with the European Community. Lacking the geopolitical significance of Poland and the sad 'advantage' of being a victim of the Western powers' betrayal at the outset of the Second World War, and simultaneously falling behind Czechoslovakia in terms of industrial development and pre-communist democratic tradition, Hungarian politicians were looking for ways to 'make up lost ground'. They were not in a position to press the economic factor, with the trade balance and the budget in a dismal state and with the impending risk of becoming just another case of Mexican-type crisis.[119] In addition, it was Balcerowicz's 'shock therapy' and Klaus's coupon privatisation rather than the late-coming Bokros plan that attracted foreign attention. And it was the Poles' reconciliation with the Germans and the argument over the future of Czechoslovakia rather than what was going on in the 'happiest barracks in the camp'[120] that were stealing the attention of foreign media and politicians. Plasser also notes the 'damage done to the collective psyche by Hungary's losing its "pioneering role" in economic transformation to Poland and [the Czech Republic]'.[121] Hungary, perhaps even more so than its regional partners, therefore had every incentive to manipulate the context of European integration into one based on pan-European liberal values rather than on economic or fiscal performance. It was in the realm of constitutionalism that a comparative advantage could be—and in fact was—gained.

The selection of a specific institutional framework designed to reflect and embody in a totemised way the polity's cognitive experience is an *orientatio* enterprise *par excellence*. There are only so many ways in which the *ontos* of the polity undergoing a thorough re-definition can express itself normatively, institutional design being one that can be established relatively rapidly. Following the demise of communism, the respective societies were modelling institutions that would capture the emerging civic spirit of the polity and present its noble side to the outside world. In Poland—claimed to be haunted by an anti-legalistic culture and accustomed to remedying any lack of cohesion of the legislative power by embracing charismatic authoritarian leaders—the selection of ontophanic institutions concerned mainly the President and the Sejm. But in Hungary, a 'country of lawyers' with a strong tradition not only of parliamentarism, but also of the judiciary's participation in the policy-making process, the pool of applicants for transitional leadership also included the Constitutional Court.

After all, both Wałesa and Havel as the banner-bearers of their respective countries' transformations were more widely known in the West than was Göncz. Neither the legislature nor Antall's cabinet was 'attractive' enough to be relied upon in the country's quest for recognition. It took Antall quite some time to distance himself from the nationalist and at times even antisemitic faction of his party comrade István Csurka and this reluctance, despite Antall's relative popularity among Western Europe's Christian Democrats, was not welcomed. The policies that the cabinet was pursuing were not much different, let alone substantially better, than those adopted elsewhere in the region. The governing coalition, for instance, was not bold enough to do away with the death penalty, as the newcomers did in Czechoslovakia, and was therefore unable to sign the ECHRFF's Optional Protocol No. 6 banning capital punishment.

So it was the Constitutional Court that struck down capital punishment. In the meantime, it announced that the country was to move in the same direction as Europe.[122] And more 'Europeanisation' of Hungarian constitutionalism was to follow, mostly by means of reliance in the Court's dicta on international standards and the case law of both the national constitutional and the transnational judiciary of Europe (and the US Supreme Court). The Court has made a name for itself both on the continent and overseas. It returned Hungary to Europe.[123] To undermine such a foreign policy asset would have been, put plainly, silly.

A few half-hearted attempts to curb constitutional review surfaced in the Hungarian Parliament after several sweeping decisions made the HCC's potential too obvious to be ignored. But the legislature's ability to curtail the Court's powers was a technical rather than a practical possibility. First, in order to modify the HACC, a qualified two-thirds majority is needed, which at the time was far from easy to amass. Secondly, the Court was operating not only under the watchful eyes of the legislature, but also under the supporting eyes of the international legal community. The Chief Justice's warning that 'if considerable limitations were imposed on our jurisdiction, then the Hungarian legislature would encounter [an] intense reaction from all over Europe and would need to give an explanation'[124] was clearly aimed at the local audience. Thirdly, in consolidating the HCC's power base Sólyom displayed Marshallian sophistication[125] In the same decision that launched Hungary on the road to Europe and made the Court the trademark of Hungarians' progressiveness, this oft-quoted passage was produced:

> The Constitutional Court must continue its effort to explain the theoretical bases of the Constitution and the rights included in it and to form a coherent system with its decisions in order to provide a reliable standard of constitutionality—an 'invisible Constitution'—beyond the Constitution; and because of this 'invisible Constitution' probably will not conflict with the new Constitution to be established or with future Constitutions. The Constitutional Court enjoys freedom in this process as long as it remains within the framework of the concept of constitutionality.[126]

Now how can you accept one part of a ruling that symbolically opened the door for your country's accession to the family of civilised nations and at once reject some other part of it? As Ackerman argues, 'a politician considering whether to defy a particular judicial judgment cannot realistically engage in a narrow cost–benefit analysis. Instead, he must engage in a broader analysis, taking into account economic and military benefits that may be lost if domestic political defiance leads to exclusion from the federation'.[127] Especially so when constitutional review establishes itself as the ultimate Europeanisation tool—'[t]he Constitutional Court does allow itself the liberty of taking part in politics, in the sense that it fights tooth and nail to integrate Hungary's constitution into international practices in terms of language, concepts, and consistency'[128]—and the environment makes it 'highly risky to criticize the Constitutional Court on intellectual or professional grounds since this would certainly be interpreted as an attempt to cast doubt on the institution itself'.[129] Trying to curb the Court's powers or defying its judgments simply became non-*salonfähig*.[130]

The story of the Constitutional Court is to a notable extent the story of the Hungarians' self-projected duty to 'make it' in Europe, to excel politically, and to prove themselves an example to the rest of the region, if not the world. It became the role of the HCC to spark up the mundane daily politics, make the country look special and give it some charisma. After the Court deliberately took up this mission its road to fame was free, for nothing short of worldwide fame has come to be expected of the Court by those who could have halted it. And the HCC was very much aware of its patriotic duty. What the then Chef Justice had to say about this is self-explanatory:

> The comparison of new solutions and the quotation of trends not only offer theoretical lessons but can also serve as a model for planned changes in the political system. This is the reason for the interest from all over the world in the output of the new courts and this offers a unique opportunity for publicity even for constitutional courts which, due to the size or importance of their countries, would never have achieved this.[131]

And thanks to the transition, the courts—but mainly the Hungarian one—believed they could become '[more] important and well known [than] they could [ever] have become as evolutionary constitutional courts solving merely routine cases, even if in an excellent manner'.[132]

It would be too harsh to describe Hungarians as 'fashion victims', especially because the fashion in question did anything but victimise them. But that the Court was allowed to impose (its interpretation of) international standards upon the legislature and, consequently, upon the population was due partly to the fact that such standards were the trend there where the country—pushed by the Court—was moving.

Czechoslovakia/Czech and Slovak Republics

Overview

In Czechoslovakia, tradition informed the establishment of constitutional review in more immediate ways than it did elsewhere in the region. Throughout the second half of the nineteenth century and in the course of the twentieth, numerous attempts surfaced locally to charge the judiciary with the protection of constitutional law. Even though most of these attempts were largely unsuccessful, it was relatively easy for the Czechoslovak post-1989 drafters to press for the incorporation of constitutional review by emphasising indigenous tradition rather than an import from abroad. Both successor states to Czechoslovakia appropriated the tradition and opted for an updated copy of the original version tracing its roots to constitutional review in the Masaryk Republic and in some ways even to the Imperial Court of the late Hapsburg era. But the context in which Czech and Slovak constitutional courts were conceived was different from that affecting the establishment of the federal court in the wake of the regime change. A few remarks are therefore warranted on how the short-lived federal constitutional court came about and operated.

Czechoslovakia's communist establishment was doubtless the least inclined among the Central European countries to pursue democratic reforms. Moreover, the hard-liners faced relatively disorganised and politically inexperienced opponents. The Slovak pre-1989 dissent was by far the weakest in Central Europe and also much less popular among the public than were insurgents elsewhere in the region. The Round Table talks were extremely short, spanning a period of a few weeks, and the content of the changeover agreement was relatively limited, concerned mainly with providing for a swift change of government and free elections, without sketching out particular policies to be pursued. At its core lay the repudiation of the constitutional clause stipulating the leading role of the communist party, the mechanism for co-optation of the insurgent leaders into the Parliament, and the provision for free elections to be held without undue delay. Moreover, the local insurgents were beneficiaries of the bandwagon effect of region-wide changes rather than of their own political savvy. Both the Czech and the Slovak transition agencies were not only the last in the region to stage a 'revolution' but, judged from the distance of a decade, also a little incompetent in getting done what they set out to achieve. And out of luck, too.

In order to pursue any thorough legal and economic reform, a viable arrangement of relations between the two republics had to be found. That it never was found can be attributed to several factors. First, Havel failed to transform his personal charisma into institutional consolidation as much as Wałesa did, although I find him less at fault for this than many others do.[133] Secondly, there were serious cultural misunderstandings inhibiting effective bargaining at federal level. The Czech political elite was breathtakingly ignorant of the Slovak socio-political context and made more mistakes in trying to police the younger brother than proved to be bearable. The Slovak leadership, struggling with internal conflicts and the growing unmanageability of the emerging popular hero Mečiar, would vent its inferiority complexes by testing the patience of its Czech partner. Thirdly, there were serious systemic obstacles to finding a viable agreement on the future of the common state. The communist constitution, due to its anti-majoritarian provisions aimed at disguising the post-1968 arrangements as an 'authentic federation', served to frustrate most attempts at national policy making in general and established prohibitively stringent criteria for constitutional amendments in particular.[134] This very 'ban on majority rule', courtesy of former President and Party Leader Husák, hindered any meaningful transformation of the constitutional framework cursed—or blessed, depending on one's understanding of an authentic federation—by the rule of parity and super-majority voting requirements. The systemic constraints combined with substantial disagreements within the Slovak representation over the proper manner of Slovakia's emancipation within the federation. This state of affairs made any solution to the issue of division of competencies between the two republics difficult both structurally and politically, and provided some rationale for referring the incomplete aspects of the agenda to a supra-political authority. The vividness of the federalism issue, one of the main *raisons d'être* of constitutional courts in general, thus helped the re-birth of the Czechoslovak one, too. Symptomatically, its first decision concerned the highly sensitive issue of division of competence between the federal and the Slovak ministries of telecommunications, an issue that the federal legislature was unable to resolve in an unambiguous way.

There were other factors conducive to the establishment of a constitutional court. Havel presented the draft Constitutional Act on the Czechoslovak Constitutional Court (CSCC) in response to a parliamentary debate on the Bill of Fundamental Rights and Freedoms,[135] and the act was adopted three weeks after the Bill of Rights. The Czechoslovak leaders also anticipated that the country would soon adhere to the ECHRFF. The clause in the Czechoslovak constitution providing for the supremacy of international human rights agreements over ordinary legislation implied that an arbiter should be instituted to assess conformity of national laws to rules of higher normative force. Similarly inviting was the simmering controversy over how to understand certain provisions of the Bill of Rights, especially those related to so-called 'positive rights'.

But the fact that Czechoslovakia formally instituted constitutional review before anyone else in Europe might have turned out to be an eternal curse. It took until November 1991 to promulgate the implementing act on the CSCC,[136] and the President appointed the first justices only in January 1992. They had the power to decide on conformity to the federal constitution of federal statutes, as well as on conformity to ratified international human rights treaties of both constitutional and statutory acts. The CSCC was also competent to furnish abstract interpretation of the constitution and review individual complaints alleging violation of a right provided for by the constitution or a ratified international human rights treaty. The Court, however, lasted a mere eleven months during which it managed to issue decisions on the merits only in a handful of cases. When judged in light of the context in which it was working—the domination of the issue of 'state and legal arrangements' between the two nations—and the short time it was given to operate, its interpretive enterprise could hardly have been more extensive and its legacy more relevant. After all, the Czech Constitutional Court refers to the former federal Court's case law on a regular basis and relies heavily, for instance, on the concept of equality elaborated by the CSCC.[137] Yet the role of the CSCC in the political and institutional turmoil of 1991–1992 was peripheral. With the exception of its decision to validate most provisions of the lustration law contested by a large faction of the Federal Assembly, the CSCC's case law did not give rise to as heated disputes as, for instance, some of the PCT's or the HCC's rulings on measures of transitional justice or economic legislation. It also suffered no significant politically motivated blows and was, to say the least, a tolerated feature of the transitional environment.

The CSCC was unable to overcome by itself the impasse in institutional reform. The political helplessness of the so-called pro-federal and pro-reform forces contributed significantly to the growing feeling of incompatibility between the paths of societal development in the two republics and, consequently, to the split of the country. In the end, separation, although in a very peculiar way, did lead to progress in constitutional reform. Slovakia adopted its first democratic constitution in September 1992, to be followed by the Czech Republic three months later.

By 'virtue' of splitting, both successor states have overcome the indefinite nature of their constitutional orders. The adoption of 'real' constitutions brought about some institutional consolidation, whether one found its particular aspects desirable or not. The different ways in which Hungarian and Polish lawmakers responded to the issue of provisionality—the former opting for an inflated engagement of a constitutional court in the elaboration of foundational arrangements, the latter postponing any relevant extension of its authority—were inapplicable to Czechoslovakia's successor states because that particular issue simply was not on the table. Quite the contrary—being able to assess the neighbour's experience with an overly powerful constitutional judiciary and one struggling with crippled authority, the Czech and Slovak drafters opted for adjudicative equipment for their constitutional courts that in general terms reflected the Austro-German standard.

Legal Culture

Modern Czech constitutional history traces its roots to the enlightened absolutism of Maria Theresa and Joseph II, which proved decisive for the unification and codification of Austrian and, by extension, Czech law. It also laid down foundations for the tradition of monistic law making by a central authority, so different from the fluidity of sources of law in Hungary. The local legal scholarship internalised, and was partly also the source of, the principles constituting the axiological basis of the bureaucratic revolution of Joseph II, especially the superiority of reason and the belief in enlightened governance by and through law. The Josephinian reform paved the way for overcoming particularism and estate personalism in the realm of law and governance[138] and proved favourable to the germination of legalism and, in a way, the rule of law.

In the Czech lands, the local origins of an institution resembling the functions of contemporary constitutional review can be found in the 'Kroměříž Proposal' of 1848, which followed the transfer by the Emperor of the *Reichstag* session from Vienna to the Moravian town of Kroměříž.[139] This draft constitution of the Austrian state, which the Czech lands were an integral part of, was influenced by the constitutions of the United States and France and contained a catalogue of fundamental civil rights to be protected by the Supreme Imperial Court.[140] The *Reichstag* session was cancelled in March 1849, which prevented implementation of both the document and the court. The ensuing Stadion constitution, imposed in March 1849, kept the catalogue of rights but no reference to any particular body charged with their protection.[141] The civil rights were then jettisoned by the so-called Silvester (New Year's Eve) patents and remained outside constitutional protection even after the 1861 February Constitution had been instituted. It was in the so-called December Constitution of 1867—consisting of a series of acts—that the nineteenth-century German theory of a government ruled by law found its institutional expression. The Imperial Court (IC), established by Act 143/1867, was empowered to carry out functions that were similar to some aspects of contemporary constitutional review. It was, for instance, competent to hear complaints of individual citizens alleging breach of their political rights guaranteed by the December Constitution. The IC, however, lacked the authority directly to invalidate a challenged act.[142] A similar scheme was in place in Slovakia until 2002, as within the review of a particular category of *inter partes* decisions the Court was competent to find unconstitutional interference with rights but precluded from annulling any such decision.

After Czechoslovakia's foundation in 1918, the competence of the IC to hear individual complaints alleging breach of political rights was transferred to the newly constituted Supreme Administrative Court (CSAC).[143] The CSAC, however, had no power to review the constitutionality of any acts of the government. Its competence in the area of protection of constitutional rights was limited to the review of the legality as opposed to the constitutionality of the challenged act. Unlike the IC, however, it had the power to annul the contested act. This was similar to the introduction of judicial review of administrative acts in Poland and Hungary in the 1980s where the main rationale was to prevent abuse by administrative agencies of their discretionary powers. Interestingly, the provisionality of transitional arrangements served to limit the powers of judicial review in 1918–1920 Czechoslovakia in a way similar to the effect that the interim nature of the Polish 'Little Constitution' had on the powers of the PCT until 1997.

In 1920, constitutional review was established on the basis of Kelsen's model.[144] The Constitutional Court was called to examine the conformity to the constitution of statutes and measures issued by the National Assembly, that is, to perform abstract posterior review. Its rulings were binding on the legislature, the executive, the administrative agencies, and the ordinary courts. When judged through the prism of contemporary reality, the main systemic defect of the Czechoslovak Constitutional Court was its inability to review individual complaints, which were to be dealt with by the CSAC. The main practical defect of the Court in protecting the constitution lay in its extreme self-restraint. Indeed, it exhibited such passivity that scholars discussing development of continental constitutional review tend to ignore it completely. Throughout its existence, the Court did not hold unconstitutional a single statute.[145] The Austrian court, rightly heralded as the antecedent of contemporary constitutional review in Europe, deviated more notably from, and was less of a captive of, the *Zeitgeist* than the Czechoslovak Court.[146] What seems more important, though, is that the seed planted in the nineteenth century did, by virtue of Czechoslovakia's joining Austria in the project of constitutional review, catch hold in the Czech (and Slovak) tradition.

Institutions such as a constitutional court naturally could not flourish under the two totalitarian regimes that followed the first split of Czechoslovakia in the late 1930s. The presence in the country's legal thought and practices of the concept of constitutional adjudication nevertheless was not completely erased. A Czech scholar points out that even during the Protectorate of Bohemia and Moravia (1939–1945) some bodies of the interim exile cabinet, such as the State Council and the Council of Law, served to perform functions of constitutional review.[147] The Slovak Constitution of 1939–1945 also provided for a constitutional court, and a statute regulating its operation was promulgated in 1942. Typically for a totalitarian regime, the Constitutional Senate did not issue a single decision.[148] Several influential constitutional drafts advocating constitutional review surfaced in the course of the 1946–1948 democratic intermezzo, too.[149] Under the communist regime, the notion of parliamentary supremacy was as rigid in Czechoslovakia as it was elsewhere in the region. Yet a formal procedure for non-judicial constitutional review was provided for even in the 1948 Constitution, which gave this power to the Presidium of the National Assembly. The 1960 Constitution transferred that authority to the plenary session of the National Assembly. To charge a legislative body with control of legislative and executive acts may seem too patently pointless to be discussed at any length. However, a hint of federalism-based, but centralism-oriented, constitutional review was in fact in place, as the National Assembly had the power to annul statutes adopted by the Slovak National Council, cabinet decrees, and any decree issued by a municipal authority. A more serious attempt to subvert the unity of political power occurred in 1968 when the new constitution introduced a constitutional court with relatively extensive authority. Once again, constitutional review remained confined to law in books.

Despite its failures, the Czechoslovak project of constitutional review was more elaborate and more vivid in local legal consciousness than it was in Poland or Hungary. Its more or less regular re-emergence in the history of ideas and institutions on the territory of Czechoslovakia was to bear fruit when the time was ripe. Indeed, one of the very first policy proposals of Havel's Civic Forum—prepared by a group of legal professionals in the late 1980s and later adopted by the Civic Forum as the basis for its early constitutional agenda—included a constitutional court, the powers of which were conceptualised along the lines of the German Constitutional Court's competence. It therefore came as no surprise that a prominent Czech constitutionalist described the establishment of constitutional review 'as a matter of course'.[150]

There are similarities between the Czech and Slovak legal cultures that are readily apparent to any student of the two countries. It is nevertheless necessary to distinguish between the development of law on the territory of Slovakia and the Czech legal tradition, not so much because the outcome was different but because the process was. The history of the Slovaks is tied to Hungary as much as it is to the Czech lands. Until 1918, and in various areas of law even afterwards,[151] Slovaks were subject to, and used, the same practices and institutions as Hungarians. The Czechs were, to varying extents and in various ways, subject to the universal applicability of Austrian law from 1620 until 1918 and in some areas—for example, commercial law—even after that. The Austro-German theory and culture of law informed Czech legal development more than any other jurisdiction in the region. This can hardly be said about Slovaks or Hungarians, who were directly under the jurisdiction of Austrian law for a mere decade in the second half of the nineteenth century. There were therefore conflicting influences at work after Slovaks joined with Czechs in their common state. During the First Czechoslovak Republic and even after the Second World War a tension was visible in Slovak law between the legacy of customary law and the formalist legalism of the Vienna–Prague axis. Legal dualism was in place until 1950 when civil law was codified. Until then, the ordinary courts, in a way similar to the Hungarian ones, used customary law on a par with statutory law.

Nevertheless, the entire interwar period was characterised by the Slovaks' intense wish to repudiate everything that bore connotations of the 'gaol of nations' era and thus all that was Hungarian.[152] This was the time when Slovaks were adopting into their repertoire of social behaviour new practices and cognitions, and anti-Hungarian sentiment worked in favour of the 'Czech way'. Andrej Hlinka, Slovakia's uncontested political and spiritual leader from the 1910s to the 1930s, summed up the idea as follows: 'Let us not avoid the question, let us say openly that we support a Czechoslovak orientation. The thousand-year marriage with Hungarians has failed. We have to part ways.'[153] Many, if not most, legal instructors in interwar Slovakia were Czechs and many of them remained after the Second World War. When their immediate influence combined with the almost universal fluency of local lawyers in German, there were no barriers left to impede the import of ideas of the Viennese School. This legacy was never lost and in the realm of legal culture the less distant Czech-bound past has by now completely undone the more distant experience informed by centuries of domination by, and coexistence with, the Hungarians.

It is in the understanding of legalism and constitutionalism, and the way these notions translate into juristic practices, that the similarities between Czechs and Slovaks are most apparent. A local scholar argues, for instance, that what left an imprint on Slovak law in the area of constitutional rights protection was the fact of common Czechoslovak statehood in general, and the new-found ability of Slovaks to petition the

CSAC with rights-based grievances in particular.[154] The Vice-President of the SCC points out that the European and Central European constitutional standards were mediated to, and internalised by, the Slovak political culture through Czechoslovak statehood.[155]

True, Slovakia lacks the experience of a sustained development of statehood. It has struggled constantly for cultural and spiritual autonomy, while at the same time self-consciously welcoming the penetration of its psyche by outside influences. Western models of governance dominate the local topography but in Slovakia's political traditions, and social and cultural paradigms, Byzantine features of the conceptualisation of public authority can also be detected. By encompassing the experience of the Western as well as the Eastern world, Slovakia is more similar to Poland and Hungary than it is to the Czech Republic.[156] But in the realm of legal culture, Slovakia's professional elite helped to domesticate and internalise in the course of the twentieth century the Austro-German/Czech model—one of monistic lawmaking enriched by the normativism of the Vienna circle and fostered by the local variation of the pure theory of law.[157] This heritage serves to preserve the paradigm of objective legalism, which on the one hand establishes a normative hierarchy of rules and requires protection of constitutional against statutory norms, but on the other limits legal rationality to deductive logic and formalism. This is one of the main reasons—if not *the* reason—why a justice of the CCC describes local ordinary adjudication as tainted by formalist mannerism,[158] and why Slovak legal academia regularly derides the judiciary for its defensive formalism based on a purely grammatical interpretation of norms.[159]

Traces of the Slovaks' adherence to the organic development of constitutional review in the Czech lands can be detected not only on the level of general functional conceptualisation, but in some more specific aspects, as well. The rules governing the appointment of the CCC and SCC justices are one such example, as the current appointment procedures are strikingly similar to the manner of appointment of the Imperial Court justices. While in 1869 the IC members were appointed by the Emperor based on a proposal from the *Reichsrat*, in the Czech Republic the authority is currently vested in the President on the basis of a Senate proposal.[160] The traditional involvement of the head of state in staffing the constitutional court remains even stronger in Slovakia where the President selects the justices from those proposed by the Parliament (10 out of 20 before 2002, 13 out of 26 from 2002), and appoints the Court's Chief Justice.[161] The President also had the right to appoint one-third of the justices (and the Chief Justice) under the First Republic's Constitution. In contrast to this pattern, both in Hungary[162] and Poland,[163] the constitutional court members are elected by the respective parliaments.

Transitional Political Economy

The Czech constitution was adopted in December 1992, following a relatively short period of deliberation. Due partly to its indisputability in general terms, constitutional review did not make it onto the list of the constitution makers' primary concerns.[164] The enacting statute,[165] therefore, was not ready when the state came into existence, and it took until July 1993 to have the first twelve justices sworn in. (The remaining three justices were appointed later that year.) However, while in Poland the lawmakers' preoccupation with setting the boundaries for interaction between and among the bipolar institutions of the legislative and the executive branches marginalized constitutional review as a subject matter of the reform debate, the higher degree of internalisation by the Czechs of the concept of constitutional adjudication helped to position the CCC more favourably than was the case with the PCT. Indeed, the original delineation of the authority of the Czech Court proved to be of sufficient complexity and fit with the general framework to insulate it from demands for either a reduction of powers, as was the case with Hungary, or their enhancement, as was the case in Poland and Slovakia.

The adoption of the Slovak constitution followed a thorough drafting enterprise spanning the period 1990–1992. Even though the last draft was prepared in a hasty and secretive manner and gave rise to bitter political divisions in the Parliament, the provisions on the Constitutional Court were virtually uncontested. The Slovak cabinet presented its first draft statute on constitutional review as early as July 1990, and in 1991 the Slovak National Council adopted a constitutional act on the SCC, followed by the relevant statutory enactment. This indicated not only a tendency towards a higher degree of institutional and political autonomy from the federal structure, but also a thorough internalisation by the local drafters of the concept of constitutional review. Because of the then Slovak government's preoccupation with the issue of federalism, no justices were appointed and the Slovak Constitution then abrogated the respective federal-era acts on constitutional review by setting forth a new regulation of the issue. The Act on the SCC was promulgated in January 1993,[166] and despite some controversy over who could appoint the justices in the absence of a serving president, the Court held its first session in March 1993.

In spite of some relevant differences between the CCC's and the SCC's concrete review competence, the very availability of a constitutional venue for complaints against *inter partes* decisions illustrates the effect that the country-specific variations of the state-centric political economy have had on the design of constitutional review. Unlike the Czech Republic and Slovakia, neither Poland nor Hungary has equipped its constitutional court with 'true' concrete review authority.

Reitz argues that behind the concept of concrete review lies the 'iron hand of the market' idea: 'the benefit of judicial review for the legal order will emerge from each individual's pursuit of his or her own interests in concrete suits'.[167] It is not a coincidence that the region's best-equipped and most elaborate system of concrete review, assigning a significant role to the individual's own effort to achieve vindication of his rights through a concrete dispute resolution mechanism, came into being in the Czech Republic. Not only was the Czech transitional elite the most vocal in its adherence to such free-marketeers as Smith or Hayek, but also the public seemed to have internalised the ideals of individualism, reduced government, and set free initiative to a larger extent than was the case anywhere else in the region. Measures aimed at fostering these ideals were advocated by the political leadership and largely supported by the population.

It may appear as mere speculation to extend this link to the conceptualisation of constitutional review. Some of the patterns of socio-political orientation of the respective polities reflected through their wider political economies, however, seem to have translated into particular designs of constitutional adjudication, as well. There are, for instance, some illustrative data available on the Central Europeans' cognitive conceptions of the meaning of democracy. In 1995, 16 percent of Poles and 14 percent of Hungarians stated that social values were central to their understanding of democracy, while 38 percent and 31 percent respectively indicated that it was freedom that they identified with democracy. In the Czech Republic, only 3 percent picked social values as opposed to 58 percent who opted for freedom. Only 4 percent of Slovaks preferred social values, while 59 percent went with freedom.[168] While the preference for social values suggests a significant role for the integration of individual interests into a community-friendly canon and for general social cohesion, the emphasis on freedom indicates preference for individual interest. In turn, while abstract review requires a petitioner to act as a trustee of the public good,[169] the ability to challenge *inter partes* decisions indicates a preference for an unmediated pursuit of personal interest at the constitutional level.

The above noted variations of political economy and their internalisation by the public can partly explain why no pursuit of personal interest is required for filing a petition with the Constitutional Court in Hungary; why in Poland claims of rights infringement had to be channelled through institutional mediators serving to reinforce the integration and cohesion of personal interests; and why in both the Czech and the Slovak Republics mechanisms were provided for that stressed individual effort and required concrete personal interest to be at stake in any individual application for a remedy of constitutional defects. The structuring of the Czech and the Slovak constitutional review so as to allow citizens to petition a constitutional court with concrete grievances may be one of the reasons why 23 percent of Czechs and 22 percent of Slovaks disagreed with the phrase 'People like me have no influence on government', while only 10 percent of Hungarians and 8 percent of Poles were ready to disagree.[170]

Transitional Leadership

In the Czech Republic, the context within which roles of transitional leadership were assigned and seized did not favour the rise of the Constitutional Court to the centre of constitutional politics. Since the Czech elite would incessantly boast of the country's political and economic advancement and its better preparedness for European integration compared to that of the rest of the region—an attitude stemming from a sincere belief in their superiority—the search for a comparative advantage in the realm of constitutionalism did not seem of immediate urgency. Unlike in Hungary where it became the role of the HCC to 'sell' the country as Europe-compatible, the Czech establishment had good reason to rely on Havel's popularity and the respect—although often accompanied by personal dislike—that Klaus enjoyed among Western leaders.

Neither Havel's nor Klaus's charisma could help the Court in any significant way. Both the public and the opinion makers were at the time happy with the interaction between the two outstanding personalities of the Czech transitional environment and saw Havel's preference for 'ethical and non-political politics' as a good counter-balance to Klaus's utilitarianism and pragmatism. In other words, Klaus had a clear mandate vigorously to pursue his economic reform and market the country among Europe's technocrats, while Havel had a clear mandate to provide a philosophical touch to the transition and market the country among Europe's romanticists. This peculiar division of labour was seen as an asset in itself and the rationale for providing for an additional leadership variable seemed weak.

Moreover, Klaus's contempt for anyone attempting to restrict his grand plan of economic reform was widely known. He would regularly complain of his coalition partners' inhibiting the reform plans and went to great lengths to argue that if transition was to succeed, things would have to go as envisaged by his party. The circumstantial restrictions of Klaus's agenda were already deemed too broad because he had to govern within a coalition rather than on his own. Moreover, systemic restrictions were in sight, as the constitution laid down the foundations for an upper chamber that could reduce Klaus's manoeuvrability in the policy-making process. To extend these inhibitors any further would simply be at odds with the idea of unifying pro-reform forces behind a particular concept of transformation; an idea which, initially at least, exemplified the new elite's approach to reform and was also supported by the mainstream media. Accordingly, the constitutional judiciary was not granted the authority to launch substantive attacks on policy choices on its own—as was in some ways the case of Hungary—but was to rely on petitions by a parliamentary faction or the President. Similarly, the President was not equipped with the authority to initiate preliminary review—powers that both the Polish and the Hungarian presidents were given—and no preliminary review as such was provided for.

As for Slovakia, it certainly could have used a public-relations asset in its quest for foreign political acknowledgment. The country lacked any significant advantage in either the realm of economic policy or the general political outlook. Slovakia's image in the EU and the Council of Europe, not to mention among the NATO hawks, suffered and the government's tense relationship with the Hungarian minority as well as its autocratic tendencies were a source of concern. Slovakia made it to the OECD only several years after its neighbours did, and before Haider's rise to power in neighbouring Austria led to an unprecedentedly severe reaction by the EU, the Slovak government was the only one in the region to have been officially reprimanded by the EU through a diplomatic *démarche*. But Slovakia's leaders appeared unfazed and kept giving the West more and more reasons to disqualify Slovakia as an applicant for NATO and EU membership. Instead of trying to compensate for diplomatic or economic failures by putting the emphasis on constitutional culture—from which the HCC and by extension ethnic Hungarian citizens benefited immensely—Mečiar would recite his mantra of Slovakia's vital geopolitical importance to the West.

Moreover, transitional leadership roles were already predetermined at the time of the SCC's conception. Mečiar was the nation's 'founding father', one with a clear vision of how to shepherd his herd. He sincerely believed that he was the only politician available who could instil order into the transitional chaos. An assertive constitutional court fond of challenging the cabinet's policies was therefore the last thing he needed to make his way of politics and policy making prevail. It seems, however, that he did not pay enough attention to the Court's abstract review equipment and it all went differently than planned, as the SCC proved to be one of the more efficient, if not the only, instruments capable of inhibiting the authoritarian tendencies of the then Slovak leadership.

As 'chance' would have it, the pool of 20 prospective justices for the first Slovak Court was selected by a parliamentary majority dominated by Mečiar's Movement for Democratic Slovakia (MDS). Then followed a controversy over whether the authority to appoint members of the SCC was among those powers that were to be performed by the Prime Minister in the absence of a serving president. Mečiar seized the opportunity and, acting in his capacity as president-in-lieu, appointed the 10 members of the SCC. He also appointed a "former member" of the MDS as the Chief Justice. The selection did bear some fruit, but less than Mečiar had hoped, as he was not diligent enough in "his" selection of a number of other justices. Over time, the SCC became one of the more substantial obstacles to arbitrary government. Its prominence rose especially after Mečiar's 'second coming' in 1994, and by the mid-1990s the Court had established itself as Slovakia's only institution capable of providing a link to Western Europe and its *Rechtsstaat* culture. This was a development that the governing majority did not expect, did not like and about which there was not much it could do. When the SCC invalidated a controversial Ministry of Health decree, Mečiar did not hesitate to call it a 'sick element of the political scene' and tried to mobilize public opinion against it. He also cancelled the Chief Justice's entitlement to an official car and a bodyguard.[171] In terms of structural crippling of the Court, however, Mečiar limited himself to having one of his loyal sidekicks propose an amendment to the court's statutory regulation. Neither the verbal nor the institutional campaign met with any success. It was the central role of the SCC in helping to preserve the democratic outlook of the country that made any attacks on its decision-making powers highly controversial both politically and doctrinally. Even more so than in Hungary, to question the SCC's authority to operate actively in constitutional space became non-*salonfähig* among those who liked to see themselves as democrats.

In the realm of concrete review, however, there was hardly any chance for the SCC to assert itself as the leader of the judicial branch. The commission in charge of the constitutional draft was chaired by Karol Plank, a respected and seasoned legal academic with strong links to judges of high ordinary courts and the entire 'judicial lobby'. (Plank was subsequently appointed Deputy Chief Justice of the Supreme Court.) Even though it was known at that time that the Czechs were going to conceptualise their constitutional court differently and that there were problems attendant on the HCC's and PCT's confinement to abstract review, a deliberate decision was taken to insulate ordinary adjudication from the SCC's scrutiny as far as possible. The drafters' schematic approach to the notion of judicial independence, their deliberate confinement within the boundaries of the Kelsenian concept of constitutional review, and possibly also their own personal preferences prevented the Court's conceptualisation as primarily a judicial authority. And when the need for adjustments became apparent, the context again worked against extending the SCC's concrete review competencies. First, there was no qualified majority available in the Parliament willing to consider constitutional and statutory amendments to that effect. The governing coalition simply did not like the Court and had no reason to try to help it. Secondly, the Court is located 300 miles away from the capital, while the Parliament and the Supreme Court shared adjacent buildings until relatively recently. Therefore, conditions for informal interaction between the judicial lobby and the parliamentarians were clearly favourable. The SCC thus was left to struggle on its own with systemic inhibitions on its operability in the realm of incidental protection of rights, an endeavour that proved too large a task for the self-conscious justices. As the review of the SCC's case law will show, the consequences were rather unfortunate.

PART II

CHAPTER 3

ADJUDICATIVE APPROACHES

In Part I, I offered a description of the environment that produced and harboured constitutional review in Central Europe. I also provided a preliminary sketch of the different versions of constitutional review in the region, locating the source of decisive influence in the interplay of various factors stemming from both the 'triple-past' and post-revolutionary development. In Part II, I identify the characteristic features of the respective constitutional courts' jurisprudence and the variables that shaped it in the most relevant way. I am thus concerned with what the courts made of the powers they were given and the constitutional texts they were to interpret, and why.

In this chapter, I examine the effect that the scope and the structure of the respective courts' decision-making authority had on their jurisprudence. Following a brief introduction, I will deal with the topic within sub-sections devoted to individual countries. I will first concern myself with the degree to which the institutional environment and the interactions it produced were either conducive to, or inhibited, an assertive involvement of a constitutional court in the process of policy making. I will assess the impact on jurisprudence of those elements of a court's authority that generate its law making instincts and thus facilitate (or impede, if absent) judicial activism. I will then assess the impact on jurisprudence of those elements of a court's authority that generate its judicial instincts and thus facilitate active judging, that is, the kind of instruments that a constitutional court could use in order to perform functions traditionally assigned to judicial bodies, especially the resolution of concrete cases and controversies and, within that, the provision of remedies for incidental violations of individual rights. Simultaneously, I will explore both the ways in which the respective courts tried to manipulate the scope and the structure of their competence so that it would fit their notions of the proper kind of judicial engagement in the project of founding, and the factors determinative of the courts' attendant choices of adjudicative methods.

FRAMEWORK

Legislating

The prime feature of the conceptualisation of constitutional review in Hungary is the HCC's (self-)appointment as guardian of the *ruptura pactada*. The HCC's powers were, and remain, much more extensive than those of any other court in the region and the same can be said about the leeway it was granted in adjusting the adjudicative equipment to its own liking. In addition, some important layers of the local legal culture proved favourable to the HCC's performance of a policy-maker's role. Accordingly, the Hungarian Court emerges as the most assertive negative legislator in the region and as a true co-leader in the process of Hungary's legal and social transformation.

In Poland, largely because of the marginalisation of the issue of constitutional review in the transitional discourse, the adjudicative authority of the Tribunal remained adversely affected by the circumstances surrounding its conception, and some specific parts of the case law remained subject to direct control by the Sejm. Also, the tradition of courts acting as agenda-setters for legislative reform is much weaker in Poland than it is in Hungary. Accordingly, the Polish Tribunal emerges as willing to assist the legislature in its efforts to complete the transition rather than to mount obstacles to it.

The Czech and the Slovak Courts were to occupy a middle ground between the Hungarian model of juridical democracy and the Polish model of political supervision of constitutional review. Both courts were equipped with an *instrumentarium* that can be described as reflecting the continental standard. In addition, legal consciousness in neither the Czech Republic nor Slovakia is particularly open to judicial law making. Indeed, were it not for the flagrant violations of the constitution by Mečiar's entourage, the SCC would most likely be as shy in overruling the legislature's policy choices as the Czech Court has been throughout the 1990s.

Judging

As much as the ability of a constitutional court to invalidate a statute because of its lack of conformity to the constitution is a yardstick of its conceptualisation as a negative legislator, it is the ability to scrutinize and invalidate a decision of an ordinary court and/or an administrative agency that indicates its conceptualisation as a *court*. The lack of the latter competence is the one defining feature that the schemes of constitutional adjudication in Poland and Hungary shared. Therefore, despite significant differences in the degree of their adjudicative autonomy and the correspondingly different implications for their jurisprudence, both the PCT and the HCC have been operating under one particular constraint—lacking the authority to scrutinize decisions of judicial or administrative agencies, their ability to adjudicate disputes of constitutional relevance has been confined to abstract review.

It is necessary at this point to explain my position on the abstract review/concrete review dichotomy. Stone Sweet and several other scholars subsume under the concrete review equipment the authority of an ordinary court to refer to a constitutional court a question of law determinative of the matter at hand.[1] I beg to disagree. I understand the referral procedure to have the same effects as the 'true' abstract review procedure. First, it is aimed at a generally binding normative act rather than a decision of a law-implementing agency. Secondly, the outcome of that review is of universal application, that is, it has *erga omnes* effects. The only difference concerns the body authorized to initiate constitutional review. While in the case of 'true' abstract review the respective competence belongs to specific public officials—the list is typically some combination of a parliamentary faction, the President, the cabinet, and the Attorney General—an interlocutory appeal can be filed by an ordinary judge who reaches the conclusion that, or incurs doubts whether, a statute she is to apply is unconstitutional. It may be argued that since a judge's application for the scrutiny of a statute derives from her experience with it in a particular adjudicative setting, the difference between such a review and that initiated by a political authority is readily apparent. But this is what the CCC, for instance, has to say about review upon judicial referrals:

> The nature of the review of the constitutionality of a contested statutory provision is one of abstract norm control because in assessing the constitutionality of the provision, the Constitutional Court takes a decision without dealing with, or assessing, the concrete issue which is the subject matter of ordinary adjudication

> proceedings and which led the ordinary court to motion the Constitutional Court to provide a decision on the constitutionality of the provision to be used in that concrete affair.[2]

According to the SCC, any referral by a court of general jurisdiction to the Constitutional Court of a question of law is to be deemed a motion for abstract review of the compatibility of legal acts.[3] The Polish Tribunal on the one hand understands judicial referrals to be a form of concrete review,[4] but on the other suggests that even constitutional complaints initiate the review of the law, not the way it is implemented by a court or other public agency.[5] Czeszejko-Sochacki adds that petitioners whose rights were found to have been violated by the Tribunal through the constitutional-complaint procedure 'have won against the legislator', not against a court or an administrative agency.[6]

Indeed, what falls under any kind of review *in abstracto*, whether initiated by political agents or by courts, or even by a constitutional complainant, is law as made, and what falls outside it is law as applied. Accordingly, abstract review can serve to develop general facets of the constitutional landscape but in terms of addressing individual grievances leaves much to be desired. It does not extend to the very realm where rights infringements are most likely to occur, that is, where the citizen and a public authority intersect on a daily basis. True, the scrutiny of normative acts can prevent many wrongs by setting strict conditions for the performance of administrative competence. In this respect, the constitutional courts have repeatedly indicated that any interference with individual rights had to be implemented via statutes and that administrative agencies were not to be allowed to restrict the enjoyment of rights by means of issuing sub-statutory regulations. It is, however, by definition difficult to bind the bureaucracy—'gifted' with a special psyche putting administrative expediency ahead of any less tangible values—by rules prospectively constraining its discretionary authority.[7] The legislation can delimit the general scope of the administration's competence and set forth standards to be followed by it but that is as much as it can do. After all, the bureaucrats' reliance on internal instructions, methodological guidelines and other acts the knowledge of which by the public is effectively precluded appears to be as widespread now as it was in the previous era. A Polish scholar, pointing out that 'the administrative body is not bound by anything', laments the 'lack of legal protection in which an arbitration or execution of action is alleged to have violated human rights',[8] and does so for a good reason. After all, 'the office water cooler is not likely to be the locus of transformative constitutional dialogue'.[9]

In short, there is a significant difference between the *Kassationseffekt* and the *Edukationseffekt* of a constitutional court's activity. The lack of a constitutional-complaint procedure in pre-1997 Poland, and its applicability to statutory and sub-statutory acts in Hungary and post-1997 Poland, did not prevent impressive achievements in the realm of *Grundrechtsdogmatik* but, by definition, kept the protection of rights by means of constitutional review within the boundaries of abstract interpretation. Within such a scheme, addressing an individual grievance is not the core concern of constitutional adjudication but merely an incidental by-product of the elaboration of doctrinal concepts. In other words, abstract review powers equip the courts with tools designed to protect the logical coherence of the legal order rather than to provide a concrete remedy. The outcome of abstract review, whether initiated by an ordinary judge or a political authority, infuses constitutional standards into the law making process and is clearly not aimed at the same actors as is an invalidation of a judicial or administrative decision, which invalidation, in turn, remedies a violation committed outside the legislator's immediate influence.

In addition, abstract review makes it difficult for the affected courts to fully implement Ackerman's suggestion—one that he addressed to the Hungarian Court in particular—that 'rather than confining their attention to a few political hot potatoes tossed to them by government officials' the justices should devote more of their time to 'the plight of an ordinary man or woman arbitrarily arrested by the police, or the casual suppression of speech by a local potentate.'[10] Abstract review forces even a constitutional complainant to phrase his claim not as invoking a particular entitlement but as necessary for the convalidation of the body of constitutional values and principles. Even a constitutional complainant therefore operates as a trustee of public good, and not of individual interest.

Contrary to their above counterparts, both the Czech and the Slovak Courts were equipped with powers that allowed them to examine the constitutionality of judicial implementation of law. But while the Czech Court enjoys full concrete review authority—for it can review and invalidate a decision of any public authority—the corresponding authority of the Slovak Court was until 2002 confined to decisions of state and municipal administrative bodies. The Czech design thus follows the German model, as it allows for constitutional complaints against judicial decisions. The Slovak design shared important similarities with the Austrian model, preventing a constitutional court from invalidating decisions of the ordinary courts. What may seem a mere nuance in the overall concrete review equipment proved vital for the degree and the quality of protection of individual rights. The supervision by means of constitutional review of the performance of ordinary courts became the bulk of the Czech Court's activity and unearthed numerous violations of constitutionally guaranteed rights taking place within ordinary adjudication. Slovak citizens were denied similar protection and to some extent the fault lay with the overly cautious SCC.

Repairing

The targets of the constitutional courts' efforts to manipulate or to repair the institutional design varied. Even though the most obvious restrictions of the Tribunal's authority concerned its relationship with the legislature, it was the Sejm's transitional leadership that the Tribunal felt most at ease deferring to. On the other hand, it was mostly at the ordinary courts that the PCT aimed the manifold creative techniques it tried to employ in order to make the most of the instruments it had at hand. Accordingly, the Tribunal's attempts to emancipate itself as the supreme interpreter of the constitution were confronted with heavy resistance by the ordinary judiciary. The Czech Republic shared the experience[11] and in its efforts to bind the ordinary courts with its interpretive guidelines the Polish Tribunal shares some important similarities with the Czech Court. The Slovak Court, on the other hand, was almost as reluctant as the HCC to supervise ordinary adjudication. Indeed, while the PCT and the CCC were largely at ease with their parliaments' efforts to establish themselves as transitional leaders and focused heavily on the constitutionally proper implementation of legislative policies by agencies charged with their application,[12] both the Hungarian Court and the Slovak Court were more willing to leave the ordinary courts alone and instead engaged in confrontation with the parliaments. One notices here the effect of bicameralism, which provides for a non-judicial instance of filtering dubious legislative measures. Neither Hungary nor Slovakia has a second parliamentary chamber, and although the lack of it certainly does not in itself explain the issue, it did provide an additional rationale for the oppositions' flights to the constitution. The counter-majoritarian tendencies of both the HCC and the SCC also were underlined by their efforts to Europeanize the local constitutional landscape. In Hungary, this process was taking place within a more or less standard political system and reflected competition between the different transitional players as to who would feed the local obsession with the West. It also was in conformity with the Court's self-understanding as the ultimate enforcer of modernity. Hardly any trace of either a standard political culture or the governing elite's effort to impress the West, however, could be detected in Slovakia at the time. The SCC's judicial activism reflected not so much its self-understanding as an autonomous agent of social change as its efforts to act as the last bastion of the rule of law in a country where the establishment proved indifferent, if not hostile, to the idea of Euro-Atlantic integration. In other words, the political circumstances relegated Slovakia's project of developing customary constitutional practice—a process which can be initiated and sustained by means of constitutional adjudication and in the course of which 'those who govern... make sense of their own role in the political system, and of how they are expected to interact with other actors'[13]—to a marginal position, as it became a mere by-product of the SCC's efforts to save the very fundamentals of democratic government.

COUNTRY SPECIFICS

Poland

Judicial Activism

Overview

There is a peculiar causal chain to the PCT's colloquy with the legislature within which two inter-related paradoxes emerge. The first paradox lies in the fact that the crippling of the Tribunal's powers has not prevented it from actively responding to the exigencies of transition by furnishing through constructive interpretation those tenets of constitutional law for which the law makers were unable to provide. The second paradox lies in the fact that the Tribunal completed a full circle, as even upon emancipation it proved willing to employ its activist approach in the service of a particular ideological concept of transformation. It thus both fell victim to, and internalised, its conceptualisation as a transitional assistant rather than a transitional leader, that is, as a body assigned the role of assisting the legislature in advancing a new social agenda rather than autonomously delineating the basic contours of the country's transition.

As much as the Tribunal's deference to the legislature was largely a function of the design-related features of Poland's framework of constitutional adjudication, there was more to its acceptance of the assistant's role. It is the local legal consciousness with its sets of professional as well as personal cognitions and ethics, and with its relatively firmly established notions of justice administration and public governance, that provides the missing links in the above causal chain. Indeed, the justices' tradition-informed self-understanding as constitutional adjudicators and founders has proved to be as relevant to the PCT's jurisprudential profile as the imperfections of both the institutional design and substantive constitutional law. In other words, the Tribunal's adherence to a mode of political economy that favoured implementation of public policy choices by legislative or, at times, even administrative means was to some extent deliberate, as it reflected the PCT's perception of its proper role both as a court of law and as an agent of social transformation. It was, again, the interplay between the exogenous constraints and the various layers of local legal tradition that informed constitutional jurisprudence in the most significant way and made the Tribunal a quintessential product of Poland's legal consciousness.

That the Tribunal continued to display deference to the Sejm even upon finalization of the institutional framework and the positioning within it of constitutional review therefore came as less of a surprise than did its previous efforts to neutralize the deficiencies of Poland's transitional higher law. Although the completion of the process of institutional design making in 1997 did away with both the provisionality constraint and the PCT's subordination to the Sejm, the Tribunal continues not to shy away from lending the legislature a helping hand. Its continued readiness to exhibit considerable self-restraint in reviewing transition-related policies suggests that it was as willing as it was forced to grant the legislature broad *Spielraum* in establishing the new regime. Both the justices' ideological inclinations and their adherence to a particular concept of constitutional review therefore account for the Tribunal's permissive attitude to the fostering of a new social agenda by predominantly legislative means as much as does the framework within which it used to, and continues to, communicate with the legislator.

The context in which the Tribunal operated during the constitutional *provisorium* requires a few general observations. It is worth repeating that one of the reasons for the marginalisation of the Tribunal in the post-1989 constitutional reform was the believed-in robustness of Poland's transitional agreement. Given the representativeness of the parties to the Round Table talks, the need to establish an apolitical guardian of the transformation was perceived as less urgent than it was in Hungary or the former Czechoslovakia. However, the integrity of the changeover agreement proved illusory as early as 1990–1991. This is what Skapska has to say about the celebrated RT talks: 'The initial contract, known as the "Round Table Agreement" was concluded by representatives of the ruling communist party... and that part of the democratic opposition which was ready to compromise. Some of its important proceedings were not public at all, and these were not subjected to sustained, public critical evaluation.'[14] She also noted that 'the paradigm of consensus and a round table [was] losing its legitimising potential'.[15]

The notion of a sustainable compromise thus became somewhat discredited, and when applied it worked in an ironic way. First, the Sejm naturally was to serve as the principal forum for establishing political consensus. Secondly, however, the emphasis on legitimacy, representativeness, and, ultimately, consensus worked against establishing a threshold for entry to the Parliament, used widely in proportional electoral systems. This very omission enhanced the paralysing effect of bitter inter-factional divisions over fundamental issues of polity orientation. Such friction seem inevitable in the period of transition and may even be healthy in helping to bring about standard political parties organized around group interests more coherent than hatred for a common enemy. But the particularization of political interest also was conducive to unstable government and left Poland with institutional arrangements that were not fully capable of responding to the challenges of transition. The PCT, for instance, was invited to participate in the resolution of political disputes without being able to enjoy structural guarantees for general obedience with its rulings.

On the one hand, it is precisely in a multi-party system, especially one affected by shattered political power, that overruling a constitutional court's decision is more of a theoretical device than a common practical solution. Brzezinski informs us that it was by virtue of Polish politics being haunted by frequent impasse and static in the area of constitutional reform that the justices of the PCT felt invited to introduce 'new principles which political elites would not otherwise get to'.[16] The Sejm itself became aware of its inability to cover by legislative activity various areas of law that were either in need of reform or were unregulated by explicit legal rules. This awareness often served to shift significant portions of law-making responsibility to the Tribunal and gave it considerable leeway in shaping the country's newly emerging constitutional landscape. Moreover, it was in the context of fragmented political power that the PCT could feel relatively safe in defying the legislature. The more difficult it was to amass two-thirds of the quorum, the greater was the probability that the rulings of the PCT would sustain examination by the Sejm. Despite fierce criticism of the PCT's approach to some of the politically sensitive issues, it was relatively seldom that the Sejm could find enough voting capital to undo a PCT ruling.

On the other hand, the Tribunal did work under the watchful eyes of the legislature. Between 1990 and 1999, the Sejm overruled a PCT ruling on 10 occasions, which represents approximately 10 percent of cases in which a statute was found unconstitutional.[17] What was a relatively seldom occurrence in absolute numbers was a frequent enough occurrence to pierce any veil of ignorance as to how far the PCT could go in undermining the parliament's regulatory capacity. If it did not want to have its decisions overruled on a regular basis, the Tribunal simply had to take into account political considerations in addition to the legal ones. These are not mutually exclusive and the dialogue is, of course, subtler than that. Stone Sweet points out the tendency—becoming dominant in large parts of the European constitutional space—of judges to act as legislators, and vice versa. Judges 'consider the potential impact of decisions being contemplated because they seek compliance on the part of the parties and because they are concerned with their own political legitimacy'.[18] The notion that constitutional courts offer reasons and furnish rulings capable of inducing the law makers' compliance is not alien to constitutional theory. Bickel phrased it elegantly: 'the task of the Court is to seek and foster assent, and compliance through assent'.[19] The way that the colloquy between a legislature and a constitutional court works thus may have two directions: not only do law makers adjust their decisions to the anticipated attitude of the court, but the members of the court also produce rulings that have a chance of being implemented without undergoing distortion by the parliament's politicised scrutiny. The fact that in the post-1997 era the relative number of statutes found unconstitutional is twice what it used to be under the previous scheme speaks volumes about the effect on the Tribunal's self-awareness of its wider operative environment.[20]

Either way, the frequent frictions both between and within the bicameral legislature and the binary executive prevented the emergence in Poland of an unambiguous and generally accepted transitional leader. This allowed the PCT to keep shaping the country's newly emerging constitutional landscape. In a way, the circumstances served to neutralize the design's adverse effect on the Tribunal's attempts at emancipation. The PCT, however, could not fail to notice the need for efficient policy making in a country whose process of transformation suffered from deep and ostensibly insurmountable divisions across the political spectrum. This gave rise to a particular paradox. It is a legitimate assumption that in the absence of an uncontested leader, be it the legislature or a holder of a top executive office, the space opens up for a constitutional court to step in and assert itself politically. This did happen in Poland to some extent but not necessarily to the detriment of the governing majority, and the Tribunal's emancipation certainly benefited the legislature more than did the parallel activity of constitutional courts in Hungary or Slovakia. The Tribunal's weak position as a negative legislator certainly played a major role in its somewhat cautious communication with the Sejm. However, as noted by Garlicki, also the new political situation induced the justices to be more sympathetic to efforts serving the institution of a new social order.[21] Accordingly, being 'aware of the unusual historical nature of the recent transformation',[22] the PCT often invoked the particular needs of systemic transition as a factor to be taken account of in its decision-making and as legitimising measures that would not be legitimate had the new regime been stabilized. In this vein, the Tribunal conceded, for instance, that the 'transition from the authoritarian state to a state ruled by law may exceptionally warrant action which could not be justified under normal circumstances'.[23] The polity's desperate need for a necessary minimum of political consensus led the PCT—on some sensitive issues at least—to abstain from challenging, if not to welcome, the rare occurrences of such consensus and at once take sides in the attendant disputes. Garlicki noted that, especially during the early years of transition, the PCT identified with Solidarity's philosophy and was often willing to provide the Sejm and the cabinet with enough *Spielraum* to perform their leadership roles.[24]

There are numerous examples indicating that the Tribunal not only thought it vital to pay attention to the general political climate and to include in its considerations the political elite's anticipated reaction, but also professed a distinct legal and moral philosophy. Neither the PCT's awareness of the frequent lack of political will in the Sejm to overrule a particular holding nor the eradication of constraints attendant on its authority have undone the Tribunal's readiness to defer to the legislature on some key issues.

The adoption of the new constitution in 1997 signalled the end of the transitional era in various ways. The completion of constitutional reform was, among many other things, expected to do away with most of the limitations imposed upon the PCT's adjudicative authority. With respect to the Tribunal's relationship with the Sejm it indeed did so, as the findings of unconstitutionality of statutes are now to be final.[25] The PCT also can review legislation for its conformity to binding international treaties, which authority it lacked before reform. In addition, it acquired the power to decide competence disputes between certain government authorities. On the other hand, the PCT is now bound to apply for an opinion of the cabinet in each case in which a holding of unconstitutionality could result in financial costs unforeseen by budgetary legislation.[26] It also has lost the power to initiate proceedings on its own motion.

Nevertheless, the most significant design-related imperfections, which in the previous era served to confine the PCT's role to that of an advisor to the legislature rather than its supervisor, were largely eliminated. The same cannot be said of the Tribunal's understanding of transitional constitutional review, which it continued to view as a vehicle of transformation policies arrived at via legislative deliberation.

Jurisprudence

The first turn. Before 1989, the Tribunal adhered to the notion of constitutional review as an assistant to the legislature and tended to protect legislative supremacy against sub-statutory abuse rather than challenge the Sejm on constitutional grounds.[27] In the meantime, it managed to stand up against the cabinet's excesses on several occasions,[28] and exceeded the expectations of both the ruling power and those who were at first sceptical of its relevance to the country's legal development.[29] Despite the Tribunal's gradual self-release from the socialist notions of law and government, it was to become the 'real thing' only after Poland's liberation from both foreign and domestic oppressors.

The fall of the old regime brought about vigorous emancipation of constitutional review. The PCT became more active in the scrutiny of statutes, and in response to the incoherence of both the constitutional law and the political arena rapidly rose to a position in the country's constitutional politics that went beyond its original conceptualisation by the constitution makers. The most visible displays of the Tribunal's rising to the occasion concerned its employment of the *Rechtsstaat* and equal-protection clauses.

The Tribunal's efforts to compensate for the positive-law constraints imposed upon its own adjudicative authority were less frequent than its parallel efforts to compensate for the deficiencies of substantive law, but were neither less controversial nor less relevant. These efforts were both aimed at the Tribunal's confinement to abstract review—on which efforts more later—and concerned with its leverage against the Sejm and the executive. By creatively interpreting the rules governing its own operation, the PCT, for instance, attributed to itself the power to review statutes ratifying international agreements to be entered into by Poland and, by extension, these international agreements as such.[30] The Tribunal also found itself competent to review a resolution of the Sejm ordering the Interior Minister to provide detailed information on former collaborators of the communist security agency and held the resolution incompatible with several constitutional provisions.[31] In a similar vein, it subsumed under its abstract review authority the Sejm's Standing Order.[32] The PCT also held that once it finds a bill to be in conformity with the constitution, the President is bound to sign it, and vice versa that the President may not sign a bill held unconstitutional within preliminary review.[33]

The PCT often would select those of the various plausible interpretations of the governing text that served the expansion of its decision-making autonomy *vis-à-vis* the Sejm. In one of the relevant decisions, the Tribunal held that if the Sejm fails appropriately to deal with a statute held unconstitutional within six months of delivery of the ruling to the speaker of the Sejm, the statute ceases to be valid.[34] The fact that both the constitution and the PCTA were silent on the issue of what happens if the Sejm neither overrules the PCT's finding of the unconstitutionality nor fails to overrule it by a qualified majority within the six-month period did not prevent the Tribunal from establishing the rule by means of interpretation. In a later case, it was precisely the lack of explicit constitutional provisions regulating the matter at hand that the Tribunal interpreted as preventing inference of the rule by means of interpretation. The issue was whether a preliminary-review finding of a bill's unconstitutionality could be subject to parliamentary reversal. The PCT answered the question in the negative.[35] So while in the first instance the PCT invented the effect of the six-months rule to strengthen its leverage against the Sejm despite a lack of regulation, in the second instance it held that since there was no rule to provide *expressis verbis* for the Sejm's reconsideration, such a rule could not be inferred.

The Tribunal did prove a little more timid than the HCC in interpreting the framework within which it was to exercise its authority. It would, for instance, repeatedly point out that it lacked the mandate to review domestic law for its conformity to international treaties and, accordingly, refused to apply international law as an autonomous normative standard for constitutional scrutiny.[36] So while the PCT did not shy away from enhancing its authority by means of creative interpretation, it did so mostly in response to a lack of rule rather than in conflict with a rule provided, a tendency discernible in, and typical of, all aspects of its interpretive constructivism.

The Tribunal's extraordinary interpretive creativity was mostly a function of the exigencies of Poland's transition, haunted by the provisionality and, consequently, the incoherence of constitutional arrangements. When judged from the vantagepoint of constraints imposed upon its decision-making authority, the Tribunal's emergence as an active maker of constitutional law did come as a surprise. But the one area of jurisprudence that offers a constitutional court the best opportunity to either assert itself as a transitional leader or defer to the legislature's leadership concerns the quintessential transitional measures, namely those effecting retribution and indemnification policies. Here, the Tribunal's record is more ambivalent. Its belief in the need to give Poland's public life a tangible and orderly face, as well as its growing sense of fiscal responsibility, precipitated the second turn.[37]

The second turn. The first opportunity for the Tribunal to align itself with the new regime came with the 1990 Pension Act which reduced certain allowances for former high-ranking officials of Poland's communist party. The Tribunal decided to prioritise a commonsensical notion of justice over formal legality, as it stated that the 'constitutional protection of vested rights applie[d] *particularly* to rights fairly obtained'.[38] In the review of the statute providing for the transfer to the state treasury of all of the Party's assets, except for membership fees, the PCT strengthened the attendant qualification by holding that the principle of vested rights could be 'enforced *only* with regard to those rights [that were] acquired in a lawful and morally unquestionable manner'.[39] The Tribunal relied on this line of reasoning in a series of subsequent decisions, for example, in its scrutiny of the 1993 Pension Act which cut pensions of those formerly employed by the repressive machinery of the communist state.[40]

Transitional specifics are most readily invoked in connection with repressive retribution policies. Here, too, the PCT proved ready to both lend support to particular ideological concepts advanced by the new establishment and evidence its willingness to defer to the legislature's efforts at transitional leadership by refraining from institutional hostility, namely by refusing to take its competence to the limit and force the Sejm into an open confrontation. Instead, it preferred to appear open to dialogue. The 1991 amendment to the Law on the Main Commission for the Investigation of Nazi Crimes in Poland allowed for the prosecution of 'crimes against individuals or groups of individuals, committed by authorities of the communist state, or tolerated and instigated by those authorities' before 31 December 1956.[41] The PCT found certain aspects of the statute too broad to be within the boundaries of constitutionally permissible retroactive prosecution. But it also held that to adhere in this particular case to the otherwise universal prohibition of retroactive legislation 'would be incompatible with the basic principles of justice'.[42] Rather than invalidating the statute and leaving it at that, the PCT issued an advisory opinion in which it clearly expressed what it would deem acceptable retroactive legislation and provided the Sejm with clear enough hints as to what it should do in order to pass constitutional muster. This typifies the PCT's understanding of itself rather as a catcher sending his pitcher signs as to what kind of a throw may make a strike than as a batter keen to send a fast ball up into the stands. It also resonates with Calabresi's notion of the proper role of judicial/constitutional review, which is 'to make the starting point from which legislatures are called to respond'.[43] And it very much resembles the kind of constitutional comity that Wedgwood describes as a situation in which 'the Court seeks to generate consensus and recognizes other law-speaking bodies as deserving weight'.[44]

More troublesome, however, was the PCT's handling of a decree issued by the Ministry of Education and allowing religious instruction in state schools. After upholding the regulation in a clear departure from the previously rigorous scrutiny of sub-statutory acts, the Tribunal held a closed meeting subsequent to which it sent the Sejm a memorandum stating that the Religious Education Act of 1961 was in violation of the constitution and should be amended.[45]

Indeed, the PCT's ability to appreciate the emergence of a new social and political agenda did not concern only the typical transitional legislation, namely that dealing with retribution and compensation policies. It also extended to issues of religious instruction, freedom of speech, and abortion. These cases, dealt with in more detail in the section on the PCT's interpretive enterprise, are illustrative of the elbowroom that the legislature and the cabinet enjoyed courtesy of the Tribunal's adherence to their policy agendas. In these and other cases the Tribunal allowed for an extensive statutory qualification of the relevant rights not only by other rights, but also by general clauses, such as those anchoring social justice or public interest. It was in the realm of welfare policies that this tendency and the Tribunal's 'second turn' became most apparent.

The Tribunal's ruling on the 1991 Pension Act, which it invalidated in part by holding that 'the possibility to revoke benefits once granted is very limited, regardless of the state's financial situation',[46] gave rise to fierce criticism across both the political and the academic spectrums. The Tribunal reacted by stepping back a little and then further. The first thing it had to learn was to justify its deference doctrinally. Accordingly, in outlining the general interpretive guidelines for the enforcement of social rights the Tribunal held that economic rights '[could] be subject to more stringent restrictions than personal or political rights and liberties'.[47] It stated that it was only the essence of a right that enjoyed constitutional protection, and that regulations prospectively limiting the existing entitlements were in conformity to the constitution.[48] The PCT also said that several of the non-classical rights, for example, the right to health protection and to assistance in case of working incapacity, or the obligation of the government to help alleviate the housing situation of families, should not be understood as sources of subjective entitlements but rather as expressing the programmatic orientation of the state. Most importantly, the legislator must not infringe upon rights set forth by the constitution unless it is provided by the constitution that further statutory regulation can specify the extent to which a given right may be enforced. As such a mandate for statutory specification is traditionally the rule rather than an exception in the realm of social rights, the PCT's deference to the legislature's choice of welfare policies appears acceptable from the vantage point of both mainstream constitutional theory and the given political and economic circumstances. In fact, that approach might have been not only legitimate, but also necessary. As there was no revolutionary break with the previous legal order, a vast number of provisions enacted by the communist legislature, including welfare policies, remained in force. Many of these policies, however, proved a hindrance to the efficient functioning of the new political and economic system. Sure enough, the economic situation of Poland made it difficult, if not impossible, for the government to fully uphold the level of public reliance on the existing social entitlements. Garlicki points out that part of the explanation for the centrality of social rights in Poland's constitutional adjudication lies in the fact that systemic transformation made certain infringements into established social entitlements necessary.[49] As the economic crisis worsened, it became increasingly difficult for the Tribunal to question the government in its efforts to limit the social safety net.

Not that it would concede absolute leeway to the Sejm in welfare regulation. Not willing to let the legislature completely decompose the social safety net, the PCT was later on to compensate for its deference by relying on the notion of 'orderly law making' as the evaluative criterion for the performance by the legislature of its policy-making role. Even more importantly, it remained insistent that it was the legislature's duty to provide for *vacatio legis*, that is, a transitional period necessary for the citizens' adjustment to the reduction of social entitlements.[50]

But the Tribunal made it known that it was aware of the peculiarity of a situation in which the new government found its policy discretion circumscribed by generous welfare promises it neither had made nor was able to fulfil. Therefore, since the constitutional delineation of social rights dated back to a different socio-economic system, according to the Tribunal it had to be brought in line with the new context.[51] Accordingly, the justices preferred to invalidate statutory reductions of welfare rights by pointing out inequality in the distribution of the burden rather than relying on the generous constitutional clauses of socialist origin.[52] Another way of 'updating' the constitutional text was to understand the content of social rights 'primarily as a catalogue of values that should be taken into account and protected within the implementation of social justice'.[53] The PCT thus conceded that special circumstances, such as a drastic deterioration of the economic situation, might justify retroactive interference with social rights.[54] It also conceded that exceptions applied to rights the enforcement of which carried a financial burden, and established the notion of 'the state of particular economic hardship' as limiting the full applicability of the respective rights. In a later decision, the Tribunal even found budgetary equilibrium to be an autonomous constitutional value,[55] and held that under exceptional circumstances interference with contracts already concluded could be deemed constitutional if such interference was justified by efforts to preserve the budgetary balance and the state's capacity to fulfil its fundamental obligations.[56] The Tribunal pointed out that since 'it [did] not bear responsibility for the creation and realization of the state budget, it could not excessively constrain the Parliament's freedom to perform its constitutional authority'.[57] Displaying growing willingness to accept diminution of social entitlements, the PCT also learned to refuse to extend the principle of legal certainty to the provision of certain welfare services.

Domestic legal academia largely supported the PCT's taking account of, and elaborating upon, the new constitutional axiology and welcomed its tendency to interpret dynamically those normative acts that were enacted after June 1989 and 'thus arose from a different social, political and economic reality'.[58] Scholarship also adhered to the notion that 'values anchored by law in general and the *Rechtsstaat* principle in particular… were to be balanced against the social axiology of political and economic reforms'.[59] Accordingly, by taking into account the need for incremental deconstruction of the former structure of social relations, the PCT often proved willing to let the legislature do that which, because of the historically contingent mode of the regime change—based on a compromise with the incumbents—could not have been completed within the revolution. Tadeusz Zieliński, the former Polish ombudsman, offers a self-explanatory excursion into the ways of legitimising that approach: 'During turbulent systemic changes it is… unavoidable that politics may dominate over law in the sense that anachronistic law cannot hinder bold political decisions whose purpose is to adapt existing laws to the requirements of the new system.'[60] After all, it is, according to the Tribunal, precisely in the period of constitutional transformation that the power of the legislature to promote particular political and economic goals is of particular importance.[61]

The interpretive tools employed by the PCT to justify its permissiveness varied. In general terms, the PCT would adhere to the assumption of a 'rational lawmaker',[62] which assumption it said was a logical component of any functional interpretation of the constitutional text.[63] In some instances, the Tribunal would approach the legislature as the 'perfect lawmaker' possessing the requisite knowledge of matters subject to its regulation.[64] The Tribunal would find an additional rationale for its deference in what Kozak denotes as the assumption of coherence as regards the legislature's hierarchy of values.[65] Kozak also points out that the PCT would at times change its *façon de parler* and approach the legislature as the 'historical lawmaker', using stenographic records of parliamentary deliberation and invoking legislative intent within its interpretive arguments.[66]

The assumption of a 'perfect lawmaker' allowed the PCT to locate the source of rationality in parliamentary deliberation. It was by virtue of understanding the legislature as encompassing both reason and will that the Tribunal often displayed a permissive attitude when confronted with the need to recognize other law-speaking bodies as deserving weight and thereby generate consensus. Indeed, the 'Constitutional Tribunal does not claim to have a monopoly on establishing interpretations of the Constitution. If there is no evident infringement of constitutional norms the Constitutional Tribunal has no reason to question the practice of uniform application by constitutional organs implementing them.'[67] Unlike in Hungary, where it is in conformity with the local tradition for social change to be facilitated through a relatively autonomous judicial elaboration of legal standards, the one legitimate forum in which to produce binding public choices in Poland was the realm of representational politics.[68] Simply, the Tribunal whole-heartedly embraced Professor Holmes's anxious suggestion that constitutional review should not serve to undermine the policy-making capacity of the parliamentary forum and thus jeopardize its newly found democratic legitimacy.[69]

No third turn. The 1997 constitutional reform released the Tribunal from most of the institutional inhibitions impacting its operability as the country's super-legislator. The self-imposed inhibitions, reflecting the PCT's understanding of its own role in the government's endeavours, remained largely unaffected. True, the Tribunal appears to be more confident in the scrutiny of normative acts for their conformity to acts of higher legal force. While in 1997 it found unconstitutionality in 15 out of 65 applications (excluding constitutional complaints), the ratio jumped to 28 such findings out of 62 applications in 1999 and remained at a similar level in 2000 (25 findings of unconstitutionality out of 61 applications, excluding constitutional complaints). The PCT also continues to emphasize the imperatives of 'orderly lawmaking' and keeps protecting the basic tenets of its established case law, such as the principles of *vacatio legis* applicable to *pro futuro* restrictions of existing entitlements, proportionality in statutory restrictions of constitutional rights, and many other similar jurisprudential essentials.

Still, the Tribunal does not seem to have undergone a principal change of consciousness as to its operability as an agent of social transformation. It continues to emphasize that it is 'not called to control the opportunity and pertinence of solutions adopted by the legislature... The point of departure is always the presumption of the legislature's rational action and of the conformity of laws to the constitution.'[70] The Tribunal therefore must not 'interfere with the legislature's prognoses and choices',[71] and 'should intervene only in cases where the legislature steps over the limits of its regulatory authority in as drastic a manner as to make the violation... of constitutional clauses obvious'.[72] Indeed, only 'drastic and obvious deviations from rationality' warrant the Tribunal's interference with legislative activity.[73] Simply, it is not the role of constitutional review to assess whether 'the legislature produced the most appropriate and comprehensive regulation... as that falls under the autonomy of the legislature, which bears political responsibility to the voters'.[74]

It is also indicative of the Tribunal's continued sensitivity to the government's financial situation that in two out of the three cases in 1999 in which it applied for an opinion of the cabinet as to the possible budgetary consequences of its ruling, it ended up finding conformity to the constitution of the contested statutes.[75] In 2000, the Tribunal inquired as to the financial implications of its decisions on eight occasions, eventually finding unconstitutionality in three cases. Further, protection of vested rights still is to cover only just and rational expectations,[76] budgetary difficulties may allow for the restriction or even cancellation of the mandated indexation of state-budget-dependent employees,[77] and to subject addressees of law to different conditions is still to be deemed in conformity with the principle of equality if such a differentiation fosters social justice.[78] Most importantly, the Tribunal has lost nothing of its belief that some fundamental morality constitutive of the regime's axiological foundations is to be applied as a yardstick of constitutionality. In its holding on the adjustment of certain pension entitlements, the Tribunal held unconstitutional a legislative differentiation between pensions of civil and military participants in resistance, noting the constitutional relevance of the purpose of the respective entitlements—granted on the basis of participation in resistance and honouring the merits of Polish citizens who struggled for the sovereignty and emancipation of their homeland.[79] Applying the same approach, but with a different outcome, the PCT later upheld a statutory amendment which made it impossible for certain former members of the communist party to be granted the status of combatants and thus receive the relevant pension entitlements.[80] Similarly, a provision excluding any amnesty for certain types of criminal offence committed by state officials between 1944 and 1989 was found constitutional, not least because justice required it so.[81]

However, the most illustrative example of the Tribunal's continued permissiveness as regards those legislative measures that reflect its own moral, ideological, or axiological preferences is its handling of politicians' efforts to use their differing attitudes towards the communist past as benchmarks of their political agenda. In 1998, the PCT invalidated within preliminary review a single provision of a statute allowing for the dismissal of judges who during the communist regime 'failed in their duty to remain independent' and did so on procedural rather than substantive grounds.[82] Later in 1998, the Tribunal validated on two occasions the principal provisions of lustration legislation mandating public officials to declare whether they had ever collaborated with the communist secret service.[83] In 1999, the Tribunal held unconstitutional, on more or less technical grounds, a few provisions of the purgation-oriented law on public service, but upheld several of the statute's exclusionary rules.[84] Several years after the Hungarian Court had pointed out that, owing to the passage of time, lustrations could not be deemed to serve the needs of transitional justice, as well as several years after the lustration law became obsolete in Slovakia, the Polish Tribunal remained open to the notion that transitional justice might require constitutionally ambivalent measures. The concerns as to whether those who came to be known as the 'dark forces of the past' would attempt to subvert the new order were entirely legitimate in the early 1990s. Although not accepted universally, a constitutional court's tolerant attitude towards purgation measures advanced by the legislature was understandable, as it answered legitimate concerns about the fate of the transition. One is left to wonder, however, why the PCT continues to be lured into assisting the parliamentary majority in its purgation efforts at this point in Polish history. Is it because of how easily the communists got away with their betrayal of the nation that the Tribunal keeps acting as a champion of historical justice? Or is the relatively recent constitutional validation of purgation measures a kind of concession offered to the right-wing parties for their failure to achieve much success in influencing the final wording of the 1997 constitution?

On the other hand, it must be noted that in 2000 the PCT held that to subject to a lustration procedure a person who resigned from a public office or aspired to take such an office while simultaneously confident on the basis of the then valid regulation that no lustration procedure would be performed was contrary to the principle of legal certainty and other principles constitutive of a democratic *Rechtsstaat*.[85]

One way or another, the Tribunal is continuing the trend of upholding rights-based challenges to legislative solutions to moral dilemmas only to the extent to which these challenges do not work against a particular ideology. This tendency suggests that despite completion of constitutional reform, the notion of transitional specifics is alive and well, at times allowing politics to get the better of law. It also exemplifies the settling in of a particular mode of constitutional discourse, one in which the constitutional court is there to assist rather than to rule the legislature. That the Tribunal remains insistent on not being competent to control the opportunity and pertinence of solutions adopted by the legislature, and that it sees the assumption of the legislature's rational action as the starting point for any constitutional scrutiny, points to a gradual domestication of a concept of constitutional review that is not only feasible and legitimate, but that may even reflect the standard continental model more accurately than does, for instance, the Hungarian one. But that the PCT remains ready to provide assistance to the legislature on various purgatory measures suggests the presence of concrete ideological conceptions regardless of changes in design or text.

The Tribunal's contribution to the founding of an operational and legitimate government indeed might have been less controversial were it not for its intermittent, and deliberate, succumbing to the prevailing political ideology. One should, however, again remind oneself of the context in which the PCT was working. Put at a considerable disadvantage *vis-à-vis* the Sejm, faced with constant confusion on the political podium, and aware of the public's demand for order its manoeuvrability was correspondingly limited. No less important is that the Tribunal's idea of founding reflected paradigms rooted in Poland's legal consciousness and thus entailed a vision of a nation-state in which elected officials, be it the parliament or a charismatic authoritarian leader, make the decisive calls as to the society's basic orientation, and constitutional review is to step in only in the case of a flagrant deviation from the main course. This is what the Tribunal seems to have been aiming for and this is what it accomplished.

Active Judging

Overview

In the preceding section, I argued that the PCT attempted to overcome the implications of the deficiencies of its abstract-review equipment only to the extent that it did not question the legislature's prominence in the policy-making process. The delineation of the Tribunal's concrete-review powers suffered from substantial defects, too. In addition to design-related constraints, such as the unavailability of a constitutional complaint, the wider context affecting constitutional adjudication provided further obstacles, as the ordinary courts proved heavily resistant to the imposition by the PCT of binding interpretive standards upon their decision-making. In this realm, however, the Tribunal tried thoroughly to compensate for the attendant deficiencies. In its efforts to neutralize the most debilitating effects of the institutional design of constitutional review in general and the protection of rights in particular, the Tribunal would: (i) locate in the *Rechtsstaat* clause several mechanisms aimed at protecting a citizen, the most prominent of which became the extensively conceptualised right to court, and (ii) throw itself into an intense colloquy with Poland's high courts, namely the Supreme Court and the Supreme Administrative Court, in an attempt to make the ordinary courts follow in their adjudication constitutional case law. Whether and how much it succeeded I will assess in the sub-section on jurisprudence. Before that, however, a few more remarks follow on the adjudicative instruments available to the PCT and the environment in which it was to employ them.

Provisional period. The Tribunal's role in the protection of rights was relegated to abstract review. Its inability effectively to address violations of individual rights was partly compensated for by the empowerment of other authorities traditionally competent to protect rights. The Supreme Administrative Court (PSAC), for instance, was assigned the role of supervising the legality of administrative decisions and thus of correcting the adverse effects they might have on the protection of citizens' individual rights.[86] As the review of merely the formal legality of administrative implementation of law proved inadequate, the PSAC's powers were later enhanced to include the review of the substantive propriety of administrative decisions. By acting as an instance of cassation within the realm of administrative law, the PSAC did a fair job in strengthening the position of individual citizens *vis-à-vis* the executive power. It comes as no surprise, then, that the number of petitions to the PSAC increased from 15,212 in 1991 to 62,297 in 1998, and continues to grow.[87] The PSAC's engagement in a dialogue with the PCT was of particular benefit to the quality of rights protection, as the PSAC would derive its jurisprudence from such Tribunal-made concepts as the citizens' confidence in government, legal certainty, right to court, fair trial, vested rights or *vacatio legis*. A similar judicial discourse—albeit mostly going in the opposite direction—took place between the Supreme Court (PSC) and the Tribunal, as the latter would not shy away from taking advantage of the complex jurisprudence of the PSC in the area of personality rights and their protection by civil law. The PCT used this material, for instance, in human dignity and right-to-privacy cases.[88]

The Office of the Ombudsman, too, compensated in part for both the exclusion of citizens from abstract-review standing and the lack of constitutional complaint. Not only did the appointment of the first ombudsman considerably raise the awareness of Polish citizens of their newly acquired status *vis-à-vis* the government,[89] but she also undertook to 'bombard' the PCT with petitions alleging rights violations. The subsequent ombudsmen continued the tendency and the office became the most active of all authorities competent to motion the PCT, with the number of ombudsman's petitions totalling approximately 130 in the 1990s.[90] Yet the effect on the citizens' insulation from intrusion by the government remains disputable, for exposing violations rather than redressing them is as much as an ombudsman can do. To use the words of Poland's second ombudsman, he had a big mouth but very short arms. Ironically, the then ombudsman Tadeusz Zieliński argued vigorously against providing the PCT with the power to hear constitutional complaints—an attitude described by some insiders as stemming from a wish to preserve the ombudsman's quasi-monopoly in the realm of rights protection—and his successor could not conceal personal satisfaction when the first years of the new instrument offered less impressive results than might have been expected.[91]

There were, however, systemic deficiencies attendant on the pre-1997 rights protection scheme other than the crippling of the PCT's authority. First, the ordinary courts lacked the mandate directly to apply the constitution in their decision-making.[92] It was decided by the Supreme Court in 1957,[93] and generally accepted until recently, that in implementing the relevant law, judges were competent to refuse to apply a sub-statutory act if deemed in violation of a statute,[94] but were not competent to refuse to apply a statute and base their findings solely on the constitution. Although the PSAC grounded a few of its decisions exclusively and directly in the constitution, using, for instance, the principle of equality as a normative basis for its rulings,[95] in general it tended to apply constitutional provisions in conjunction with ordinary laws and as a guide for statutory interpretation.

Secondly, rather than invalidating the defective regulations—which, after all, it had no power to do—the PSAC would disregard them in its adjudicative practice or, more seldom, refer them to the PCT through an interlocutory appeal. As Kabat points out, any decision of the PSAC implying illegality of a sub-statutory regulation had no effect on the validity of the regulation, and in any future proceedings the administrative agencies theoretically could use it as fully applicable.[96]

Thirdly, the referral competence, the use of which could lead to invalidation by the PCT of defective legal rules, was confined to appellate courts, leaving the first-instance courts outside any discourse with the Tribunal and delaying the constitutional scrutiny of statutes relevant to the matter at hand. Moreover, even the eligible courts, including the PSAC and the PSC, were reluctant to engage the PCT in their interpretive endeavours and relied on the referral procedure to a much lesser extent than would be desirable from the vantagepoint of an intense intra-judicial colloquy. Between 1990 and 1999, the PCT decided on the basis of interlocutory appeals from all the ordinary courts combined in 17 instances. The situation slightly improved only with the extension of the referral competence to all the affected ordinary courts, regardless of their rank.

Fourthly, the insufficient constitutional regulation of the relationship between national and international law affected the jurisprudence of the ordinary courts even more than it did that of the Tribunal. On the one hand, there were signs that the courts were gradually becoming accustomed in their decisions to referring to the relevant international law. In 1987, the Supreme Court rejected the idea that judges could be bound to apply international treaties in their adjudication,[97] yet in 1991 the PSC itself understood the ICCPR as self-executing, and directly applied its Articles 4 and 15.[98] The PCT then held in 1992 that the courts were bound to apply international treatises *ex proprio vigore*,[99] and later conceptualised ratified international agreements as 'an integral element of the system of the Polish state' and thus as 'directly binding and applicable'.[100] The growing willingness to implement international law by ordinary courts became especially visible after the coming into force of the ECHRFF. On the other hand, a direct reference to the case law of pan-European judicial authorities was seldom the basis for interpretation, and international law was used in parallel to domestic law rather than as an autonomous normative basis for a particular decision. The Polish judges were careful to apply international norms *contra legem*, and well aware of the fact that statutes were to serve as the primary normative basis for their decisions.

Any applicant to an ordinary court who claimed a violation of her rights therefore had to be advised to base her claim on a particular statute in force. Several pieces of rights-protective legislation—for example, that regulating political rights and due process guarantees in criminal law—were enacted after the change of regime. Nevertheless, parts of the relevant legislation raised doubts and reservations as to their conformity to international standards, as was the case, for instance, with pre-trial detention procedure.[101] The substantive human rights law was not fully remodelled and the rights-enforcement mechanisms were incomplete. The Tribunal elevated the right to court to a constitutional principle but the framework of justice administration did not offer a fully satisfying basis for the redress of individual grievances. Osiatynski points out that 'over half of the complaints concerning the violation of constitutional rights sent by citizens to the Sejm's, the President's, the Ombudsman, and the Helsinki Committees are about violation of rights by courts and not by the administration or the Parliament'.[102] The practical reality served to reinforce the positive-law limitations, as justice administration in Poland—as well as in other post-communist countries—suffered from serious wounds inflicted upon it by the previous regime. The relatively low prestige of the judicial profession all over Central Europe—the degree varies slightly between the respective countries—results in the understaffing of courts, exposing them to caseloads they are unable to deal with effectively. This in turn leads the public to look for extra-legal ways of dispute resolution and often induces sentiments bordering on resignation concerning the availability of justice. The length of judicial proceedings is lamented as almost prohibitive,[103] and is generally expected to rise, the situation being particularly bad in the realm of civil and commercial law.[104] Add to this the widespread suspicion of the judiciary's lack of resistance to corruption and the right to court, even though incontestable in theory, appears to be a rather imperfect solution, one that requires additional guarantees to be of much use.

Moreover, systemic deficiencies attendant on the incidental protection of rights in Poland affected not only ordinary citizens, but had adverse consequences for the country itself. The number of complaints filed against Poland at the ECHR, for instance, is by far the highest in the region and the overwhelming majority of them allege violation of the right to court or unreasonable delays in ordinary adjudication.[105]

Reform. The rights-protective instrumentarium that the PCT was equipped with by the 1997 Constitution is claimed by some authors to be just about perfect.[106] How far does it really go? Far enough to be short of perfect.

Important steps were taken to enhance the PCT's competence in the realm of rights protection. It now has the power to assess the conformity of national to international law. What the PCT was doing previously in a quasi-clandestine way—namely substantiating its interpretation by reference to binding international agreements—it can now do on the normative rather than the axiological level, using international norms as a direct source of law. Given the current pace of the internationalisation of human-rights guarantees and the level of protection that transnational instruments and their attendant case law provide, this inclusion in the Polish constitution can only be welcomed.

Yet diversion of the PCT's attention from abstract review to adjudication of cases and controversies was not the path taken. True, the long anticipated procedure for filing constitutional complaints was established, allowing the PCT to hear claims of violation of rights alleged to have resulted from application of law by a court or a body of public administration. It is, however, precisely in the regulation of the constitutional complaint that the constitution maker went only half way, and the issue merits detailed examination.

First, the review of constitutional complaints concerns solely the universally binding normative acts, that is, statutes and sub-statutory regulations. As such, it is a mixture of referral procedure and abstract posterior review of constitutionality. It extends from judges to the litigants the right to apply for the PCT's holding on the constitutionality of a statute dispositive of the litigated matter. In the meantime, the review is posterior rather than anterior, as it applies to situations in which an ordinary court implicitly finds the respective statute to be in conformity to the constitution. The combination of the lack of authority to issue universally binding interpretations of statutory law and the applicability of constitutional complaints only to normative legal acts deprives constitutional review of an instrument that would allow it effectively to supervise the extent to which ordinary courts adhere in their adjudication to the Tribunal-made standards of constitutionality. In and of itself, the transfer of the power to issue universally binding interpretive guidelines from the PCT to the PSC is a positive step towards reducing the Tribunal's abstract review equipment. In combination with the exclusion of judicial and administrative decisions from the PCT's scrutiny, it is, however, a step towards stripping constitutional review of its *raison d'être* in the realm of rights protection.

Secondly, the Tribunal may not adjudicate *ultra petita partium*, that is, in excess of a petition. Since any constitutional complaint must apply for invalidation of a universally binding normative act rather than an individual judgment in order to be certified, under certain circumstances the Tribunal may face a no-win situation. It can either invalidate a statute even though the statute may be perfectly constitutional under a particular interpretation, or refuse to do so even though it may believe that the individual judgment did not do justice to either the statute or the claimant. Here, the PCT faces a particular dilemma. It is well established in both the doctrine[107] and the PCT's case law that it should declare a statute constitutional if it is possible to interpret it as conforming to the constitution, even though the ordinary court interpreted it in the dispute at hand in a different, unconstitutional way. However, if the PCT holds a contested norm to be in conformity with the constitution or a statute while at the same time arguing for a particular interpretation, it has no way of providing for the courts' observance of that interpretation. Thus, if the Tribunal locates the source of unconstitutionality in judicial interpretation of a statute and not in the statute itself, in order to both provide a remedy to the affected claimant and be on the safe side with respect to judicial interpretation of the given law in the future, it should strike down the statute. Moreover, not only is the PCT unable to invalidate an ordinary court's judgment, it is also only the finding of unconstitutionality that allows for the re-opening of the respective proceedings.[108] Ironically then, the constraint put on the PCT's adjudicative powers can in fact serve to constrain the legislature, as it may induce the Tribunal to invalidate more statutes than it would were it empowered to rule on the ordinary courts' judgments.

To add to the deficiency of the scheme, if the contested statute ceased to be effective before the Tribunal issued a ruling the proceedings had to be stayed. Constitutional complainants were thus left with no possibility of applying for a constitutional remedy even though their rights might have been violated. The 2000 amendment to the PACT corrected this flaw, allowing the PCT to complete proceedings even in the case of previous derogation of the contested statute, as long as it is necessary for the protection of constitutional rights and liberties.[109]

Thirdly, in order for a constitutional complaint to be formally perfect and thus admissible, stringent criteria must be met. The complaint may be filed only upon the exhaustion of all the available administrative or judicial proceedings, including the instance of cassation.[110] Also, before a final judgment is issued, no party to the proceedings has the authority to motion the PCT on the issue of law, as such a motion falls within the exclusive discretion of the respective court. Given the usual length of a three-instance judicial procedure and in light of the courts' reluctance to furnish the PCT with their own referrals, this puts the claimant at a disadvantage. Moreover, even if non-conformity to the constitution is eventually declared by the PCT, the affected judgment is not invalidated and proceedings are merely reopened. Thus, even if the applicable statute is invalidated, the redress of the grievance that gave rise to the dispute is simply deferred. Further, the PCT may, if it finds it appropriate, postpone the derogation of the contested act for up to 18 months in the case of statutes and up to 12 months in the case of sub-statutory decrees following the publication of the unconstitutionality/illegality finding.

The exclusion of individual decisions from the scope of the Tribunal's review, in combination with some other tenets of the 1997 reform—such as the transfer from the PCT to the Supreme Court of the authority to issue universally binding interpretation of statutes—suggests that the latter court's quest for interpretive autonomy has borne fruit. It is indeed difficult to conceive of compelling arguments for keeping the PCT confined within the boundaries of abstract review other than the PSC's largely successful campaign to be conceptualised as the ultimate protector of rights.[111] It therefore appears that in exchange for its strengthening *vis-à-vis* the Sejm the PCT had to pay by losing ground against Poland's high courts. The systemic inhibitions attendant on the operation of constitutional review in Poland thus may have simply changed from legislature-centred to court-centred. Or, to put it more mildly, the transfer of certain abstract review powers to the PSC and the PSAC[112] was not accompanied by a correspondingly significant increase in the Tribunal's concrete review powers.

The matter is more complex, however. The new regulation, for instance, widens considerably the judicial venues for addressing citizens' grievances. Pursuant to Articles 77 and 78 of the constitution, claims of rights violations can be pursued within ordinary adjudication. In addition, Article 8.2 of the constitution states that 'provisions of the constitution apply directly unless provided otherwise by the constitution'. Therefore, while on the one hand the new regulation transferred parts of the PCT's authority to the ordinary courts and thereby weakened its centrality in Poland's rights discourse, on the other hand it made the right to court all the more relevant.[113]

The ordinary courts' capacity to hear claims of rights violations and directly apply the relevant constitutional provisions indeed appears a more significant enhancement of the rights protection scheme than does the incorporation of a constitutional complaint. The current scheme may well account for the surprising fact that fears that the anticipated influx of constitutional complaints would render the PCT's protection ineffective proved to be unfounded.[114] The constitution's direct applicability by ordinary courts, however, also provided a new battleground for recurring confrontations within the Polish judiciary. While a significant part of domestic legal academia supports the notion that ordinary courts are not bound by a statute if they come to believe that it is unconstitutional, others, including justices of the Tribunal, think that a court may never refuse to apply a statute by alleging its unconstitutionality without referring the issue to the PCT. This dispute not only continues to shape legal discourse in Poland, but also bears heavily on the conceptualisation of judicial review. If ordinary courts are allowed to disregard a statute in their decision-making, it is a revolutionary development in Polish legal tradition. It suggests a move towards a system of diffuse constitutional review with the Supreme Court on the top, and thus a conceptualisation of justice administration bearing more resemblance to common-law countries than to continental legal systems. The matter is extremely relevant to the intra-judicial colloquy, as there does not appear to be any reason for an ordinary court to refer an issue of law to the Tribunal if it may perform constitutional review on its own. This temptation may prove too strong to resist especially for the highest-instance ordinary courts. It is therefore a considerable step forward that the authority to refer an issue of law to the PCT was extended from appellate courts to any adjudicating court. This extension bore fruit in 1999 when six of the 10 judicial referrals received by the Tribunal came from district or regional courts. In 2000, seven of the nine interlocutory appeals that were decided on the merits originated with courts other than the PSC or the PSAC.

Jurisprudence

The right to court. The PCT's efforts to compensate for its own jurisdictional limitations by vigorously emphasizing the right to have one's claims addressed by the judiciary form one of the very cornerstones of its jurisprudence. The PCT began to elaborate upon the right to court shortly before the change of regime and thus before the *Rechtsstaat* clause was inserted into the Polish constitution. In its first decision on the issue, and without yet using the notion of the right to court, the Tribunal relied on Article 56 of the constitution—stipulating that administration of justice in the Republic of Poland was to be carried out by courts and that the powers and organization of the judiciary were to be specified by statute—and held that administrative agencies lacked the competence to resolve certain indemnification claims, as such claims were to fall under the authority of courts.[115] After the *Rechtsstaat* clause came into force, the PCT combined the principle of the state ruled by law with Article 56 and introduced an individual right to court as, 'although not expressly provided for in the constitution, stemming from its Article 1 and Article 56 (1)'.[116] The extremely general language of the respective constitutional clauses did not prevent the PCT from making use of the same combination in subsequent decisions,[117] although it began to find additional doctrinal support in international instruments, especially the IPCPR and later, upon its ratification in 1993, the ECHRFF.

The Tribunal's seminal ruling on the right to court dealt with the 1990 Act on Border Guards, depriving border officials of the possibility to appeal their transfers and dismissals to administrative courts. The PCT held that the right to court was of such importance in a democratic state ruled by law that any interpretation aiming at its restriction would be in conflict with the fundamental elements of the Polish Republic.[118] It further found the right to court to include the right to a fair and public hearing in matters relating to the defence of legal interests, whether of civil or administrative origin.[119]

The Tribunal later extended the right to court to foreigners put under arrest,[120] and invalidated provisions granting control over deprivation of liberty to the PSAC instead of a court of general civil jurisdiction.[121] In the latter ruling, it stated that the possibility to file a petition with the PSAC did not offer an effective guarantee of rights, as it required exhausting the first-instance administrative procedure, followed overly lengthy proceedings, and required the filing of a petition with a court through an administrative organ or a cassation instance.

The right to court became so fundamental an element of the PCT's transitional jurisprudence that it did not need to rely on the textual improvements offered by the 1997 constitutional reform. The Tribunal simply continues to understand the right to court as an incontestable part of the citizens' expectations of the government and as an essential element of the rule of law. The possibility of having administrative decisions reviewed by the administrative court, for instance, is according to the Tribunal one of the most important constitutional principles.[122] Accordingly, a rule which excludes from administrative judicial review a decision to issue or not to issue a security certificate designed to enable a person to access classified information violates the constitutional right to court.[123] The Tribunal also has extended the ambit of the right to court by holding in 1998 that judicial review had to be provided in every case of expropriation of goods, even if it concerned confiscation of narcotic substances.[124] Building on a vast body of related precedents, the PCT has come to understand the right to court as encompassing the right to have one's claim addressed by an impartial and independent court, the right to have procedural rules observed by the court in accordance with the demands of justice, and the right to receive a ruling on the adjudicated claim.[125]

The right-to-court jurisprudence typifies the Tribunal's attempts to overcome the defects of its adjudicative toolbox. By emphasizing procedural guarantees of rights protection, the Tribunal balanced its own willingness to grant the Sejm considerable leeway in substantive policy making by making sure that the policies' implications for their addressees could be examined by courts if necessary. Also, in order to alleviate its own incapacity to furnish concrete remedies for rights' infringements, the PCT tried to locate the corresponding authority in the ordinary courts. It was, however, precisely in its interaction with the ordinary courts that the

PCT's efforts to compensate for the imperfections of the institutional framework of rights protection, especially its campaign to neutralize the impact of the abstract review trap, faced serious impediments.

Intra-judicial colloquy. In order to ease the systemic deficiencies of the adjudication framework, the PCT borrowed from the Italian constitutional doctrine the notion of a living law, according to which statutes are to be reviewed for their constitutionality based on their interpretation by the law implementing agencies, especially the judiciary. The PCT itself, however, qualified this notion by insisting that this technique be applicable only if the given interpretation of the contested regulation is well established in the case law. 'It is only if no doubt appears that the provisions have acquired in practice a content contrary to the Constitution or the laws that a decision would be justified holding thusly understood provisions as unconstitutional or illegal'.[126] So the Tribunal obliged itself to look for an interpretation allowing for constitutional validation of the contested statute. 'If, in light of grammatical interpretation, the given norm may be understood in different ways, the interpretation that guarantees conformity to constitutional principles must be adhered to.'[127] This imperative wording, however, did not translate into ordinary case law as thoroughly as the PCT had hoped and the ordinary courts often took the 'must-be-adhered-to' suggestion to mean that it may be adhered to at their discretion.

The Tribunal therefore attempted to pursue other interpretive methods—one was to interpret judicial referrals as mandatory, the other to issue universally binding interpretations of statutes. It thus tried to make certain that even if reluctant to engage the PCT in their adjudication, the ordinary courts would abide by its decisions. In combination with its insistence on the availability of judicial venues for the protection of rights, the Tribunal's interpretive interventions in ordinary adjudication might appear a promising tool to counter-balance its confinement to abstract review. Both these methods, however, proved a source of profound disagreement between Poland's judicial authorities and were regularly defied by their addressees, the ordinary courts.

The friction between ordinary and constitutional judiciary was fed mainly by the rivalry between the Tribunal and the PSC. One of the PSC justices argued in academic terms, for instance, that since the PCT was not a court, it should not interfere with the interpretive enterprise of the ordinary courts.[128] The following view of one of the Supreme Court judges sums up neatly the PSC's take on the Tribunal's position within the Polish judiciary:

> [C]reation of the Constitutional Tribunal means that the legislator adopts as his own the position that the constitution could be and should be subjected to the court's jurisdiction, which is out of the question. For this reason the whole matter must be reframed. The problem is not whether the constitution can be used in the jurisdiction, but which court should be allowed to utilize it. The opinion that the Constitutional Tribunal should enjoy this right, but the Supreme Court should not, would have to be based on very strong arguments. These arguments do not exist.[129]

Indeed, one of the very few issues related to the Tribunal's authority *de lege ferenda* that gave rise to a controversy during the deliberation over the 1997 Constitution was whether the Supreme Court was to be bound by the PCT's interpretations. According to Czeszejko-Sochacki, the universally binding effect of the PCT's rulings was explicitly anchored in the 1997 constitution precisely because of 'the damaging practice, which—as is illustrated by the Supreme Court—attempted to relativise the universally binding effect'.[130]

The issue of the binding nature of the PCT's interpretations of statutory and constitutional law involved Poland's judicial authorities in their most serious disagreement. The tension, more or less latent in the early 1990s, surfaced in a dramatic fashion when the PSC issued a ruling according to which 'a decision of the Constitutional Tribunal does not have any immediate effect, which would deprive the contested statute of its binding character and, moreover, excludes the possibility of negating such a statute (by other means, e.g. within ordinary courts' adjudication) until the Sejm decides to amend or cancel the statute in whole or in part'.[131] The PSC further opined that even if the Sejm upheld the finding of unconstitutionality, the respective statute would remain valid until its explicit modification by the legislature.[132] The PCT reacted by holding that if the Sejm does not make a decision to overrule or uphold its finding of unconstitutionality within six months of receiving the ruling, the respective statute loses its binding force upon publication by the Chief Justice of the relevant resolution.[133]

Despite the PCT's efforts to the contrary, it was apparent that the ordinary courts were less than willing to observe its interpretive endeavours. The ruling in which it interpreted in a radically different way from both the PSAC and the PSC the interest accrual on outstanding remuneration for police officers and border guards[134] triggered another heated dispute between the Tribunal and the Supreme Court. In addition to rejecting the interpretation of both the PSC and the PSAC, the Tribunal held that should a statute be found unconstitutional on the basis of which statute an ordinary court issued its ruling, the respective proceedings had to be re-opened and the PCT's interpretation adhered to by the adjudicating court.[135] Following this decision, the Supreme Court held that the ordinary courts were not obliged to observe in their adjudication the universally binding interpretations of the PCT.[136] Trying to hold ground, the Tribunal reiterated the position that its interpretations of statutes were binding upon all organs and authorities, and that court judgments and administrative decisions issued on the basis of an interpretation subsequently held unconstitutional were to be corrected in accordance with the relevant procedure.[137]

However, some of the Tribunal's efforts creatively to interpret the adjudication scheme in order to compensate for the shortcomings of its competence were deemed controversial not only by the ordinary courts, but also by Polish scholarship.[138] On a general note, the PCT's authority to furnish universally binding guidelines on statutory interpretation, although explicitly provided for by the constitution, was at odds with the fact that in civil-law systems the *Rechtsintegration* function is traditionally attributed to the highest-instance ordinary court. Moreover, the commentators were not completely at ease with so-called interpretive sentences in which the Tribunal would hold a statute constitutional only if interpreted by courts in a particular way. Since only the holding of the decision, and not the dictum, is effective *erga omnes*, the Tribunal would insert the interpretation into the sentence.[139] True, according to Article 190.1 of the Constitution, any ruling of the PCT on the constitutionality of a normative act is universally binding. But, as Jozefowicz points out,[140] neither the constitution nor the PCTA offered an unambiguous basis for inserting a particular interpretation into the holding instead of keeping it within the dictum. Although Garlicki takes a different stance on the issue,[141] he concedes that the Tribunal has no tools available to impose its particular interpretation upon the ordinary courts, and must therefore rely on the persuasiveness of its legal argumentation.[142] Given the ordinary courts' reluctance to feel bound by the PCT's interpretive decisions, this seems, and has proved to be, shaky ground.

The rivalry between the Tribunal and the Supreme Court extended beyond the issue of who was authoritatively to interpret Poland's law. Another of their controversies concerned the vitally important referral procedure, one of the very few instruments allowing for something akin to concrete norm control under the Polish constitution. Before 1997, the PSC would interpret the referral authority of appellate courts as implying the possibility, rather than the obligation, of a court to refer an issue of law to the PCT.[143] Following the promulgation of the new constitution, the PSC found additional support for its defiance of the PCT in the immediate accessibility of the constitution to ordinary courts. It held that should a court believe a particular statute to be unconstitutional, it could refuse to apply it and then base a finding exclusively on the constitution.[144] Even the traditionally more Tribunal-friendly PSAC takes the same stance on the issue.[145] Professor Sanetra, a justice on the Supreme Court, repeated on several occasions that any court in session could apply the constitution directly and did not have the duty to refer a constitutionally dubious statute to the PCT.[146] Professor Rymarz, a justice on the Tribunal, agrees.[147] The PCT's justices Safjan, Garlicki,[148] and Kolasiński,[149] as well as several Polish scholars,[150] argue, however, that if an ordinary court incurs doubts about the constitutionality of a normative act determinative of the pending matter, it is obliged to refer the issue to the PCT.

As with interpretive sentences, the mandatory nature of judicial referrals does not seem a black-and-white issue, either. Both Article 193 of the constitution and Article 3 of the 1997 Act on the Constitutional Tribunal (PACT) state that 'any court *may* refer a question of law to the Constitutional Tribunal as to the conformity of a normative act to the Constitution, ratified international agreement or statute, if the answer to such question of law will determine the matter pending before such court'. The relevant text thus suggests that judicial referral is optional rather than mandatory. The competing visions of judicial protection of rights notwithstanding, it works in favour of the individual petitioner if a court in charge of his claim may disregard a dubious statute, for such a practice reduces both the length of the proceedings and other technical obstacles attendant on a full-scale review by the Tribunal.[151] One way or another, there were only three rulings issued on the basis of interlocutory appeals in both 1997 and 1998. The Supreme Court referred to the PCT for the first time under the new constitutional regime in November 1998.[152] Although nine decisions were issued on the basis of judicial referrals in 1999, not a single one came from the PSC. Given both the continued inability of citizens to challenge individual decisions at a constitutional level and litigants' inability to initiate constitutional review on their own motion, the referral procedure remains crucial to the Tribunal's access to the less abstract elements of its constitutional decision-making. Although there seems to be hope that the ordinary courts will co-operate rather than compete with the Tribunal, it remains difficult to assess whether there is in fact a firm tendency emerging among them to accept, where applicable, the co-operative engagement of constitutional review.

The effectiveness of the protection of rights will largely depend on the quality of institutional dialogue between the PCT and the ordinary courts, especially the Supreme Court.[153] The history of that colloquy, although not warranting complete despair, is far from offering an overly optimistic prognosis. Garlicki expresses in diplomatic terms his concern that the relations between the PCT and Poland's high courts may reduce rather than enhance the level of individual rights protection.[154] The new constitutional regulation, however, gives no reason to believe that the PSC will soften its assertive attitude towards the Tribunal. Moreover, the fact that the divisions extend from within the judiciary into academia suggests that neither of the two main rivals is able to point to, and rely upon, unequivocal doctrinal support.

It is in this context that the early experience with constitutional complaint may seem a cause for concern.[155] After no complaints in 1997, 168 were filed with the PCT in the following year.[156] Out of those, however, only 22 were admitted for a full hearing and only one decision—unfavourable to the claimant—was actually issued.[157] In 1999, nine decisions on the merits were issued out of 185 petitions that reached the Tribunal and were classified as constitutional complaints,[158] with four unconstitutionality findings.[159] The same number of unconstitutionality findings issued upon a constitutional complaint applies to 2000—four out of 10 decisions on the merits.

Early experience also proves well founded some of the concerns outlined above. Many petitions were rejected because the petitioner either failed to pay the respective court fee, or identified a judicial decision rather than a normative act as the subject matter of his complaint, or filed the petition without first exhausting the cassation instance.[160] More than two-thirds of complaints received by the PCT in 1999 were rejected because they were not filed by an attorney at law.[161] In one documented case, the petitioner missed the deadline for filing a constitutional complaint because of his alleged inability to find an attorney, a necessity pursuant to the law.[162] To add to the technical constraints, the Tribunal defines as inadmissible constitutional complaints alleging a violation of rights set forth only by international agreements and not by the constitution itself.[163] It is then of no surprise that the first ruling favourable to a constitutional claimant—and only the second final judgment on a constitutional complaint in the first 14 months of the new constitution's being in force—came in February 1999.[164]

Even though the constitutional complaint is gradually becoming a more popular element of a citizen's arsenal in her quest for protection, it appears that judicial review rather than constitutional review may in future play a more important role in the incidental protection of individual rights. This is a development that both the PSAC and the Polish Supreme Court have helped to foster. As for the former court, it is growing in doctrinal sophistication and enjoys a rich capital of public confidence. As for the Supreme Court, it has referred to constitutional provisions in 60 decisions in less than two years since the coming into force of the new constitution.[165] It now boasts a relatively rich constitution-related case law, ranging from the principle of equality to the right to property, freedom of assembly, right to court and even jurisprudential issues as delicate as the sources of law or their intertemporality. Whether the exclusion of judicial and administrative decisions from the scope of the PCT's review will prove to be a cause for serious concern as to the quality of the citizen–government relationship therefore remains to be seen. The Tribunal after all does have access to various tools it can use in order to assert its relevance as the protector of rights. Even though the new constitution has proven less of an enhancement of concrete constitutional review than many had hoped, it does provide the PCT with enough textual material to further develop its *Grundrechtsdogmatik*. And after a decade-and-half of elaboration, that may well be what the Tribunal is both accustomed and most happy to do.

Hungary

Judicial Activism

Overview

The Hungarian system of constitutionality protection is heavily biased in favour of abstract review, facilitating the Court's active involvement in the policy-making process. The HCC exploited this adjudicative equipment to the limits of political and doctrinal feasibility, and even creatively manipulated it so that it would serve its own idea of the proper kind of constitutional review. It strove, and largely managed, to modernize Hungary's law and provide the country with a *Grundrechtsdogmatik* fully comparable to that of the Western democracies. The Court, however, was mostly concerned with producing scholarly commentary rather than with taking on the judicial robe. Its perception of the role it should play in the period of transition was not only informed by institutional choices made at the time of regime changeover but reflected tradition, too. The indigenous legal consciousness served to reinforce the impact of design and fuelled the Court's law-making tendencies. Relying on the local paradigm of judicial activism, the HCC found the judicial robe too tight for its taste and felt compelled to police those within its reach; and a long reach it was indeed.

At the time of the RT talks in 1989 when the reconstruction of the Hungarian constitution was being intensely deliberated and the foundations for the country's constitutional reform were laid down, the question as to who should be appointed the engine of transformation revolved around the Parliament–President dichotomy. Given the strong tradition of parliamentarism in modern Hungary and the Parliament's relatively liberal demeanour both shortly before and during the regime change, the legislature came to be seen as the more or less true embodiment of the polity liberated from oppression. A weak presidency was instituted,[166] and a considered decision was made and transplanted into the text of the constitution to conceptualise the Parliament as the prime leader in the process of transition.

Yet in comparison to most of the world's constitutional courts, and especially in comparison to the PCT struggling with various systemic inhibitions, the HCC's adjudicative equipment was impressive, to say the least. According to the September Pact, adopted at the Round Table talks in 1989, the HCC's role was to 'contribute to the creation of a state built on the rule of law, protect the constitutional order, and safeguard the separation and balance of power'.[167] This particular wording did not find its way to the constitution[168] and was slightly enriched in the HACC, so as to include other roles, such as the protection of constitutionally guaranteed rights. It suggests, however, that those in charge of shaping constitutional review thought it proper to conceptualise the HCC as a decision-making authority *sui generis*, resembling more than anything else a tribal counsel of elders. That it would be the Court that would most intensely and most significantly challenge the Parliament's transitional leadership occurred to the relevant political agents only after the HCC had produced its first far-reaching decisions. But despite frequent claims that the drafters of both the 1989 amendment to the constitution and the HACC had no idea what the Constitutional Court was about, there are indications at the level of constitutional regulation that in general terms a deliberate decision was made with regard to the HCC's positioning within the framework of government. The fact that unlike in Poland, Czech Republic or Slovakia, the HCC is not regulated within the constitution's chapter on judicial power offers a first hint, albeit a superficial one. There is no role for the HCC in justice administration in Hungary as, pursuant to Article 45 of the constitution, this is the exclusive provenance of ordinary adjudication. There is, however, much more on the part of the text of both the constitution and the HACC.

In addition to powers typical of continental constitutional courts—namely review of generally binding normative acts for their conformity to the constitution—the HCC was granted competencies the range and combination of which is without precedent in the history of constitutional review.[169] The standing to initiate post-enactment review of statutes and sub-statutory regulations for their conformity to the constitution is open to everyone,[170] without any qualifications, while review of conformity to international treaties of national law may be motioned only by enumerated government authorities. Until 1998, the Court had the authority to perform *ex ante* review of draft legislation on the motion of the Parliament, parliamentary committees or a group of at least 50 parliamentarians at any stage of legislative deliberation. The pre-enactment review standing is now open only to the cabinet and the President, and is limited to bills pending promulgation. Based on a Court precedent, however, it includes the review of draft legislation for its conformity to international law. Still within preliminary review, the legislature may initiate the Court's assessment of the constitutionality of the Standing Order of Parliament. The Parliament, the President and the cabinet may motion the HCC to assess conformity to the constitution of an international treaty pending ratification. The Court has the authority to resolve competence conflicts between the different government agencies, between local and national administration, as well as between the different municipalities. It can intervene in cases of manifest unconstitutionality, for example, in the case of omission by the respective authorities to enact legislation or sub-statutory norms required by the constitution. The Court's power to shape law is considerably enhanced by its discretion over the temporal effect of its decisions, as it can invalidate the contested norm from a particular date in the future, from the date the respective decision appears in the official gazette, or, if it finds it warranted by legal certainty imperatives or an important interest of the petitioner, even retroactively.[171] An ordinary court may file an interlocutory appeal with the HCC to determine whether a statute or any other legal instrument relevant to the case at hand is constitutional. Unlike in Poland, the right to motion the Court with an interlocutory appeal is not limited to the adjudicating court, but extends to the litigants.

The HCC was thus packed with adjudicative tools that strengthened its capacity to legislate. What it lacks is the ability to hear constitutional complaints against individual decisions. The *actio popularis* allows anyone to contest legislation without any personal interest being at stake but limits the applicability of a constitutional complaint to normative acts on the basis of which an individual decision was issued. When viewed in isolation from the bulk of the HCC's powers, the omission of a 'true' constitutional complaint—that is, one aimed at *inter partes* decisions of public authorities—served the legitimate purpose of preventing the Court from becoming an appellate court. The overall structuring of its adjudicative authority, however, contributed to the HCC's failure to become a court at all, and created an institutional environment that enabled and encouraged delegation to the court of policy disputes rather than concrete rights grievances.

Other features that are by definition conducive to the involvement of a constitutional court in the law-making process—such as the lack of a second legislative chamber designed, inter alia, to filter constitutionally dubious measures, emphasis on abstract review enhanced by the possibility of *ex ante* review, and the President's constitutional veto allowing him to motion the court—were all in place in Hungary. Solid foundations were thus laid for what has become one of the principal features of Hungary's post-revolutionary development, namely the double-leadership in the process of transition of the Parliament and the Constitutional Court, fed throughout the transition period by their quest for political relevance and, in consequence, recurrent confrontation.

As much as the external constraints imposed upon its adjudicative authority translated into the Polish Tribunal's case law, the HCC's extensive *instrumentarium* proved similarly effective. There were, however, several other factors only remotely related to the design to help the Court to preserve its role in bringing about social change and base Hungary's transformation in a double transitional leadership; that of the governing majority and constitutional review. One was the Court's ability to diversify its 'competence portfolio', so to speak. Not only could it rely on powers provided by the constitution as well as on public approval—both of which it could eventually lose—but it was also able to draw on international recognition. The Europeanisation mission, displayed initially in *Capital Punishment* and the retribution rulings, allowed the HCC to foster its agenda without having to defer to the incumbents on every occasion. In addition, a paradox similar to that noted in the case of Poland also can be detected in Hungary, only this time in reverse order. The

Parliament, the cabinet and to some extent also the President have advanced their claims to leadership in the process of Hungary's reconstruction as a liberal democracy. The space for the Court to put itself at the helm of social reform thus appeared fairly limited. The HCC, however, had fewer reasons than the PCT to worry about the effects of fragmentation of political power and the governing majority's ability to function as a policy-setter. By virtue of being a supreme authority in a unitary state with a single-chamber legislature, the Parliament's policy-making capacity is limited by very few structural obstacles—were it not for constitutional review, it would enjoy almost unlimited leeway within the political process.[172] In addition, the Hungarian voting system—being a combination of proportional and first-past-the-post features—proved conducive to strong parliamentary majorities. Add to this the fact that, similarly to Germany, a cabinet dismissal depends on a so-called 'constructive motion of non-confidence', which means that the cabinet may be effectively voted out of office only if there is a new designated Prime Minister enjoying majority support in the Parliament. The Hungarian political arena was therefore much more stable and coherent than the Polish, the Slovak, and, a few years into the transition, even the Czech one. Every single post-communist cabinet in Hungary finished its term in office and enjoyed a workable majority in the Parliament, a feat unparalleled anywhere else in the region. The very strength and stability of the Parliament gave the HCC less reason to sympathize with the legislature's policy-making efforts and made it less inclined to lend the law makers a helping hand than the fragmentation of transitional politics in Poland gave the PCT. The difference in the courts' approaches to their legislatures illustrates the contingent nature of Holmes's concern that activism of constitutional courts may undermine the institutionalisation of the national parliaments' authority and legitimacy.[173] When trapped between the need to Europeanize the local legal landscape on the one hand and the need to allow for efficient policy making on the other, the HCC tended to emphasize the former aspect as the core of its mission and distanced itself more than the PCT and the CCC from the Charybdis of unconstrained efficiency.

Not that the HCC has been completely free of turns similar to those that have taken place in Polish constitutional development. In the realm of restitution policy, for instance, the Court went the entire way from rejecting restitutions in principle to allowing the legislature to have it almost the very way it wanted it from the beginning. Similarly, the HCC eventually let some of the retribution measures pass constitutional muster despite the initial refusal. But even after partial retreats, the Court continued to both legislate more assertively and affect the policy outcomes of parliamentary deliberation more thoroughly than any other court in the region. The most significant change thus came only with the completion of personal restructuring of the HCC in 1998 when the new justices embarked on a different path of constitutional adjudication, narrowing both the scope and the depth of their review.

Jurisprudence

Rise to leadership. Ironically or not, it was thanks to, not in spite of, the Court's refusal to attribute decisive normative significance to the transitional specifics that it became much more of a transitional leader than any other constitutional court in the region. Sólyom argues that 'from a legal point of view, transition was accomplished the moment Mátyás Szűrös shouted "Hungary is a republic" through a window in the House of Parliament on 23 October 1989',[174] and goes on to insist that the Court's activity should not be explained as a reaction to the transition but rather as a 'normal development'.[175] The HCC tended to orientate its jurisprudence prospectively, refusing to draw any argumentative support from the widely suggested need to first face the past and then build the nation anew. The combination of focus on posterity with preference for normality translated heavily into the HCC's case law, and its prospective constitutionalism was radically different from the PCT's and the CCC's efforts to assist the reconstruction of their polities according to the insurgents' agendas.

Indeed, the legislature began to feel the impact of constitutional review immediately upon its institution, as the HCC did not shy away from coming forward with its own transitional agenda, using the concept of prospective constitutionalism to obstruct some elementary transitional measures adopted by the Parliament, such as the lifting of the statute of limitations for crimes left unpunished for political reasons or the restitution of property nationalized during socialism.

The seminal transition ruling, the notorious *Zétényi*, illustrates both the Court's take on the relevance of transitional specifics and the peculiarity of the Hungarian kind of judicial activism. Both the PCT and the CCC found the notion of the 'state ruled by law' to warrant retroactive justice. The HCC based its rejection of retroactive justice on the very same concept, and argued that the principle of legal certainty, as the cornerstone of the rule of law, did not allow for any *ex post facto* criminal prosecution. Watching the courts apply the same law to a radically different effect must fill every legal realist's heart with joy. Indeed, one is tempted to view the difference in the respective courts' approaches to the issue as a mere display of the justices' individual political preferences.

The variances emerging in the region in the realm of transitional justice nonetheless were as much conceptual as they were political. True, *Zétényi* might seem an extension of some aspects of the deal made at the Round Table talks between the reform-friendly communist leadership and the opposition, and the Court's approach an effort to preserve to the maximum possible extent the *ruptura pactada*. On a doctrinal note, however, the HCC went to great lengths to argue against value judgments or the preference for the basic principles of justice to formal legality. In the Court's view, legal certainty trumped substantive justice. Contrary to what both the PCT and the CCC stood for, the Hungarian Court said that 'the basic guarantees of the rule of law [could] not be set aside by reference to historical situations and to justice as a requirement of the state under the rule of law... Legal certainty based on formal and objective principles is more important than necessarily partial and subjective justice.'[176] The HCC argued that the ban on *ex post facto* criminal punishment, as well as the lack of former owners' entitlements to property seized by and under the former regime, was the necessary result of Hungary's transition-of-choice and thus a reflection of the uninterrupted continuity of the rule of law.

The very concept of the paradoxical revolution by the rule of law, however, was largely of the Court's own making and the Parliament was faced with its implications for its own elbowroom *ex post facto*, so to speak. Moreover, as the Court rightly anticipated that the Parliament would not be too keen to subscribe to its peculiar interpretation of what the change of regime was meant to bear, the justices did not hesitate to appoint themselves the guardians of this paradoxical revolution. Indeed, one of the most significant aspects of *Zétényi*'s idiosyncrasy and 'indigenousness' is undoubtedly the Court's messianic mission, the wish to save the people from their weaker selves, prevent distraction from the road to European salvation and hold high the torch of the rule of law to mark the boundaries of what is, and what is not, allowed in a civilized world. Where did this boldness of the self-appointed saviours come from?

This is what the then Vice-President of the HCC has to say:

> It is fair to say that, until the end of the nineteenth century, the courts played a pre-eminent role and that the development of the judicial system was a vital priority... Our first king and his successors, the various presidents, [all] gave prominence to case law... The courts have played a principal role in our legislative sys-

> tem and... we have reason to hope that our region will see the birth of a new era that places great value in courts. The judiciary can look back upon a solid foundation of traditions. I would call it a sacred tradition and we must now assume this heritage and transform it to meet the needs of the future.[177]

It thus was the strength of legal rationality elaborated upon and brought to life by courts that was to facilitate the polity's redemption and advancement. The notion that the way ahead must be enlightened by the champions of law and reason rather than the champions of politics and will can be identified already in the formative period of modern Hungary, that is, in the period of its emancipation as a constitutive element of the Austro-Hungarian monarchy. The Court's belief in the purity of legal dogmatics and rational legal analysis led it to monopolize constitutional interpretation, transcend the unstable political arena, and prefer its own constitutional 'idealism' to the 'pragmatism' of the incumbents.[178]

Both *Zétényi* and the early decisions on compensation policy also reflected two inter-related layers of the country's quest for recognition. One layer, aimed at the outside world, was informed by the Hungarians' wish to excel in the region, acquire distinct 'Western' credentials, and set an example to the 'backwardish' Eastern Europe.[179] But since the legislature failed to account for this particular psychological trait, the space opened up on the domestic scene for the HCC to steal from the Parliament the spotlight of constitutional transformation by catering to the need of the polity to display itself to the outside world as truly European. In comparison to the PCT's reaction to the Stalinist crimes statute, which exposed the Tribunal's readiness to help the law-making pitcher strike out the bad guys, *Zétényi* and the early compensation cases demonstrate that the HCC was eagerly waiting for a fast ball to score some home-runs of its own. As the then Chief Justice informs us, *Zétényi* was a deliberate deviation from the closely scrutinized approaches of the Czech and Polish courts, and—something which makes the HCC's decision appear even more courageous—also of the German Constitutional Court. Sólyom argues that the invisible constitution—that is, reception and adoption of contemporary constitutional thinking and dogmatics—would be usable in the Czech Republic and in Slovakia as well, and in other countries of the region'.[180] Needless to say, it was the HCC that saw itself at the forefront of this contemporary constitutional thinking. Sólyom lamented, for instance, that it was "a terrible waste that their rulings have not yet been published in impeccable English,"[181] undoubtedly for the 'people who are internationally minded'[182] to learn their lesson in European constitutionalism.

The Court's approach to the notion that the exigencies of systemic transformation should (not) translate into constitutional jurisprudence was selective. On the one hand, the Court did take note on a few occasions of the special circumstances relating to the change of regime. It did so, for instance, when it permitted the legislature to account in the statutory resolution of proprietary grievances for the historically unique change of the political system.[183] The HCC invoked historical exceptionality also in *Restitution of Church Property*. In *Incitement*, it referred to the past both as a negative referent and as extending into the contemporary era the unique historical circumstances of which provided a ground for differentiating between incitement to hatred and 'mere' denigration.[184]

On the other hand, the Chief Justice pointed out that the outcome of the Court's interpretation would often depend on the way the issue was approached: that is, presented either as a question of facing the past or one of providing solutions for the future. The Court opted for the latter as the default mode of approaching transition-related issues. It thus managed to structure even the model case of 'coming to terms with the past'—that is, the lustration issue—as 'entirely independent of the original goals of the lustration laws'.[185] According to the Court, 'the constitutional issue at the crux of the matter involves striking a balance between circumscribing the circle of individuals at issue and information on them of public interest',[186] and is therefore a perfectly 'normal' question of constitutional significance. Several years before the Polish Tribunal still found it feasible to deal with the past via purgatory measures, the HCC held that the lustration act had to be 'examined in view of present-day, normal legal conditions characteristic of a constitutional state. Owing to the passage of time, the legal peculiarities of the transition period can today hardly be validated within the framework of obligations presumed by a constitutional state.'[187] Similarly, the Court deliberately phrased even the restitution of church property not as an issue of compensation for past misdeeds but as a solution contributing to the contemporary society's functionality. The preference for normality was also behind the Court's rejection of the qualified-majority rule for statutory implementation of constitutional rights, as it implied that the 'peculiar political circumstances of the transition' have passed, rendering the special rule irrelevant.[188]

The HCC's refusal to attribute decisive significance to the peculiarities of transition and its insistence on 'normal' constitutional development extended beyond the realm of typical transitional policies. Unlike the PCT, which would respond to the exigencies of economic transformation by permitting legislative curbing of welfare entitlements, the HCC often went the other way. The Court's double switch on the issue of interest rates offers a fine example. In 1990, it held that neither the de-monopolization of banking industry nor inflation could justify a unilateral change of interest rates.[189] The then Chief Justice remarked at the time that this decision 'made it very difficult, though not impossible, to use inflation as an argument for raising interest rates'.[190] A year later, in the immediate wake of dramatic inflation, the HCC held the *ex post facto* raising of interest rates on publicly provided housing loans to be compatible with the constitution under the *clausula rebus sic stantibus* rule.[191] But in 1995, the Court explicitly refused to allow any further inflation-induced increase in interest rates since, as the Chief Justice put it, 'the transition or "system change" occurs only once'.[192] In other words, transitional specifics may not be relied upon as a default device legitimising measures that would not be constitutionally perfect under 'normal' circumstances.[193]

Moreover, unlike the Polish Tribunal, which would often justify its serving of the Sejm's transitional agenda by references to extraordinary historical or economic circumstances, the HCC presented itself as the depository of the paradox of the rule-of-law revolution, rejecting the notion that laws adopted in the past would be imbued with less normative force than those adopted after the change of regime. While the PCT held that the pre-1989 law had to be interpreted in light of the change of regime, the Hungarian Court '[did] not distinguish between preconstitutional and postconstitutional law'.[194] Its insistence that the 'fundamental guarantees of the rule of law may never be denied by reference to historical circumstances'[195] suggests that the HCC would have a hard time accepting the PCT's justification of measures unjustifiable under normal circumstances by reference to specific transition-related circumstances. The argument that transitory period might require specific legal solutions or that extra-legal variables—other than those of the HCC's own making, that is—should be accounted for in constitutional adjudication simply was not an argument the HCC was fond of using. It held in *Zétényi*, and did not revoke later, that political considerations were excluded from its scrutiny, and that the principle of legality required that the very norms regulating the legal system be applied without further conditions.

The discretion that both the PCT and the CCC were willing to grant their legislatures in the realm of welfare policies was considerably narrower in Hungary. In the notorious series of cases dealing with the government's austerity plan, the HCC interpreted certain welfare rights as worthy of the same level of protection as property rights,[196] and struck down a number of provisions of the amendments to social security legislation. In doing so, it deliberately refused to make itself aware of the economic consequences of its holdings and, again in stark contrast to some of the PCT's decisions in the same area, rejected the notion of economic emergency as a constitutionally relevant argument. It is indeed the absence of a certain line of argumentation rather than a presence of some other that speaks volumes about the Court's approach to transitional specifics. In response to the turmoil following its early holdings on fiscal legislation, the PCT came forth to the voices calling for more flexibility in evaluating the normative ambit of welfare rights. Accordingly, it established budgetary equilibrium as a constitutional value and held that the imminence of an economic crisis might justify constitutionally ambivalent measures. This lesson the HCC was not willing to learn. Rather, it tended to disregard financial considerations as qualifiers of the enjoyment of constitutionally protected rights. Instead of accounting for the impact its holding might have on the country's welfare reform, it based the rejection of austerity measures on its own understanding of certain social security benefits as purchased rights. In a truly peculiar exercise of legal analysis, it also invoked its own previous ruling in the abortion case, implying that the legislature had an obligation to guarantee living conditions for future generations and provide incentives for childbearing.

Overall, the HCC was much less forthcoming to the legislature's implicit demands for 'transitional leeway' than were the PCT and the CCC. It also proved less willing to engage in sorting out claims of historical injustice, or to approach the protection of rights with an eye to their impact on the government's economic performance. On the one hand, the HCC's regular—but not absolute—refusal to help the legislature to account for injustices committed in the previous era, or to overcome constitutional requirements for the sake of economic policy, often made the *entente* between the Court and the Parliament quite 'un-*cordiale*'. On the other hand, it allowed the Court to try to portray its decision-making as informed by legalistic rather than political considerations.

Partial retreat. But not everything would always go the way the HCC wanted it to go. The Parliament had enough stamina continuously to mobilize political capital to challenge the Court's holdings—to, as Seitzer puts it, brush itself off and charge again and again, seeking to preserve, if not extend, its policy-making discretion.[197] Unlike the Sejm, which realized that it could rely, in some ways at least, on the PCT's willingness to uphold the relatively rare occurrences of parliamentary consensus, and therefore asked for and was given a certain degree of the benefit of doubt, the Hungarian Parliament—facing a formidable opponent in the HCC—would try hard to get its act together. Klingsberg noted both the Parliament's increasing dislike of the Court's stealing its spotlight in the transition[198] and the awareness of the justices of using judicial capital wisely.[199] In the early 1990s, Ackerman praised the Court for its early retribution and compensation case law but at once voiced a serious concern: 'the Court cannot expect to play this positive role over the long run without displaying much more political prudence... It is only a matter of time before the Court's abstract resolution of an unending series of burning disputes will generate an overwhelming reaction by parliamentarians who will destroy such a politically exposed institution.'[200] His and similar warnings of the HCC's ultimate vulnerability were not lost on the justices.

The series of rulings on compensation policy illustrate both the Parliament's indefatigable brushing off and the corresponding decrease in the intensity of the Court's charges against it. Indeed, as the Parliament became painfully aware early in the innings that the Court would regularly send its fastballs to the outfield, it began to pitch some curve balls. The HCC had to find a way to respond. It soon found itself trapped between its own paradox of the rule-of-law revolution disallowing any discontinuity between the former and the current legal regime, and its simultaneous awareness of the political necessity to allow to stand those measures of land reform it previously deemed inappropriate. In response to the growing lack of support either in the political arena or among the commentators for the HCC to keep refuting legislative efforts at restitution—according to a first-hand account by Páczolay, the Court feared a 'revolution'[201]—it stepped back from its previously uncompromising attitude and over a series of related decisions eventually let the legislature have it almost the very way it wanted it.

Originally, the Court based its review of compensation policies on the principle of uncompromising equality, which was to prevent any discrimination between former owners and non-former owners. It gradually retreated from these stringent criteria and, instead, 'rested on deference to nominal legislative justifications'.[202] It would not, however, step down from the position that former owners had no enforceable entitlements to their former property. It opted for the principle of 'novation', which was to enable the government to ignore the legal nature of the origin of certain property grievances. But even though the Court thought that 'the content and boundaries of "novation" had been exhaustively detailed in the Second, Third and Fourth Resolutions',[203] the legislature found it difficult to figure out exactly how far that principle could carry its restitution efforts. This difficulty suggests how cumbersome was the Court's attempt to provide a legalistic disguise for the shift in opinion on property restitutions. It therefore completed the retreat in *Compensation V* and explained: 'The term "novation" is not used... in its ordinary civil law sense. The term "novation" in the court's usage is a simple and convenient shorthand to indicate that the legislature is permitted to take into account the unique historical circumstances of the change of political system in its statutory resolution of proprietary grievances.'[204]

The HCC's tactical savvy also came to light in *Restitution of Church Property*. Here, the HCC used the notion of social functionality of the Church to overcome the requirements of equality, which in *Compensation I* seemed invincible and upon which subsequent petitioners tended to rely. In addition, the Court paid notable lip service to the Parliament's regulatory autonomy and came forth to the legislature both by allowing for the return of real estate to the affected religious organizations and by considerably curbing the scope of the two-thirds majority rule for the statutory regulation of rights.[205]

One could argue that what I label 'permissiveness' in the case of the Polish Tribunal is euphemistically dubbed 'political savvy' in the case of the HCC. But the Court's retreat in the realm of compensation, and partly also in the realm of retributive measures, served to preserve the accumulated judicial capital and was far from suggesting surrender. Most importantly, the Court qualified its deference by more than merely face-saving measures. It deferred to some of the Parliament's fundamental assumptions underlying the restitution scheme only after the legislature adjusted its approach to the HCC's position in some significant ways, for example, by acknowledging that pre-Second World War owners should be taken account of in the compensation policies—a move that both the CCC and the SCC refused to require of their legislatures. The Court also kept open the space for further interference, as it insisted that although differential treatment might be permitted, the pool of beneficiaries of property transfers had to be enlarged so as to include all similarly positioned groups. And should disadvantaged groups be identified in the future, the Court said it was ready to speak up on their behalf. It made good on this promise when it found unconstitutional legislative differentiation between financial compensation to be granted to relatives of victims of state terror on the one hand (30,000 Hungarian forints [around 100 US dollars in spring 2002]) and financial compensation to be granted to victims of false imprisonment on the other (1,000,000 Hungarian forints [around 3,500 US dollars in spring 2002]). It even obliged the government to revise the provision so as to make eligible for the newly stipulated amount also those who had already been paid the 30,000 forints.[206]

Further, the HCC would pay lip service to the legislature's policy-making capacity in order to window-dress its assertiveness but would at once outline in detail the boundaries of permissible action. This is exactly what it did in the first abortion case, in which it left it to the legislature to make the crucial decision on the legal personality of a foetus and in the meantime suggested relatively elaborate guidelines to be followed by the Parliament in regulating the matter. Similarly, the Chief Justice, in his concurring opinion in *Capital Punishment*, explicitly stated that to alter the meaning of the Constitution was the exclusive province of the legislature yet simultaneously argued that in interpreting the text the Court was not to be in any way bound by the legislature's intent, whether known or unknown.[207] The Court also scored some considerable clear-cut victories, the most impressive of which concerned the realm of personal data protection, as it refused to bow to the legislature and disallowed any extension of the deadline it had previously set for legislative reform of the personal identification number (PIN) system. In consequence, it managed to have its standards fully incorporated into the respective legislation. The very fact that the HCC would advance its own complex substantive constitutional agenda and, despite occasional setbacks, largely get away with it shows how different was the positioning and the operation of constitutional review in Hungary from that elsewhere in the region.

Activism continued. The Court's tendency to juxtapose rights against the government's duty to act illustrates another unique element of the HCC–Parliament colloquy. What merits special attention here is that the Court transcended the traditional negative rights/positive rights dichotomy—it did not confine the notion that government was bound to act as much as to refrain from action to the realm of welfare rights, but extended it to freedoms commonly conceptualised as requiring non-interference. It held, for instance, that 'the state's duty to "respect and protect" fundamental rights [was] not exhausted by the duty not to encroach on them but incorporate[d] the obligation to ensure the conditions necessary for their realization'.[208] In other words, the protection of rights comprises at once the state's duty to refrain from action and to act, as 'the Constitution... demands that the State engage in affirmative protective action on the one hand and self-restraint on the other hand'.[209] In the first abortion decision, that requirement included not only the state's duty to refrain from compulsion in the realm of freedom of conscience, but also the duty to render possible the meaningful alternatives of its exercise and 'to guarantee the conditions that are necessary for the freedom of religion to prevail'.[210] Similarly, the requirement of the state's neutrality with respect to religion was found to entail more than mere restraint, as 'it is the State's obligation to ensure a field for manifesting, teaching and following in life one's religious convictions, for the operation of churches as well as for rejecting religion or keeping silent on it'.[211] The Court also pointed out the government's constitutional duty to provide public organizations with financial means necessary for their operability and autonomy from the state.[212] The Court later relied upon the government's 'duty to secure the conditions of life for future generations'[213]—with which it was charged in the abortion decision—in *Social Security Benefits*. Here, the HCC reminded the Parliament of the society's 'elementary right linked to having an active population in the future', translating into, for instance, the government's obligation of 'guaranteeing the living conditions of future generations',[214] or 'its obligations to protect the mother, the family and the child.'[215] Moreover, the government has to make sure 'that both natural and legal persons be able to plan with good grounds in making their economic, family or livelihood-related decisions'.[216]

In the lustration decision, the HCC inferred from the principle of legal security the duty of the legislature 'to ensure the effective operation of the procedure and administrative institution it created by guaranteeing the necessary authorization in the form of legal provisions'.[217] The freedom of expression was found to require detailed legal regulation of financial, procedural, and organizational solutions pertaining to public radio and TV operations, such a requirement stemming from the state's 'obligation to secure the conditions necessary for the creation and maintenance of the functioning of democratic public opinion'.[218] The administrative regulation of public media was thus found unconstitutional predominantly because of the government's insufficient performance of its regulatory duties, 'because of the absence... of guarantees against undue influence from any source'.[219] From Article 70 (K) of the Constitution—providing that claims arising from infringement on fundamental rights and objections to the decisions of public authorities regarding the fulfilment of their duties may be brought before a court—the Court inferred the duty of the government to establish institutions whose task it is to impose penalties for the violation of the consumers' rights.[220] Shortly and clearly, 'the protection of the constitutional order and the protection of citizens' rights is the Government's constitutional duty ([Art. 35 (1)] for which it may be held accountable.'[221]

How strong were the normative implications of the government's general duty to provide for its citizens' well being became most obvious in the case dealing with minors' membership of homosexual advocate groups and the case concerning the right to a healthy environment. In the former, the Court held that 'the right of the child to protection and care at the same time establishe[d] the duty of the State for the institutional protection of the child's personality development. This protective duty of the State [could] result in restricting the fundamental rights of the child.'[222] The HCC held that the government was bound to avert risks related to the child's pursuit of activities that could prove harmful in the future. According to the Court, none of these duties could be delegated to the parent.

But inasmuch as the HCC would regularly co-relate rights to the duty of their affirmative promotion by the government, in the environmental protection case the 'duty' element was found to constitute the core of the given right. The Court held the right to a healthy environment to be 'exceedingly dominated and determined by its objective aspect of institutional protection' by the government.[223] Referring to one of its earlier decisions, the Court re-emphasized, 'the duties of the State [had to] include the protection of the natural basis of life and extend to the establishment of institutions for the management of non-renewable resources'.[224]

The above sketch does not cover all the displays of the Court's insistent pointing out that the proper manner of governance entails more than abstention from inflicting harm. What it does demonstrate is that the HCC was not willing to let the legislature take its regulatory duties lightly. The Court feared normative vacuum and had almost no confidence that the political arena would be capable of an acceptable self-regulation.[225] The Court's distrust of the will- rather than reason-producing fora and its insistence on comprehensive legal solutions are a natural sapling of Hungary's tradition pursuant to which law is the primary, if not the exclusive, instrument of social change. The assignment by the HCC of affirmative duties to public authorities indeed served to accelerate development in various areas, for example, in the realm of data protection, mass media, organization and functioning of the judiciary, and so on. The Court's basking in the spotlight of the country's constitutional politics also served purposes not immediately related to that or another constitutional issue, such as the 'marketing' of the country as modern, liberal, progressive—read 'European'. All in all, the HCC established itself as the engine of Hungary's transformation into a country respectful of individual rights, achieved impressive results in modernizing Hungary's law, and must be praised for its willingness to challenge the indicia of unconstrained majoritarianism. The Court's tendency to assign tasks to, and distribute positive obligations among, institutional actors across the government suggests, however, how peculiar was the HCC's positioning in Hungarian constitutional politics and how different the Sólyom court from a court. It also suggests how far the HCC has gotten in resembling a model of constitutional politics that Stone Sweet says is irreversibly to dominate European constitutional space—a model in which law making is judicialised, constitutional courts legislate, and the boundaries delineating the different branches' operational ambits become increasingly blurred.[226]

Nonetheless, there appear signs of a growing willingness on the part of the HCC to vacate the realm of founding that it co-occupied so vigorously during its formative years. Rather than writing their own masterpieces of constitutional theory, the new justices seem to be content with deciding fairly simple matters by fairly simple means,[227] without reaching 'far beyond' the issue at hand and without feeling compelled to provide for solutions to outlive the present era and cast a shadow into a distant future. In invalidating a simple-majority amendment to a statute adopted by a two-thirds majority, for instance, the Court, instead of engaging in a discussion of the substantive aspects of the amendment, pointed out that a statute adopted by a qualified majority simply could not be amended by a lesser majority, and, in my opinion correctly, left the issue at that.[228] Similarly, in holding unconstitutional a statutory provision allowing the Interior Minister to decree the location of zones where prostitution was to be permitted, the HCC pointed out the violation of the municipalities' regulatory autonomy and did not engage in any material discussion of the merits of the so-called 'tolerance zones'.[229] On a different note, the new Court seems to have stepped back from the Sólyom court's insistence on the constitution's value neutrality, as it held the constitution to be based on specific values and to lack of protection of speech inconsistent with such values.[230] It also suggested a certain deviation from the preceding case law on the applicability of public order as a legitimate objective for restricting free speech.[231] It nonetheless appears that of the various legacies of the Sólyom Court, the Németh Court prefers the emphasis on a normal development to the invisible constitution. What Scheppele denotes as formalism[232] others may view as a display of the Court's coming to grips with the fact that the golden era of founding—giving it the opportunity to speak out even if not asked and inviting it to speak more loudly than a constitutional court is expected to in 'normal' times—may indeed be over.

Active Judging

Overview

In the preceding section, I argued that the transitional institutional and political environment, as well as various layers of the country's legal consciousness, proved a fertile soil for the HCC's policy-making activism. While the Court's operability in shaping Hungary's law could hardly be overestimated, its ability to administer justice suffered from serious imperfections. Unlike the Polish Tribunal, however, the HCC did not appear particularly interested in neutralizing the effects of its confinement to abstract review and contributed on its own to the diminution of the judicial elements of its identity. It would creatively manipulate its adjudicative equipment, but would do so mostly with the enforcement of abstract constitutionalism in mind, functioning in the capacity of a shaper of law rather than its administrator. Put simply, as much as constitutional adjudication in Hungary benefited from the fact that it was serviced by the most powerful court in the world, it also suffered from the failure of that court to ever become a court.

Throughout the region, constitutional jurisprudence was heavily informed not only by the design within which constitutional courts were to operate, the shape of which was largely outside their immediate influence, but also by procedural rules allowing for some degree of interpretive autonomy in their adjustment by the respective courts. Even more so was this the case with Hungary, as the HCC had more freedom than any other court in the region to manipulate the scheme within which it was to adjudicate.

The Hungarian constitution delineates constitutional review in rather general terms and the HACC contains only the most fundamental procedural rules for the HCC's operation. Neither of the above acts expressed so clear a preference for that or another mode of proceedings that the Court could not deviate from it. In fact, the HCC was left to elaborate the details of its functioning by means of an internal regulation, subject to parliamentary approval. It was for no fault on the part of the HCC that such approval never came about, unlike the internal regulation itself. The operational features of the HCC therefore were largely of its own making, and its self-conceptualisation accounted for the practice of constitutional review as much as did the relevant black-letter law. In Sólyom's own words, "the Constitutional Court had exceptional freedom to define its political importance and role, but its legal character in a narrow sense as well".[233]

Sólyom titled his recent work on HCC as *Constitutional Judiciary in a New Democracy*, but in the HCC's actual practice, the adjective proved much stronger than the noun. As Sólyom himself concedes, the Court was facing a puzzle whether its primary role was to "ensure abstract constitutional order or to remedy individual injuries affecting fundamental human rights'.[234] It made a decision to concern itself with the general integrity of law rather than its incidental implications for a particular claimant. Instead of becoming an authority attempting to focus on specific controversies, the HCC conceived of itself as a body whose mission was 'to build a system of dogmatic, an edifice of constitutional law' and 'to make statements… valid beyond the case being treated'.[235] Under such a scheme, 'individual cases are significant only as elements achieving acceptable aggregates'.[236] The emphasis, as Galligan phrases it, is not on accuracy and propriety in each case,[237] but on jurisprudential consequences transcending individual interest and affecting the polity at large. The petitions, after all, do nothing 'but get the C[onstitutional] C[ourt] machinery going'.[238]

Several aspects of the Court's practice corroborate the ex-Chief Justice's confession. The HCC, in the internal regulation of its proceedings—the so-called Court Rules—decided to employ inquisitorial rather than adversarial procedure and, in addition, pushed the former to its limits. It decided, for instance, to orientate its deliberations around written depositions and limit the number of public hearings to the minimum possible extent.[239] The HACC does provide for both closed-door proceedings and reliance on written depositions. However, it also provides for the participation in the HCC's public sessions of various public authorities and other persons invited by the Chief Justice before a closed session is convened. By regularly convening a closed session at the very beginning of the proceedings, the Court used to circumvent this rule and effectively limit public participation in its proceedings. Brunner also points out that the Court Rules go against the HACC in that they allow the HCC to gather all evidence necessary, while the HACC expressly forbids any means of acquiring evidence other than those enumerated in its Article 25.[240]

The HCC's reluctance to provide for an adversarial procedure also has shown itself in its failure to account in deliberation for the petitioners' statements at public hearings in those rare cases when such hearings did take place, to identify petitioners in the rulings, and, in general, to understand as relevant the petitioners' legal arguments and reflections of the issue. Sólyom said that the Court did not feel "strictly bound by the petition but use[d] it as a procedural starting point in order to render decisions concerning constitutional provisions as often, and as soon, as possible'.[241] Accordingly, the 'Court usually prefers general arguments, which are effective far beyond the question in the given case when through this generality even the supposition of positive or negative bias may be prevented'.[242] The HCC thus felt free to review also those provisions that the applicant did not contest. If there were a link between the challenged provisions and those that the Court took for review in excess of the petition, it would invalidate the latter ones as well.

Both Páczolay[243] and Brunner[244] argue that the Court's choice corresponded to the nature of the powers granted to it. Indeed, since there is no veritable constitutional complaint, concrete controversies between two clearly identifiable and opposing actors seldom are a basis for the HCC's decision-making. The preference for written depositions was partly due to the overflow of petitions, which rendered regular public trials unmanageable. And to understand petitions loosely and as merely a starting point comes naturally if a petition could be submitted by anyone, and, unlike elsewhere in the region, the HACC did not require the petitioner to either have a lawyer draft the complaint or represent the petitioner in the proceedings at the Court. Sólyom therefore may be right to argue that the HCC's institutional character of its own choice fitted the underlying assumptions about the role of constitutional review in Hungarian constitutional discourse.[245] There certainly is a link between abstract review and the failure to operate as a court. However, it does not appear that it would necessarily have to be as strong as it happened to be in Hungary. The Polish experience, for instance, suggests that the Hungarian path was not the only option available. In the realm of rights protection, the powers of the PCT are no less linked to abstract review than are those of the HCC. Nevertheless, its former Chief Justice Zoll underlines the PCT's 'very positive experience' with public hearings and the participation of a wide range of agents therein, which according to him 'plays a great role for the development of legal culture in general'.[246] Public hearings take place on a regular basis also within the abstract review proceedings of the Czech and Slovak constitutional courts. The HCC's emphasis on a non-public and non-adversarial mode of proceedings is the first in a long line of indicia suggesting that instead of engaging in dispute resolution the Court decided to act as the ultimate custodian of the law's coherence at the most abstract level. In other words, it thought that its vocation was to become an enforcer of modern constitutionalism, an imposer on the domestic legal culture of values transcending both the 'visible' text and the particularities of a given case.

Constitutional 'judiciary'. Not that the HCC would be happy with every aspect of its confinement to abstract review. It attempted, for instance, to neutralize the politicians' tendency to stampede to the Court with their agendas and engage it in delicate political disputes. The fact that the HCC soon became a venue of first rather than last resort for both the parliamentary factions and the executive indicated its political relevance, but at once made it extremely vulnerable to accusations of excessive judicial activism. The HCC was, for instance, repeatedly asked to sort out tensions between the President and the cabinet through an abstract interpretation of constitutional provisions relating to presidential powers.[247] Further, in order to avoid an open clash with a coalition partner, Prime Minister Antall shifted political responsibility from the cabinet to the HCC by demanding an advisory opinion on a highly controversial restitution bill (*Compensation I*).[248] In 1991, the Minister of Finance presented the HCC with several drafts of legislative proposals and asked it to provide the Ministry with guidelines as to further elaboration of the drafts (*Rabar*).

At that point, the Court became aware of the pitfalls of its permanent and unconstrained availability to politicians and, for the sake of its own survival as a constitutional court, decided that the time was ripe for it to refuse any such invitations and, consequently, to give up some of its competencies. Accordingly, it denied that it had jurisdiction to review ideas subject to development in a variety of directions, as such a review would 'inevitably result in the Constitutional Court taking over the responsibility of the legislative and even the executive power and thereby creating some sort of government by the Constitutional Court'.[249] In response to a petition by a group of parliamentarians seeking pre-enactment review of an indemnification-related legislative proposal, the HCC held that unless a bill was exempt from further modification it could not fall under its jurisdiction (*Compensation II*). The concept of a moot claim proved strict enough to render this mode of adjudication virtually obsolete.[250] The HCC's insistent refusal to engage in quasi-legislative preliminary review eventually led the lawmakers to strike some of the related provisions out and preserve standing in this realm only for the President and the cabinet.[251]

Yet it is difficult to view the HCC as an innocent victim of the politicians' excessive reliance on extra-parliamentary fora. True, it decided against the employment of those of its powers that were least compatible with traditional notions of constitutional review. The justices both complained about, and tried to put limits on, the frequent efforts of the political factions to align the Court on their side and use it against their opponents. The HCC, however, did contribute to this state of affairs. Unlike the Polish Tribunal, which stressed that it did not 'claim to have monopoly on establishing interpretations of the Constitution... and ha[d] no reason to question the practice of uniform application by constitutional organs implementing them',[252] the Hungarian Court never saw itself 'bound by the constitutional practice of other state organs'.[253] Sólyom informs us of the HCC's refusal to 'say that it is possible to fill any gaps in the constitution by the practice of the state organs, concerned, that is, by political bargains'.[254] Even when it refused to admit the motion for pre-enactment review in *Compensation II*, the HCC did not pass on the opportunity to 'summarize its theoretical stance' and informed the Parliament of the criteria required in order for the respective measures to be constitutional. Similarly, even though it refused to solve the issue of constitutional permissibility of abortion in definite substantive terms, it produced a complex summary of its doctrinal position on the issue and handed to the Parliament fairly elaborate guidelines on how to proceed with the respective regulation. As noted—and, interestingly, with unequivocal approval—by one Hungarian scholar, 'not only the standards of constitutionality but constitutional life as a whole was stemming from the jurisprudence of the Constitutional Court'.[255] The Court itself proudly proclaimed that 'the development that political conflicts are solved by the judiciary and according to legal rationality can be rightly called the judicialisation of political power'.[256] After all, the Sólyomian version of 'constitutional reality is inconceivable without a monopoly over the interpretation of the constitution'.[257] It is thus not wholly surprising that political factions understood the HCC's insistence on having a monopoly on explaining the country's supreme law as an invitation to the Calabresian flight to the constitution on every possible occasion.

The HCC's approach to those elements of its abstract review equipment that enhanced its capacity to legislate was selective rather than unequivocally dismissive. In *Rabar*, the Court held that any application for an advisory opinion had to be based on a concrete constitutional problem related to a concrete constitutional provision.[258] In a later decision, however, the HCC rejected those parts of a petition for an advisory opinion that were related to a concrete situation, and held that in order for such a petition to be proper it would have to give the Court the possibility to give 'a properly abstract answer to be compulsorily applied in all cases in the future'.[259] In its later take on advisory opinions, the Court dubbed the resolution of concrete cases as one of the two extremes from which it tried to stay away and argued that only issues requiring an answer 'beyond the particular problem that concerned the petitioner'[260] fell under its authority to interpret constitutional provisions. The Court was apparently—and understandably, too—willing to give up powers that made it vulnerable to political pressure. However, it would simultaneously interpret those it wanted to keep as requiring that it give general solutions for posterity rather than become enmeshed in concrete controversies. In other words, Ackerman's suggestion to focus on the plights of ordinary men and women rather than those of government officials was accepted only in part; confining itself to such plights simply was not the Court's idea of founding.

The Court's failure to diversify its contribution to constitutional development and its ambition to deepen those tenets of its authority that did not have much to do with the way the judiciary is traditionally thought to operate did not necessarily serve to undermine the quality of rights protection. After all, the *Grundrechtsdogmatik* that the HCC developed by means of abstract review bears comparison to established constitutional regimes across the globe. In some ways, however, the adverse consequences of the Court's entrapment within abstract review were readily apparent.

First, the Parliament appeared unfazed by several unfavourable holdings, aware of the Court's lacking a sword: that is, its ultimate inability to enforce the case law. The HCC felt free to assign homework to the lawmakers but had no way of making sure that the homework in fact would be done. The deadline set by the Court for the replacement of an unconstitutional media regulation, for instance, passed unobserved by the legislature and the HCC eventually gave up, leaving the Parliament to figure out the 'deadline' on its own.[261] In a delayed response to the Court's ruling, which held part of the Penal Code unconstitutional, the Parliament amended the respective provisions of the Penal Code by striking out the affected section and transplanting it into the section that the HCC had found constitutional! It was seven years after its first ruling that the Court got to deal with the issue again, being bound to acknowledge that what has been declared unconstitutional in its previous holding had ended up being 'hidden' by the Parliament under a different clause.[262] In its first abortion decision, the HCC elaborated complex criteria for legislative regulation of the issue. When the new abortion law was enacted, its incompatibility with the Court's guidelines gave rise to a number of petitions.

The Court, however, put the petitions on the back burner and invalidated parts of the law because of their vagueness only five years after it had received the first petitions challenging the law.[263] It even postponed the effect of its decision for over 19 months. The HCC's inability to hear petitions against individual decisions causing direct and immediate harm allowed it to deal with certain matters less seriously than one would expect from a self-proclaimed guardian of a coherent constitutional order. It is a legitimate assumption that were a constitutional complaint available and petitioners were allowed to challenge individual decisions, the HCC would feel pressed to address these and other issues with more diligence. But because of its preoccupation with leaving a legacy of an elaborate edifice of constitutional law, the Court felt free to take its time to keep refining the dicta over and over.

Secondly, Scheppele notes that a vast number of petitions alleged violations of rights by means of administrative decisions. Based on lack of competence, the Court would automatically screen these petitions out. Hungary lacks a specialized administrative tribunal and although ordinary courts do have the authority to review administrative decisions, certain kinds of decisions are excluded from the scope of judicial review. It is precisely in the absence of a separate judicial authority authorized to review administrative decisions that a constitutional court's ability to evaluate the constitutional conformity of administrative decisions is of the utmost importance to the quality of rights protection. There are after all telling examples in the region. In Poland, administrative judicial review alleviated the adverse impact on the protection of rights of the Tribunal's abstract-review trap. The lack of a coherent system of judicial review in the Czech Republic led to the intense involvement of the CCC in the scrutiny of administrative decisions. Moreover, to rely on the ordinary courts' readiness to implement in adjudication the relevant constitutional-review-produced abstract interpretation of the constitution or on their diligent supervision of the administrative authorities has shown to be an insufficient solution across the region, as the ordinary courts themselves proved to be in need of supervision.

Intra-judicial colloquy. Indeed, the region-specific deficiencies of the rights-enforcement mechanisms did not escape Hungary, either. As Bard points out, 'claims originating from violations of basic rights... are normally rejected unless they invoke an explicit provision in the implementing legislation'.[264] The administration of justice in Hungary suffers from material and personal shortcomings to an extent comparable to the rest of the region. The plague of positivism haunting ordinary adjudication in the post-communist world is less widespread in Hungary but not completely absent. Sajó summarised the first half of the decade in the following terms

> Courts are not particularly eager in responding to rights claims. In five years of democracy, in not a single case did an ordinary Hungarian court ground its decision on the fundamental rights provisions of the Constitution, and only exceptionally does an ordinary court refer a law, in relation to a pending case, to the Constitutional Court for review. The legal processes are slow and compensation for rights violations is often inadequate, even in cases of human rights violations.[265]

While the Polish and the Czech constitutional courts would do their best to counter similar tendencies on their home turf, the Hungarian one, partly because of the structure of its authority and partly because of its own fondness for abstract constitutionalism, felt less inclined to engage in confrontation with ordinary adjudication. The HCC nonetheless was not completely oblivious to the deficiencies affecting justice administration. It held, for instance, that even administrative decisions based on the agencies' discretionary powers had to be made subject to judicial review.[266] Also, even though the HCC was, as Brunner points out, generally reluctant to use its discretion in determining the temporal effect of its decisions in favour of the petitioners, it would in certain cases attempt to provide an effective remedy by invalidating the contested legal provisions with an *ex tunc* effect, that is, retroactively.[267] The Court used this technique—similar to the Austrian concept of rewarding the petitioner for raising the claim (*Ergreiferprämie*)—for the first time in 1990 when it held the contested norm void *ex tunc* with respect to the petitioner and *pro futuro* with respect to everyone else. Based on Article 43.3 of the HACC, retroactive invalidation became a rule in cases in which criminal conviction was based on a statute subsequently found unconstitutional by the Court—a new trial must be granted to all who remain adversely affected by the invalidated norm—but is generally inapplicable in civil or administrative cases. The HCC's tendency to require complex institutional guarantees and legal schemes so as to decrease the likelihood of repeated occurrences of the same kind of grievance is another display of its willingness partially to compensate for its emphasis on the elaboration of a commentary to the constitutional text rather than on dispute resolution.

Most importantly, the Court's efforts to react appropriately to the limitations of the Hungarian design of constitutional review—for example, to shift part of the responsibility for the protection of rights to the ordinary courts—enjoyed a friendlier intra-judicial colloquy than was the case elsewhere in the region. The scheme within which the HCC was to interact with the ordinary courts proved conducive to parallel rather than competitive performance of certain judicial functions. The advisory opinions as separate binding interpretations, for instance, concern only the constitution, excluding ordinary legislation. The HCC's role in the realm of integration of law therefore does not overlap with the Hungarian Supreme Court's *Rechtsintegration* function as directly as the PCT's interpretation of statutes interfered with the activity of the Polish Supreme Court before the 1997 reform. This fact naturally decreased the likelihood of friction between the highest judicial authorities in Hungary. Scheppele noted that the HCC and the Supreme Court simply made a deal as to the division of labour between them.[268] Indeed, the Court stated that any decision of the Supreme Court was outside the scope of constitutional review and was therefore unamenable.[269] Also, when the ordinary courts voiced their disagreement with the Court's finding in a paternity case in which it invalidated a court ruling,[270] the HCC simply refrained from the practice.[271] Instead, it would regularly invite the ordinary courts to apply constitutional case law to particular fact patterns in their adjudication[272] and insist on leaving 'differentiated consideration of the characteristics of each individual case to the ordinary courts'.[273] The Court came forth to the judiciary also when it declared as constitutional the lack of the ombudsmen's powers to scrutinize and challenge deficiencies in ordinary adjudication.[274] Whether the above practice necessarily benefited the quality of rights protection is open to question but the relatively friendly interaction between the HCC and the ordinary courts may well account for the fact that the number of judicial referrals is in Hungary notably higher than elsewhere in the region.[275]

There also seems to be a general sense of improvement in terms of implementation by the ordinary courts of constitutional standards. They do remain reluctant to accept the idea that the HCC should be able to interfere with their interpretive enterprise. Brunner, however, points out that while most interlocutory appeals to the HCC were in the earlier period initiated by the litigants and not by the judge, the courts are now becoming more active in motioning the HCC.[276] Most importantly from the point of view of rights protection, even the ordinary courts of first or second instance are gradually becoming accustomed to referring in their decisions to international human rights law. On this note, Mavi points out a case in which a county court rendered its judgment on the basis of principles established by the jurisprudence of the ECHR,[277] something difficult to conceive of elsewhere in the region.

That being said, one notices that even though communications between the different judicial authorities served to alleviate, partially and indirectly, some of the adverse consequences of the Court's confinement to abstract review, its decision to keep out of the realm of justice administration certainly helped to make the intra-judicial discourse relatively amicable. The overall institutional environment provided important incentives for the HCC to make that decision. It was, however, also its own susceptibility to the gravitational pull of constitutional politics that made it difficult for the Court to focus on the provision of remedies for incidental violations of individual rights. The leeway that the HCC was granted in bringing about its own unique law of constitutional procedure suggests that the Hungarian version of constitutional review did not come about only by virtue of constitutional and legislative authorization. The decisions that the HCC made in specifying its *modus operandi* reflect its self-understanding as an enforcer of abstract constitutional order and its approach to the individual citizen as a trustee of the public good. It appears that in the mind of the majority of justices, the overwhelming abstract review equipment was not so much a necessary evil as a welcome invitation for the Court to do what it thought it was proper for a constitutional court to do.

However, there are increasing calls for a reshaping of the Court that would reduce the load of its abstract review powers and authorize it to review decisions of ordinary courts and/or public administration authorities. In its own draft of the HACC, the HCC suggested the same path.[278] It is difficult to foresee where the Court will find itself a few years from now. As in the case of the Polish Tribunal, the growing significance of ordinary adjudication for the protection of fundamental rights may decrease the Court's burden in various ways. If it combines with the reduction of its abstract review powers, the HCC may eventually get to inhabit a constitutional space that will allow it to free itself of the immense pressure of having to found a modern nation and, at last, become a 'normal' constitutional court.

Czech Republic

Judicial Activism

Overview

On the level of generalities, the CCC's adjudicative equipment allowed for assertiveness in the policy-making arena. Some particular features of the Czech scheme of constitutional adjudication, however, affected the CCC's operability as an active law maker. These include stringent voting requirements for statute invalidation, extensive concrete-review competence diverting the Court's attention from abstract review to the scrutiny of individual decisions, or the somewhat restricted applicability of certain kinds of international treaty in the review of domestic legislation. In addition, the traditional theory of separation of powers and the political economy resulting therefrom proved to be deeply rooted in the local public governance culture, conceptualising the legislative process as the preferred mode of policy making. Moreover, not only the CCC's self-understanding as a constitutional adjudicator and as an agent of social transformation, but also the justices' ideological inclinations led the Court to embrace the ideology on which the new regime was founded and defer regularly and consistently to the Parliament's key policy choices. After all, the CCC's jurisprudential agenda of value-laden constitutionalism, which was to serve the needs of substantive justice and was to reflect the jusnaturalist revival, coincided to a notable extent with the agenda of the post-revolutionary leadership. The Court's principled commitment to the way of transition originally pursued by the new political establishment nonetheless led it to demand from subsequent representations that they display the same level of engagement in effectuating transition as the Court itself was offering. Gradually and somewhat reluctantly, the CCC's record in the scrutiny of legislation is beginning to match its achievements in the realm of concrete review.

The Czech Court came equipped with a relatively broad abstract-review authority. It has the power to review statutes for their conformity to the constitution and international human rights treaties, as well as to review other generally binding normative acts, including those issued by municipal authorities, for their conformity to acts of higher normative force. The Court also has the authority to hear complaints of municipal authorities against illegal interference by the cabinet with the right to local self-government, and to resolve competence disputes between regional administration and municipal authorities.[279]

This equipment, in and of itself, does not have definitive explanatory value. It does provide space for the Court to attempt to assert itself as a relevant player in the law-making process, although to a lesser extent than does a scheme allowing for preliminary abstract review and/or findings of legislative omissions in addition to repressive norm control. The wider institutional framework, however, contained features which in various ways served to qualify the general layout of the Court's authority.

The first such feature to be noted is the existence of a second legislative chamber designed, among other things, to filter dubious measures and thus reduce the possibility of the Court's involvement with the more political aspects of legal discourse. The Czech Senate was established in 1996 and since conception it has faced indifference, even hostility from both the general public and various segments of the political arena.[280] In addition, it has at times capitulated to the naked wielding of power by the leadership of the two major political parties and thus failed to affirm its own *raison d'être*.[281] It also proved a relatively minor factor in feeding the Court's caseload, especially in the early years. On the other hand, the Senate is gradually becoming accustomed to exercising its veto authority and enriching legislative deliberation, which practice decreases the likelihood of having policy disputes resolved at the level of the constitutional judiciary. Moreover, some of its occasional referrals enabled the CCC to impact a handful of major transformation policies.

Secondly, the structure of the Court's authority proved conducive to the diffusion of its adjudicative focus. Given the extensive concrete-review equipment and the large number of individual petitions resulting therefrom, the CCC's attention was divided between abstract review of policy choices and the assessment of their practical implications for individual claimants. Moreover, the ability to concern itself with the application of law onto individual fact patterns allowed the Court whole-heartedly to subscribe to the notion of minimal judicial interference with legislative judgments. The dilemma attendant on abstract review—that is, whether to refuse to annul a statute and thus accept the risk of its unconstitutional interpretation by the ordinary courts or invalidate the law and thus cross swords with the legislature, even if it might not be necessary—was less of a concern to the CCC than it was to the PCT or the HCC. Knowing that if a given statute proves susceptible to an interpretation contradicting the constitution it would have a chance to assess it, the CCC was often ready to restrain itself without feeling remorse. The possibility of reviewing individual decisions in addition to legislation therefore played an important role in preventing the Court from becoming a prominent policy maker instead of a court.

Thirdly, the local conceptualisation of the primacy of international law over domestic law had a visible effect on certain tenets of the CCC's case law. Pursuant to Article 10 of the Czech Constitution, ratified and published international agreements on human rights are superior to statutes. Thus, in order for an international treaty to have precedence over a provision of domestic law it must be promulgated as a treaty on human rights. Such treaties are different from other international agreements in terms of the voting procedure, too, as they have to be ratified by a constitutional majority, that is, three-fifths of all the members of the lower parliamentary chamber, the House of Representatives. On the national level, it is within the sole discretion of the legislature which treaties it will incorporate as human rights treaties. Malenovský describes this situation in the following way: 'The Constitution gives an incorporation "monopoly" to the legislative body, as it specifies that Parliament itself is sovereign to determine which treaties may be applied by the Czech judiciary, including the Constitutional Court.'[282] He also points out, however, that in practice the cabinet plays the key role, as the Parliament tends not to question the treaties' classification by the executive. The Parliament's monopoly affects only treaties adopted prior to the coming into force of the Czech Constitution. It is within the discretion of the Constitutional Court to classify treaties ratified by Czechoslovakia before 1 January 1993 and binding for the Czech Republic as one of the two successor states.

This arrangement may seem of minor significance but it often proved decisive for the disposition of claims alleging lack of conformity to international law of domestic regulations. First, only a small number of international treaties ratified after 1992—and thus falling within the Parliament's incorporation monopoly—were voted upon as human rights treaties. The International Labour Organization (ILO) Convention on the Abolition of Forced Labour, for instance, was ratified as a non-human rights treaty. Secondly, even when the classification enterprise falls upon the Court, its interpretation tends not to be extensive. When reviewing the constitutionality of elimination of the statutory ban on nighttime labour of women, the CCC refused to apply as higher law ILO Treaty No. 89, classifying it not as a treaty on human rights but only as a treaty on conditions applicable to the employment of women.[283] The ILO treaties in general were not the preferred reference point for the Court, as it regularly held them not to be treaties on fundamental rights and thus inapplicable as the yardstick of the scrutiny of statutes.[284]

Moreover, the Court would occasionally commit inconsistencies even when interpreting international-law instruments that it found applicable.[285] In general, it simply found domestic human rights law to offer more extensive protection than most international documents. And within the category of international treaties allowing no doubt as to their human-rights status, the CCC felt most comfortable working with the ECHRFF, while other international human rights documents received considerably less attention.[286]

Furthermore, only a plenary session of the CCC is competent to exercise abstract review and votes of nine justices—three-fifths of the Court's members—are required for statute invalidation. This is a significantly higher threshold than that required elsewhere in the region,[287] with the exception of pre-2002 Slovakia where seven of the 10 members constituted the minimum quorum but the votes of the majority of all justices were required for statute annulment, which in practice amounted to a three-fifths majority.[288] In Poland where the Tribunal has the same number of justices as does the CCC, the scrutiny of statutes and international agreements falls within the authority of a five-member panel whose decisions are adopted by a simple majority.[289] In Hungary, eight members of the plenary session constitute the relevant quorum of which a simple majority decides, with the Chief Justice (or Deputy Chief Justice) casting the decisive ballot in case of a tie. The difference between the levels of protection granted to legislative choices in the respective countries is considerable, as three justices in Poland and five justices in Hungary may under certain circumstances annul a statute while at least nine are required to do the same in the Czech Republic.

Similar restrictions apply to standing requirements. In the case of constitutional review of statutes, only the President and a group of parliamentarians can motion the Court.[290] In the case of review of sub-statutory norms, either the cabinet or a group of parliamentarians (smaller in number than that required for the review of statutes) is competent to motion the Court. Every other constitution in the region extended this capacity to various other bodies. Hungary, with its *actio popularis*, is, of course, a special case. Even in Poland, however, standing in the realm of abstract review was granted to a number of authorities, including the Attorney General, the Head of the Supreme Control Office, the ombudsman, the Chief Justices of the Supreme Court and the Supreme Administrative Court, and various public corporations.[291] Slovakia, sharing a similar scheme of constitutional review with the Czech Republic, also provides for more generous standing rules. True, the legislative minority has the best incentive to challenge majoritarian policy choices at the constitutional level. But the wider the access to abstract review, the more exposed is its subject matter. The restrictive standing criteria, even in conjunction with the previously noted limitations, certainly do not offer a definitive explanation of the issue. When read in context, however, the institutional framework within which the CCC was to exercise its authority does provide some understanding of its lesser engagement in the policy-making process.

The peculiarities of local political development indeed proved highly relevant to the degree of the CCC's activism. The Czech political scene was dominated by a coalition of rightist and centrist parties for most part of the decade. Even President Havel, although in disagreement especially with Klaus' party on some particular issues, shared with the coalition the general understanding of how reform was to proceed, and, at least initially, used his referral authority to a considerably smaller degree than did presidents elsewhere in the region. The overwhelming majority of petitions applying for abstract constitutional review of legislative measures therefore originated with the parliamentary minority. Its political operability, however, was extremely low. The dominant position of the governing coalition, especially during the first electoral term of 1992–1996, reflected the population's preference for policies pursued by the government. Antall's cabinet in Hungary managed to harbour a level of public support similar to that enjoyed by Klaus's coalition. In Hungary, however, the opposition was less tainted with the unpopular 'leftist' stigma than the then largest opposition party in the Czech Republic, the Left Bloc, dominated by the communist party. Because of its affiliation with many former dissidents, as well as its constructive demeanour during the changeover talks, the Hungary's parliamentary minority simply had a better image and was seen as an element constitutive of, and compatible with, the new regime to a much larger extent than was the parliamentary minority in the Czech Republic. Moreover, Antall's cabinet managed to alienate the liberal media while Klaus's cabinet, initially at least, enjoyed treatment by the mainstream media that bordered on devotion. Most of the transformation policies enjoyed the whole-hearted support of a majority of experts, the media, and the public. Since the overall atmosphere in society was conducive to labelling substantive challenges to the new Czech elite's wielding of power as undermining the transition and as a complot of so-called dark forces, it was politically counter-productive to mount such challenges. The legitimacy of the Klaus way of transformation ostensibly was beyond any doubt. To question the rationality of his policies was simply at odds with Czech society's immersion in an orgy of self-congratulation for its superiority to the rest of the world, with the possible exceptions of Reagan, Friedman, and Thatcher. Both the politicians' and the media's insistence on the Czech Republic's invincibility in the race for European integration consistently reiterated those beliefs. Obstructing government policies thus was less than *salonfähig*: it was reactionary. The polity's psychology was not inclined to tolerate let alone welcome the opposition's flights to the constitution. The *Zeitgeist* of the early years of the Czech Republic was therefore much less permissive to interference by constitutional review with efficient policy implementation than it was, albeit for different reasons, in Hungary and Slovakia.

The CCC's own commitment to the ideology underlying the new regime only reinforced the impact of the external environment. Several former dissidents and people with, to say the least, an uneasy attitude towards the communist regime were appointed to the Court. For many of the CCC's justices, it felt natural to support the new establishment's thorough attack on the past. Unsurprisingly then, the parliamentary minority—the one channel of mounting challenges to legislative solutions that is usually relied upon in abstract constitutional review schemes and at once is one of the very few so authorized channels in the Czech Republic—saw most of its attempts to foster a 'soft' version of transition rejected by the Court. Consequently, it lost confidence in constitutional review as a possible counter-balance to the government's efforts at an unhindered transition. It is telling of the relevance of the immediate political context that attacks as thorough as those aimed by the respective losers of the legislative battle in Hungary at the very philosophy of restitution policies or lustration measures were never mounted in the Czech Republic. The lack of such challenges reflected, among other things, their perceived futility. Indeed, as confessed by Justice Holländer, the Court 'enjoys' a rather bad reputation among Czech left-wing politicians.[292] The ensuing review of the case law will demonstrate that the Court largely deserved it, as it proved much less forthcoming to the opposition's normative challenges than did the HCC or the Slovak Court.

Jurisprudence

Assisting historical justice. The first opportunity legally to effectuate the victory of the new ideology came with the left-wing parliamentarians' petition against the Act on the Lawlessness of the Communist Regime and the Resistance Against It. This statute, although declaratory in part, served the same purpose as did the Stalinist crimes legislation in Poland, and the Zétényi Act and its follow-ups in Hungary. The CCC validated the act in its entirety.[293]

It held, in stark contrast to the concept of neutrality advocated by the HCC, that the constitution was not based on value neutrality, but contained certain regulatory ideas reflecting fundamental and inviolable values of a democratic society. This was the first in a long line of decisions in which the Court indicated a strong preference for the material understanding of the rule of law: 'The Constitution... does not bind the positive law only with formal legality but subjects the application and the interpretation of legal rules to their material content, and requires that law respects the fundamental values constitutive of a democratic society'.[294] According to the Court, this approach rejects the idea of a formal *Rechtsstaat* and thus denies legitimacy to a regime based solely on law's formal rationality. The role of the constitution cannot be limited to setting procedural standards and laying out the institutional framework for the exercise of public power because, the Court stated, such a constitution would allow different kinds of political content to be poured in it. In this vein, the justices pointed out the unfortunate historical experience that the Weimar democracy and post-1948 Czechoslovakia had with these 'positivist' constitutions. Rejecting the 'law is law' principle, the CCC expressed uneasiness with a state of affairs that would allow injustice to stand because of law, again in direct opposition to the opinion of the HCC that law must prevail over demands for substantive justice.

This, however, was only an academic entrée to the key issue, the lifting of the statute of limitations for crimes committed during the *ancien régime* and left unpunished for political reasons. Here, the difference between the CCC's and the PCT's approaches on the one hand and that of the HCC on the other was most significant. The Hungarian Court insisted on absolute protection of procedural guarantees and invoked the notion of constitutional criminal law to disallow any retroactive punishment, regardless of substantive justice. The Czech Court argued that the issue of procedural requirements relating to criminal prosecution, and even more so the issue of the statute of limitations, were outside the constitutional regulation of rights. It pointed out that the Charter of Rights explicitly regulated which crimes might be prosecuted but remained silent on how long they could be prosecuted. The Court further argued that the provision lifting the statute of limitations was not a constitutive norm but a declaratory one, reflecting the fact that both the willingness and the effort to punish the respective crimes were absent during the previous era.

Rejecting the argument of legal certainty professed so vigorously by the HCC, the Czech Court insisted that to interpret the constitution as preventing retroactive punishment for the relevant crimes would be 'meaningless', as it would prefer the legal certainty of the perpetrators of these crimes to the legal certainty of citizens and so certify the communist regime as a *Rechtsstaat*. In addition, it would contradict Article 9.3 of the Czech Constitution pursuant to which 'the interpretation of legal rules shall not justify actions aimed at eliminating or undermining the foundations of a democratic state'.

The CCC's 'lawlessness of communism' decision was even more permissive than the PCT's parallel holding on the Stalinist-crimes statute. The Tribunal held even under the Sejm's watchful eyes that in order to be upheld as conforming to the constitution criminal action to be punished retroactively would have to be sufficiently specified.[295] Unlike the PCT, the Czech Court had no immediate reasons to suspect that, should it decide against the legislature, it would be overruled. And yet the only relevant criteria set by the Czech statute and upheld by the Court concerned the requirement that crimes committed during a specific period of time were left unpunished for political reasons.

The various saplings of the main retribution legislation that followed and were referred to the Court gave the justices further opportunities to assist the legislature in deconstructing the web of privileges stemming from the communist era. In a decision parallel to the PCT's ruling on the protection of vested rights of pensioners formerly employed by the state's repressive machinery,[296] the CCC upheld a statute which took away certain layers of financial remuneration for members of the military. Based on the statute, years served in the repressive machinery of the communist state were not to be counted towards the stipulation of certain allowances to which military personnel and other employment categories were legally entitled because of the hardship attendant on their respective professions. Here, the Court held that unequal treatment was constitutional if carried out in public interest and for public benefit. As much as 'fostering the principles of democracy and human rights is undoubtedly in the public interest... it is not in the public interest to favour activities that were, whether directly or indirectly, aimed at suppressing human rights and the democratic system'.[297] The CCC invoked the notion of the moral and political unreliability of those who in the past had served the suppression of human rights and democracy, and pointed out how absurd it would be to demand from a democratic government that it remunerate people who, according to the lawlessness statute, engaged in condemnable activities. But it again went even further than the PCT when it stated that it did not matter whether the affected persons were, or were not, members of the Party, or whether they were 'a directly important, principal and decisive element, or merely instruments (certainly conscious) or captives of their own kind of those who actively implemented the regime'.[298] Moreover, the Court rejected the argument that the statute adversely affected also those who were certified by the respective civic committees as loyal to the democratic regime and as capable of serving it. It stated that that certification was 'only a display of the generosity and humaneness of the democratic system towards its opponents'.[299] This is different not only from the 'batting practice' of the HCC; it is also different from the catching and signalling by the PCT: on the issue of transitional justice, the Czech Court was an all-star relief pitcher happy to finish the game off with no runs and no walks.

The CCC also upheld a statute changing tenured positions of university professors into temporary contracts.[300] The Czech labour code requires complex and stringent criteria for termination of indefinite-period employment. According to the respective statute, however, labour contracts of academics concluded for an unspecified period of time were to be transformed into contracts the validity of which would expire *ex lege* within approximately one year upon the adoption of the statute. This measure was thus aimed at purging academia of those members who were thought to have discredited themselves during the previous regime.

The profile of cases that never reached the docket of constitutional review is as telling of the ideological and political context—that the CCC's take on transitional justice was both a result of and helped to foster—as is the case law upholding the contested legislation. First, the legislature's attempts to do away with the most debilitating aspects of the socialist-era economic and welfare regulations were immune from constitutional arm-wrestling to a much greater degree than they were in Poland or Hungary. In other words, the general political and social environment was more supportive than was the case elsewhere in the region not only of the purgation measures but of the economic 'shock therapy', too. Accordingly, a relatively low number of statutes instituting welfare reform made it to the CCC.

Secondly, the vast body of restitution and rehabilitation laws was not contested in principle, for example, by challenging the legislature's thorough interference with established property relations. The left-wing opposition was aware of both the futility of these challenges and their political counter-productivity. Rather, inconsistencies in, and restrictions of, the access to restitution were the most frequent subject of constitutional challenges mounted against the different indemnification policies. So, when certain tenets of indemnification policies were held unconstitutional, in most cases it was so because they were deemed too restrictive and in need of expansion.

Thirdly, there was no confrontation between the Court and the legislature on the issue of lustration until late 2001. The Czechoslovak Constitutional Court upheld, with some minor exceptions, the widely criticized lustration law before the CCC was established and the issue was not submitted for review thereafter. In 1995, the validity of the lustration law was prolonged until 31 December 2000. Havel refused to sign the amendment, using roughly the same arguments as the HCC, that is, that lustration was an exceptional measure justified in times when the revolution's achievements could be jeopardized but served no legitimate purpose and was unduly discriminatory under ordinary circumstances. After Havel's veto was overruled, no petitions against the law appeared at the CCC. In 2000, the Parliament prolonged the lustration law again, this time until the promulgation of a statute on the civil service. The CCC dismissed on formal grounds the challenge against the prolongation. In December 2001, it reviewed the matter on its merits but adhered to the ruling of the CSCC, including the exceptions.

The case law on indemnification policies and their implementation by the ordinary courts and administrative agencies constituted a large portion of Czech transitional jurisprudence and was most illustrative of the Court's deference to legislative solutions. Justice Cepl's belief that 'without rehabilitation, restitution and lustration, there would be no transformation'[301] proved to be the majority view, and the restitution and rehabilitation policies enjoyed almost as much support from the CCC as did those aimed at retribution. As a general rule, the Court would defer to the legislative stipulation of eligibility criteria for indemnification claims, with one significant exception. In one of the first decisions on the issue, the Court held that to exclude from indemnification citizens who did not satisfy the additional requirement of permanent residence on the territory of the Czech Republic was a violation of various provisions of constitutional stature.[302] The CCC held that to establish criteria for the kind of property to be restituted was within the legislature's discretion, as the purpose of the policy was to indemnify only the most serious wrongs. To restrict the pool of the respective beneficiaries by additional subjective criteria, however, would be unconstitutional. The subsequent claimants, alleging discrimination between different categories of beneficiary, tended to rely in their arguments upon this holding of the Court, mostly to no avail. The CCC upheld, for instance, the criterion of nationality,[303] the restriction of certain indemnification entitlements to legal persons,[304] the temporal restriction of restitution claims to the beginning of the communist regime,[305] the preferential treatment granted to individual farmers in the case of transfer of agricultural land,[306] the restriction of indemnification to a particular category of wrongs to those subject to racial discrimination,[307] and the differentiation between different categories of descendent of the original beneficiaries.[308]

The differences between the approaches of the region's constitutional courts to the legality of the former regimes proved crucial for their evaluation of transitional justice, including the property-related aspects. The HCC, in line with its insistence on formal legality of the socialist era, came up with the principle of novation reflecting the lack of enforceable entitlements to property taken away under the previous regime and allowing the government to ignore the legal nature of the origin of their property grievances. Not so the Czech Court, which would repeatedly point out the illegality underlying the entire operation of the communist regime. Accordingly, it understood restitution as an 'elimination of the illegality of property transfers' and as reflecting the 'duty to restitute the original legal state of affairs'.[309] Also, while the HCC saw extensive restitution to be at odds with some elementary aspects of economic reform—for example, large-scale privatisation—the Czech Court would refer to the social urgency of 'completing the economic reform, the integral part of which is also the transformation and privatisation of agriculture, including the restitution of property taken away illegally'.[310] The Court's belief in restitution as a constitutive element of political, economic, and social transformation proved solid enough to allow for the imposition of financial sanctions upon natural persons who as agents of agricultural cooperatives inhibited the restitution process by failing to observe the relevant laws.[311] The CCC perceived the legislature's vigour in punishing those who obstructed the indemnification process as serving the society's need for the establishment of a viable economic basis for democratic transition. After all, protecting constitutionality entailed the protection of the very process of economic reform.[312]

Similarly to their Polish colleagues, the Czech justices would often point out the exclusive policy-making competence of the legislature and the lack of their own capacity to substitute political will with judicial rulings. Accordingly, following the initial round of indemnification policies the CCC adhered to the legislature's new stand on the issue and legitimised partial deviations from the general scheme. It rejected, for instance, a petition challenging the constitutionality of a statute precluding restitution for those who satisfied the nationality criterion only after the term expired for filing their claims.[313] Similarly, a statute mandating that the affected persons apply for financial compensation instead of *restitutio in natura* in case the contested property was already privatised was found to protect the principle of legal certainty and vested rights.[314]

But neither the lack-of-competence argument nor the Court's belief in the superiority of the legislature in the policy-making process was strong enough to undo the justices' belief in the ideological underpinnings of indemnification policies. Illustrative of the depth of its ideological commitment is the Court's reaction to the attempts to narrow the scope of restitution claims by the social democratic administration that came to power in 1998 and was supported by deputies many of whom were previously less than enthusiastic about the early indemnification policies. According to the so-called transformation statute adopted in 1992, the respective beneficiaries were to be issued their full property shares in agricultural cooperatives upon the expiration of a seven-year period. Shortly before the end of the period, the statute was amended so as to replace this entitlement with a bond to be paid in 20 years at 2 percent interest or, alternatively, a property certificate to be paid in 15 years, with no interest. Here, the principle of legal certainty and the principle of citizens' confidence in law were found to trump the legislature's policy-making capacity.[315]

The Court's fondness for restitution and its readiness to compensate for the Parliament's lack of commitment to provide indemnification to former property owners also led it to invalidate a statutory rule, which precluded restitution of national cultural sites before an act on the protection of such sites was enacted. The Court deviated here from the rule of assuming both the rationality and the legitimacy of legislative measures on the issue of coming to terms with the past because it did not 'share the opinion of the legislature that there was a rational purpose for excluding national cultural sites from the ordinary restitution process'.[316] The CCC's case law on quintessential transitional measures was at times rather selective in its approach to the principles of legal certainty and vested rights,[317] but none of the inconsistencies were of such degree or relevance as to question the Court's alignment with those who shared the belief that no indemnification meant no transformation.

Assisting economic reform. As in the case of Poland, the Czech Court's refusal to interfere with the legislature's regulatory performance extended from transitional justice into the realm of economic policies. Here, however, the CCC had less work to do than did the PCT or even the Hungarian Court, as the pool of agencies with standing to initiate constitutional review was considerably narrower and the government's efforts to downsize the welfare state more appreciated.

On a general note, the CCC held—together with other courts in the region—that the legislature had a 'substantially wider space' for regulation in the economic realm than it did in the case of statutes directly related to fundamental human rights and freedoms.[318] This implicit classification of rights into classical first-generation rights and the second- or third-generation rights, with corresponding differences in their susceptibility to statutory qualification, resonated well with the dominant attitude among the Czech political frontmen, and can be witnessed in various shapes and forms across post-communist Europe. The consequences of this conceptual approach for the normative significance of a particular right, however, varied significantly from one country to another.

The Czech Court, for instance, upheld a statute which subjected the additional income of pension recipients to mandatory contributions to pension and unemployment funds.[319] Both the petitioners and the dissent argued that to require such a contribution from those who by definition could never become unemployed and who have already fulfilled their duty of contributing to pension insurance was to subject them to a discriminatory hidden tax. The majority rejected the argument as unreflective of the fact that any social security system was a mixture of the solidarity and the equality principles. According to the Court, to find a balance between those principles is the prerogative of the legislature. Most importantly, social security allowances such as retirement pensions are not property rights and ought not to be protected as such. Interestingly, the Polish Tribunal held to the same effect a few years later.[320] Compare this to the striking down by the HCC of significant elements of Hungary's welfare reform. Not only did the Hungarian Court understand certain social security allowances as purchased rights, but also its line of reasoning suggested that the parliament's policy-making prerogatives were subject to the Court's understanding of equality, legal certainty, and the government's duty to account for the well-being of its citizens in general.

The above and several other decisions reflected the Czech Court's conceptual take on the extent and nature of the legislator's competence to implement new economic or social policies. According to the CCC, the social urgency of adopting new policies and a 'higher degree of intensity of public interest... justifies a higher degree of interference with the principles of equality and citizen's confidence in the new legal regulation'.[321] This sounds rather innocent. What the CCC seems to have meant, however, is that the legislature was permitted to interfere with established contractual relations if it so wished. The most illustrative case concerned lease agreements entered into before certain provisions of a statute on national enterprises came into force. These leases were to be terminated *ex lege* in the case of the winding-up of a given national enterprise, regardless of the term for which they were concluded and with no attendant indemnification. Although it is difficult to imagine a clearer case of retroactivity, the CCC dubbed this regulation as 'falsely retroactive'—and thus acceptable—and pointed out that public interest in the privatisation of national enterprises served to qualify the principle of citizens' confidence in law. In a bizarre mode of reasoning, the Court argued that upon the coming into force of the contested provision, the respective lessees had to become aware that once the national enterprise was wound-up, their leases would expire. That those lessees had no way of predicting that such a law would be promulgated when they entered into their contracts was an argument that the CCC did not wish to pursue.

Similarly to the *Wesengehalt* doctrine of the HCC and the PCT, the Czech Court insisted on restricting the normative ambit of a right to its essence, and thus protecting against statutory qualification only the right's fundamental tenets. In this vein, it held that 'the legislature [could] not be denied the right to newly regulate social relations in every realm where it [found] it necessary and meaningful for the sake of the public interest, unless by doing so it would undermine the very essence of fundamental rights and freedoms'.[322]

But the one concept that the CCC certainly was not going to pursue was egalitarianism in social policy. As a general rule applicable to interpretation of equality across its normative ambit, the Court would regularly point out that equality could be invoked as a constitutional entitlement only in relation to an autonomous fundamental right protected by the relevant documents.[323] Referring to the concept of equality elaborated by the short-lived constitutional court of Czechoslovakia, the CCC would never tire of emphasizing that 'in order to perform its functions, the government may grant to certain groups less benefits than other groups... but may do so only by invoking public values'.[324] When applied in the realm of welfare policy, the notion of equality indeed proved of low significance. Like the PCT, which found certain social rights to reflect the programmatic orientation of the state rather than to constitute subjective entitlements, the CCC held the equality principle to serve the function of 'an ideal typical category expressing objectives that cannot fully reflect social reality and can be achieved only approximately'.[325] Also, 'if inequality of social relations is to affect fundamental human rights, it must achieve a degree that somehow questions the very essence of equality'.[326] This, again, sounds more innocent than it actually is. By rejecting egalitarianism, the CCC seems to have meant that the legislature could subject the same group of professionals to different requirements. The case concerned a statute that required architects, construction engineers, and technicians to undergo an authorization procedure before a certain date. Those who did not follow the statute, however, fared better because very shortly before the adjustment period expired the Parliament abolished the authorization requirement. Two groups thus emerged within a single industry: one meeting the criteria set by the statute, one free-riding on the legislature's whim, which whim the Court dubbed as 'the current legitimate political will of the Parliament expressed in the form of a statute'.[327]

The very notion of equality came in handy, however, when an amendment to the Labour Code lifted a ban on both the night-time labour of women and the assignment to business trips of pregnant women and women nursing small children.[328] The CCC, in a Lochner-like argument, pointed out that to disallow elimination of the general prohibition of nighttime labour of women would amount to unequal treatment of, and discrimination against, women. It also argued that the contested amendment attempted to adjust labour regulations to new trends so that the labour law would facilitate, rather than inhibit, the country's economic development. Indeed, greater flexibility in the labour market rather than equality seems to have been at the core of the Court's concern, as it could—and in fact did on other occasions—resort to invoking 'public values' as justifying unequal treatment.

Seeking jurisprudential autonomy. The Court's awareness of the need to assist the effectuation of the new economic and social paradigms proved to be a significant element of its consciousness as a constitutional adjudicator. The CCC therefore tended to challenge the legislature especially in cases that raised doubts about the Parliament's readiness to do the same. The less glamorous the Czech way of transformation proved to be, the less willing was the CCC to give it the benefit of the doubt. Accordingly, its acceptance of the notion of transitional specifics gradually eroded. In its early case law, the CCC refused to invalidate a provision of the Civic Code which transformed *ex lege* all previous quasi-tenancies of lodgings into legally protected tenancies, with all the corresponding implications for the protection of tenants at the expense of landlords. This holding was of far-reaching significance, as it constituted a lock-in situation for the landlords, making them unable unilaterally to increase the rent or terminate rent agreements unless they met the stringent criteria set forth by the applicable law.[329] Seven years later, however, the CCC based its related holding on largely the same argument it had previously rejected, namely that under the existing scheme many real-estate owners were in fact forced to finance part of the cost of rent. The Court pointed out that a legal cap on the amount of rent imposed upon only a specific group of owners was discriminatory and imposed undue financial burdens on some landlords while excluding others from the same obligation.[330] The Court therefore invalidated the Ministry of Finance decree stipulating a maximum rent for the most common type of lease agreement. Unwilling completely to do away with the protection of tenants, however, the CCC postponed the coming into effect of its decision until the end of 2001.

The fact that the Polish Tribunal had held to the same effect[331] a few years earlier than the CCC offers an interesting insight into the ways in which particular rather than general features of institutional design affect constitutional jurisprudence. While the PCT as an abstract-review venue was open to a wide range of agents, the Czech standing rules made the CCC's review of social and economic policies dependent on petitions submitted to it by the left-wing parliamentary minority. One could hardly expect social democrats and communists to attempt to undermine the protection of the lower middle class, which is the one segment most likely to be affected by rent deregulation. Since the Court did not dare to launch deregulatory policies at the very beginning of its operation, it had to wait, despite all commitment to the free market paradigm, for a group of right-wing senators to give it another chance.

The Court professed its dislike for continued preservation of interventionist regulatory practices also by invalidating a statutory provision which allowed the cabinet to stipulate the nominal value of private health care services to be reimbursed by the health insurance companies. Its growing uneasiness with governmental interference led the CCC to annul cabinet decrees establishing different quota for different domestic producers of sugar and milk.[332] Even though it would be harsh to present the Court as a champion of *laissez-faire* capitalism, its eagerness to eliminate remnants of protectionism from a wide variety of legal regulations is a significant element of its transitional jurisprudence, and suggests what the justices have openly professed in early retribution decisions, namely that ideological foundations of the legal order were to serve as important guidelines in interpreting the law.

The Court's eagerness to effectuate the ideological distancing of the new regime from the past extended to the realm of classical rights and freedoms, too. Not that the CCC would completely free itself from considerations of administrative expediency. It would, for instance, happily defer to the Parliament's regulation of matters related to citizenship or permanent residence.[333] Still, the Court often exhibited praiseworthy concern for certain politically and socially vulnerable segments of society. It invalidated, for instance, a statutory provision allowing immigration authorities to expel a foreign national without giving the expelled person the possibility to personally attend appeal hearings.[334] On the same issue, it invalidated a provision preventing judicial review of expulsion decisions,[335] and later annulled a provision allowing police authorities to detain any person reasonably presumed to have entered or residing illegally on the territory of the Czech Republic.[336] The Court also struck down a provision allowing the head of a penitentiary institution, rather than a criminal court, to decide upon the transfer of an inmate to a different penitentiary.[337] After a long colloquy with the ordinary courts and other law-implementing agencies, the Court decided to invalidate a provision of the Police Act which stipulated a 24-hour detention period parallel to the one provided for by the Penal Code.[338] In a similar vein, the CCC annulled a provision that did not allow defendants to challenge the prolongation of their custody, and struck down the rule allowing for anonymous testimony.[339] Based on a petition filed by President Havel, the Court also invalidated a rule mandating criminal prosecution of the defamation of the Parliament, the Cabinet, and the Constitutional Court.[340]

As long as the government's policies corresponded with the CCC's anti-communist, freedom-over-equality, individual-over-government approach, its involvement in constitutional politics was relatively unobtrusive, even delicate. It was especially upon the institution of the social democratic administration in 1998 and the attendant deformation of the political scene by the infamous 'opposition agreement'[341] that the CCC began actively to assert its counter-majoritarian features. It held unconstitutional, for instance, various tenets of the electoral reform aimed at manipulating the framework of elections in favour of the major parties.[342] Only a few weeks later, the Court continued its recent vigorous emancipation when it struck down several provisions of the act on the financing of political parties, again aimed at decreasing state allowances for the smallest Czech political parties and extending the availability of public funds to the established ones.[343] Losing patience with the long-term neglect by the political arena of the deficiencies of the judicial review system, the Court annulled, with *pro futuro* effect, the entire Chapter V of the Civil Procedure Code, which served as the basis for judicial review of administrative decisions throughout the 1990s.[344]

The CCC's increasing interference with the majority's political agenda—and the growing number of Havel's motions to the Court—generates the same kind of conflict that emerged frequently within Hungarian constitutional politics in the early and mid-1990s. Moreover, the legislature appears even more ready than the CCC for open confrontation—in less than a month after the Court held unconstitutional a 100-percent increase in public subsidies for a political party (from 500,000 Czech crowns per parliamentary mandate to twice the amount), the Parliament enacted a new amendment to the statute, decreasing the amount found unconstitutional by a mere 10 percent. So, while the ordinary courts tend to defy the CCC's judgments less than that they used to, the legislature appears willing to take defiance of constitutional case law to new heights. The detrimental potential of the above trend for the culture of constitutionalism in the Czech Republic is readily apparent and may become even more dangerous when the new—and possibly less confident, less seasoned, and thus more sensitive to political demands—justices are appointed in 2003.

The preceding excursion into the CCC's jurisprudence illustrates its self-positioning within the processes of societal transformation. The Czech and the Polish constitutional courts alike were relatively lenient in supervising measures meant to serve the institution of a new legal, social, political, and economic order. In both cases, the indigenous legal consciousness proved favourable to the validation by means of constitutional review of the legislator's supremacy in the policy-making process. Indeed, both courts relied on the traditional separation-of-powers theory as an essential *Kompetenz* guideline, suggesting wide discretion for the legislature in the process of implementation of constitutional mandates, especially in the realm of economic and welfare policies. The degree to which either court's permissiveness not only was a function of the design of constitutional adjudication but also reflected its preference for a particular mode of transformation appears similar, too. But while the PCT was confronted with a wide range of petitions based on very diverse political and ideological notions waiting to be accommodated, the Czech Court focused less attentively on interests with a chance of being invoked and considered within the legislative process, such as women's employment conditions or pensioners' social security rights. However, when the level of parliamentarians' caution and political self-consciousness proved prohibitive to legislative reform—as it did, for instance, with respect to rent or private health care regulation—or when constitutionally imperfect rules remained in force largely out of convenience (as they did, for instance, in various matters related to due process rights of foreign nationals or criminal defendants) the Court would accept the invitation and intervene on behalf of those unaccounted for within parliamentary deliberation.[345] Moreover, its selective rather than unequivocal deference outside transitional justice, as well as its growing readiness to correct a wide range of legislative failures, suggest that the CCC was capable of autonomous thinking and that it carried out a fair amount of work in founding the Czech Republic as a modern liberal democracy.

Active Judging

Overview

In the preceding section, I argued that the environment in which Czech constitutional adjudication was operating throughout the 1990s did not allow for the translation of the Court's relatively extensive abstract-review equipment into intense judicial activism at the legislature's expense. The Parliament, after all, took care of many of the CCC's preferences. In the realm of concrete review, however, substantial disagreements over the implementation of law arose between the CCC and the ordinary courts. In order both to see the purpose of the different legislative policies prevail over their necessarily more narrow textual delineation and to effectuate the natural-law revolution, the Court tended to require from the ordinary courts that they interpret law teleologically and account in their decision-making for substantive justice. The CCC's concrete-review authority was not completely free from ambiguities, but it did prove helpful to the accomplishment of its mission.

There are three kinds of constitutional complaint available within the Czech scheme of concrete review: (i) a municipal council can motion the Court to set aside illegal interference by the government with the right to local self-government; (ii) a political party can file a petition against its dissolution or other decision affecting its activity; and (iii) the 'true' constitutional complaint, that is, one filed against an effective decision of a public authority infringing upon a constitutionally guaranteed fundamental right or freedom. The third kind constitutes the overwhelming majority of the CCC's concrete review jurisprudence, and is a significant portion of its decision-making enterprise in general. Its applicability to action by *any* public authority proved of decisive importance for the Court's emergence as the highest *court* in the country.

Several other features of the Czech rights-protection framework contributed to the vastness of the CCC's concrete-review case law. First, it was only in December 2000 that an ombudsman was appointed in the Czech Republic. The lack of this venue for hearing citizens' grievances—one which proved highly relevant in both Poland and Hungary—arguably increased the number of petitions filed with the ordinary courts and, because of the courts' own deficiencies, subsequently with the Constitutional Court as well.

Secondly, in spite of being mentioned in the Constitution, the Supreme Administrative Court—which proved so instrumental in compensating for the restricted authority of the PCT in Poland—hitherto has not been established in the Czech Republic. The CCC therefore acted as the appellate, or in some cases even as the first, instance of judicial review of administrative decisions. What could often be handled within judicial review, if it were available, thus became an issue for constitutional review.

Thirdly, international law, including human rights instruments, was completely disregarded in adjudication throughout the communist era. Even though the judiciary was relatively well purged of those of its members that could, with some ideological flavour, be described as reactionary to the new regime, the lack of experience in applying international law, let alone prioritising it against the applicable statutes, remained pervasive amongst the judiciary. The same can be said about the traditional mode of interpretation, which was based on reciting positivist mantras, often to rather ridiculous effect. The courts proved largely unwilling to do away with the emphasis on formalist and purely grammatical interpretation of law, which tendency naturally translated into numerous violations of constitutional rights within the judicial process itself.

Jurisprudence

Intra-judicial colloquy. The CCC understood the deficiencies affecting judicial protection of rights as an invitation to intervene actively in ordinary adjudication, and the various doctrinal by-products of the CCC's rulings in the realm of concrete review, such as the vigorous rejection of excessive formalism or the emphasis on teleological interpretation, proved highly relevant to the emergence of the Czech kind of constitutionalism. Given the Court's unsatisfying experience with the level of the ordinary courts' appreciation of its efforts to infuse constitutionality standards into the realm of law implementation, however, it often felt compelled to subsequently repair the given law through abstract review, too.

In general, the Court stressed that if it were possible to interpret a rule in a way that would allow for its application in accordance with the constitution's mandates, such an interpretation had to be preferred to the rule's annulment.[346] The no-derogation-unless-necessary rule is a sensible exercise of judicial self-restraint and a standard element of constitutional jurisprudence across the globe. However, it often proved inadequate in the practice of rights protection in post-communist Europe, and the Czech Republic was no exception.

It was the growing mistrust of ordinary courts and other law-implementing agencies that led the CCC occasionally to deviate from the rule of non-derogation. It was, for instance, 'forced' to invalidate a provision of the Police Act stipulating a 24-hour detention period,[347] as the relevant authorities, including the ordinary courts, consistently interpreted it differently from the CCC. [348] It also observed that 'to leave the assessment of proportionality between public interest in the prohibition of residence for an alien on one side and the protection of the alien's fundamental rights and freedoms on the other can hardly be left in the hands of public authorities... if they are to apply a law the conditions and limits of which are insufficiently defined',[349] and invalidated the contested provision, although a constitutionally feasible interpretation could indeed be inferred from it. Following a number of cases in which it found the petitioners' procedural rights to have been violated because of an ordinary court's arbitrary action, the CCC invalidated a provision of the Civil Procedure Code allowing an ordinary court to proceed *in camera* regardless of the parties' preference.[350] The Court also invalidated a provision similar in effect but related to a different kind of procedure.[351]

As was the case elsewhere in the region, the ordinary courts—and among them especially the Supreme Court—would regularly question the ability of the CCC to impose upon them a duty to follow in their adjudication its interpretation of law.[352] This resistance would amount at times to an overt disregarding of any part of a CCC's ruling other than the holding itself. In *Ružička*,[353] the Supreme Court acted in direct conflict with the Court's decision because it simply disagreed with it. But the most heated confrontation between the respective judicial bodies concerned the issue of criminal prosecution of conscientious objectors. The CCC held on several occasions that to punish those who refused to be drafted into mandatory military service repeatedly—that is, upon every receipt of a draft—was a violation of the *ne bis in idem* (double jeopardy) clause. In its first decision on the issue, the Court concluded the dictum as follows: '[T]he Constitutional Court expects that this principal decision will guide ordinary courts in their future deliberations on the extent of punishment for those who permanently refuse military service.'[354] Those expectations proved false, as the ordinary courts would furnish the same rulings again and again, only to have them subsequently cancelled by the CCC.[355] The friction reached its climax when the Supreme Court, upon annulment of its decision through constitutional review,[356] issued the same decision again, without providing any evidence as to why the facts of the case could possibly lead the CCC to deviate from its previous holding, and simply noting its disagreement with the Court's and the petitioner's interpretation. The CCC subsequently annulled that decision[357] and emphasized that the binding nature of its decisions was the *conditio sine qua non* for effective constitutional review. That, however, was not the end of the story, as two justices of the Supreme Court subsequently refused to hear the matter by invoking bias, which bias they found constituted by their different legal opinion on the issue. Eventually, it took an intervention by the Justice Department to have the issue settled.

The Supreme Court's tendency to defy the CCC's interpretive efforts not only found some support within Czech legal scholarship,[358] it also extended to the lower-instance courts. In one criminal case, the appellate court explicitly rejected the CCC's interpretation of the adjudicated issue.[359] And in a restitution case, another appellate court confessed self-assuredly that it 'decided deliberately in conflict' with the relevant case law of both the Constitutional Court and the Supreme Court because 'it did not agree with the opinions formulated therein'.[360]

'Constitutional' judiciary. The frequent displays of the ordinary courts' urge to undermine its interpretive enterprise led the Court to step beyond its conceptualisation as a specialized tribunal and act as an appellate instance, a step it would vigorously deny taking. As a general rule, the Court held that it was neither an appellate court nor a body hierarchically superior to ordinary adjudication. Accordingly, its role in the supervision of ordinary courts was to be confined to reviewing 'the procedural purity' of judicial proceedings.[361] The CCC pointed out that it was not authorized to evaluate the assessment of evidence by the ordinary courts even if it did not agree with that assessment.[362] In the end, it is

always the adjudicating court that has the right and the duty to assess all the evidence.[363] The Court also explicitly refused to find itself competent to carry out its own investigation and assessment of the facts of a case, as that was the prerogative of ordinary adjudication.[364] To supplement or modify the ordinary courts' factual findings was found by the CCC to be outside its authority, since that would make it operate as an appellate court.[365] To re-evaluate the evidence as gathered and assessed by the ordinary courts would require the CCC to gather evidence on its own,[366] conflict with the CCC's consistent case law,[367] and interfere with the exclusive competence of the ordinary courts.[368] It is the framework of ordinary adjudication that is assigned the role of correcting and eliminating mistakes in the assessment of facts, and the CCC cannot substitute it by remedying such mistakes.[369]

That was to be the general rule. The number of exceptions that the CCC made to that rule suggests, however, that it was as much of a window-dressing device as was the HCC's verbal adherence to the legislature's supremacy in the policy-making process. The tendency of the Czech and the Hungarian Courts to first pay lip service to the decision-making autonomy of the 'opponent' and then implicitly curb that autonomy thus illustrates which tenets of their judicial activism these courts found to be most sensitive from the vantage point of *Kompetenz* legitimacy. The Czech Court was relatively deferential to the legislature, and its occasional interference with a legislative judgment on some particular issue did not require extensive justification, as it was a correctional device rather than a display of the Court's competitiveness in principle. In the case of ordinary adjudication, however, the CCC would intervene so frequently and so expansively that it felt obliged to offer a verbal affirmation that there indeed was some concrete meaning to the judiciary's independence and decision-making autonomy. While the HCC would repeat that it was not a legislator and then legislate, the Czech Court would insist that it was not a court of high appeal and then act as one.

First, the CCC would annul a judicial decision not only because of a court's failure fully to observe the petitioner's due process rights, but at times would do so also because it reached a different conclusion on the evidence gathered. In such cases, the Court would qualify the above 'rule' by pointing out the necessity of a link between evidence and its assessment on one side, and the legal conclusion on the other. According to the Court, if there is an extreme discrepancy between the assessment of facts and the attendant legal conclusion, the right to a fair trial is violated.[370]

Such an extreme discrepancy was found, for instance, in a case in which an ordinary court found the petitioner guilty while the CCC thought the evidence was insufficient.[371] At times, discrepancy did not even have to be extreme, as 'significant discrepancy' and the failure to interpret a statute on the basis of its overall structure were found to constitute sheer arbitrariness.[372] Is this not a disagreement with assessment of evidence, which the Court previously found to be an insufficient basis for annulment on constitutional grounds? If re-evaluating evidence assessment really fell outside the scope of the CCC's authority as a protector of constitutionality, why would it ever make the effort to justify its decision to uphold a contested ruling by pointing out that it 'finds the evidence assessment... to be fully compatible with constitutional principles and agrees with the conclusion as formulated'?[373]

An early decision of the Court also suggested full discretion of the ordinary courts as to which evidence to admit and which to reject. The CCC held that it fell within their exclusive competence to decide what evidence should be admitted and whether and to what extent it was necessary to allow for additional evidence, as well as to evaluate the parties' motions for admission of evidence. To use the Court's own words, 'the decision on the *extent* of admitted evidence is within the *exclusive* competence of ordinary courts'.[374] This competence proved less than exclusive, however, and the CCC felt authorized to remedy not only the ordinary courts' failures to draw from the available evidence what it thought was the proper conclusion, but also their decisions on the extent of admitted evidence. What was originally described as full discretion thus came to include, inter alia, the duty of an ordinary court not only to concern itself with a party's motion for admission of evidence, but also exhaustively to describe in its reasoning the process of evidence gathering and assessment,[375] and, if it denied such a motion, to provide convincing reasons for the denial.[376]

Similarly, while some of the Court's rulings indicate its unwillingness to carry out any fact-finding activity or to gather evidence,[377] some others are based precisely on that enterprise. During its review of a senatorial candidate's petition, the CCC, for instance, examined electoral petitions and had its own staff count the number of valid signatures on them.[378] In another case, the CCC examined the correspondence of litigants assessed within the original proceedings and thoroughly examined the relevant data.[379] In yet another decision, the Court pointed out that it was not bound by the factual findings of the ordinary courts and did some investigation on its own.[380] Simply, 'an intense effort is devoted to the assessment of factual aspects of the matter in the dicta of the Constitutional Court's decisions'.[381]

The above variances in the CCC's take on the ordinary courts' procedural autonomy are a perfect illustration of the impact of design. The constitutional complaints in the Czech Republic are randomly assigned to four three-member panels, which have universal competence, that is, do not operate only within a specific area of law, as is the case in Germany. Two votes are thus enough to find either violation or non-violation. Given the complexity of issues, as well as the necessary variations between the fact patterns of individual cases, there is considerable likelihood of different approaches to principally analogous situations. Also, the respective panels tend to cross-reference their own rulings rather than those of other panels when deciding analogous cases. Indeed, the first, and to some extent also the second, panel of the Court tended to be substantially more permissive of the ordinary courts' decisions on admissibility of evidence than did the third or the fourth panel.[382] To suggest that, were certain petitions assigned to a different panel, a remedy might have been granted is speculative but not entirely implausible.

This inconsistency may seem too high a price for the availability of constitutional complaints. A few things should be considered, however. First, the caseload within concrete review makes it virtually impossible to have the plenary session adjudicate upon constitutional complaints. After all, flaws in the CCC's case law are widely believed to be a result of the overload of work that the justices are exposed to, not their lack of qualifications.[383] But unlike the HCC, which allows itself the luxury of putting petitions on the back-burner and finds only six to 10 issues a year to be of constitutional importance,[384] the Czech Court deems constitutionally relevant matters that its Hungarian counterpart would never even look at. So Halmai may dub the operation of a multiple-panel scheme a failure,[385] but both those petitioners who have been granted relief by a constitutional court for incidental violations of their rights, be it in Germany or the Czech Republic, and those who have been denied that venue in Hungary would probably phrase the matter a little differently.

Secondly, all the Court's panels seem to share general assumptions as to the level of protection to which a petitioner is in principle entitled. What cuts across the entire Court without reservations is the justices' dislike for 'excessive formalism' and their fondness for an extensive and justice-informed interpretation of procedural rules. This leads the CCC to require from the ordinary courts that they refrain from interpreting restrictively the rules excluding certain matters from judicial review[386] and display sensitivity in dealing with petitions suffering from minor procedural flaws.[387] The tendency to annul judicial decisions because of formalist interpretation, to label such interpretation unjust,[388] and to emphasize 'the logic, the purpose and the meaning'[389] of the text can be detected across the Court's case law.

Thirdly, even though the CCC would initially insist that it lacked the authority to scrutinize the constitutionality of an ordinary court's decision with respect to substantive rights,[390] it would on many different occasions state that in reviewing the constitutionality of an individual act of public authority it was not only concerned with procedural purity, but also called to evaluate the constitutionality of interpretation and application of substantive law.[391] Despite occasional variances in the assessment of the ordinary courts' procedural discretion and the corresponding difference in the degree of their insulation from constitutional review, the CCC's approach to the incidental protection of rights therefore was among the most generous not only within the Visegrád region, but also in Europe as a whole.

The Court's friendly face. Taking the step from mere procedural legitimisation of ordinary adjudication to a thorough assessment of cases in their complexity led the CCC routinely to step up on behalf of restitution/rehabilitation beneficiaries or criminal defendants. The Court's default approach in both these realms was, one might say, petitioner-friendly. In the realm of indemnification policies, the CCC concerned itself with correcting narrow interpretation of restitution/rehabilitation entitlements and derided ordinary courts and administrative agencies for achieving solutions which, despite conformity to the text's literal reading, it deemed blatantly unjust. The CCC displayed the same level of sensitivity also in the realm of criminal law, and the number as well as the variety of decisions in which it held for a petitioner against a law-and-order implementing agency was impressive.

A significant portion of criminal law cases in which the CCC did not shy away from finding a violation of constitutional rights dealt with custody matters.[392] The Court also opted for an extensive interpretation of a witness's right against self-incrimination and incrimination of close relatives,[393] the right to counsel,[394] and the availability of complaints against a wide range of procedural decisions of a criminal court.[395] The CCC tended to invalidate decisions of criminal courts and other prosecuting agencies especially on the basis of due process rights but it also rendered void a number of guilty verdicts because it found the evidence insufficient.[396] Even more daring was the Court's finding for a police officer who had accepted a bribe in exchange for arranging that someone would not be taken into custody. The CCC held that because of the police's involvement in setting him up, the petitioner's due process rights were violated, and in general restricted the applicability of entrapment practices by law enforcement agencies. The Court did not fail to grant the same degree of protection to aliens facing custody,[397] deportation,[398] or unlawful searches,[399] either. In an illustrative case, the CCC held that renunciation of certain procedural rights by a Vietnamese woman—although generally acceptable—could not be deemed valid, as she was inexperienced in, and intimidated by, criminal proceedings in a foreign environment, and thus barely aware of the consequences of her decision.

The above sketch is not self-serving, as it was the thorough and extensive supervision of ordinary adjudication—grounded firmly in the extent of the CCC's concrete-review authority—that made the Czech Court look and operate so differently from the HCC, the PCT, or even the Slovak Court. It is impossible to conceive of any other court in the region bothering with the assessment of evidence on the basis of which a defendant was convicted of rape, or pondering how intense were the emotional links between an alien facing deportation and his child. This is, in a way, a live example of a constitutional court concerning itself with quotidian plight of the world's most ordinary inhabitants instead of engaging, in academic seclusion, in a never-ending colloquy on policy choices. No other constitutional court in the region could or would have ever invalidated a judicial ruling through reliance on the *in dubio pro reo* clause,[400] and no other constitutional court in the region thus came to be more of a court than the CCC.

It is fitting to conclude this section with a brief discussion of a paradigmatic case which illuminates most of the relevant tenets of the CCC's jurisprudential agenda, and provides a striking illustration of the benefits attendant on the ability of a constitutional court to review practical implications of a law generally held to be compatible with the Constitution.[401] The case concerned, symbolically enough, a restitution claim filed by a citizen of the Slovak Republic before the division of Czechoslovakia. According to the applicable law—upheld by the CCC itself within abstract review[402]—only the citizens of the Czech Republic were eligible for property restitution. Both the Land Office and the Regional Court therefore rejected the petitioner's claim. The CCC invalidated both decisions as infringing upon the principle of non-retroactivity and pointed out that dogmatic interpretation of the issue would work against the underlying purpose of indemnification policies. In addition to being intuitively right, the decision demonstrates: (i) the Court's general deference to the legislature's choice to restrict eligibility in the restitution process to Czech citizens, for this very choice was the basis for the contested decisions; (ii) the selective approach of the CCC to the principle of non-retroactivity, as it was generally lenient in reviewing the retroactive effect of indemnification claims within abstract review;[403] (iii) the Court's preference for extensive interpretation of restitution policies if it could benefit the claimant; (iv) the Court's dislike of positivist interpretation, as it rejected a 'dogmatic' approach to the issue as inappropriate and unjust; (v) the Court's emphasis on procedural purity and wide accessibility of judicial venues of rights protection, as it found the petitioner's exclusion from access to appellate proceedings a violation of his due process rights; and (vi) the Court's Elyian features, as it stood up on behalf of a foreign national whose interests could hardly be considered, let alone protected, within the political process.

As in the realm of abstract review, the defining elements of the concrete-review case law were a function of both the design and the Court's internal cognitive environment. As regards the former, the CCC pointed out that because of the 'non-existence of the Supreme Administrative Court provided for by the Constitution, it [was] forced to correct the courts' legal opinions in cases adjudicated within the system of administrative judicial review'.[404] The wide accessibility of constitutional complaints against both administrative and judicial decisions led the Court to supervise ordinary adjudication and induced its active judging. The design therefore accounts for the CCC's very ability to police the ordinary courts. The content of this policing, however, reflects both the Court's fondness for a particular concept of justice and its adherence to teleological interpretation of law. The assertiveness of the Court *vis-à-vis* the ordinary courts served to advance causes for which it exhibited a preference also in its colloquy with the legislature: for example, extensive interpretation of restitution claims, strict observance of due process rights, protection of unpopular groups such as aliens, criminal defendants or conscientious objectors, and, in general, adherence to the material understanding of the rule of law. Even in areas where the framework of constitutional adjudication was tainted with ambiguities and where the Court had to confront almost uniform resistance by its judicial counterparts, it asserted itself as the leading court of the country and did so mostly for the citizens' benefit.

Slovak Republic

Judicial Activism

Overview

Slovakia's framework of constitutional adjudication was designed so as to favour abstract review—more so than in the Czech Republic but less than in Poland or Hungary. The standing in the realm of abstract review is open to a number of authorities and the catalogue of measures subject to the Court's scrutiny is relatively extensive. The operative context throughout the 1990s reinforced this underlying bias. The government's authoritarian tendencies and the frequency and poise with which it would disregard constitutional imperatives indicated clearly that efficient rather than legitimate leadership was to dominate Slovakia's transitional equation. The SCC thus found itself operating in an environment that not only encouraged delegation to it of policy disputes, but in which such a delegation proved necessary for the preservation of the very basics of the rule of law. The Court accepted the invitation and, instead of diversifying its contribution to the country's constitutional development, focused on making a good use of its counter-majoritarian arsenal. Between 1994–1998, when the danger of authoritarianism seemed most imminent, it invalidated in whole or in part approximately 60 percent of the contested regulations. But instead of employing its adjudicative equipment to either help consolidate the axiological foundations of the emerging regime (such as the PCT or the CCC) or impose its vision of a great society upon the political arena (such as the HCC), the SCC was forced to try saving the nation rather than founding it. The more ignorant the then governing majority would become of the exigencies of the European integration process or of the essentials of liberal democratic constitutionalism, the more focused and more narrow the Court's adjudicative efforts. As much as the mode of the SCC's abstract review was prohibitive in that it served to frustrate the government's attempts at establishing unconstrained majoritarianism, it also was defensive in that the Court was mostly concerned with remedying frequent and apparent excesses rather than with developing and asserting an autonomous jurisprudential agenda.

The one factor of utmost relevance to the specifics of Slovakia's constitutional jurisprudence was the country's political development. Indeed, the context of transitional politics served to highlight certain features of institutional design while suppressing others.

In mid-1992, Vladimír Mečiar, an excellent communicator, once a student in the Soviet Union and a man with no political scruples, scored a clear electoral victory. This very fact proved fatal to Czechoslovakia as a common state, Slovakia's ambitions with respect to the EU and NATO membership, inflow of foreign investment and the country's ranking in acknowledged economic-performance rating schemes. Not only that, but Mečiar's authoritarian style cast a long shadow over both the government's quotidian operation and the functioning of society at large. Following another electoral victory in 1994, Mečiar found a relatively reliable vehicle for his authoritarian endeavours in a coalition with a radical left-wing party and a radical right-wing party, which coalition enjoyed a comfortable majority in the Parliament (the National Council). Although it was short of disposing of a qualified majority of votes required for constitutional amendments, its control of the legislative process was almost complete. The coalition, for instance, deviated from the established standard of proportional representation of parliamentary factions in parliamentary committees, which have a crucial role in legislative proceedings. Most opposition leaders were assigned to the committee of least political relevance—that on environmental protection. The coalition enjoyed a comfortable majority in every other committee, which made the drafting process a rather smooth one. Given its sheer manpower in the National Council, the coalition's agenda would usually be passed rapidly and in full.

Moreover, Slovakia's legislature is unicameral and thus lacks an additional parliamentary instance which could filter the most flagrant excesses of the lower chamber. The lack of any meaningful parliamentary deliberation, and the lack of a second legislative chamber that would be capable of reducing the speed and the vigour of Mečiar's policy agenda and partly neutralizing his attempts at self-aggrandizement at the expense of other agencies, induced the frustrated opposition to seek refuge in the SCC. The President's ability to veto a bill and return it to the legislature for reconsideration was an institutional barrier of minor significance until the late 1990s, as the veto did not raise the threshold for re-adoption of a bill and the same number of votes—that is, a simple majority of the quorum—was required for passing the statute. Lacking powers that could do more than merely delay by a few weeks the promulgation of legislation, lacking in charisma that could enhance his claim to leadership and lacking in powerful political allies that could enhance his manoeuvrability, President Kováč became rapidly accustomed to rely on his ability to motion the Court for either an annulment of a statute or an abstract interpretation of the constitution.[405]

The diversity of political visions within the legislative minority, its poor performance in public opinion polls, and the damage done to Kováč's image by an international arrest warrant issued by German authorities against his son further enhanced the incapacity of either the President or the opposition to make a difference on their own. Most major media were during the early years of Mečiarism aligned on Mečiar's side, too. Only gradually have the industrial lobby and the opinion makers become concerned by the government's failures in the foreign-policy and economic arenas. It was only in the late 1990s that societal polarization became too pervasive to be tolerable. This was a context that not only enabled, but also vehemently encouraged a political minority to commission a conceptually apolitical authority with policy review. The Constitutional Court, after all, was the one instrument ready to compensate for the political failures of Slovakia's struggling 'democrats' throughout the era of their splendid isolation from both power and responsibility.

The SCC therefore was exposed to partisan bickering of self-absorbed politicians ready to throw at it any hot potato that they would come across. The overwhelming majority of Kováč's abstract-review referrals to the Court were in one way or another related to his own powers. The opposing parties' inability to sort out their claims within the parliamentary forum engaged the SCC in disputes of a purely political nature. In this state of affairs, those who governed were not ready to 'make sense of their own role in the political system, and of how they [were] expected to interact with other actors',[406] but were mostly interested in either completely eliminating competing visions of social development, as was Mečiar's agenda, or having the Court educate their opponents, as was the opposition's agenda.

It was in this context that the standing rules, and within them the ability of the Attorney General to motion the Court, could have become particularly relevant to judicial elaboration of constitutional law and more helpful to the development of constitutional doctrine than were opportunities offered by petty politics. This was to some extent indeed the case. The attorney general was the most active authority to petition the SCC, which found approximately 75 percent of his petitions substantiated and warranting a holding of lack of conformity.[407] It was the attorney general who had the SCC speak on issues such as a sub-statutory regulation of the right to free health care, municipal regulation of the right to privacy or property, and various other issues with immediate effect on citizens' standing vis-à-vis public authority. Were the access to abstract review limited to a group of deputies and the President, as was the Czech case,

Slovakia's constitutional discourse most likely would be completely dominated by policy and *Kompetenz* disputes, with a few rights-oriented challenges thrown in here and there for the sake of variety. On the other hand, the attorney general was a political appointee and none of the office holders showed much interest in crossing Mečiar's path by contesting the major tenets of his policy. The fate of the attorney general who once did so and challenged the constitutionality of a decree issued by the department of health offered both sides a telling story—the decree was held unconstitutional and the attorney general replaced. A peculiar division of labour thus gradually emerged in motioning the Court—the attorney general would refer to the SCC issues lacking in politically explosive potential (mostly municipal and sub-statutory measures) while the opposition and the President would challenge those policy choices that they were unable to influence within the legislative process.

There were other displays of the capacity of political development and some design-related technical arrangements to penetrate constitutional adjudication and heavily qualify the implications for the Court's jurisprudence of the overall institutional framework. Voting requirements for invalidation of a statute, for instance, were until 2002 practically as strict in Slovakia as they are in the Czech Republic—six of the 10 justices (and all justices but one of the minimum quorum of seven) had to concur in order to hold that the Constitution was violated. In both countries, an abstract-review petition thus may be dismissed without any ruling on the merits simply because the plenary session fails to muster the requisite majority of votes for a holding of either conformity or non-conformity. Yet since the Slovak Court was to some extent divided along lines of political sympathies—this alignment became rather apparent especially towards the end of its first term—and since it also strove to maintain an appearance of impartiality, this would occur more often in Slovakia than it would in the Czech Republic. A number of challenges to constitutionally dubious legislation therefore were dismissed because of politically informed friction among the justices or their lack of willingness to 'favour' one side of a dispute over another.

Similarly, both the CCC and the Slovak Court are authorized to adjudicate electoral matters. As the Slovak political environment was much more polarized and the struggle for influence less cultivated than it was in the Czech Republic, instances of alleged election-related violations of the Constitution were more frequent and the SCC's attendant case-law more extensive. As for constitutional review of municipal decrees, both countries suffered from an ambiguous constitutional regulation of the municipalities' regulatory autonomy and, consequently, their tendency to exceed mandates granted by the Constitution. Yet the ability of a regional body of state administration to challenge municipal decrees in the Czech Republic, and the fact that in Slovakia only the central political institutions—preoccupied with their own conflicts—were able to do the same resulted in a higher number of petitions to the CCC and its more diverse jurisprudence in the area.

Jurisprudence

Not going anywhere. In Slovakia, there is a conspicuous absence of a particular trait of transitional constitutional jurisprudence, which sets the SCC apart from its regional counterparts—its almost complete lack of involvement in sorting out arguments over the methods and the content of transitional justice. There were no arguments because there was hardly any justice sought.

The worldlier of Slovakia's opinion makers tend to ridicule the notion of the 'Slovak specifics' advocated and acted upon by many local potentates. This notion, trivial as it is, came to mean that Slovakia should not copy its Visegrád neighbours in their race to the finish line of political, economic, and military integration in West-sponsored international organizations.[408] It also came to mean that as thick a line as possible should be drawn between the communist past and the not-so-post-communist present. The reason for the lack of challenges mounted against retribution measures was simple—almost no retribution measures were implemented. The federal lustration legislation, although perfectly valid and enforceable even after the split, never made it from the books into action, and because of its overt disregard by the relevant Slovak authorities and the lack of public demand for its observance it soon became obsolete. The only lustration-related holding issued within abstract review came in very shortly after the Court's establishment. It concerned a statutory elimination of lustration requirements for one category of public servants and their continued effect for another category. The SCC found this to constitute unequal treatment and absolved the members of the police force and the prison wardens of the duty to document that they had never been members of the communist secret security agency.[409]

More importantly, retributive measures of similar scope to the Hungarian Zétényi Act, the Stalinist-crimes amendment in Poland, or the Czech lawlessness-of-communism statute were neither adopted nor seriously pondered in Slovakia. The one legislative act which acknowledged the illegitimacy of the communist regime was voted upon by a Parliament in which former members of the communist party constituted a majority. The result was symbolic in more than one sense. First, the statute of limitations was not lifted—it was suspended for crimes for which it has not yet expired. Secondly, no former official was ever effectively convicted on the basis of the statute. Thirdly, on display here was political calculation rather than considered self-reflection. Similarly, unlike both the PCT and the CCC, which have allowed for the reduction of certain social entitlements of pensioners who were formerly employed by the regime's repressive machinery, the Slovak Court never had to face this particular issue.

The rapid and extensive infiltration by former communists of the major transition agencies relegated Slovakia's project of coming to terms with the past to the realm of virtual reality. The top offices were throughout most of the decade inhabited by politicians who were at one time or another members of the communist party. Between 1994 and 1998, the President, the Prime Minister, the Speaker of the Parliament, and the Chief Justice of the SCC were former members of the party. The same applies to the post-1998 era, except for the Prime Minister. The truth commission designed to document and investigate communist crimes—having a staff of a few hundred in the Czech Republic (the 'Benda Office') and of a few thousand in Germany (the 'Gauck Committee')—was established in Slovakia only in 2000, is run by a Czech national and has two (!) full-time employees. How could any retribution policy have been implemented in this country?

The fate of the other sibling in the family of transitional-justice measures—that is, restitution policies—was only slightly better. The HCC struggled with this issue on numerous occasions, and a local commentator describes the first seven years of Czech constitutional review as aimed at 'helping out restitution beneficiaries'.[410] Not only in Hungary and the Czech Republic, but also in Slovakia, the restitution legislation had serious implications for, and shaped in manifold ways, the entire legal order. It speaks for itself that until 2001 there was only one abstract-review petition (filed in 1998) directly related to the statutory delineation of the restitution beneficiaries' entitlements.[411] The petitioner, a group of parliamentarians, argued that to subject property return to a statute of limitations was in violation of several constitutional provisions, including the right to property, the right to court, and the rule of law. The Court rejected the argumentation and, unlike the CCC but in line with the HCC's take on the issue, pointed out that restitution beneficiaries were not to be approached as owners but rather as applicants for a renewal of their property rights. Accordingly, it was legitimate for the legislature to subject restitution claims to an expiration period. But the petitioner also challenged a statutory rule which had been in force for almost 10 years and which excluded national cultural sites from the standard restitution regime. This is the very same rule which the Czech Court found unconstitutional because it effectively prevented return of property rights to specific categories of real estate. The Slovak Court dismissed the argument and whatever one thinks of property restitution, it did so in a silly way. It did not concern itself either with the fact that there was a statutory rule capable of precluding indefinitely certain categories of former owners from applying for a return of their property, or with the rule's possible implications for the principle of equal protection. It simply stated, 'it [was] up to those who [had]… legislative initiative to decide when the respective bills would be drafted and when and in which form they would be adopted by the Parliament'.[412] What the Czech Court devoted a comprehensive ruling to, the Slovak Court figured out in a single paragraph. What is even more striking is that the SCC did not hesitate to point out that the relevant act on national cultural sites was not yet adopted in the Czech Republic, either. The fact that this was the very reason why the CCC invalidated the related restriction was somehow lost on the Slovak Court.

That the first direct challenge against some fundamental aspects of restitution policy was filed only in 1998[413] indicates that the SCC's disinclination to either pursue historical justice—as did the PCT and the CCC—or at least comment on it in a thorough and extensive manner, as did the HCC, might not have been entirely its own fault. In a way, it reflected (the absence of) public demand. After all, what is one to make of the fact that the one case dealing with mandatory transfer to the state treasury of the Communist Party's property concerned the issue of whether stationery with an acquisition value lower than 5,000 Czechoslovak crowns (then approximately 150 USD) fell within the scope of property to be returned?[414] The rule of permanent residence as an eligibility requirement, found unconstitutional by the CCC in 1994, also was never contested at the Slovak Court.[415] Apparently, the original ethos of the 1989 revolution—favourable, among other things, to restitution of various kinds of rights, including those related to property—has taken almost no hold in Slovakia's political mainstream. But unlike the Czech Court, which managed to preserve, even cultivate, that ethos in spite of multiple changes of cabinet, the Slovak Court does not seem to have ever believed in it.

Indeed, the SCC was reluctant to pursue the project of coming to terms with the past even when given a chance. It could care less, for instance, about the implementation of restitution policies through ordinary adjudication. It said in 1994, within concrete review, that it was not within its competence to redress injustice committed through specific property wrongs.[416] Accordingly, when faced with a restitution-related claim a few years later, the SCC refused to hear the application in part and dismissed it in the rest.[417] It then comes as no surprise that in the index of its case law for 1993–1999, the Court lists four decisions altogether under the rubric 'restitution' and is yet to issue a restitution-related ruling in which it would find for a petitioner.[418]

The government officials compensated for their lack of interest in the pursuit of transitional justice by providing the public with a spectacle of confrontations and, consequently, offering the Court a chance to join in. This also was the case in Hungary and Poland, and lately in the Czech Republic. In short, all the region's constitutional courts had a fair share of inter-branch disputes to deal with. The difference between the respective countries as to the extent to which these disputes were related to specific substantive issues of constitutional relevance and reflected a disagreement over who was to pursue a particular vision of social and legal development and how, may be said to have been one of degree rather than kind. After all, the former Hungarian President Göncz had his issues with Prime Minister Antall and so did Havel with Klaus or Zeman, and Wałesa with almost everyone who was not clearly aligned on his side. In Slovakia, however, the practical implications and the intensity of personal dislike between the respective officials were so pervasive as to really amount to a difference in kind. Indeed, a significant portion of the governing majority's transitional agenda focused merely on how to debilitate the opponent's operability in daily politics.

Halfway up. The aftermath of the 1994 parliamentary elections indicated clearly that the political arena was ready to exploit constitutional review for the pettiest of partisan goals. First, Mečiar's Movement for Democratic Slovaka (MDS) applied to the SCC for the annulment of electoral results of the Democratic Union (DU),[419] partly because it was founded by deputies who had defected from Mečiar's party and partly because the annulment would give the new coalition a constitutional majority. A few days later, the DU applied to the Court for the annulment of electoral results of the MDS.[420]

The Court dismissed both electoral complaints, emphasizing that it lacked the requisite authority. This was the beginning of a tendency that would regularly resurface in the Court's jurisprudence—at times, it would prefer the appearance of impartiality to full and effective exercise of its powers. In other words, in arguments of a purely political nature, the SCC often would rather find lack of competence than speak on the merits of a dispute. (Even the second Slovak Court, appointed in 2000, continued the trend when, for instance, it refused to speak in material terms on the hottest political/constitutional issue of that year, that is, whether early elections could be held on the basis of a referendum.[421])

Nonetheless, the governing majority's authoritarian tendencies soon became too obvious to be taken lightly by the SCC. The coalition diversified its arsenal of political harassment by, for instance, establishing investigative committees which were authorized to carry out different procedural measures usually granted to law enforcement agencies, for example, to summon citizens and interrogate them, and were to be employed to investigate the DU's participation in the preceding national elections. The Court found investigative committees to be acceptable in principle but without a sufficient mandate in the text of the Constitution, and held the amendment unconstitutional. The coalition, however, had both a wide range of instruments and enough stamina to keep generating more sophisticated harassment. In part, it was aimed at reducing the institutional competencies of political opponents, in part it was aimed at centralizing power in general. It is telling that eight out of nine meritorious decisions issued as abstract constitutional interpretations during Mečiar's era dealt in one way or another with the restriction by other agencies of presidential powers. In all but one instance,[422] the SCC found the President to have been in the right.[423]

Many applications with which the SCC had to deal reflected political pettiness rather than the urgency of the given issue. In the wake of the 1994 elections, for instance, the interim government resigned *en bloc*, and the President accepted the resignation and dismissed the cabinet. According to the constitution, the outgoing cabinet was to perform its care-taking functions until the appointment of a new cabinet. The newly elected parliament, however, voted against two individual ministers and demanded that the President dismiss them. The Court argued that the dismissed cabinet performed its functions *ex constitutione*, that there was no constitutionally relevant relationship between the outgoing cabinet and the new Parliament, and thus no possibility of dismissal.[424] The SCC also was invited to establish authoritatively the exact term of the President's office. The petitioner, a group of coalition deputies, argued that the President was to leave office five years after his election. The President argued that his term expired five years after his inauguration. The difference was two weeks but even that was too long for the coalition to live with. The Court again sided with Kováč.[425]

The coalition's tendency to curb the opposition's *Spielraum* extended from implementing the existing constitutional and statutory mandates (being the subject matter of abstract-interpretation procedure) to making new ones (being the subject matter of abstract-review procedure). The Parliament, for instance, modified its rules of procedure so as not to allow a deputy to speak during deliberation in anything other than the official language (that is, Slovak) and to divide the 15-day period available for the President to veto a statute into various segments, giving the President only four days to either sign the bill or return it for reconsideration. The Court came out in favour of the President on the issue of the veto period but disagreed with his challenge against the mandatory use of Slovak language in parliamentary deliberation.[426]

Many of the governing majority's measures ending up at the SCC were simply infantile displays of self-aggrandizing politics. Many others, however, were of structural significance in that they were aimed at changing the framework of public governance so as to secure for the coalition an institutional framework that would allow it to pursue its goals with as few restrictions as possible. The National Council, for instance, amended the respective legislation so as to strip the President of his authority to appoint the Chief of Joint Staff. This the Court deemed unconstitutional.[427] When the same issue surfaced with respect to the head of the intelligence agency, the Court failed to muster the requisite number of votes and had to dismiss the motion.[428] It was thus by a single vote that the ground was laid for political terrorism of the intelligence agency the consequences of which still haunt Slovakia today. (Paradoxically or not, a lesser degree of judicial self-restraint in the above and a number of other cases would have been extremely beneficial for democracy in Slovakia, both from the short-term and the long-term perspective.) The campaign against the President then continued both outside and within the Parliament. As displays of public dissatisfaction with its government were becoming more vocal and more frequent, the National Council attempted, for instance, to take away from Kováč the power to evaluate and act upon citizens' petitions applying for a referendum, and to have him bound by the Parliament's decision on the matter. This, too, the SCC found unconstitutional.[429]

Kováč, although enemy number one of the coalition, was not its only designated victim. At approximately the same time as the Hungarian Court invalidated the rule allowing a public prosecutor to interfere with judicial decisions, the Slovak legislature extended the parallel competencies even further, giving the Attorney General, the Chief Justice of the Supreme Court, and the Minister of Justice the authority to appeal for a variety of reasons valid and enforceable judgments of ordinary courts. The SCC held this extension unconstitutional in part, but rejected the challenge against the authority of the respective agencies to appeal judgments issued in violation of the law.[430] Another illustration of the government's attempts to centralize power across the realm of public administration came with the statute on procurature. It gave the prosecutorial office an independent status and equipped it with a number of competencies, ranging from supervisory to controlling to repressive, and applicable against a wide range of authorities, including administrative agencies and municipal authorities. Symbolically, the act was to become enforceable two weeks before it was actually published. The Court invalidated the provision effectuating the act before its publication, as well as those of the contested provisions that it deemed in excess of the constitutional mandate for the performance of prosecutorial activities, especially those subordinating administrative and municipal agencies to the procurators' decision-making authority.[431] However, some of the contested provisions were left untouched because the requisite number of votes was not mustered for either a finding of conformity or a declaration of non-conformity.

Another of the few areas in which competing visions were as relevant as were competing egos was the realm of economic policy and within it especially the different privatisation methods. Here, the agenda revolved around how to allow for the smooth transfer of national property into the hands of 'honest Mečiarist entrepreneurs', as the party line would have it.

In November 1994, during an all-night parliamentary session, the newly emerging coalition completely shut the opposition off from parliamentary deliberation and took the country over by means of a legislative storm. In the course of it, the parliamentary majority managed to adopt a number of flagrantly unconstitutional measures, especially as far as privatisation was concerned. The SCC's docket became filled with the opposition's petitions soon afterwards.

It was, in fact, the coalition's attempt to redefine the framework of economic reform that gave the SCC the first real opportunity to affect the progress of transition. The series of related rulings began with a statute retroactively invalidating all privatisation decisions issued by the previous cabinet between the elections and the institution of the new cabinet. The SCC found the statute to be in violation of several constitutional provisions, mostly those related to separation of powers.[432] The new privatisation agenda also equipped the Fund of National Property (FNP)—staffed with political appointees—with as many competencies as possible. This was the part of the agenda with which the Court was least happy. It annulled, for instance, an amendment to the privatisation act, which transferred from the cabinet to the Presidium of the FNP the authority to effectuate direct sale of national property.[433] The Court also invalidated a rule that gave the FNP preferential status—a 'golden share'—in corporations in which it owned shares.[434]

Despite the setbacks it suffered because of constitutional review, the coalition's demonstrations of force intensified with new elections approaching. First, the National Council amended the statutory framework for municipal elections. Among other things, it set forth stringent eligibility criteria for candidates for municipal offices, requiring one year of permanent residence in the respective municipality. It also disallowed any campaign messages to be aired through local TV and radio broadcasting. As a distant shot at gerrymandering, seats in municipal offices were to be divided according to the proportion of the respective ethnic minority in the overall local population. Further, standing in judicial proceedings instituted against an electoral competitor by an opponent was to be limited to the complainant and thus exclude the party against which a judgment was being sought. The SCC found all of the above provisions unconstitutional but again left some others in force, in part because it disagreed with the challenge and partly because it failed to establish the requisite majority of votes for either holding.[435]

The above act was only an entrée to the amendment of rules governing the national elections. The new legislation addressed all the major concerns of the governing coalition, especially the fact that the pre-electoral coalition of centrist parties began to fare better in the polls and that the most popular TV station in Slovakia was not as happy with Mečiar's politics as he—given his alleged involvement in granting the station a license to broadcast—rightly expected. The new rules thus stipulated that electoral campaign could be carried out only through public radio and TV stations, all under relatively direct control of the parliamentary majority. Pursuant to the amendment, no campaign messages were allowed in excess of the airtime offered by the two public media and divided evenly between the relevant parties. Similarly to the act on municipal elections, standing in certain electoral matters was to be limited to the complainant and exclude the competitor against whom a judgment was being sought. Most importantly, a member of a political party could not run on the ticket of another party even if it was a joint ticket of various parties forming an electoral coalition. This was a rule that affected the opposition in the most direct way, as it had planned to run with a list of candidates belonging to different parties but listed jointly on one ballot. This also was one of the rules which the Court did not invalidate, arguing that it did not prevent equal access to elected offices as the petitioner had argued. What the SCC did find unconstitutional was restrictions imposed upon campaign broadcasting, as well as the lack of access of the affected party to judicial proceedings instituted against it.[436]

Many similar examples abound, but what the preceding excursion into the SCC's decision-making activity establishes in unequivocal terms is that throughout the 'dark ages' of Mečiarism Slovakia's political space and, consequently, constitutional jurisprudence were dominated by the coalition's efforts to eliminate or reduce its opponents' institutional operability.[437] The issues, which gave other courts in the region their distinct faces—for example, church–state relations (Poland, Hungary), right to life (Poland, Hungary), restitutions (Czech Republic, Hungary) or welfare and labour policies (Czech Republic, Poland, Hungary)—were either completely absent in the SCC's case law or were of only marginal significance. Not that the SCC would never touch on issues bearing relevance to the protection of specific human rights or fundamental freedoms. It spoke within abstract review on, for instance, freedom of speech, right to court, right to health care, property rights, language rights of national and ethnic minorities, or litigants' equal protection in civil procedure. The Court was nonetheless forced to employ its abstract-review equipment mainly to deal with instances of an overt abuse of legislative or executive power and the attendant attempts at political and institutional aggrandizement. Its perception by the public therefore was determined mostly by its attempts to prevent further deconstitutionalisation of public governance.

True, other constitutional courts in the region have at times been victimised—sometimes willingly, sometimes not—by so-called political priorities. But the SCC appears to have been more of a captive of the political context than any of its regional counterparts. The Czech Court and the Polish Tribunal strove to preserve the original ethos of their countries' revolutionary emancipation and policies rooted in it. The HCC even developed on its own an ethos attendant on the change of regime. Any such ethos—that is, one that would orientate its jurisprudence—the Slovak Court was both deprived of and unable to 'fabricate'. Its involvement in the founding therefore was relegated to preventing the founding fathers from transporting the country a few hundred miles east, into the universe of Byzantine-like authority.

The methods which the post-1998 coalition has been using in order to pursue its policy agenda appear to be more cultivated and respectful of the constitution, and the burden it imposes upon the Court's docket is correspondingly smaller. There were, for instance, only two holdings issued in 2000 on the constitutionality of statutes, and during the three years of its operation the coalition was found by the SCC to have adopted an unconstitutional statute in only two cases.[438] The political arena nonetheless continues to involve the SCC in issues that should not be able to make it through the legislative process. In late 2000, the Parliament adopted a statute mandating political parties to adjust their statutes so as to prevent multiple party memberships. In spite of vocal protests by a number of legal experts—and reservations expressed by a number of coalition parliamentarians, too—political bargains between the different party leaders proved stronger than the relevant constitutional imperatives. The statute was then referred to the SCC by a group of parliamentarians who had voted for the statute only a few weeks before. One of these deputies even drafted the petition, represented the petitioner in the proceedings at the SCC, and, after the Court had found non-conformity, thought it appropriate to label the ruling a 'victory of the constitution over politicking'![439] A similar situation occurred in 2001 with respect to a statute on public administration reform.[440]

Halfway down. The survey of its way to the centre of constitutional politics focused on the SCC at its counter-majoritarian best. As I pointed out at the outset of this section, however, the prohibitive aspects of the Court's judicial activism were only half the story. The other half shows a court on the defensive, struggling not only with a determined opponent but also with its own deficiencies—partly imposed, partly self-inflicted.

The SCC faced the pressure at once to protect constitutionality and/or legality against abuse and to refrain from provoking the country's founding fathers, that is, the abusers themselves. I am not suggesting that the aggressive campaign launched by Mečiar against the SCC after it struck down two health care-related executive decrees scared the justices away from issuing unfavourable rulings.[441] I do contend, however, that not the vulgar warnings themselves but the suggestion that the Court was undermining the 'Slovak way' of transformation was not completely lost on some of the justices.

In addition, the SCC did not feel that, given the society's growing polarization, it had the mandate unambiguously to side with one camp or the other. Not only the public, but also the Court had its share of internal conflict to deal with. It is known, for instance, that some of the justices had informal affiliations with either the coalition or the opposition, and were at times voting also according to their sympathies. Justice Drgonec, for instance, said, after having left the Court in 2000, that Chief Justice Čič perceived him as an obstacle to performance by the SCC of tasks allegedly given to Čič by his former party colleagues from Mečiar's MDS.[442]

The reinforcement by the political context of systemic deficiencies thus again proved to be the principal source of difficulties for the efficacy of Slovakia's constitutional review. The issue of the voting rules provides a relatively tangible interface between the systemic and the contextual variables. Many contested provisions 'fit' for a finding of unconstitutionality persevered simply because the votes were split, reflecting the deepening of doctrinal and political schisms within the Court. Rather than struggling for constitutional justice at all costs, the SCC as a whole would often prefer not to 'favour' one side over the other in order to prevent exposure of the fact that the reasons for its lack of unity on some fundamental issues might have been informed by the justices' personal politics. Whatever their motivation, in the case of applications dismissed because of a split vote no reasons for either position were ever sketched out.

Further, the rules of procedure are structured so as to induce time-consuming proceedings. The rapporteur first examines whether the application meets all the statutory requirements for a review on the merits and then presents his report to the plenary session for deliberation and a vote on the application's admission for further proceedings. The defendant must be given the possibility to file a written response, to which the applicant has the right to respond. Then follows the actual review of the case by a rapporteur and usually a few rounds of plenary deliberation. No time limits apply to any of the above actions, except for those stipulated by the Court itself. The parties also are entitled to present their cases at an oral hearing, and in cases of high political relevance this used to be the rule rather than an exception.[443]

There also is a lot that the Chief Justice himself or any justice rapporteur can do to reinforce the debilitating effect of the exogenous constraints. The Chief Justice, for instance, may assign the incoming petitions practically to any rapporteur he wants and thus make sure that the 'right' justices deal with a controversial issue. In the realm of abstract review, this was in fact a rather common practice. The rapporteur may repeatedly ask the parties for their statements, or allow for a postponement of oral hearings and thus make sure that the constitutional resolution affects the ongoing practice only after it achieves its primary goals.

Indeed, within the review of the series of privatisation-related measures, the Court usually took several months to arrive at a decision—seven to ten months on average in the case of measures found wholly or partly unconstitutional. Given the complexity of the adjudicated issues and the necessity to observe procedural requirements, this period did not seem unreasonable *per se*. The problem lay with the SCC's inability either to hold unconstitutionality with an *ex tunc* effect or to suspend effect of the contested regulations upon receipt of the application for a review on the merits.[444] This the legislator was perfectly aware of and would therefore promulgate measures which were unconstitutional on the face of it, but which could be expected to remain in force for a sufficient period of time to make the possible constitutional remedy largely symbolic. Because of the time gap between the coming into force of a regulation and the staying of its effect by virtue of a Court decision, national property of immense value was transferred on the basis of rules eventually declared to lack conformity to the Constitution. The economic implications of the Court's case law were thus largely symbolic.

The restructuring of the coupon privatisation scheme—developed by Klaus during the federal era and later adopted in independent Slovakia—exemplified the SCC's halfway climb to the centre of local constitutional politics. The post-1994 majority substituted coupons that any citizen of 18 years or older could have used to purchase shares in designated companies with government bonds, to mature by the end of 2001. The Court completely let the opposition down on this matter, as it upheld all but one of the challenged provisions.[445] It pointed out that coupon holders were not shareholders and that their property rights therefore by definition could not have been retroactively violated. The Court also stated that the new regulation was in the public interest and that in limiting the coupon holders' previously instituted entitlements the government satisfied all the constitutional criteria applicable to property rights limitations. It pointed out that

> economic measures, even if they do not provide for continuity with previous economic policy, can be at any time regulated in a manner that is in conformity with the Constitution of the Slovak Republic. In this respect, the requirement of legal certainty is met if universally binding legal acts are not amended accidentally and subjectively but only in accordance with the constitution and an objectively established state of social development, which grows faster or slows down based on the needs of the society.[446]

Despite the cumbersome wording—with its apparent Marxist underpinnings—the essence of negative legislating was on display here. But the Court's self-conscious decision not to overheat the discourse and its tendency to proceed with 'all deliberate speed' proved much more worrisome with respect to the already noted amendment to the election law. The petition was filed on 30 June 1998, a few weeks after the statute was adopted and a few days after it came into force. The elections were planned for 28–29 September 1998 and the petitioner therefore asked the Court to apply Section 26 of the SACC, that is, grant the issue priority status. The Court had done so before and was explicitly allowed to do so under the SACC. Nonetheless, the ruling, which held unconstitutional various rules governing the elections, was issued six months after the elections took place.[447] One is left to wonder what is the source of legitimacy of a government operating on the basis of a primary delegation of power, which took place under rules violating the *Grundnorm*, and what kind of Court it is that establishes that as a *fait accompli*?

In some ways, then, the case of Slovakia's constitutional review refutes, or maybe just proves an exception to, Stone Sweet's claim that '[t]he more politically controversial the policy conflict to be resolved… the more we will expect the court to produce: a partial victory for both the opposition and the government; a complex constitutional justification for its decision; and a set of rules governing how such issues ought to be settled in the future.'[448] In a number of controversial cases, the SCC produced a mere dismissal because of a split vote, offered no justification whatsoever for either position and no rules to govern similar matters in the future, and, by failing to address the claim, in effect granted complete victory to the majority. This, however, corroborates the claim I am advancing throughout this book (and that Stone Sweet often tackles from a different angle), that is, that subtleties of political development, and even some purely personal aspects relating to constitutional discourse, are capable of substantially modifying the effect on a court's jurisprudence of factors of more general nature and scope.

Indeed, it is in the displays of the Court's lack of confidence as a policy-maker and agenda-developer that my main theme re-emerges, that is, the interdependence, and the combined effect on jurisprudence, of factors of different nature and origin. The lack in the local legal tradition of the judiciary's involvement in injecting into the legal order substantive policy-oriented elements undoubtedly was a significant part of the rationale for the SCC's employment of passive virtues within the review of economic and welfare policies, but even more so the exigencies of political development and the attendant self-positioning by the SCC within the framework of founding. The Court, for instance, acted in a principled manner in most of the cases having to do with the harassment of the President or the opposition. Had it not done so, all the indicators of Slovakia's affiliation with Europe, fragile as they were, would be erased from the country's foreign-policy portfolio. But when the original *orientatio* guidelines did not have to be preserved but rather elaborated upon, the SCC tended to leave that elaboration up to the elected officials. In other words, to let the government restructure, for instance, the different privatisation methods or the wider economic framework was not necessarily putting the integration process in direct jeopardy, even though it might have provided excellent opportunities for clientelism and corruption. The SCC therefore tended to scrutinize rather leniently the kind of measures that many other constitutional courts—not least the Czech and the Polish—felt could be subsumed under the legislature's regulatory prerogatives. That approach not only reflected the SCC's understanding of a proper way of facilitating social change by means of constitutional review, but also was strategic in allowing the Court to defend against illegitimacy accusations its mission of Europeanising domestic constitutional politics.

Many Slovaks who originally feared that a Court handpicked by Mečiar would become a mere puppet-institution might be inclined to view its performance as a good point in case for the struggle-for-constitutional-justice claim advanced by Schwartz. Indeed, if preserving the very fundamentals of the rule of law is what a constitutional court should confine itself to doing, the SCC has done very well. It is beyond question that it was instrumental in helping Slovakia's transitional political environment sustain attempts at the deconstruction of its democratic foundations and in cultivating the country's legal discourse. One should, however, not ignore the fact that the overt violations of the constitution by the Mečiar-led administration made the SCC's struggle for constitutional justice 'easy' in the sense that it was invited to perform its counter-majoritarian mission in fighting laws and decrees flagrantly exceeding the applicable mandates. The Court displayed courage mostly with respect to issues in which solutions other than those it adopted were hardly conceivable. On more polemical issues, it often proved self-conscious, self-restrained, and on the defensive. Unlike other courts in the region—struggling to pursue autonomous visions of constitutional development and assert these visions either against the legislature (HCC) or the ordinary courts (PCT and CCC)—the SCC lacked the requisite degree of enthusiasm for developing an autonomous jurisprudential agenda. In terms of adjudicative equipment, it could hardly have asked for more. It was the exigencies of the political environment that delayed the SCC's coming of age as a doctrine-developer. As the Slovak communists would say, it was 'a victim of circumstances'. If that is so, the Court could not have copied its *populus* any better.

Active Judging

Overview

In the preceding section, I argued that the design of Slovak abstract review allowed the SCC to counter the government's proclivity to pursue its transitional agenda without observing the applicable constitutional restraints. Any limitations attendant on the Court's judicial activism were either self-imposed or contextual, or had to do with some technical arrangements relating to the efficacy of constitutional review. The framework of concrete review suffered both from some fundamental systemic deficiencies and from the SCC's lack of focus on their elimination.

Until 1 January 2002, several competence- and enforceability-related deficiencies served to reduce both the range of issues fit for adjudication within concrete review and the capacity of the Court to address and remedy the alleged violations of constitutional rights. Pursuant to the SACC, the Court was competent to hear a constitutional complaint only if: (i) it alleged a violation of a right that either was expressly listed in the Slovak Constitution or could be inferred from such a right; (ii) it alleged a violation of a right for the protection of which there were no other judicial venues available; (iii) it alleged a violation of a right infringed by a valid and enforceable judgment of state administration, regional administration, or municipal authorities; (iv) it was filed within two months of the date of coming into force of the contested decision; and (v) if all other remedies—including the so-called extraordinary appeals, where applicable—were exhausted.[449]

The SCC has been applying these stringent admissibility criteria to the fullest extent. Accordingly, meritorious decisions issued on the basis of constitutional complaints were an extremely rare occurrence in the Court's case law. Until 2002—that is, during almost nine years of the Court's existence—there had been 10 (!) findings issued upon constitutional complaints, and in only eight cases did the SCC find for the complainant. Originally, the low number of holdings on the merits stemmed from the lack of established cognitions among the applicants as to the ambit of applicability of a constitutional complaint, and the Court's propensity respectively to 'educate' the complainants. One notes here the effect of the lack of an ombudsman's office in Slovakia, as a large number of complaints that have reached the Court's docket clearly would have been more suitable for handling by an ombudsman. Accordingly, the SCC dismissed the vast majority of complaints—in 1995, for instance, only one finding was issued out of 172 constitutional complaints filed with the Court. Consequently, the citizens' reliance on constitutional complaint as an effective way of addressing violations of constitutional rights diminished. In 1996, only 28 constitutional complaints were filed and in 1997 only 30. Gradually, the petitioners have developed a habit of relying on the other instrument of constitutional protection of individual rights, the so-called petition.[450]

The petition was available for any natural or legal person alleging that their rights had been violated, without further qualification. There were no restrictions listed as to who was eligible to file a petition, against what kind of a decision, and within what time limits. On the other hand, it was completely within the SCC's discretion whether it granted a writ of certiorari and admitted a petition for a hearing on the merits or not. Yet because of the heavily restricted ambit of constitutional complaints, the Court has been admitting all petitions that it thought satisfied the formal criteria. Not that these criteria were particularly loose. The Court, for instance, was bound to dismiss a petition that it deemed manifestly ill-founded, not competent to hear, filed by an unauthorized person, or to which there was not attached a power of attorney for a qualified lawyer.

But the most serious defect of the petition procedure concerned the Court's inability to invalidate a decision held unconstitutional. Until the adoption of a constitutional amendment in 2001, neither the Constitution nor the SACC provided for a rule governing the procedure following a holding of unconstitutionality in relation to a petition—or such, at least, was the SCC's interpretation of the matter. In other words, it was within the affected agency's discretion whether it re-opened the proceedings, issued a new decision in accordance with the Court's opinion, or simply left the matter as it was.[451] Unsurprisingly, the latter option used to be the option of default. This was another 'Slovak specific'—a decision held within the petition procedure to be the immediate cause of violation of fundamental rights could be fully enforced against the party whose rights were violated. Accordingly, the ECHR did not understand the petition procedure to be the kind of remedy that would have to be exhausted before relief could be sought at supra-national level.[452]

Nonetheless, the petition became a motion of default for non-institutional applicants. While in 1995 there were still twice as many constitutional complaints as there were petitions, the ratio has rapidly reversed in response to the Court's evolving jurisprudence, and the number of petitions stabilized at about five times the number of constitutional complaints. As admissibility criteria were much stricter for the latter applications, the ratio of holdings was even higher—for the eight meritorious decisions on constitutional complaints there were about 110 that were issued on the basis of petitions.

It was again the combination of the design and the context that made the SCC's concrete-review performance as pervasively affected by the heavy reliance of the political arena upon constitutional adjudication as was its jurisprudence in the realm of abstract review. The SCC's extensive competence in the adjudication of electoral matters, for instance, induced the delegation by political agents of their grievances to constitutional review. Similarly imposing upon the Court's docket was the frequency of rights violations committed by the governing coalition against its political opponents. In addition, both the political forum and the media paid great attention to a case law that was touching upon issues of immediate political relevance and, in a way, pressed upon the Court to keep itself occupied with inter-partisan bickering. Simply, both the lack of venues that could effectively address ordinary citizens' complaints and the failures of the available protective mechanisms were only of secondary concern to the SCC's critics.

Factors outside the Court's field of immediate influence—that is, both its powers and the overall context in which it was to function—therefore were not particularly favourable to its focus on 'minor' and 'trivial' grievances of non-institutional applicants. But these factors were not the only barriers involved, and the Court has done its fair share in reinforcing them.

It found it improper, for instance, to apply rules governing the constitutional-complaint procedure analogically within its handling of petitions, which in practice came to mean that almost all of its human-rights rulings issued within concrete review were only of declaratory effect.[453] The SCC also understood its capacity to supervise ordinary adjudication to be rather narrow and refused to deal with the merits of a vast number of petitions alleging incorrect procedure or interpretation on the part of the ordinary courts. On a more specific note, it also developed a tendency to scrutinize within preliminary proceedings the merits of individual petitions more strictly than those of abstract-review motions.

There is, of course, more than *denegatio iustitiae* to the SCC's concrete-review jurisprudence. In the ensuing excursion, I will deal with three major themes: (i) the intra-judicial colloquy dominated by the Court's unwillingness to confront ordinary adjudication, and its incapacity, partly self-imposed and partly informed by the design, to address a wide range of wrongs; (ii) the review of issues of immediate political relevance and the inability of the Court to grant relief, affected again both by its own caution and the design; and (iii) the Court's rising to the occasion by either hearing a case or furnishing a remedy, or both, mostly in order to prevent further de-Europeanisation of local legal discourse and practice.

Jurisprudence

A missing court. I have already pointed out that in both the Czech Republic and Poland, the interaction between the constitutional court and the ordinary courts, especially the respective Supreme Courts, was extremely problematic. To use this term to describe the situation in Slovakia would be an understatement. If asked to respond to a petition alleging its unconstitutional action, the Slovak Supreme Court often responds by emphasizing that it does not fall under the scope of constitutional review and is therefore incapable of being a party to the proceedings at the SCC, and in general finds it inappropriate to explain its actions or decisions.[454] How has it become this daring?

It was in 1993 that the SCC exhibited for the first and last time an instinct of assertiveness against an ordinary court. The case concerned unlawful deprivation of liberty—more specifically, internment in a psychiatric clinic. The SCC first held that the petitioner's personal liberty was violated and then did what it would never do again. It simply said that the contested judgment was to lose effect and ordered that the petitioner be released and his personal liberty restored.[455] This might strike one as a sound way to proceed; soundness, however, was hardly a concern in what happened next.

First, a number of high-ranking members of the Supreme Court 'summoned' some of the justices to a meeting during which serious objections were voiced against any interference by the SCC with ordinary adjudication. The majority at the Court then held the affected decision unfit for publication in the official collection of decisions and decided to make it as secret as possible. And then the whole idea of an intra-judicial colloquy fell through. The rest is a different story.

It is illustrative of the SCC's changed consciousness that it would specify the framework within which the intra-judicial colloquy was (not) going to take place by means of denial of competence. First, the Court held that it was not competent to review the ordinary courts' decisions contested by means of a constitutional complaint[456] or to annul them even if contested by means of a petition.[457] Then followed a ruling that the SCC lacked authority to ever review the legality of ordinary adjudication proceedings.[458] But the one case that indicated unambiguously the SCC's conceptual approach to the scrutiny of ordinary adjudication by means of concrete constitutional review concerned, symptomatically enough, a petition challenging an ordinary court's decision to deny return of real estate property. The petitioner argued that the respective courts failed in their duty properly to assess all available evidence and draw proper legal conclusions from it. However, as the SCC responded, constitutional review and ordinary adjudication

> are two separate, mutually independent and procedurally self-contained systems of justice administration.... The autonomous and equal status and mission of these two systems prevent any kind of mutual superiority or inferiority... The constitutional court is therefore not authorized to annul decisions of ordinary courts, suspend their enforceability or review whether the ordinary courts have carried out and properly evaluated all the necessary evidence.[459]

It became a doctrinal cornerstone of the SCC's scrutiny of ordinary adjudication that it did not have the power to 'review whether facts were or were not correctly assessed in ordinary adjudication and what factual and legal conclusions [an] ordinary court inferred from the assessment of facts'.[460] No matter how informed by the context the Court's partial evacuation of constitutional justice administration was,[461] I find some of the consequences objectionable.

In 1995 an officer of the intelligence agency was dismissed by the head of his department. He appealed within the applicable time limit to the director of the intelligence agency who was the one authority competent to dispose of the appeal. Pursuant to the relevant law, however, appeals are to be filed not with the authority competent to review them, but with the first-instance body. By the time the agency's director referred the appeal to the head of the department so that the head of the department could then properly refer the appeal to the director, the time limit for the appeal had expired. The Supreme Court dismissed the officer's complaint without reviewing its merits and simply stayed the proceedings, pointing out that it had the power to review only properly appealed administrative acts. The officer then filed with the SCC a petition alleging violation of his right to court. The Court refused to hear the petition in part and denied relief in the rest. It stated that the officer had addressed his appeal to the wrong body, that the competent body had received the appeal after the time limit had expired, and that the attendant consequences could not be undone by means of constitutional review.[462] Compare this kind of struggle for constitutional justice to all those decisions of the Czech Court in which it derided ordinary courts for sophisticated formalism resulting in the denial of the right to court. Compare the absolute lack of criticism of this and similar decisions either in the Slovak law journals or in the media with their intense focus on the Court's handling of politicised disputes between elected officials. In light of this comparison it becomes clear why the relative number of judgments issued by the ECHR against Slovakia is four times the number of judgments issued against the Czech Republic.[463]

Further, the SCC would find itself unauthorized to intervene even if an ordinary court committed substantive errors.[464] No relief was therefore granted to a petitioner who was dismissed from work on the basis of a disciplinary measure, which one court deemed void but upon which another court relied as valid and thus justifying the dismissal.[465] So, 'even though the courts' improper procedural action... can lead to violation of litigants' right to a fair trial (including their fundamental rights as parties to judicial proceedings), the very fact of proceeding upon, and deciding, [a claim] demonstrates that the fundamental right to judicial protection... was respected'. Allegations to the contrary are therefore manifestly ill founded.[466]

The SCC's insistence that it was not called to supervise the legality of ordinary adjudication extended to matters of much higher significance than labour disputes. The Court, for instance, refused to hear a petition challenging a decision of the Supreme Court not to deal with a 'complaint for violation of law' filed by the Attorney General to contest the petitioner's criminal conviction.[467] The Court argued that only the Attorney General, and not the petitioner, was entitled to file the respective complaint. Accordingly, it found no causal link between the petitioner's right to judicial protection and the action by the Supreme Court, and held the petition manifestly ill founded. This warrants repetition—the Attorney General found the contested criminal conviction to have been issued in violation of law, to the petitioner's detriment; the Supreme Court refused to deal with the merits of his complaint because of procedural defects; pursuant to the SCC's case law, the Attorney General himself could not have filed the constitutional petition; *summa summarum*, the petitioner's allegations that his access to court was unduly restricted were manifestly ill-founded.

To sum up the extent of the SCC's (lack of) authority with respect to ordinary adjudication, 'the Constitutional Court... does not have the power to review, uphold, let alone annul either the procedural or the meritorious decisions of ordinary courts'.[468] It also 'lacks authorization to review the observance by ordinary courts of statutory law in their proceedings and decisions'.[469] Naturally, then, allegations of the courts' failure to observe the relevant law in their decision-making generally were deemed manifestly ill-founded. Manifest lack of merits and the lack of competence: the Court's two favourite ways of saying that it was not really a court.

Nevertheless, the insulation from constitutional scrutiny of ordinary adjudication was not complete. One of the few areas in which the Court would consistently prove strict enough to keep finding violations by the ordinary courts concerned the right to have one's claim adjudicated without unreasonable delay. The frequency and the conceptual similarity of claims in this area allowed the Court to develop a coherent doctrine of assessment of unreasonable delays and it is now the most extensive and most elaborate part of its concrete-review jurisprudence.[470] Its assessment of unreasonable delays is standardized along the lines of criteria used by the ECHR, but is in some ways even broader—the Court has extended the protection against unreasonable delays from judicial proceedings to proceedings before a branch office of the internal revenue service,[471] and has found the right to timely adjudication applicable also to preliminary-injunction proceedings.[472]

Politicians' court. There were two basic types within the concrete review of cases of high political relevance. The first is the more obvious: adjudication of electoral complaints, which applies to both national and municipal elections. There were 10 complaints filed in relation to the 1994 national elections but the SCC dismissed all of them. The reasons ranged from manifest lack of merits to the Court's very strict interpretation of its competence in the matter at hand. The applicants learnt the lesson, and there were no complaints filed after the 1998 elections. If it did not concern Slovakia, one could deem it a paradox that no electoral complaints would challenge elections that took place on the basis of statutory rules some of which the SCC later held unconstitutional within abstract review.

The ratio of applications to rulings was slightly better as far as municipal elections were concerned. Out of more than 100 complaints, eight decisions on the merits were issued. The design and the context combined interestingly in this area. On the one hand, the SCC can within the adjudication of electoral complaints annul the contested elections, invalidate the contested electoral outcome, or even annul a decision of the electoral commission and proclaim as elected the candidate whom it thinks properly elected. This the SCC may do in reference to both national and municipal elections. On the other hand, the SCC also seems to be taking into account the factor of political and doctrinal feasibility of judicial interference with parliamentary elections, and the attendant potential of society-wide conflict. Accordingly, while within the scrutiny of complaints against national elections the Court would try to find an interpretation that would allow it to vacate the area and deny relief, in the less attended to, and less explosive, area of municipal elections the SCC would not always shy away from implementing the available instruments. In a few cases, the Court annulled the elections because it found them to have taken place within an unconstitutional framework;[473] in other instances it quashed the election of a single officer;[474] and in other cases still it simply instituted a different candidate, as it concluded that the votes had not been counted correctly.[475]

But it was the petition-based case law that illustrated most visibly both the kind of issues that the SCC was forced to deal with because of Slovakia's political development and the deficiencies attendant on its concrete-review instrumentarium.

One of the measures adopted by the new parliamentary majority in order to intimidate the opposition was the establishment of an interim commission—composed exclusively of the then coalition deputies—designed to investigate the content of petitions filed by the DU in order to run in the elections. The interim commission had the petitions delivered to its offices from the Ministry of the Interior archives, unsealed them, reviewed the personal data of people who had signed them, made copies of the petitions, and distributed them to other bodies. One of the DU's supporters filed a petition with the Court alleging violation of his right to privacy and the protection of personal data. The SCC found the commission's actions authorized except for the copying of petitions.[476] Although indicative of future developments, this was nothing compared to what was yet to come.

In 1995, President Kováč's son was abducted and forcibly transported to neighbouring Austria where he was arrested on the basis of an international arrest warrant issued by a German prosecutor. It became apparent soon after the kidnapping, and has seemed beyond doubt ever since, that the operation was carried out by the Slovak Intelligence Agency, possibly at the request, or with the approval, of then Prime Minister Mečiar.

What was more relevant to the case at the SCC was that the competent Slovak authorities refused to apply for Kováč Jr's extradition to Slovakia even after he was indicted at home for fraud, which application the criminal code explicitly mandated. The petitioner argued that the failure of the Ministry of Foreign Affairs to apply for his extradition violated his right freely to enter the territory of Slovakia, his right to defence and counsel, his rights to inviolability of private and family life, his freedom of movement, and the constitutionally mandated protection of family life and parenthood. The Court found the petition substantiated only with respect to the right of any Slovak national to enter freely Slovakia's territory. This was moral rather than legal satisfaction, as the law did not foresee any implications of a holding of unconstitutionality issued on the basis of a petition. In the case of Kováč Jr, moral satisfaction was more or less everything that he was seeking. The case of Gaulieder, another victim of Mečiar's not-so-cold war with his political opponents, was different.

Gaulieder ran on MDS's ticket in 1994 and like other candidates of the party signed a blank resignation from parliamentary office to be deposited with the party's leadership and used whenever the need would arise. After he publicly voiced his disagreement with some of Mečiar's policies, it became clear that the party was going to try to make him leave office. Gaulieder therefore repeatedly said both in public and in the Parliament that he did not intend to step down and that any document presented to the contrary would indicate against his will. The Speaker of the Parliament then received by ordinary mail service the resignation letter, and the National Council consequently adopted a resolution in which it took account of Gaulieder's resignation. Gaulieder applied to the SCC, arguing that his right to resign from parliamentary office had been violated because his public revocation of the resignation had not been respected. The Court agreed with the petitioner but argued that it lacked the power to annul the resolution, by which means he was effectively deprived of his mandate.[477] It also dismissed a related petition, filed by an opposition deputy against the resolution of the National Council by means of which a new deputy was instituted into Gaulieder's office and his mandate certified.[478]

By continuing to legislate with the successor to Gaulieder's parliamentary seat, the National Council confirmed that it held the Court's decisions in utter disrespect and would ignore them at will. The case thus finally brought to the attention of the media the lack of a mechanism for the enforcement of constitutional law *sui generis*. But it also exposed the

SCC's defensive posture, that is, its refusal to confront the majority by *struggling* for constitutional justice. In the case at hand, a struggle would probably amount to more than the Court's allegations of its incapacity to either annul the very parliamentary resolution it found unconstitutional or hold against the certification of the substitute parliamentary mandate.

Life was indeed not easy for either Slovak politicians or 'their' Court. After one of the deputies of the Slovak National Party died, his seat was to be taken by a deputy who ranked next on the party's ballot in terms of preferential votes. The rules are very clear and in the case at hand the applicant's mandate should have been certified automatically, so to speak. The party leadership, however, became suspicious of the new deputy's political reliability and nominated a different candidate. The National Council then adopted a resolution to that effect. The unsuccessful candidate applied to the SCC for relief and asked the Court to oblige the Speaker of the Parliament to remedy the situation. The SCC took the usual seven months to arrive at a decision in which it found violation of the petitioner's right to be elected, and argued vehemently for the observance by all the government authorities of the principle of legal certainty.[479] The ruling, however, again was only of declaratory effect, as the Court found itself without any power to oblige the Speaker as required in the petition. The legislature thus continued to operate with two members whose mandates were certified in violation of the relevant constitutional provisions.

There was still more to come and more of the same. Over the years, Slovakia's establishment discredited itself enough to make the country unacceptable as a candidate for NATO membership. The government, looking for an alibi for its deliberate political failure, initiated a referendum with three questions relating to Slovakia's application for NATO membership. Simultaneously, a group of opposition deputies launched a campaign for popular presidential elections. Based on the petition's compliance with the respective statutory criteria, the President—who is the one authority competent to declare a referendum—added a fourth question, on whether the President should be elected by popular vote rather than by the legislature. The complete subject matter of the referendum was then published in the Official Gazette. Subsequently, the Central Referendum Commission approved the default ballot and stamped all the ballots that the Ministry of the Interior was to distribute around the country. The Minister of the Interior, however, decided to issue ballots excluding the fourth question. The requisite stamp was 'stolen' and the invalid ballots stamped and distributed. The public ignored the referendum, and the SCC received a petition shortly thereafter. The applicant argued that his right to participate in a referendum as declared by the President of the Republic, as well as his right to participate directly in the governance of public affairs, had been violated. Seven months later, the Court agreed with the petitioner.[480] The remedy? The usual—none.

The question arises whether the Court's contribution to legal certainty could only have been verbal—that is, whether the alleged lack of competence to grant relief was as insurmountable as interpreted. The answer to the Court's *Kompetenz*-restraint again points to political circumstances. On the one hand, the SCC was more or less ready to subject the governing majority to European standards of political culture. On the other hand, any hint of a step beyond its powers would expose the Court to vehement accusations of illegitimate behaviour, undermine the merits of the core of its decisions, and put its Europeanisation project in jeopardy. It remains open to question, however, how much good to the country's prospects of integration the Court's verbal-only mode of protection of the rule of law has done. After all, one could phrase the question less charitably: was the Court so brave in holding against the perpetrators because it was guided by the European integration-related imperatives or because it knew that the consequences for the governing majority of its noble declarations were at best indirect?

Nevertheless, some of the justices learned the lesson and proved that when political priorities so required, ways could be found of circumventing systemic deficiencies. Their opportunity finally to demonstrate creativity came only in the last weeks of the Court's first term. Shortly before his dismissal in 1998 and acting in his capacity as president-in-lieu, Mečiar issued an amnesty for any and all criminal actions relating to the abduction of Kováč Jr and the referendum-sabotage by the former Minister of the Interior. As the original amnesty was not far-reaching enough, Mečiar issued a new one in order to complete the insulation of his allies, and possibly of himself, from eventual post-electoral prosecution.[481] After the 1998 elections, criminal prosecution was initiated against some of the incriminated members of the Slovak Intelligence Agency who have subsequently applied to the SCC for protection. In the first case, one of the Court's panels dismissed the complaint, alleging lack of competence. The other case, however, was assigned to a different panel 'in order to achieve balance'.[482] Despite six years of constant refusal to annul any decisions contested by means of a petition, despite the obvious self-serving nature of the amnesty and despite the fact that it used to dismiss individual petitions out of hand throughout its operation, the respective panel agreed with the petitioner, annulled the investigator's decision and effectively stayed the ongoing criminal prosecution.

The ruling was so out of line with the Court's case law and so lacking in persuasive legal argumentation that it prompted some of the best legal minds of the country to label it as a direct attack on the rule of law.[483] However, it made several things clear. First, the alleged inability of the SCC to quash individual decisions within the petition procedure seems to have been a matter of interpretation rather than an insurmountable necessity. After all, the Court had done a similar thing at the very beginning of its operation when it ordered a petitioner's release from a psychiatric clinic.[484] The French say that once is never but twice is a habit. The answer to the question why the Court has not developed this habit more thoroughly may be self-consciousness and self-restraint informed by judicial philosophy or judicial politics in addition to, and at times maybe even in spite of, the applicable text.

Secondly, the ruling made transparent the victimization by Slovakia's political development of constitutional review, as it proved right those who suspected the SCC to have been internally divided along lines of political affiliation. The Court simply lost most of the capital of public confidence it had accumulated by standing up against Mečiar on previous occasions. As 'chance' would have it, this time in reverse order, a few months after the controversial ruling was issued the terms of all but one of the justices expired and the new coalition, together with Mečiar's victorious rival in presidential elections, has had an important say in choosing the new members.

A slightly different Court. As the justices were nearing the completion of their terms, they became more ready to judge, and by judging to make constitutional law. The main reason was their growing awareness that the Court's lack of capacity/readiness effectively to remedy a certain category of constitutional rights infringements was resulting in an increasing number of applications being filed with the ECHR. It probably is not a coincidence that in the wake of a series of judgments issued by the ECHR against Slovakia, the number of findings on individual applications increased from three in 1996 to 18 in 1998 (first two judgments against Slovakia in 1998), then jumped to 33 in 1999, and remained at about 30 in 2000 (several more judgments against Slovakia in the course of 1999 and 2000). By admitting a higher number of petitions for a full hearing, the SCC tried to make itself seem an available—if not necessarily efficient—venue of redressing individual violations of rights, and thus influence in some ways the admissibility decisions of the ECHR. The fact that some applications were filed in parallel both at the SCC and the ECHR also made the justices 'nervous' and induced their closer scrutiny; after all, no member of a national constitutional court is pleased to see his ruling 'overruled' by an international court.

In one of the cases illustrating the justices' rising awareness, the Court again found itself unauthorized to quash the contested judgment but did not leave the matter at that—instead, it went to notable lengths to emphasize that the Supreme Court had a duty to remedy the situation, and indicated that the ECHR would most likely find a violation of the respective rights if Slovak authorities granted no relief.[485]

The Court's gradual opening to a variety of normative challenges and propositions also suggested attempts to leave a doctrinal legacy which would overshadow the years of denial of competence and petitioner-unfriendliness. Indeed, the SCC became more active not only from a procedural point of view, but also in terms of material scrutiny. It was especially one of the two panels that tried to show petitioners its friendly face—somewhat unexpectedly, given the Court's propensity to resist suggestions to complement protection offered by ordinary adjudication. The said panel proved very petitioner-friendly in dealing with a petition alleging the failure of a district office (a body of regional administration) actively to protect a child's well-being. The case was filed by a mother of a little girl who had been bullied over a period of time and even physically attacked by one of her classmates. The attacker was too young for any criminal prosecution but the mother repeatedly asked the social-care division of the district office to take protective measures. The district office had not taken any action and the SCC found its omission to have constituted a violation of rights under the 1989 Covenant on the Rights of Children in connection with the right to inviolability of personal and family life under the Slovak Constitution. The Court stated that 'all government authorities competent to act in relations regulated by the Covenant [had] a duty to carry out effective measures designed to protect rights guaranteed by the Covenant',[486] and found the district office's failure to consider measures to protect the petitioner's daughter to have constituted a breach of duties set forth by the Covenant and the Constitution. This was one of the few instances in which the SCC has found the courage to say that the so-called negative freedoms were co-related to the government's positive duty of active and effective protection, a line of reasoning that was one of the trademarks of the HCC's human-rights jurisprudence.

The attempts to leave a lasting imprint on the country's constitutional discourse combined with the Court's sensitivity to European transnational law in a ruling in which the application was dismissed within a paragraph or two but space found for a rather peculiar analysis, as the SCC found it possible to have a petition filed against it. 'By such a petition it is possible to allege a violation of a petitioner's rights by either a decision of the Constitutional Court, or other action or omission by the Constitutional Court, that is, a violation committed in disposing of a petition, or in other kind of proceedings, not only those of concrete, but also those of abstract review of constitutionality.'[487] Paradoxically or not, the petition was held manifestly ill founded and the petitioner advised to seek relief with supra-national judicial authorities.

A radically different Court? The Court's increasingly assertive approach in the realm of concrete review reflected not only the need for a thorough Europeanisation of the local legal topography, but also some significant changes in the context in which it operated. Ordinary adjudication, for instance, gradually lost its aura of purity, if it had ever had one. In several highly publicized cases concerning serious criminal action, the respective courts failed to complete their proceedings before criminal defendants had to be released from detention because of expiration of the applicable time limits. In a number of cases, criminal defendants were released on bail under extremely suspicious circumstances. Several judges were indicted for possession of narcotics, illegal possession of weapons, or other improper behaviour. The Chief Justice of the Supreme Court is under suspicion of having forged an official document, and one of his allies on the bench accepted at a reduced price services from a party to a pending litigation at the Supreme Court. The SCC itself found constitutional rights to have been violated by ordinary courts on numerous occasions. So first the context changed and then followed some design-related adjustments.

Reflecting upon the increasingly untenable deficiencies of the petition procedure, and the attendant exposure of Slovakia to supra-national judicial authorities, the recent constitutional amendment (March 2001) modified the respective provisions so as to allow the SCC to annul judgments of the ordinary courts and grant 'equitable financial satisfaction' for rights' violations committed by any of the government agencies. This extension of the SCC's powers came into effect only on 1 January 2002, and therefore could not yet translate into jurisprudence. The other adjustments were less direct but of more immediate impact. In 2000, a number of former judges and attorneys with expertise in civil and criminal procedure were appointed to the Court, which means that there are now more practitioners than academics on the bench. The new Chief Justice

Mazák also restructured the SCC's internal organization so as to operate with three instead of two panels. The new professional profile and the different working methods allowed for increased efficiency in dealing with individual petitions, and the number of decisions issued within concrete review is considerably higher than it was during the Court's early years.

In general, the new tendencies emerging in the Court's case law suggest a higher degree of the justices' readiness to concern themselves with issues previously deemed 'unworthy' of the SCC's attention. The first panel, for instance, found violation of the right to privacy and the constitutionally mandated protection of family life in the case of a petitioner who had to vacate a subsidized municipal lodging despite being on a list of applicants for such a lodging.[488] Interestingly, the Court found the fault to have lain with the ordinary court reviewing the vacation order, not with the municipality itself. A different panel extended the applicability of due process rights from criminal defendants to persons who had already been convicted, despite contrary indications in the constitutional text.[489] Somewhat in contrast to its earlier case law, the Court also stipulated that any denial of competence by an ordinary court resting on formal or procedural grounds had to be assessed in light of the right-to-court guarantees.[490] Illustrative of the changes in the SCC's self-understanding was its approach to a petition that did not satisfy the statutory requirement of qualified legal representation. The petitioner argued that his right to court was violated because of his being obliged to have a legal counsel in extraordinary appeal proceedings.[491] Instead of dismissing the application out of hand, the Court explained that it had decided not to demand from the petitioner the requisite proof of legal representation because 'he would thus be asked to fulfil the very duty which he deems a violation of his constitutional right'.[492] Also, 'given the special circumstances it is necessary to give the petitioner an answer to the question… whether it is permissible under the Constitution to make effective access to a high court subject to qualified legal representation'.[493] The panel ended up dismissing the application for other reasons, but in contrast to the first Court's propensity not to give substantive answers 'unless necessary', it offered the petitioner a relatively thorough explanation of the purpose of qualified legal representation in certain kinds of judicial proceedings. This took place at a time when the Court, alleging lack of competence, dismissed an abstract-interpretation application filed by a group of parliamentarians.[494] Only a couple of years ago, the approach would most likely have been the opposite. Is this 'pay-back time' for years of clogging the Court by politically motivated petitions? There are reasons to hope so.

The most significant display of the SCC's increased sensitivity to the incidental protection of non-institutional applicants came with the justices' decision to continue hearing so-called petitions despite the fact that the constitution-maker committed a mistake by derogating the petition procedure from 1 July 2001 and making the new concrete-review regulation enforceable only from 1 January 2002. Although reluctantly, the Court preferred continuity in rights protection to strict observance of its mandate, arguing that its general conceptualisation as a protector of constitutionality did not allow it to vacate for six months the realm of incidental review.

The new Court is apparently trying to establish a distinct identity. It is, however, difficult to assess whether the implications for its jurisprudence of some novel arrangements, both those provided for by the constitution-makers and those implemented by the SCC itself, will be of lasting and pervasive effect. Nonetheless, it appears that the second Court not only will have at its disposal more efficient instruments of incidental rights protection, but also will be willing actively to implement them. As the need for close supervision by the SCC of political processes has decreased considerably, the context, too, has become more favourable to a focus on concrete review. No less importantly, the citizens' confidence in the availability of constitutional protection of rights appears to be on the way to restoration. If the SCC continues to deliver, such confidence may even be justified.

CHAPTER 4

INTERPRETIVE TECHNIQUES

In Chapter 3, I discussed the effect on Central European constitutional case law of various features relating to the design of constitutional adjudication. I argued, however, that the different adjudicative approaches of the respective courts had proven to be a function of factors more complicated than the relative exposure or insulation of a constitutional court to or from other policy-making or adjudicating fora. In this chapter, I focus on the effect on the courts' interpretive techniques of texts that were made available to them. I argue that the provisionality or finality of foundational arrangements had far-reaching consequences for the respective courts' approaches to constitutional interpretation, but also pay attention to variables transcending the relevant texts' extent and quality, such as the justices' professional cognitions and ideological inclinations, or the traditional local interpretive codes.

FRAMEWORK

As much as 'a constitution... declares the revolution over and substantively complete',[1] a series of constitutional amendments arguably does so to a lesser extent. The fact that both the Hungarian and the pre-1997 Polish constitutions were explicitly acknowledged and widely understood to be temporary was not lost on the two courts. Even though the provisionality constraint served to limit the authority of Polish constitutional review in manifold ways, the underdeveloped constitutional base led the Tribunal to use the *Rechtsstaat* and equal-protection clauses to elaborate a complex doctrine based largely on extra-textual considerations. In Hungary, the provisionality of foundational arrangements induced what

Sajó described as *horror vacui*,[2] the fear that a normative vacuum could put the progress of transition in jeopardy. It became the role of the HCC to make sense of the different pieces of the patchwork and play an active role in delineating both the content of the different rights and the structure of relations between the branches of government. Both the Polish Constitutional Tribunal (PCT) and the Hungarian Constitutional Court (HCC) have thereby introduced to their audiences a number of complex jurisprudential doctrines deriving from theories of law and government rather than extending from the available texts.

Provisionality also entailed revolutionary impurity. Accordingly, the Polish Tribunal found it legitimate to continue effectuating the revolution by, for instance, interpreting welfare rights under a new axiology—one that was to reflect the systemic changes and the shifting ideological conceptions. The curbing of privileges of former party cadres, for instance, also suggested that the PCT was ready to complete what could not have been completed by means of the original deal with the communist incumbents. It was thus partly because of the impurity of the transitional arrangements that the Tribunal could undertake the vacuum-filling role as extensively as it did.

Similarly, when the 'provisionality boost' combined with the Hungarian courts' traditionally lesser respect for codified law, as well as with the vulnerability to accusations of illegitimacy of the post-1989 arrangements, it was logical for the HCC to keep stepping outside the textual foundations of the new order. The then Chief Justice reminded us that because of the infirmity of the constitutional framework, he and his colleagues 'decided to build a dogmatic system that was independent of the unstable political arena, and would outlive the present constitution'.[3] The distant perspective of a new constitution led the HCC to use the generous provisions concerning its authority to overcome both the provisionality and the impurity of constitutional arrangements by elaborating upon an invisible meta-constitution, which was to both outlive the present constitution and be superior to any subsequent ones. As much as the Sólyom Court insisted on normal development, it also showed a lack of respect for the constitutional patchwork, and by means of guarding the paradoxical rule-of-law, revolution continued to foster a particular understanding of the change of regime.

The circumstances were radically different in the Czech and Slovak Republics. The Czech and Slovak constitutions did declare the revolutions over and substantively complete. While both Hungary and Poland were still in midst of a constitutional period rather than a constitutional moment of self-definition,[4] and their higher law patchworks were more prone to constructive interpretation than to mere preservation, it was natural for the Czechs and, above all, for the Slovaks, to hang onto the achievement of the new beginning, not the least for symbolic reasons.[5] Since the text was both definite and legitimate,[6] the constitutional reviewers themselves internalised the notion that their role was to protect the framework of achievements rather than to construct positive higher law. Neither the Czech Constitutional Court (CCC) nor the Slovak Constitutional Court (SCC) felt compelled or free to step outside the text on a daily basis, so to speak. Neither court, for instance, enhanced its competence by means of interpretive creativity as extensively as the PCT or the HCC. The bulk of the CCC's and SCC's decision making was a relatively straightforward exercise of comparing a statutory or administrative measure to the constitutional mandate of either the legislature or the executive, that is, reviewing whether the affected law making agency accounted for the explicit limitations of its authority.

The respective courts' responses to a questionnaire circulated at a conference of European constitutional courts offer circumstantial evidence of the differences in their understanding of the proper kind of constitutional interpretation. This is all that the Czech Court offered in response to a question on its role in constitutional development: '[a] stabilising one'.[7] The more loquacious Slovak Court argued that its role was to preserve the integrity of constitutional principles and act as a factor of stability.[8] Both the PCT and the HCC provided much more elaborate accounts. The PCT stated that its case law was to 'elaborate the development of the law according to constitutional principles'.[9] The HCC pointed out that it 'took a rather activist position in both reshaping the legal system and balancing the conflicts of the political powers.'[10] The ensuing review of jurisprudence will offer more immediate displays of constructivist/preservationist tendencies but the terminology is telling—stability and preservation on one side, active elaboration and development on the other.

There are, however, differences not only among, but also within, the provisionality/finality groups. The Hungarian Court, for instance, not only had to worry less than the PCT about its adjudicative equipment and had more elbowroom in adjusting the operational rules to its own liking, but it also had more text to work with. There were fewer lacunae to be filled by means of constitutional interpretation in Hungary than there were in Poland and, accordingly, fewer substantive provisions had to be 'invented'. The Polish Tribunal has often acted as a constitutional emergency unit, that is, has made law mainly in order to provide for those layers of constitutional law that were, for reasons having to do with Polish politics in the transitional period, outside the legislator's reach. The HCC's constructive interpretation, on the other hand, reflected its self-understanding as a monopolist shaper of the country's constitutional law. So while the PCT would construct mostly in response to a lack of rule rather than in conflict with a rule provided, the HCC would not shy away from adjusting an explicit rule to legal dogmatics of its own making. This difference again can be traced to the respective countries' legal traditions. Dzialocha, a former Justice of the PCT, argues that 'to understand *ius* as a binding law let alone as a better law than *lex scripta*... is at odds with the legal consciousness of both the citizens and the state officials implementing law [in Poland] and it also finds no support in the manner in which lawyers have been trained in this country for at least one hundred years'.[11] On the contrary, a Hungarian scholar rejects the invitation to understand *ius* as extending from, and dependent upon, *lex*, and implies a preference for the former.[12]

The kind of interpretive sophistication, imagination, and sense of historical and professional vocation that tended to be dismissive of the text as the supreme interpretive guideline also can be detected in the jurisprudence of the Czech Court, which was to work with a 'real', conceptually permanent constitution. True, the Czech constitution was drafted more hastily than the Slovak one, and was preceded by less intense scholarly deliberation. Since the Czech opposition at the time was numerically and politically stronger than the Slovak one and since without its approval the constitution would not pass, the bargaining was affected by a desperate need to reach a compromise, which was not really the case in Slovakia. In the end, the Czech constitution proved to be much more a final product, as it did not become subject to as thorough and as frequent amendments as the Slovak constitution. And yet, even though less willing than the Polish Tribunal or the HCC to rely on the extra-textual universe as a default interpretive device, the Czech Court would imbue the text with a particular value content and strive to have other agencies observe this content in their decision making. The SCC, on the other hand, found itself bound by a constitution which the legislature regularly disregarded during Mečiar's era and which was declared in need of thorough reconstruction post Mečiar. And yet the Slovak Court tended to take the text at its face value and the furthest it would go would be to interpret it functionally, that is, to approach the relevant constitutional provisions with regard to the overall textual structure.

Both the nature and the intensity of the courts' interpretive creativity and the goals it was meant to serve varied. The PCT, for instance, often employed its technique of qualifying individual rights by abstract clauses in order to support a specific legislative choice. Similarly, the CCC's value-laden constitutionalism did not, at least until very recently, serve to undermine the Parliament's prominence in the policy making process. The Slovak Court was far less creative than either of the two courts and yet almost as much of a counter-majoritarian instrument as was the HCC. These differences suggest that the provisionality/finality of constitutional arrangements was an important, but not the only factor in play. In other words, a court's assertive communication with the legislature did not necessarily translate into constructivist interpretation. And vice versa, the permissive mode of abstract review did not necessarily entail interpretive restraint. Again, then, variations in the courts' self-understanding as institutions and in the justices' legal and moral philosophies accounted for the different jurisprudential outcomes as much as did factors immediately linked to the applicable textual frameworks.

COUNTRY SPECIFICS

Poland

Overview

The lack of a coherent and stable parliamentary majority opened up space for constitutional jurisprudence to play a major role in fixing the gap-ridden texture of Poland's pre-1997 constitutional law. The PCT accepted the invitation. It provided for many of the parts missing from the fabric of interim arrangements, looking for guidance outside the underdeveloped text and subjecting the emerging practices in the realm of constitutional politics to the suprapositive principles it deemed endemic to a *Rechtsstaat*-kind of democracy. Constructing a missing rule if necessary instead of evading hard cases by pointing out the unavailability of textual mandates became a routine practice for the PCT. The very same fragmentation of the transitional arrangements that allowed the Tribunal to get away with infusing suprapositive layers into the legal system simultaneously led it to approach the constitution as an axiological depository of values. This approach translated into some questionable tenets of its *Grundrechtsdogmatik*. The constructivist nature of the PCT's interpretive enterprise thus proved to be a double-edged sword: it would in many instances result in the 'invention' of a right neglected by the written text, and at other times allow for the limitation of that or another right by the Tribunal's extensively charitable understanding of such constitutional generalities as the principle of social justice or public welfare.

Various of the Tribunal's previously noted interpretive 'inventions', including the notion of living law, the right to court, or interpretive sentences were a result of the PCT's efforts to repair the institutional design, especially that concerning the incidental rights-protection scheme. The imperfections of the text proved similarly inviting. Following the change of regime, Poland kept the catalogue of rights set forth by Chapter VIII of its communist constitution and modified it only slightly, just enough to eliminate the most blatant inconsistencies with the modern liberal understanding of rights. Chapter VIII, typically of a socialist regime, focused on social rights and did not include such basics as the right to privacy, the right to judicial redress of grievances, the right to freedom of movement, the right to organise in trade unions, the right to participate in state and municipality administration, the right to information, or the right to citizenship.

The 1997 constitution both gave Poland an extensive catalogue of rights and consolidated the Tribunal's authority to review domestic legislation for conformity to international law. Both features found their way into the jurisprudence and a handful of decisions document the Tribunal's tendency to combine novel substantive provisions on rights with its newly acquired authority to scrutinise domestic law for its conformity to international agreements. Several areas of case law nonetheless suggest continuity rather than change. Some of these areas do not give rise to any reservations, be it the *Rechtsstaat*, the right-to-court or the equal-protection jurisprudence, but some—for example, the relatively recent case law on purgation measures—do. All in all, while the enhancement of the Tribunal's powers does not seem to have cured all its deferential instincts, the enrichment of the available text served to attenuate its constructivist tendencies.

Jurisprudence

The Rechtsstaat clause. Due to the lack of some key constitutional provisions, the PCT was bound either to give up on the availability of certain rights or to construe them as implicit in the text at hand. It went with the latter option and decided to approach the constitution as an axiological depository of values and principles.

Accordingly, the Tribunal held the constitution to consist of norms, principles, and values, most of which it found implicitly contained in the *Rechtsstaat* clause. It also held the very principles it found to be emanating from the *Rechtsstaat* clause to include additional sub-layers anchoring more particular principles all of which could be invoked as sources of law either on their own or in conjunction with other principles. The *Rechtsstaat* clause thus was found to include numerous penumbras giving rise to rights, principles, or values unaccounted for by the text. Its reach was immense, as the Tribunal derived from it a vast range of concepts, including that of non-retroactivity of laws, respect for human dignity, right to life, proportionality in legislative regulation of rights, the right to privacy, citizens' confidence in government, protection of vested rights, or clarity and precision of law.

The *Rechtsstaat* clause also helped constitutional review to free itself from some of the most debilitating *Kompetenz*-constraints. Unable to invoke international human rights treaties as an autonomous source of rights or obligations, the Tribunal used to refer to international instruments in two ways: it would either invoke international law within an interpretive argument, as an additional source of doctrinal support,[13] or refer to the particular international legal norm 'in parallel to the *Rechtsstaat* clause', as a non-autonomous basis of scrutiny, holding that the obligation to abide by international commitments resulted from Article 1 of the constitution.[14]

The constitutional arrangements on the separation of powers were only slightly more elaborate and up-to-date than those concerning human rights. They did not, for instance, explicitly anchor either the very principle of separation of powers or any of its saplings, for example, the notion of checks and balances. The Tribunal none the less located the separation-of-powers principle in the *Rechtsstaat* clause.[15] But the founding enterprise, and within it the quest for leadership by President Wałesa against the legislature and the cabinet, and vice versa, required the Tribunal to provide for more than the constitutional essentials. It therefore regularly engaged in the positional adjustment of law to concrete fact patterns by delineating permissible modes of interaction between the different branches of power. To provide a short demonstration of its daily bread of constructive interpretation, it is worth mentioning that the Tribunal: (i) stipulated repetitively and thoroughly what the principle of judicial independence entailed *vis-à-vis* the executive branch;[16] (ii) dealt with the overlapping competence of the cabinet and the legislature in budgetary matters,[17] and with the Sejm's capacity to interfere with the cabinet's privatisation policy;[18] (iii) defined the position of the Senate in, as well as other elements of, the legislative process;[19] (iv) specified the procedure for presidential ratification of international agreements;[20] (v) interpreted the authority of the cabinet to countersign presidential acts;[21] and (vi) specified the extent of the President's authority to dissolve the legislature in case it should fail to approve the annual budget act.[22]

There are numerous other displays of the PCT's interpretive creativity which indicate its deep engagement in the project of founding. Rather than pointing out each and every one of them, I shall rather note that behind the inference of numerous constitutional principles from the *Rechtsstaat* clause lay their inaccessibility through literalist or originalist interpretation and, simultaneously, their understanding by the Tribunal as indispensable for Poland's evolution into a standard constitutional democracy. The PCT's constructivist constitutional landscaping thus was a way of responding to 'the necessities of Poland's post-communist transition, defining parameters of law-making particularly in areas untouched by constitutional reform'[23] and offering general—or less so—guidelines for the functioning of public authorities pending the adoption of the Constitution of Poland. Rather than merely deciding petitions on their merits, preserving higher-law achievements against the current majority or consolidating the established notions of constitutional government, the Tribunal, even though lacking the power to make law in the traditional sense of the word, did more than simply give normative effect to the existing provisions or apply them in an extensive way. It was inventing—or, put more mildly, unearthing—those tenets of constitutionalism that it believed necessary for the completion of Poland's transition to a democratic *Rechtsstaat*.

Nevertheless, circumstances that force a constitutional court to rely heavily on the extra-textual universe can hardly be deemed entirely favourable. Indeed, the very same context that allowed the Tribunal to identify constitutional norms outside the available text, elaborate a complex constitutional axiology, and, in most cases, even get away with it, led it on some occasions to employ interpretive techniques that in the end served to undermine its achievements in the realm of *Grundrechtsdogmatik*.

Rights qualification. The Tribunal's approach to the constitution not only as a source of enforceable legal provisions, but also—and mostly—as an axiological depository of values and principles reflecting the new ideology had a far-reaching effect on its jurisprudence. As many subjective rights were missing, the Tribunal had to invent them as values or principles and, consequently, apply them as such, that is, as subject to optimisation with other values and principles found to be encompassed, explicitly or implicitly, by the constitution. This corresponds to the dichotomy of subjective rights/objective principles offered by Schlink with respect to the jurisprudence of the German Constitutional Court (GCC).[24] Schlink argues that rights understood as objective principles rather than subjective entitlements 'guarantee the citizen entitlements only in accordance with what is legally and actually possible'.[25] When juxtaposed against other rights or state interests, their mutual balancing under the familiar proportionality/rationality test is required. In short, rights as principles are not trumps; rather, the relative optimum among the different principles is sought.

In looking for interpretive tools that would enable it to approach rights as principles rather than as subjective entitlements, the Tribunal derived from the GCC-made principle of *praktische Konkordanz*, requiring constitutionally protected values to 'be harmonised with one another' and 'preserved in a creative tension'.[26] It also applied the GCC's principle of proportionality, including the *Wesengehalt* doctrine according to which the government may never interfere with the essence of a given right.[27] There is, however, only a short—and barely noticeable—step from balancing rights and interests in order to find their relative optimum to employing interpretive techniques that tend to qualify rights by extra-legal considerations of various kinds and thus relativise their normative content. The PCT took this step often enough to make it a distinct aspect of its jurisprudence.

The lack of certain specific rights provisions naturally led the PCT to rely heavily on the general clauses. But it would assign priority to general clauses over particular rights even when the latter were available either through the text itself or through the emerging jurisprudence. Indeed, the very fact that certain rights-as-principles were invented by the Tribunal rather than explicitly anchored in the text allowed it to attribute to them a lower status in the value hierarchy than to those expressly provided for. The PCT held that since explicitly anchored in the *Rechtsstaat* clause, social justice trumped principles not expressly provided for, for example, protection of vested rights or legal certainty. Social justice, however, was also found to trump the right to property, anchored in the very text of the constitution, as, according to the Tribunal, 'fundamental personal needs' were to be distinguished from other aspects of property, the lack of protection of which was not unconstitutional if social justice justified statutory restrictions.[28] In fact, social justice may allow retroactive interference with vested rights if, for instance, inflation and a change of economic situation warrant such interference.[29] The revindication of property acquired in violation of basic equity is therefore legitimate, as it protects those who were previously deprived of the property rather than those who were unjustly enriched.[30] Further, property rights may be subject to statutory qualifications as long as such qualifications are based on constitutional provisions, especially those protecting the public interest.[31]

The Tribunal's use of the public interest clause would at times be rather peculiar. It held, for instance, that since society was in need of the services provided by the Voluntary Fire Brigades, granting them the license to sell liquor while simultaneously denying the privilege to other private or public corporations did not infringe upon the principle of equality.[32] According to the Tribunal, the Brigades' preferential treatment was a function of their different legal status and should be understood as a relief of public expenses. That may not be the best legal reasoning. More importantly, the tendency to allow for an extensive qualification of rights by reference to extra-legal considerations, whether economic, sociological, or moral, also extended to those relatively few decisions of the PCT that dealt with so-called classical liberties.

Freedom of speech was among the constitutional rights victimised by their optimisation as principles. In its first review of the Radio and TV Broadcasting Act of 1992 (RTBA), the PCT disregarded constitutional provisions allowing for preventive control of speech and argued for the prohibition of any *ex ante* control of the content of speech.[33] In the meantime, however, it also stated that the freedom of speech was not absolute and had to be weighed against other rights and interests.[34] That, in and of itself, is hardly a cause for concern. What this approach entailed, however, was quite different from what one would expect, and it was in the series of freedom-of-speech decisions that the Tribunal fully relied on the concept of public interest as a universal tool for qualifying fundamental rights and liberties.

First, the PCT, relying on the explicit constitutional directive mandating harmonisation of freedom of speech and informational freedom with the protection of the community,[35] held constitutional those provisions of the RTBA that ordered public radio and TV stations to respect in their programmes Christian values corresponding to universal ethical values.[36] The Tribunal explicitly acknowledged its understanding of the freedom of speech as an objective principle when it pointed out that the issue at hand concerned 'an open and pluralistic radio and TV broadcasting system as a general fundamental principle',[37] which had to be interpreted not only under the issue-specific provisions, but also in concordance with the general clauses providing for the protection of public morality and public interest.[38] As a principle and a value, freedom of speech was to be balanced against other principles and values, which in this context were the freedom of conscience and the freedom of religion of those viewers whose religious sentiments could be offended were Christian values neglected in the broadcasting.

The Tribunal later upheld the constitutional validity of the RTBA also in its application to private broadcasters. It repeated that freedom of speech, even though a constitutional value, was not of an absolute nature,[39] and 'as a constitutional value could namely be realised in different ways and by different means'.[40] The PCT again invoked the public-wealth clause as justifying restrictions imposed upon a broadcasting that could offend the morality and well being of the community. In addition, it found the RTBA to protect only those Christian values that corresponded to the universal ethical foundations of 'Mediterranean culture'—these values therefore could not be mistaken for religion.[41]

The Tribunal approached rights as values to be balanced against each other also when it dealt with the delicate issue of separation of church and state. In the ruling on the Ministry of Education instructions allowing for religious education in public schools, the PCT stated that the principle of a lay and neutral state had to 'signify the possibility of cooperation in domains serving common interest and humans' personal development. The ethical education of the young is undoubtedly one such domain.'[42] Accordingly, religious education in public schools conforms to the constitution as long as it is voluntary, carried out under programmes autonomously drafted by the respective religious organisations, and performed by catechists appointed by these organisations. Relying on the assumption that the religious instructors' performance of educational functions served a common interest, the PCT also found that for these instructors to be remunerated by the government did not violate the prohibition of granting public subsidies to religious organisations.[43] The PCT also validated as constitutional the instructions allowing for both the display of crosses and the recital of prayers in public schools, again understanding the freedom of religion as a principle that gives the citizen the possibility to participate as much as to abstain from participation in religious ceremonies.[44]

The tendency to balance rights against some broadly conceptualised principles reached its peak in the 1997 decision on the abortion law.[45] In disallowing abortion for reasons of 'difficult living conditions' or a 'difficult personal situation', the PCT found it unnecessary to treat a foetus as a bearer of the right to life. It held instead that since life was a constitutionally protected value, it had to be protected as such against other values, for example, a woman's right to self-determination. 'In order to evaluate the constitutionality of rules allowing for abortion it is necessary to employ a method of harmonising the goods and values in conflict.'[46] The legislator must respect 'the necessity of taking into account proportionality in solving such conflicts'.[47] Understandably, then, 'it is necessary for the legislator—because of a conflict of goods representing constitutional values, rights, or freedoms—to sacrifice one such conflicting good'.[48] Moreover, to allow abortion for reasons of personal difficulty would undermine the constitutional values of human dignity and the protection of maternity and family.[49]

The above sketch does not aim to cover the entire scope and all the particular aspects of the employment by the PCT of the proportionality principle. It selects certain decisions to illustrate the PCT's efforts to compensate for the deficiencies in the law in books by taking the constitution to be a treasury of values. These efforts impacted both the mode and the content of the rights discourse. While the mode was one of approaching rights as principles and values, the content suggested that that particular technique made rights prone to relativisation not only by other rights, but also by non-rights provisions.

What the sketch also illustrates is the inadequacy of singling out individual factors in explaining this or another trait of constitutional jurisprudence. The PCT's tendency to allow for an extensive statutory qualification of rights offers, for instance, telling hindsight into its self-understanding *vis-à-vis* the legislature, and suggests that interpretive constructivism does not necessarily entail the interpreter's assertiveness against competing institutions. An equally important variable lending support to qualification of rights by other values and principles of constitutional stature is to be found in the design, that is, the domination by abstract review of the PCT's rights protective instrumentarium. It is especially in a scheme that confines a constitutional court to the scrutiny of the fit of a norm with the *Grundrechtsdogmatik* rather than of the effect it might have on a particular individual that a claimant is expected to act as a trustee of the public good. In any such system, convalidation of the entire body of constitutional values and principles is preferred to satisfaction of an individual entitlement, and the emphasis lies on potential as opposed to immediate infringements of rights. It is, after all, the scrutiny of public policy choices that allows a court to concern itself with an unidentified mass of 'Mediterranean culture'-oriented citizens.

A brief glimpse at the modern constitutional history of Poland suggests, however, that tradition was as instrumental as the more immediate institutional and textual factors in inducing the Tribunal to subject rights to a multi-layered qualification enterprise. What should be noted here, with apologies, is that it does not seem to be a concept alien to the Polish public psyche that the fate of the polity is at times, if not often, to be deemed worthier than individual interests. That certainly is not a unique position,[50] but it seems of particular relevance to Poland. Building on the traumatic experience with the *liberum veto*—suggesting that unlimited protection of rights may lead to chaos, anarchy, and eventually the very dissolution of the state—the internalisation by Poles of the concept of rights qualification caught a strong hold in their twentieth-century constitution-making endeavours. The juxtaposition of rights and citizens' duties and loyalty to the state found its way to impacting every constitution that Poland has adopted in the twentieth century.[51] Osiatynski points out that 'Poles perceive duties as the conditions of rights; the only concession to a liberal interpretation of rights is an occasional admission that an individual has rights in relation to the state, and duties in relation to the society'.[52]

Despite all the rights talk and revival of natural law, the context of Poland's post-communist transition was an unlikely candidate to eliminate the traditional tendency to qualify individual interests by those of the polity. As Los points out, 'a careful reading of Solidarity documents... reveals that rights celebrated by this ideology were understood as community rights, or, more fundamentally, the right of the Polish nation to recover its true nature'.[53] These documents advocate a system in which 'rights and duties are determined by a functional division of labour within a community which strives to reach its organic form'[54] and in which 'there would be no opposing sides', as it becomes 'a community linked by bonds of organic unity.'[55] It is a fairly common understanding in modern Poland—informed by multi-layered historical experience—that law should be read as an instrument of social cohesion rather than as a weapon to be used by individuals against each other or the government. Adhering fully to the traditional communitarian understanding of rights, the PCT became enmeshed in, rather than imposed itself upon, these layers of local legal consciousness.

When common-interest considerations trump individual rights, the community, and not the individual, receives prime constitutional protection. In the United States, this takes place more seldom than many would like to see. Mary Ann Glendon's take on the absolutisation of rights in the country's constitutional discourse epitomises these concerns:

> Our rights talk, in its absoluteness, promotes unrealistic expectations, heightens social conflict, and inhibits dialogue that might lead toward consensus, accommodation, or at least the discovery of common ground. In its silence concerning responsibilities, it seems to condone acceptance of the benefits of living in a democratic social welfare state, without accepting the corresponding personal and civic obligations. In its relentless individualism, it fosters a climate that is inhospitable to society's losers, and that systemically disadvantages caretakers and dependents, young and old.[56]

None of this could really give rise to complaint in Poland, as the PCT clearly rejected what Holmes depicted as 'negative constitutionalism',[57] that is, an obsession with the protection of individual rights against the tyranny of the government. Quite the contrary, by reinforcing the communitarian as opposed to the proto-liberal individualistic approach to the protection of rights, and by subscribing in principle to the secular translations of various doctrinal positions of the Catholic Church, the Tribunal often rode on the wave of mainstream legal and social consciousness instead of swimming against it on behalf of the minority.

Although preference for the protection of the community is an *a priori* value judgment incontestable by dogmatic legal analysis, some worrying consequences may attend a search for common ground in the realm of constitutional adjudication. The short step from optimising rights among themselves to their qualification by non-rights considerations represents a serious conceptual difference: rather than juxtaposing rights as values of equal worth,[58] values susceptible to ideological colouring are added to the equation. This often makes the balancing rather unbalanced. It is also open to question how 'common' was in fact the understanding that led the Tribunal to read into the constitution the need to protect the universal ethical foundations of the Mediterranean culture, or the significance of religious education for Polish youth's healthy development.

It is precisely during transitional times that the Glendonian search for consensus may reinforce community-protective elements more vigorously than might actually be needed or appropriate. As long as the basics of the polity's course of development are not entrenched and the public discourse revolves around the grand themes of *orientatio*, it takes a lot of courage from any court--let alone one with limited competence—to direct the authorities' attention to the seemingly less important grievances of Mr or Ms Kowalski. The emphasis laid on rebuilding the nation or the community then translates into a correspondingly weaker status for rights as subjective entitlements, and portrays as perfectly legitimate the qualification of constituents' rights by concepts as prone to abuse as is common interest or basic fairness. And even if the plight of an ordinary citizen makes it from the bottom of the agenda to a less marginal position, it is still seen--and perhaps rightly so--as asking for more instead of less intervention by the state, and only adding to the government's duty to govern rather than the individual's right to be let alone.

Social rights revisited. In many ways, it was the immediate unavailability of black-letter law that forced the Tribunal to confront the extra-textual universe. In some other ways, the text itself proved to be a source of difficulty. The fabric of Chapter VIII, which transplanted the socialist concept of rights into the post-socialist era, naturally left a considerable imprint on the PCT's jurisprudence. It was largely, but not only, due to the domination by social rights of Poland's human rights-related texts that the Tribunal's case law revolved around issues of welfare policy, while its jurisprudence on so-called classical rights and liberties remained relatively less developed. In each and every one of his annual reports on the PCT's case law preceding the adoption of the 1997 Constitution, Garlicki was bound to note that both the public and the PCT attributed less prominence to classical rights and liberties than they did to social and economic ones.[59]

Nevertheless, as much as one could hardly blame only the lack of text for the Tribunal's obsession with a particular version of public morality and its tolerance of extensive qualification of rights, so, too, could one hardly blame only the text for the prominence in Poland's constitutional discourse of social rights. After all, social rights were a dominant theme also outside the realm of constitutional review. Most applications to the PSAC and the ombudsman, for instance, dealt with issues such as welfare allowances, housing, or labour disputes. One can therefore understand the pervasiveness of social rights in Poland's public discourse either as an indication of the legacy of citizens' reliance on government-provided welfare, or as a display of the degree of identification by the Polish public of democracy with social values,[60] or as a combination of the two. Either way, social consciousness accounted for the PCT's preoccupation with welfare rights as much as did the constitutional text itself.

The transplantation of the vast and inflexible social safety net into the new era is often deemed an easy case for the communist-legacy argument.

But there is more to it. True, 'the prior institutional framework has guided the rules of the new political game, helping to determine the interests, ideas, and goals of individual actors on questions of social policy'.[61] To conceptualise social rights as central in constitutional law, however, also reflected the traditional understanding of the individual–community relationship in Poland. In terms of axiology, one should not overstate the impact of normative theories of communism on the doctrinal underpinnings of the rights talk in Poland. One should rather note the Poles' traditional commitment to Catholicism, including its social teaching, as well as the ethos fostered by Solidarity as the secular counterpart of the Church. In a way, it indeed was the failure to modify Chapter VIII of the communist constitution, rather than a deliberate decision to include social rights in the new order, that reinforced their centrality in constitutional adjudication. The emphasis on welfare rights, however, is far from being a rare occurrence in Poland's legal history, as it can be detected in the extensive social legislation preceding the adoption of the March Constitution in 1921, as well as in the March Constitution itself. The only instance in Polish legal history in the twentieth century of leaving social and economic rights outside constitutional delineation was the negatively assessed and short-lived April Constitution of 1935, which injected authoritarian elements into Poland's framework of government and adversely affected the status of rights in general.

It is well established in Western Europe—and less so in the United States[62]—that, in light of the current level of governments' involvement in their constituents' lives, limiting rights and liberties to the so-called negative ones offers insufficient protection. Schlink summarises the postwar development in a dramatic way:

> Fundamental rights no longer protect specific freedoms of citizens against specific government intrusions, as the traditional view expected; they now protect the citizen in his entire existence against an omnipotent and omnipresent state... Everything that a citizen may demand or must accept from another citizen, he demands or accepts due to government authorisation. In the same way, all of a citizen's actions are relevant to his free development; all such actions are capable of, and in need of, protection as fundamental rights. In this world, where all spheres of freedom are fundamentally protected spheres and all limitations of spheres of freedom are state-sanctioned limitations, every problem of social life is essentially a problem of fundamental rights.[63]

The omnipresence of government was all the more relevant in Poland, a country transiting from socialism and looking for a strong hand to instil order into chaos. Such a context necessarily created a tension between the professed willingness of the new establishment to reduce the role of the state and the need to keep government protection in place to undo the most blatant failures of local versions of *laissez-faire* capitalism. On the one hand, Poland—like every other country in the region—was unavoidably heading for severe social and economic stratification, and if economic reform was to proceed, considerable material inequality was to be expected. On the other hand, a significant part of the ideal of communal relations in Poland was based on what Kedzia labels the 'arithmetic dimension of equality'.[64] To proceed with transformation in its pure free-market version, or to do so without an adjustment period, might have fitted the elite's preferences but was certainly at odds with public expectations. The tradition of holding the community responsible for an individual's well-being made it risky for the government to merely watch and let happen the rise of the *nouveau riche*, taking place at the expense of the less 'competent'. To ignore the cognitive and ideological undercurrents of social development either in the realm of institutional reform or in constitutional jurisprudence, for example, to refuse to qualify the free-market paradigm by communally internalised notions of the government's role in making one's life bearable, would therefore work against both the tradition and the transitional context. Kramer argues that it is mainly the relatively generous social safety net that serves to explain 'why calm has generally prevailed in East-Central Europe at a time when many observers feared that violent disturbances would erupt'.[65] Although certain layers of social entitlements did prove illusory under the new circumstances, it was vital to include them in the message communicated by the establishment to society at large. The immediate elimination of social rights from the centre of rights-discourse fora, including courts in general and constitutional adjudication in particular, would attack habits that have been developing for almost a century and that have evolved from mere habits into an element of one's *Weltanschauung*.

Contrary to the claims of some reputed American scholars,[66] it therefore would be the immediate renunciation of welfare rights—serving expressive as much as normative functions—rather than their gradual acculturation by the free-market paradigm that might have threatened the reform process by stripping it of public support. After all, the Tribunal did take into account the economic costs of constitutional protection of second-generation rights and proved flexible in manipulating their normative implications. Unlike in the realm of classical rights where the Tribunal supplemented the available text with rights derived from the

Rechtsstaat and equal-protection clauses, the welfare-related constitutional regulations it approached 'with considerable reluctance'.[67] Indeed, its handling of the social rights catalogue—not least in comparison with the more generous HCC—-deserves the label 'fiscally responsible'.

Continuity and change. After the new constitution was adopted, the Tribunal opted for continuity with its pre-1997 case law, especially with respect to the understanding of the *Rechtsstaat* clause which was transported to the 1997 constitution without any change. Therefore, 'where the systemic and functional context did not experience substantial modification, the new constitutional provisions conserved their old meaning'.[68] In addition, because of the halfway reform of institutional design in the realm of incidental protection of rights, it is abstract review that continues to feed the PCT's adjudication. Constitutional adjudication therefore continues to shape local legal topography in general terms, often deriving from the basic tenets of transitional jurisprudence.[69] The Tribunal continues, for instance, to understand the constitution as 'a firm objective system of values... the central role in which belongs to natural and inviolable human dignity'.[70] Therefore, even if some foundational principles 'are not explicitly anchored in the constitution's written text, they immanently derive from its axiology or the essence of a democratic state ruled by law'.[71]

Nevertheless, the availability of textual novelties did bring some new elements into constitutional jurisprudence. The Tribunal observed, for instance, that the preamble to the 1997 constitution anchored some new values, such as liberty, justice, cooperation, and dialogue. These values are to serve as evaluative criteria for any action by the government, including the legislature, in parallel to the basic orientational guidelines emanating from the *Rechtsstaat* clause. Since the PCT is now able to ground its findings in specific provisions regulating rights, it tends to make less use of the *Rechtsstaat* clause. Accordingly,

> in case a normative act is challenged, it is primarily specific provisions that must be invoked as reference norms. In such situations, there is no need to invoke the principle of a democratic state as a distinct reference norm. This principle thus serves mostly the function of an interpretive guideline.[72]

The Tribunal's willingness not to seek refuge in the *Rechtsstaat* clause unless necessary surfaced almost immediately after the new constitution and the PACT came into force, suggesting that interpretive constructivism was mostly a function of the unavailability of specific provisions. Holding unconstitutional the requirement that doctors indicate a reference number on certificates sent to the patient's employer and the social insurance authority—by which reference numbers it was possible to identify the patient's medical condition—the Tribunal stated:

> The Constitution..., unlike the previous constitution, directly refers to the right to privacy by declaring in Article 47 that everyone shall have the right to legal protection of his private and family life, and of his honour and good reputation, and the right to make decisions about his personal life. The Constitution has also introduced, in Article 51, a new category: the individual right to personal data protection, which covers, inter alia, the legal conditions under which individuals may disclose information concerning themselves, the refusal to allow public authorities to acquire, collect or make accessible information on citizens other than that which is necessary in a democratic state ruled by law.[73]

Clearly, it was difficult for the PCT to conceal the joy with which it found that 'in the present state of affairs, there is no need to add to a very broad catalogue of individual rights and freedoms, covering the categories dealt with in Articles 47 and 51, by means of referring to the [*Rechtsstaat*] clause'.[74]

Also, as the new constitution, and the ideology behind it, became less open to second-generation rights than the pre-1997 text and context, and a full-scale catalogue of rights and liberties came into force, the Tribunal's focal point of attention was diverted from social rights. Accordingly, in 1998 for the first time ever it issued more decisions on civic and political rights than on social ones, a tendency that continues to bear on its jurisprudence. Garlicki points out that it is now less welfare rights and more the right to property that the Tribunal tends to deal with frequently and extensively.[75] Nonetheless, the PCT does derive from those jurisprudential concepts and relies on those interpretive techniques that it established previously. Accordingly, the right to property is not of an absolute nature,[76] the rights' constitutional protection against statutory qualification extends only to their *contenu essentiel*, and 'stricter standards apply to the regulation of personal and political rights than of economic and social rights'.[77]

Even though the new constitution opened up for the PCT interpretive possibilities that were previously out of its reach, the text is only a part of the overall background informing constitutional jurisprudence and, in and of itself, remains incapable of overcoming the effect of other equally important variables. It appears, for instance, that both the traditional local conceptualisation of public governance and the justices' moral instincts continue to induce the Tribunal to employ its interpretive creativity to sustain rather than to undermine the dominant paradigms reflective of the specifics of the local legal and social consciousness, and thus legitimise even those normative concepts that are arguably in deviation from Western standards in that or another area of constitutional law. The post-1997 rulings on purgation measures or social entitlements of former party cadres are examples of this kind.

It is none the less thanks largely to the Tribunal's interpretive creativity in the interim era that nowadays Poland operates as a standard democratic state, and that some basic tenets of liberal democratic constitutionalism appear to be sufficiently entrenched in the country's legal discourse. As the 1997 reform did away with the provisionality constraint, and as complex and explicit constitutional and statutory provisions now regulate the PCT's operation, overt constructivism becomes a less feasible option of reacting to the operative framework. The Tribunal seems both aware of, and content with, this development.

Hungary

Overview

The series of constitutional amendments following the change of regime equipped Hungary with a workable framework of constitutional law and gave it, among other things, an elaborate catalogue of rights. The Hungarian constitution also allows for extensive implementation of international law in the realm of both ordinary and constitutional adjudication. The Court therefore had fewer immediate reasons than did the PCT to reach outside the available text; The HCC's *Rechtsstaat* jurisprudence, for instance, is more modest in extent than the Polish one. Nonetheless, the HCC's insistence on having exclusive prerogatives to explain the constitution was in no way conducive to interpretive self-restraint. Indeed, the Court not only developed a sophisticated hierarchy of rights different from the one suggested by the available text, but also did not shy away from occasionally adjusting the text of the constitution to a 'supra-constitutional' constitution based on the Court's system of legal dogmatics. Its interpretive creativity therefore was not so much a function of the lack of text as of the lack of authority that the available text had for the Court.

It is customary for constitutional courts to rely in their interpretive endeavours on tools other than the mere 'letter of the law'. The HCC, too, did not hesitate to open for itself the door to a body of a-textualities, with

Capital Punishment being a hallmark of this tendency. The Court, however, did not restrict itself to approaching the extra-textual universe as a subsidiary referential source for interpretation, but would occasionally prefer it to the available text. From its conception, the HCC embarked on a mission of perfecting both the legislation and the constitution by means of rational legal analysis, flavoured by what Sólyom dubs 'internationalism'.

Jurisprudence

Invisible constitution. To have the letter of the law, especially that of the constitution, made subordinate to, and substituted with, doctrinal concepts put into effect by a body comprised of a few lawyers might be the worst nightmare of a constitutional originalist. But for the HCC, even the constitutional text was tainted with the impurity of political will, and therefore did not possess attributes that would make it a reliable basis for Hungary's rise to exemplary modernity. It was profane, not sacred; accordingly, it was for the invisible constitution of purely rational dogmatic origin to take its place. Simply, the HCC-built 'dogmatic system... independent of the unstable political arena [was to] outlive the present constitution'.[78] Over time, the HCC has introduced various self-made notions, including the 'invisible constitution' itself,[79] the primacy of legal certainty over substantive justice,[80] constitutional criminal law,[81] and the 'novation' of property claims.

The uniqueness of the HCC's interpretive constructivism, however, does not lie in its approach to what had to be inferred because of immediate inaccessibility, but in its handling of the existing text. When a particular textual arrangement would not correspond to the supra-political world of legal dogmatics, the Court would often substitute it with a rule that was theretofore invisible but that it felt compelled to visualise for the benefit of the rule of 'law'. The making by the Court of a hierarchy of rights parallel to the one suggested by the constitution is a prime example of this tendency, but many other are available. When the qualified-majority (two-thirds of the quorum) rule for the adoption of laws related to certain enumerated rights lost its appeal for the Court, it was severely circumscribed and made virtually obsolete. The HCC concluded that to understand the two-thirds rule to be applicable to all aspects of a given right would be at odds with 'the function of the qualified majority', and invoked 'the substance of parliamentarism', 'the functioning ability of the parliamentary system', and the fact that the rule was 'incidental' as a trump of the constitutional text.[82] In a similar vein, the Court disregarded provisions allowing for preliminary review of draft legislation by labelling them as contrary to the status of constitutional review in a system characterised by separation of powers. In a much less restraining mode, it created for itself the power to review draft legislation for its conformity to international agreements.[83] Similarly, while the HACC confines the assessment of the constitutionality of treaties to those pending ratification, the Court extended its competence to treaties transformed into domestic law by the respective Act of Parliament.[84] The HCC also invented the idea of 'indirect and remote relations' in order to ease the limitations on the legislator's policy-making capacity of the constitutional requirement that any regulation of basic rights and duties had to be of statutory rank.[85] Although the constitutional text does not subject this requirement to any qualifications, to take it at face value would, in Sólyom's words be 'ridiculous'.[86]

The Hungarian Court's constructivism apparently was of a different kind than that of the Polish Tribunal. Rather than reaching outside the text to provide for a missing guideline, as the PCT would do, the HCC simply took the invisible constitution to be an inexhaustible toolbox from which invisible, but ready-for-use rules could be picked as needed to repair the text. The tendency to fix the text rather than merely to supplement it suggests, again, the Court's moving away from the implementation of law to its making.

Hierarchisation of rights. The HCC's interpretive constructivism was most notably on display in the elaboration of a complex hierarchy of rights. While the text does not contain a clear differentiation between rights, it does suggest two kinds of hierarchy: (i) there is a group of rights that are non-derogatable, that is, that may not be curtailed even during a state of emergency;[87] (ii) a higher threshold is required for the adoption of implementing legislation in enumerated cases.[88] The two groups of rights do not overlap, with three exceptions: freedom of religion, the rights of national and ethnic minorities, and the right to citizenship. According to the Court, however, this differentiation does not warrant special treatment for the respective rights as it 'does not establish a theoretically based hierarchy among rights' and reflects only 'their political importance'.[89] Political importance apparently is not enough in an interpretive universe where legal dogmatics are taken to trump the *volonté générale*.

The preference for a theory-based hierarchy of rights over the one reflecting their political importance perfectly echoes the traditional layers of the Hungarian variety of judicial interpretation. It is mechanical application of the legislature's will and the rule-dogmatism that Varga, speaking for many, deems the most debilitating deficiencies of socialist law, waiting to be undone by legal professionals.[90] After the revolution, the order of the day for Hungarian jurists was to restore the prestige of jurisprudence by aiding its emancipation from a mechanical implementation of the letter of the law into an autonomous instrument of social change. Varga also points out that in Hungary 'precedents (gained through deductive—inductive reasoning by the method of distinguishing) have been produced by judicial practice so that the actual message of the law be revealed'.[91] This certainly is not unique, but in combination with suspicion of the text as a product of political bargaining it helps to understand why in Hungary—as opposed to Poland or, for that matter, most civil law countries—the courts often deem the legislative text an imperfect source of law. This suspicion has not only informed a large part of the Court's jurisprudence, but a striking example of it also can be found in Hungarian scholarship, as Varga laments those theoretical approaches that tend to deduce *ius* from *lex*.[92]

Quite expectedly, then, the Court insisted on its freedom to elaborate the theoretical basis of the Constitution and on the superiority of this basis to the written law. Consequently, it proved much stricter than other courts in the region in understanding the legislature as encompassing reason in addition to will. As much as the Court approached the legislature as a repository of politically representative will, it still was will only and as such was subject to the scrutiny of reason possessed by the wise men on the bench. Accordingly, the HCC decided that it was not going to be 'bound by the constitutional practice of other state organs',[93] refusing to 'say that it is possible to fill any gaps in the constitution by the practice of the state organs concerned, i.e. by political bargains'.[94]

Therefore, when faced with a lack of referential sources, traditions, and routines of institutional interaction to derive from the HCC tended to resort to legal theory and philosophy. True, *dottrine* plays an important role in any legal system.[95] Yet it seems to receive special attention in Hungary. When faced with the lack of referential sources for interpretation, the former Chief Justice would not complain of the lack of established cognitions and practices in the application by public authorities of constitutional provisions, but of the lack of domestic theoretical sources, scholarly commentaries, and textbooks.[96] The local tradition again helped to fuel this tendency. I already pointed out the permeability of law, in fact its convergence with academic elaboration in both medieval and modern Hungary.[97] And Varga approvingly notes the role that 'law and its academic backing' played in modernising and Europeanising the nineteenth-century Hungarian polity.[98] The centripetal force of the legal academe proved so important that it made Budapest, the prime haven of the country's 'intellectual workshops', the de facto seat of the Court, contrary to the statutory provision locating the seat in the provincial city of Esztergom. The preference for theoreticians has also shown itself in the selection of justices.[99]

Either way, the HCC produced a rights-ladder of its own making. At the top was the value of personal autonomy, reflected through the right to human dignity, and followed by different communicative rights as off-spring of the freedom of expression.

What the human dignity clause did for the HCC was in a way similar to what the *Rechtsstaat* clause did for the PCT, that is, operate as a fountain of unenumerated rights and as the supreme orientational principle. Human dignity was first applied in a case dealing with the trade unions' capacity to act on behalf of employees without their express consent. Holding this arrangement unconstitutional, the HCC presented human dignity as the source of a general personality right, a 'mother right', i.e., a subsidiary fundamental right which may be relied upon at any time by both the Constitutional Court and other courts for the protection of an individual's autonomy when none of the concrete, named fundamental rights is applicable for a particular set of facts'.[100] As such, human dignity also includes 'the right to free personal development, to self-determination, to privacy or general freedom of action'.[101]

This was only the first indication of how prominent the principle of human dignity was going to become in the Court's jurisprudence, and the supremacy of human dignity within the catalogue of rights was soon to be reaffirmed in *Capital Punishment* and *Abortion*. In the former, the HCC emphasised that human life and human dignity formed an inseparable unity and had greater value than anything else. In concurring opinions, a person's life and dignity were found to be beyond the reach of law, superior to any legal values, and entitled to the fullest possible legal protection. The Court stuck to the strong version of human dignity also in *Abortion* in which it defined human dignity as 'a quality coterminous with human existence, a quality which is indivisible and cannot be limited, hence appertaining equally to every human being'.[102] Human dignity, however, was held omnipotent only when linked to the right to life, and in later decisions its supremacy was slightly qualified. In the case concerning paternity disputes, for instance, the Court held that it was only in conjunction with the right to life that human dignity was inviolable, and that, understood as a general personality right, it could be subject to restrictions to the same extent as other fundamental rights.[103]

The human dignity case law also served the establishment of the overall interpretive framework. In his concurring opinion in *Capital Punishment*, Sólyom not only joined with the majority's argument that life and dignity were theoretically and naturally illimitable, he also outlined the role of the Court in interpreting rights as such:

> [T]he interpretation of the Constitution shall be based in the concept of rights to be interpreted as neutral categories, the limits of which may be established with a high degree of consensus, while their content may be filled with many different value concepts... The Constitutional Court has to intervene in borderline cases to draw the line beyond which a given concept about the content of a right ('answer') may not be brought into harmony with the whole system (basic principles) of the Constitution... The Constitutional Court may establish that a given concept about the content of a constitutional right fits into the conceptual framework of the Constitution even though the legislature wished to exclude it... Of course, it is a value judgment. This is, however, the very thing for which the Constitutional Court has authorisation: to enforce its own concept on the content in order to maintain the Constitution.[104]

And that is indeed the very thing that the Court would do.

Gradually, the HCC found the human dignity clause to include several penumbras of different normative implications, and applied it in some rather unusual contexts, suggesting again a parallel with the PCT's employment of the *Rechtsstaat* clause across the subject matter of constitutional law. In the case concerning the discretionary authority of the Chief Justice of the Supreme Court and the Attorney General to challenge a final court ruling,[105] as well as in the case concerning the latter's authority to intervene in civil proceedings in the name of protection of government interests or important social interests,[106] the HCC found those powers to be in violation of the constitutional right to self-determination and thus of human dignity. Over time, the Court has extended the scope of application of the different aspects of human dignity to include: (i) freedom of conscience, (ii) the right to marry (holding unconstitutional the requirement that members of armed forces be obliged to obtain approval from their commander),[107] (iii) the right to know, ascertain, or discover one's genetic origins,[108] (iv) the right to pursue higher education without unduly restrictive qualifications (holding unconstitutional the exclusion from higher education of those who were prohibited from participating in public affairs),[109] (v) the right to form a legally sanctioned partnership between persons of the same sex,[110] (vi) the right to protection of good reputation,[111] (vii) the right of athletes to compete and change employers,[112] (viii) the principle of self-determination with regard to membership of professional organisations,[113] (ix) the right to consent to medical services or refuse specific kinds of medical treatment of persons with limited legal capacity,[114] and a good number of other cases.

Freedom of expression is another right with a 'special place among the constitutional fundamental rights... amounting to the "mother right" of different types of... the so-called "communicative" fundamental rights'.[115] According to the Court, the special importance of the freedom of expression requires that, in cases of conflict, other rights balanced against it—with the exception of human dignity, as 'human dignity may restrict the freedom of expression'[116]—must be interpreted narrowly.[117] In the HCC's view, communicative rights originating in the freedom of expression include freedom of speech and freedom of the press—the latter encompassing the freedom of all media, as well as the freedom of information—freedom to distribute and disseminate works of art, freedom of scientific research and teaching. They are also linked to the freedom of religion and conscience, and the right of assembly. As these specific rights are expressly provided for by the constitution, they could all stand on their own as sources of individuals' entitlements but given their common origin, that is, the sacrosanct freedom of expression, they have to be attended to by the legislature with particular sensitivity. Nonetheless, some hierarchy emerged among these rights as well, and it was free speech that received VIP treatment from the Court in *Incitement* and the case concerning denigration of public officials.[118] In yet another decision, however, the HCC held that because of the scarcity of technical resources the kind of freedom of expression that is serviced through radio and TV broadcasting might be subject to some issue-specific constraints.[119]

A special status was accorded to criminal law guarantees which were 'as a rule absolute in the eyes of the Constitutional Court'[120] and against which no other right or constitutional goal could be balanced. In their delineation, the HCC again 'helped' the text, as it derived several tenets of 'constitutional criminal law' from the rule-of-law and human-dignity clauses, including the principle of subjective responsibility or the right to be free from prosecution, rooted in a particular understanding of the statute of limitations.

Proportionality. The hierarchisation of rights served to attribute different normative weight to specific rights and thus provide guidelines for their mutual balancing on the vertical axis. The balancing of rights by means of their vertical hierarchisation, however, was a perfectly dependable interpretive tool only in the case of a conflict between rights of a clearly different rank in the Court's ladder. It was the principle of proportionality that was to take care of the rest.

Despite their common Karlsruhe roots, however, the HCC's approach to the proportionality principle was rather different from that of the PCT or the CCC, in that it was much less legislature-friendly. Parallel to its lesser support for the notion of transitional specifics, the HCC was also reluctant to allow for statutory restrictions on rights on the basis of references to public interest or basic fairness.

On the one hand, the HCC conceded that no rights except for the right to life were of an absolute nature, and joined the PCT in employing the GCC-made concept of balancing rights as principles and constituents of a complex constitutional fabric. Accordingly, 'the state examines the values attached to a specific fundamental right in relation to other fundamental rights, and the protection of fundamental rights is embedded in the state's protection and maintenance of the constitutional order as a whole'.[121] Also, 'the state frames laws and regulations limiting the ability to exercise individual basic rights in a manner which is cognisant of the constitutional goals and comports with the exercise of other basic rights; it promotes the fullest satisfaction of individual rights attainable from the perspective of the overall order, thereby promoting the consonance of these basic rights'.[122]

Over the years, the Court also eased the rigorous test for the permissibility of statutory restrictions of rights. The proportionality test, requiring that a legislative constraint of a given right must be both necessary for the protection of another fundamental right and a measure of the least possible intrusion, was first used by Chief Justice Sólyom in a concurring opinion[123] and later fully adhered to by the majority in subsequent decisions.[124] However, without renouncing the very basis of its proportionality doctrine, the HCC gradually stepped back from these stringent criteria. It first extended the permission for statutory limitations of rights from the protection of rights to the protection of constitutional objectives, and later even to any rational legislative purpose, as long as the given measure was both rational and necessary. In *Incitement*, the Court stated:

> [I]t is not enough for the constitutionality of the restriction of a fundamental right that it occurs in order to protect some other fundamental right or freedom, or other constitutional goal, but it is also necessary that the restriction meets the requirement of proportionality: the importance of the desired goal and the violation of the fundamental right inflicted for that purpose must be in balance.[125]

On the other hand, the Hungarian Court carefully avoided referring to the constitution as a system of values,[126] and in consequence proved stricter than the PCT in scrutinising how much weight was to be attributed to non-rights values. Accordingly, it allowed the Parliament less discretion in favouring very general and very intangible principles over particular rights, and was less willing than was the PCT to let the legislature get away with public-order or public-morality justifications of constraining via statutory measures the enjoyment of rights. According to the Court, '"public interest" in and of itself is insufficient grounds to limit a fundamental right... save where the Constitution explicitly allows this, as in the case of expropriation'.[127] In *Incitement*, it struck down as unconstitutional the clause permitting criminal prosecution of those who use offensive or denigrating expressions against the Hungarian nation, or any other nationality, people, creed, or race in front of a large public gathering. The Court argued that limiting the freedom of speech in order to provide for 'an abstract protection of the public order and peace as an end in themselves'[128] was an insufficient justification. It also stressed:

> Laws restricting the freedom of expression are to be assigned greater weight if they directly serve the realisation or protection of another individual fundamental right, less weight if they protect such rights only indirectly through the mediation of an institution, and the least weight if they merely serve some abstract value as an end in itself (public peace, for instance).[129]

In late 1999, however, the new Court qualified this notion by holding that protecting public order in those of its aspects that have to do with the community's dignity may justify legislative restrictions of freedom of speech.[130]

Progressivism. The single most important motivation behind its interpretive creativity was the HCC's wish to assert its leadership role in the process of Hungary's Europeanisation through an insistent instilling into the country's constitutional order of progressive legal and legal-philosophical concepts. As the most distinct of its features, the Court's progressivist urge was conducive to its constructive instincts in practically all areas of adjudication, but it is in the realm of rights protection that its displays were most obvious.

In the Court's view, to constitutionalise the legal landscape was to internationalise it. Thus, in *Capital Punishment*, the Chief Justice argued that since 'the decision of the CC [was] deliberately subjective and tied to history… it [was] desirable for the CC to consider the contemporary international approach'.[131] A modification of *Zétényi*'s rigid understanding of the change of regime occurred by virtue of reference to international law, too, and many other decisions could be cited to similar effect. The exercise in comparative constitutionalism became the Court's trademark, as it would regularly refer in its dicta to the jurisprudence of the ECHR, and to a lesser extent to that of the US Supreme Court or the GCC.[132] Even though without an explicit acknowledgement in the decisions themselves, Sólyom informs us that the Court drew lessons from many other constitutional courts around the globe, pointing out the borrowing from its Portugese, Spanish, Italian and Latin American counterparts.[133] Both the country's and the Court's quest for foreign credentials did not allow otherwise. Simply, '[a]ll means had to be used in order to attach the Hungarian constitutional system to Western standards of democracy'.[134] But since the Hungarian courts relied on comparative methods and drew heavily from foreign sources as early as the nineteenth and early twentieth century, the Court's tendency to make use of transnational judicial cross-fertilisation was again as much a function of the local tradition as it was of the contemporary context.

In addition to serving Hungary's integrative ambitions, internationalising the Court's case law, and, by extension, the country's constitutional politics was also a way of achieving legal and social progress. Accordingly, the HCC often went further than the jurisprudential standards of the ECHR or the leading constitutional courts across the globe required.

The realm of personal data protection, for instance, was a telling example of the HCC's efforts to modernise various spheres of legal regulation. In 1990, the Court found to be in violation of the right to privacy and the protection of personal data a regulation requiring party officials and senior officers of public organisations to furnish a declaration of their property holdings.[135] A year later, in a decision that came as a surprise to both the experts and the lay public, the HCC invoked the right to informational self-determination and declared unconstitutional the unrestricted use of the uniform PIN system. It also set a deadline for the legislature to modify the system according to the requirements set out in the ruling. The issue returned in 1994 in relation to some specific modes of the PINs' use, but the Court remained strict in its insistence on a comprehensive new solution, and held that to use a PIN to identify perpetrators of minor offences in the respective sentences or patients in documents issued by health care authorities was a violation of the respective constitutional rights.[136]

The Court also found that the right to freedom of information required that meetings of municipal authorities and the records thereof be made public.[137] In the lustration decision, the HCC held that information on public officials' activities during the previous regime was to count as public information and had to be made generally accessible. On the other hand, it held parts of the lustration law unconstitutional because of the absence of guarantees of the right to privacy and informational self-determination. The Court then continued to foster an overall reform of the data protection system—one that would provide sufficient protection of data and at once make public information accessible—when, in reference to the freedom of scientific search, it held unconstitutional the classification of certain information related to the past activities of government officials.[138]

The HCC's decisions on data protection are a microcosm of its entire adjudication, as they illustrate its characteristic features and shed light on the multi-layered motivational horizon informing its interpretive enterprise. Within the data protection case law, the Court (i) tried to shape the legal system through complex guidelines to inform legislative regulation, (ii) referred to international standards, (iii) pointed out various duties of the government to take action, (iv) in order to prevent a legal vacuum gave the Parliament the time necessary to come up with a comprehensive legislative solution, (v) elaborated in a doctrinal, concrete context-transcending way on the mutual relationship between the different aspects of informational self-determination and the right to privacy, and, overall, (vi) fostered a distinct concept of the proper handling of personal and public data in a modern society.

The HCC did not prove timid in assisting the emergence of a new system of mass media regulation, either. It insisted, for instance, that it was the legislature's duty to 'ensure that neither the organs of the state nor a specific group in society be able to influence the content of programming in such a way as to injure comprehensiveness, balance as regards coverage, and accuracy in presenting the opinions prevalent in society'.[139] In trying to modernise the regulation of media operations, the Court relied mostly on the GCC's case law. Its efforts which were aimed at achieving a pluralistic model of electronic media, however, fared with less success than those in the realm of data protection, as the HCC did not manage to cultivate the media's handling by the political sphere enough to prevent multiple occurrences of a media war, which still seems to be a favourite playground for Hungarian politicians.[140]

The same progressivist urge that the HCC exhibited in the data protection case law also lay behind its ruling on same-sex partnerships. Even though the Court phrased the problem in terms of discrimination, it implicitly undertook to modernise the law's approach to previously unacknowledged phenomena, and to bring it into line with progressive trends elsewhere, in this case particularly in Western Europe. To this effect, the HCC pointed out that the state '[could] maintain and support traditional institutions, as well as create new legal forms for acknowledging new phenomena, and with this at the same time it [could] expand the boundaries of 'normality' for public opinion'.[141] Needless to say, the Court, faithful to its leadership role, imposed upon itself the task of expanding the boundaries of normality and suggesting new legal forms.

The Court went much further than Western standards required in its decision on the right to a healthy environment. The HCC distinguished this right both from a social right and from a classical individual right, as well as from a mere constitutional goal, such as the establishment of a free market economy. Instead, it conceptualised the right to a healthy environment as 'a distinct fundamental right exceedingly dominated and determined by its objective aspect of institutional protection'.[142] Reaping rewards from its long-term tendency to impose upon the government the duty of affirmative action, the HCC held that 'the right to environmental protection raise[d] the guarantees for the implementation of the state duties... to the level of a fundamental right'.[143] The Court further linked the right to environmental protection to the right to life, dubbed it 'the objective, institutional aspect of the right to life',[144] and pointed out 'the responsibility of the State to maintain the natural basis of human life... as a separate constitutional "right"'.[145] Not willing to stop at delineating the government's duties, the HCC went so far as to argue that 'nature' and 'present and future mankind' were bearers of the right to a healthy environment.[146]

In the freedom of expression cases, especially those related to constitutional guarantees of denigratory speech and to the regulation of mass media operations, the Court drew from the experience of seasoned constitutional courts, especially the GCC, and did not deviate from the established Western standards to any significant extent. It is rather the series of rulings on data protection, self-informational determination, registered partnerships, and environmental protection that illustrate the HCC's project of modernising the local legal topography through constitutional interpretation. With these decisions in mind, there seems to be solid ground for Sólyom's claim that Hungary's constitutional development (based largely on the dogmatics of the court's making) 'did not constitute a one-way street: a new court not only received the wisdom of its elder brothers but might contribute to the common constitutional culture with its own ideas.'[147] There is no doubt that many commentators would find it dangerous to justify judicial restrictions of the legislature's policy-making capacity by, for instance, reading into the constitution the eligibility of nature and future mankind as beneficiaries of the right to a healthy environment. Others among us, however, may find some sort of solace in the fact that it was often the Court's willingness to push the boundaries of what is conceivable under rational legal analysis that would remind the outside world that there was in fact life between the Elbe and the Volga and that it might even be worthy of Westerners' attention. And one thing certainly should be conceded to Sólyom: within less than a decade, 'a body of work was completed that other courts under normal circumstances, might reach within thirty years'.[148] Even if the Court now settles for completing in three decades what under normal circumstances indeed does take three decades, its role in making Hungary what it is today can neither be denied nor done away with.

Czech Republic

Overview

The constitutional order of the Czech Republic, comprising of the 1992 constitution and a number of related acts of constitutional stature, includes a full-fledged Charter of Fundamental Rights and Freedoms comparable to rights catalogues available elsewhere in Europe and in various aspects even more extensive than the ECHRFF. Having more text to work with than the PCT and holding the text in higher esteem than the HCC, the Czech Court would neither resort to the general clauses to provide for specific rights nor establish its own hierarchy of rights. Yet there is a peculiar causal chain relating to the CCC's preservationist interpretive enterprise, similar in some ways to that of the PCT's colloquy with the Sejm. In its early decisions, the CCC imbued the Constitution's text with specific value content, and then vigorously protected this content against whoever was not ready to follow. It strove to preserve by its interpretive enterprise the constitution-makers' or the lawmakers' intent to the extent that this intent reflected the Court's perception of the ethos of the respective revolutionary achievements. In general, it would deduce constitutional or legislative intent from the text itself or access it by invoking the text's purpose and meaning. The CCC, however, espoused values it deemed foundational in so vigorous and uncompromising a manner as occasionally to implant into the text a purpose and meaning of its own making. So it would step outside the available text mostly to support the different tenets of the new regime's substantive agenda, but occasionally would do so also in order to effectuate the imperatives of natural-law philosophy to which the respective agencies had failed to attend fully within the law-making or law-implementing processes.

To understand the text as a repository of specific values and ideas, and to preserve these values through both abstract and concrete review, became a trademark of the Court's interpretive enterprise. But unlike the HCC, which would vigorously pursue its own jurisprudential agenda of prospective constitutionalism and construe progressive legal concepts that were to govern legislative and executive action, the Czech Court's interpretive creativity was preservationist both in nature and in the goals it pursued. First, the CCC's policing tendencies affected mostly the realm of ordinary adjudication. In the scrutiny of legislation, the Court's reaching outside the text generally would serve to preserve the legislature's policy choice. Secondly, the CCC's exercise in extra-textualism was clearly motivated by its willingness to preserve the achievements of the new legal ideology, stemming from the Velvet Revolution and extending to the foundation of the Czech Republic. After all, the CCC presented the value basis of the Czech society not as a concept of its own making but as 'incorporated into the text of the constitution'.[149]

Jurisprudence

Meta-constitutional law. Even though it might have happened by the invisible hand of destiny, it is probably no coincidence that the very first decision that the CCC chose to issue—concerning the illegality of the communist regime—combined both aspects of its interpretive tendencies, that is, their preservationist nature and their rootedness in meta-legal values. It set a definite, and definitely loud, tone for the Court's project of non-positivist and non-formalist constitutionalism, and at once served to evidence its readiness to protect the emergence of new values. The first ruling allowed no doubt as to the CCC's understanding of the constitution as comprised of suprapositive values, especially those that it held to be constitutive of a democratic society. According to the Court, any value-neutral constitution—that is, one that would fail to imbue the text with definite material content—was tainted with the historically discredited legal positivism and thus conceptually handicapped.

The CCC again relied on the superiority of so-called democratic legitimacy to the legitimacy of formal law when it refused to find unconstitutional the notorious Beneš decrees, which after the Second World War provided a legal basis for the mass disenfranchisement of German and Hungarian nationals living on the territory of Czechoslovakia.[150] The Court argued that democracy was not a meta-legal concept but one with concrete legal implications, and then went even further. It emphasised the continuity of values between the post-war Czechoslovakia and the pre-Munich republic founded by Masaryk.[151] It invoked the notion of 'a kind of common language, a general consensus with these values and principles'[152] as the yardstick of constitutional validity of the post-war regime. Even the ornate reasoning of the HCC would pale in comparison to the CCC's extensive philosophical excursion into the notions of guilt, collective and personal responsibility, truth, history, individual destiny, evil, and other such terms. The Court even quoted Emerson,[153] only to arrive at the end of the essay to the conclusion that to assess the Beneš decrees' constitutionality would not serve any legal purpose, as they had lost their constitutive effect and ceased to regulate existing legal relations.[154] The Beneš decrees ruling definitely confirmed that, to the CCC, the constitution of a democratic government had to go beyond procedural legitimisation and that it was the law's particular material content and the values embedded in it that distinguished a legitimate text from one whose legitimacy was crippled.

The Court's reading of the text as imbued with specific material content, as well as its insistence on a particular value profile of the new regime, often led it to solutions unforeseeable by the written law. A prime example is a case concerning the criminal conviction of a former intelligence officer who operated as a double agent in the communist era and was found guilty of criminal action against state security in the late 1970s. In 1997, the Supreme Court upheld the conviction upon appeal, pointing out that the committed acts were punishable both under the former and under the new criminal law. The CCC disagreed and reversed the conviction, arguing that espionage against the communist state, whether carried out for profit or not, could not be deemed to pose the requisite degree of threat to society.[155] According to the ruling, the

Czechoslovak state lacked the necessary attributes of sovereignty during its occupation by the Soviet Army, and the very object of the respective criminal action—that is, the external security of the state—was therefore absent.[156]

The notion of a pre-legal universe whose value hierarchy is of higher normative significance than that of law in books also found its way into the more ordinary aspects of constitutional adjudication. One of the restitution cases, for instance, dealt with the legal effects of withdrawing a property claim during the communist era. The ordinary courts, applying the relevant law, held that the withdrawal prevented any satisfaction of the claim, even under the new regulations. The CCC disagreed and argued for the possibility of 'convalidating imperfections of legal action performed during the period of servitude'.[157] After all, had the petitioner lived in a properly functioning democratic state based on the rule of law, he would never have withdrawn his claim.[158]

In no less radical fashion, the Court pointed out that constitutional scrutiny of restitution legislation was to take into account the necessity of completing economic reform in the realm of agriculture, as this reform was 'one of the guarantees against the potential reversal of the emerging democratic society back into a paternalistic state, that is, a totalitarian state based on a collectivist understanding of economy'.[159] One feels inclined to modify Justice Cepl's assertion that there is no transformation without restitution to state that there is no constitutional interpretation without ideological cognisance.

A seemingly trivial case involving the alleged failure of President Havel to meet the 15-day deadline available to him to veto a statute allowed the CCC to reiterate its understanding of the proper kind of constitutionalism. Indeed, the Court took the issue of when the deadline expired to be a 'dispute about the understanding of law in a democratic society'.[160] It is worth quoting the CCC at some length:

> The document institutionalising a system of fundamental and universally accepted values, and forming a mechanism and a process of making legitimate authoritative decisions, cannot exist outside the publicly accepted context of values, ideas of justice, and notions of the meaning, purpose, and mode of functioning of democratic institutions. In other words, it cannot operate outside the minimal value and institutional consensus.[161]

What a relief it must have been for the public to see justice prevail and find that it was the context of values and the ideas of justice espoused by the citizenry that led the Court to hold that the President had in fact managed to meet the deadline.

In invalidating a statute which eliminated certain layers of financial remuneration for specific categories of civil servants, including judges, the Court found it appropriate to invoke 'the existence of a value hierarchy forming the cornerstone and the basic cement-blocks of a society', which hierarchy was to enjoy priority even against 'ethical and legal normative systems'.[162] After all, 'legal norms share a common ground with values to the extent that they constitute a normative value hierarchy, which constitutes, establishes and organises a society'—both the legal norms and their implementation are to reflect these values.[163] As Justice Holländer puts it, a value-based application and interpretation of organic law is simply an extension of the material understanding of the rule of law.[164] Or, understanding extra-textual principles as a binding source of law, and preferring in interpretation a value hierarchy to the written law is simply an extension of the CCC's efforts to preserve the original ethos of the regime change based in some subtle ways on the primacy of natural law, and thus effectuate a revolutionary paradigm shift in the traditionally positivist local legal consciousness.

Against formalism. The Court might have tried at times too hard with its universe of *a priori* values. Yet its insistence that 'an implementation of law based solely on literalist interpretation is absolutely untenable' allowed for the extension from abstract into concrete review of the Court's rejection of formalism/positivism.[165] This approach not only worked to the benefit of individual petitioners; it became a distinct feature of, and an indispensable asset to, the newly emerging tenets of Czech legal culture.

As a general rule, the Court held:

> [T]he courts' duty to find law does not mean merely identifying direct, concrete and explicit statutory directives, but entails their duty to find and formulate that which is law even if the interpretation concerns abstract norms, constitutional principles, provisions of the Charter of Fundamental Rights and Freedoms, and obligations arising out of international treaties.[166]

The CCC's dislike of formalism and literalism showed in a radical way in a series of cases concerning candidates' eligibility for elections to the Senate. The Central Electoral Committee found several senatorial candidates to be ineligible because of formal deficiencies in their applications. The Supreme Court has upheld these findings upon appeal. The CCC, however, subsequently invalidated most of them. The fact patterns of the respective cases differed slightly but the core of the Court's argument suggested the inadequacy of formalist approaches to notions such as free competition of political parties or democratic society. According to the Court, 'these very notions include aspects exceeding the formalist positivist framework'.[167] Free political competition as a constitutional principle therefore requires that even in cases where its legislative regulation may be ambiguous, political competition must be interpreted extensively, 'so as to make it possible to vote and be elected, not the other way around'.[168] In order to facilitate and protect free competition of political parties, the courts should refrain from applying positivist interpretation of the applicable law.[169] That is the special interpretive rule governing the regulation of political competition; the general one, applicable across the legal order, requires that 'one does not search for the purpose and the meaning of a statute only in its words and sentences'.[170] Accordingly, to prefer 'considerations of suitability or practicality to law and especially to constitutional principles' is to interpret the available regulations in a manner that violates their purpose and their meaning, as well as the logic of the matter.[171] It makes for a striking paradox that similar arguments advanced in the United States in the wake of the contested 2000 presidential elections did not prevail. Ironically, solutions that 'make it possible to vote and be elected, not the other way around' were found superior to a strict interpretation of the letter of the law in a country that has cherished legal positivism for most of its existence, while in a country that likes to export its constitutional culture across the globe they were not.

The Court's readiness to 'eliminate the formalist positivist interpretive approaches' of the ordinary courts extended to the realm of civil procedure.[172] It found, for instance, certain displays of the ordinary courts' preference for 'excessive formalism to result in a sophisticated justification of an apparent injustice' and thus outside the boundaries of constitutionality.[173] Similarly, the CCC would regularly find rejection by the ordinary courts of petitions suffering from minor technical or procedural flaws to be 'unduly strict' and thus a violation of the right to court.[174] The Court would also find violation of the right to a fair trial in the case of 'insensitive and purely formalist proceedings' by an ordinary court.[175]

The Court chastised the ordinary courts mostly for their blind observance of the letter of the law, and their lack of regard for the purpose, meaning, systemic consistency, or logic of the given rule. Surprisingly or not, it proved less demanding as far as its own demeanour was concerned, as it at times fell victim to the same kind of insensitive formalism for which it used to reproach ordinary adjudication.

The CACC contains a provision precluding the Constitutional Court from adjudicating in excess of a petition. The CCC remained almost blindly faithful to this rule.[176] One of the many examples concerns a petition which applied for the invalidation of the adjective 'racial' (as in racial discrimination) as a prerequisite for the eligibility for certain indemnification entitlements. The Court held that the petition did not meet the required criteria, for pursuant to Article 87.1(a) of the CACC a petitioner may apply for the invalidation of a statute or its specific provisions. According to the CCC, the term 'specific provision' reflects 'a wholesome and autonomous disposition with normative and binding effects', which is not the case of the adjective 'racial'.[177] The Court conceded that the differentiation between racial and other forms of discrimination might indeed amount to the rule's unconstitutionality, but pointed out that judged by *formal considerations*, the respective application failed to meet the required criteria.[178] In a different case, the Court's rapporteur rejected the application for the invalidation of a statutory rule, which discriminated between the implications of an *ex lege* transfer of property and conveyance of property by contractual means.[179] Even though the rapporteur conceded that the statute's failure to treat the two situations equally did 'amount to certain inequality', and even though the Court's plenary session invoked the very same difference only a few weeks later,[180] the petition was rejected as unfounded because to abolish the contested part of the provision would render the entire clause a-functional. In a case dealing with the rule allowing for detention by police authorities of a person presumed to be an illegal alien, the Court invalidated the rule allowing for detention. But it refused to deal with the rule stipulating the period of detention in related instances because that particular rule was not the legal basis on which the contested decision was issued, and thus did not meet the formal criteria required by the CACC.[181] The debilitating effects of the *non ultra petitum* rule were acknowledged in a dissenting vote in a case in which a provision of the Civil Procedure Act was invalidated as applied for by the petitioner.[182] As a result of the Court's strict refusal to act in excess of the petition, a part of the rule was abolished that did not grant the status of litigant to a person whose rights could be affected in the proceedings, while another part of the same rule remained in force, mandating *in camera* proceedings and thus excluding the possibility of a hearing for any litigant.[183]

So while the Court was often willing to transcend the letter of the laws it was asked to review, it restrained itself in interpreting the rules of its own operation. One notices here a difference between the CCC's approach to the *Kompetenz* issue and that of the Hungarian Court. While the former court refused to understand individual applications as an invitation to shape the affected law and suggested that such a practice would amount to a transgression of its authority, the latter court used petitions to push the Parliament into large-scale legislative reforms and would not shy away from invalidating provisions that it found constitutional *per se* but inextricably related to the area of law that it felt was in need of substantial reform.[184]

Teleological interpretation. The Court's rejection of literal-only interpretation combined with its preference for teleological interpretation:

> [A] court is not absolutely bound by the literal wording of a statutory rule but may, and must, deviate from such a wording if it is warranted for important reasons by the purpose of the rule, the history of its adoption, systemic consistency or some other principle rooted in the legal order as a complex of rules compatible with the constitution.[185]

Accordingly, it is the purpose, the meaning, and the logic of a structure of a legal rule that the ordinary courts, and the CCC itself, should be primarily concerned with.

There is a vast number of cases in which statutory interpretation was found unconstitutional because it was at odds with the alleged purpose, meaning, and objective of a given rule.[186] Yet the very technique employed by the CCC to educate the ordinary courts in functional interpretation most often served to preserve the legislature's policy choices. The one realm of constitutional adjudication in which the preservation of legislative intent proved of utmost relevance to the outcome of constitutional disputes was the implementation of restitution policies. In general, 'the role of interpretation and application of law is to fulfil the will of the legislature'.[187] The ordinary courts therefore should 'not use claimants' ignorance or mistakes against the aims of restitution policies'.[188] Also, interpreting indemnification laws 'in conflict with interpretive rules according to which the meaning of individual statutory provisions must be determined on the basis of the statute's structure cannot be defined in any other way than as a violation of the principle of non-arbitrariness'.[189]

Again, the CCC proved stricter in preaching rules than in obeying them. Compare, for instance, these two takes of the same Court on the same issue, that is, the relation between literalist and teleological interpretation. According to one ruling, 'an implementation of law that is based solely on literalist interpretation is absolutely untenable. Linguistic interpretation represents only an introductory understanding of an applied legal norm. It is only a starting point for the illumination and clarification of its meaning and purpose.'[190] According to another ruling, however,

> in case of the application of a legal rule it is necessary to draw primarily from its literal wording. Only if such a wording is unclear and unintelligible, as well as in conflict with a meaning and a purpose of the rule that are unambiguous and exclusive, is it possible to prefer an e ratione legis interpretation to linguistic interpretation.[191]

The latter quote comes from a ruling which exemplifies the Court's selectivity in opting for that or another mode of interpretation. There were two conceptually identical applications contesting mandatory representation by either a member of the bar, or a corporate attorney,[192] or a notary public in the proceedings at the Constitutional Court. In the first of the two cases, a panel of the CCC, interpreting the matter *e ratione legis*, held that if the petitioner himself was a member of the bar, it was unnecessary for him to be represented by another one.[193] A different panel leaned towards ruling to the contrary on a factually different but legally identical issue,[194] and therefore applied to the Court's plenary session for a binding memorandum on the matter. The plenary session held that the meaning and purpose of the disputed rule were not unambiguous, which ambiguity warranted fidelity to the literal wording. However, even though the CCC did opt for the linguistic interpretation, it both did and did not take the wording of the text to be dispositive of the issue. First, it argued that the purpose of the rule was to assure not only a legally qualified representation of rights, but also a higher degree of objectivity in the evaluation of the merits of litigants' claims. Accordingly, that purpose warranted application of the rule regardless of the petitioners' legal qualifications. Secondly, however, the Court deemed this purpose ambivalent. To escape this simultaneous invoking and not invoking of the purpose, the CCC applied the maxim *lege non distinguente nec nostrum est distinguere*, that is, it argued that since the rule did not contain an explicit differentiation between a non-qualified natural person and a member of the bar, such a differentiation could not be inferred.

The issue of mandatory representation by a bar member of a bar member is arguably of minor social significance. It illustrates, however, the contingent nature of teleological interpretation. That a search for the law's purpose could easily lead to discriminatory implications became rather obvious in other cases, as well. Let us compare, for instance, two indemnification-related petitions both of which applied for the invalidation of statutory rules claimed to have led to unjust judicial rulings. In one case, the contested statutory criterion linked indemnification eligibility to death in a concentration camp; in the other case a statute required that the applicant for indemnification be married to the original beneficiary at the time of injury. In the first case, the petitioner's husband deceased during his transport from a concentration camp a few days after the camp was liberated. According to the CCC, it would be absurd and in conflict with the purpose and aims of indemnification policies to interpret the respective rule as preventing relief only because the decisive event occurred after the liberation of the camp. Also, 'the period during which inmates of a concentration camp were not free to leave it must be assessed individually according to the specific circumstances of a case'.[195] In the other case, however, the Court refused to grant relief to a petitioner who failed to meet the required criterion of being married to the original beneficiary 'at the time of the infliction of injury'. The fact that severe Germanisation and the incarceration of the couple effectively precluded the marriage, and that the marriage did take place when circumstances allowed it, is essentially of the same significance as the fact that people could have died in consequence of their incarceration in concentration camps even after those camps were liberated. Here, however, the Court, rather than pointing out the absurdity of strict adherence to legislative differentiation, argued that the legislature was free to define the pool of eligible beneficiaries. Moreover, in the first case the statutory rule was upheld because its sensitive interpretation in individual cases could, and in fact had to, allow for observance of the meaning and the purpose of indemnification policies. In the second case, the CCC conceded that the statute might indeed be harsh with respect to the petitioner but left the issue at that and refused to concern itself any further with the unavailability of judicial assessment of hardship caused by legislative regulation. It held that the fact that the legislator did not provide for the possibility of assessing and alleviating the attendant hardship in the course of law's application could not be deemed unequal treatment. True, the CCC relied on various legalistic arguments, pointing out, for instance, that the applicable legislation lacked an exact definition of a concentration camp, while the criterion of marriage obviously was easier to assess. But in the latter instance, it also failed to make clear that to preclude any individualised assessment of a causal link between injury and the events that preceded it was at odds with the purpose of righting wrongs. The CCC thereby has not committed a primitive, but only a 'sophisticated justification of an apparent injustice'. Most importantly, it made its favourite technique of teleological interpretation appear as arbitrary as it deemed the ordinary courts' favourite technique of literalist interpretation to be.

Proportionality. The interpretive enterprise of the CCC, with its indoctrination of the text with *a priori* values, and its subordination of the letter of the law to notions of what is meaningful and purposeful, may seem similar to that of the HCC or the PCT. The differences, however, are as relevant as are the similarities.

First, legislative intent receives much more attention in the Czech Republic than it does in Hungary. For the CCC, the aim of any interpretation is to mediate the legislature's will as faithfully as possible. Accordingly, authentic documents anchoring that will are to serve as the primary interpretive guidelines. The HCC, on the other hand, does not feel bound by the legislative intent, even if explicitly articulated.[196] Secondly, the CCC's decisions read differently from those of the Hungarian Court. No matter how far the Czech Court would go in its excursion into moral and political philosophy, its dicta would still include a meticulous examination of the relevant legal rules and their interrelation and be structured in terms of individual statutory provisions. Whether successfully or not, the judge usually attempts to get the better of the policy maker in the Czech world of constitutional justice.

But the most important difference is related to the project of rights balancing. The Hungarian Court explicitly rejected as normatively insignificant the hierarchy of rights suggested by the text, and based its rights jurisprudence on a hierarchy of its own making. The Polish Tribunal would often weigh principles explicitly anchored in the text differently from those it inferred from the available general constitutional clauses. Having access to more text than the PCT, and holding the available constitutional text in higher esteem than the HCC, the Czech Court's proportionality jurisprudence became rather 'conventional'.

In general, 'a fundamental right or freedom may be limited only in the interest of another fundamental right or freedom'.[197] In case of conflict, the affected rights are to be balanced against each other, while preserving their essence and their meaning. The balancing enterprise itself is subject to the rationality and necessity criteria. The Court offers a hint of a hierarchy when it presents a third criterion, one based on the assessment of the importance of a given right. Such an assessment, however, does not draw from some pre-established hierarchy of rights but must concern itself with empirical, systemic, contextual, and value arguments.[198] Unlike the HCC—which, for instance, prioritises human dignity and grants preferential treatment to freedom of speech, too—the CCC tends to understand rights provided for by the text as *prima facie* equal. In the absence of a clear legislative directive as to the difference in the value of the respective rights, they are to be treated as being of equal worth. Accordingly, the right to personal inviolability was held to be of equal worth with the right to a fair trial,[199] and freedom of speech equal to personality rights.[200] The one instance in which the Court explicitly attributed more value to one right than to another dealt with the legislative regulation of handgun possession. The CCC found the right to life, health, property, and other rights that could be jeopardised because of unrestrained access to handguns to be of incomparably higher value than the right to possess arms. Even here, however, the Court did not fail to mention that since the text of the Charter did not conceptualise the right to arms possession as a fundamental right, its legislative restriction by definition could not be unconstitutional.[201]

The CCC was not completely immune from subjecting rights to public interest considerations, and it is in this regard that its employment of rights-qualifying devices appears similar to the PCT's interpretive tendencies. That public interest might qualify the enjoyment of rights can be deduced *a contrario* from the Court's suggestion that 'the negative consequences of measures that restrict fundamental human rights and freedoms may not outweigh the benefits to the public's interest in these measures'.[202] The Court relied upon public interest also in its rulings on *ex lege* transformation of quasi-tenancies into legally protected ones, and on *ex lege* termination of leases on formerly national property. Nevertheless, any restriction by a general clause in principle must be based on a specific textual mandate. It is only in the case that the constitutional text expressly allows for legislative qualification of a right that that right may be properly limited.[203] Accordingly, the CCC found the institution of anonymous witnesses to be an improper legislative restriction of a number of due process rights because their constitutional regulation did not explicitly allow for any legislative qualification. Also, the Court held the restriction of indemnification eligibility by the criterion of nationality to be in conformity with the constitution only because Article 11.2 of the Charter expressly stated that the possibility to acquire certain kinds of property could be limited to Czech citizens. Since the respective constitutional provision did not provide for any other qualifying condition on the acquisition of property, any such condition imposed by the legislature—for example, the permanent-residence requirement—would be invalid.

The interpretive approaches that insulate from governmental interference only the essence of a right or require an explicit textual mandate for legislative restriction of constitutional rights can be easily detected in the jurisprudence of other constitutional courts in the region. Sharing in the use of the main orientational reference points, such as the case law of the ECHR or the GCC, the respective courts have employed similar conceptual criteria in the assessment of legislative qualification of rights. What is noteworthy about the Czech proportionality doctrine is its extensive application in the CCC's scrutiny of ordinary adjudication. As the Court held, 'it is necessary that the requirements of proportionality be applied not only to legislative activity, but to no lesser extent be followed also in the realm of judicial power'.[204] Accordingly, the Court would not hesitate to apply the proportionality principle within the evaluation of the ordinary courts' procedural decisions. It held, for instance, that to strictly follow certain formalist considerations was a *disproportionate* limitation of the right to a fair trial.[205] The CCC would also regularly re-assess the balancing of rights as performed by an ordinary court. If the Court arrived at a different conclusion on the extent of protection of one right against another—for example, personality rights against the freedom of speech—it would invalidate the ruling of an ordinary court as lacking in the proportionality aspects.

This is what happened in a case involving a newspaper article which contained a mildly critical value judgment and a couple of factual errors. The CCC rebutted the contention of the Supreme Court that the truthfulness of the communicated information was a basic prerequisite of any critical judgment. It held that 'in the case of a fundamental right as important as freedom of speech the responsibility for the truthfulness of all the information should not be insisted… as long as… the petitioner expressly linked his polemical statement to certain facts which were, after all, proven true'.[206] Another case involved two journalists of a prominent national daily newspaper who in their article expressed an unfavourable value judgment on the past activities of a local politician. They also committed certain factual errors and conceded that they had done so, but argued that the false factual assertion was insignificant. The CCC agreed and pointed out the necessity of evaluating factual errors in the context of all the communicated information and to establish an unambiguous causal link between such an error and injury to a personality right.[207] A failure to do that would violate not only the exigencies of procedural purity of judicial proceedings, but also the proportionality command. The Court's assertion that the specific nature of the periodical press makes it difficult to 'insist on absolute precision of factual assertions'[208] suggests that freedom of speech—although on a par with personality rights in terms of intrinsic value—is to be handled with care.

Since bitter political divisions—kept in a state of latency throughout the first half-decade of the transition—have recently begun to penetrate constitutional adjudication in a sharp and vocal manner, the Court's significance to Czech constitutional politics is on the rise and bound to grow. It is more than likely that, until the new justices are appointed, the CCC shall not renounce the universe of meta-legal values it has so vigorously protected throughout its existence. After all, the Court's educational project aimed at the ordinary courts has already borne fruit and there are 'many judges of lower as well as higher courts who base their decisions on judgments of the Constitutional Court without asking themselves whether precedents are, or are not, admissible under Czech law'.[209] Until changes are implemented in the realm of judicial review of administrative decisions, however, the notions of teleological interpretation and substantive justice will continue to impact the intra-judicial seminar on law and its values. Given the Court's major role in preserving the original ethos of the Velvet Revolution and its relatively unobtrusive manner of operating in the realm of constitutional politics, it is no surprise that voices are emerging in the Czech Republic that point out that the first Court will most likely be remembered with nostalgia.[210] As it appears intent on fostering its version of constitutionalism and becomes more active in policing the governing majority, it may well be that the Czech Court, instead of receiving suggestions from Sólyom to learn from the HCC, will be able to offer some inspiration of its own.

Slovak Republic

Overview

The Slovak Court took the letter of the constitution to be its supreme, and often the only, guidance, and almost completely refrained from constructing supra-positive constitutional law. The conceptual finality of Slovakia's constitutional arrangements was one of the major factors affecting the SCC's interpretive endeavours. After all, the Court was to apply the very first democratic constitution of independent Slovakia. This has served, at least psychologically, to insulate the written constitution from much tinkering by philosophers of law. In addition, the constitution's text contained an extensive catalogue of rights that did not need to be developed by means of creative inference from axiological clauses. Variables other than the text, however, proved of equal significance for the SCC's interpretive techniques. Indeed, while the text allowed for preservation, the context required it.

First, there soon emerged in the country's constitutional discourse the need to counterbalance the government's utter disrespect for constitutional imperatives. The SCC's strict insistence that the superiority of the constitution show in the daily operation of the different governmental agencies led it to require, and simultaneously serve as an example of, an uncompromising observance of constitutional mandates. To compensate for the government's lack of regard for the constitution by a faithful observance of it also served to reinforce the SCC's legitimacy. As it was rapidly dragged into extremely sensitive political disputes, and became closely watched and heavily pressured by the entire political sphere, the Court felt it had to be very careful in its reasoning. In other words, in protecting itself not only against doctrinal accusations of excessive activism, but also—and mostly—against politically motivated reproaches, it was practical for the Court to profess adherence to *lex scripta*. Therefore, instead of pursuing meta-constitutional law, the Court's mandate as perceived by the justices was to serve as an unbiased arbiter of whatever surfaced in the vulgar political discourse. The letter of the law is the one measure that is deemed relatively reliable in providing an appearance of impartiality.

Secondly, the Court was too busy protecting the constitution against frequent and flagrant abuse to have the time and space for the proactive development of an autonomous jurisprudential agenda. Even though it may seem a paradox, there were not many hard cases from a legal point of view, as the assessed constitutional violations were often rather apparent and did not require the SCC to reach far beyond the available text. The issues that allow for, and encourage, interpretive constructivism—such as freedom of speech, abortion, church–state relations, or retribution—have rarely or never reached the SCC's docket. Moreover, there was no appealing axiology available that the Court could actively foster through elaboration of values and extra-textual principles. The coming about of both the new state and the constitution was tainted by behind-the-scenes bargaining and the attendant lack of popular enthusiasm for what was happening in the public realm. Values that should have accompanied Slovakia's emancipation and that the Court could subsequently rely upon in its interpretative project were absent, and those available were what the SCC later found itself struggling against.

Finally, most justices simply lacked the ambition to try to leave a personal imprint on the country's constitutional development, and some lacked the requisite legal philosophical sophistication, too. Hence their resort to the text as the orientational device of choice.

Jurisprudence

Selective literalism. The SCC's interpretation of its own authority provides an illustrative introduction to the justices' mental universe and, consequently, the interpretive techniques they felt at ease employing. Let us start with what I understand to be the most serious interpretive failure of the SCC, that is, its handling of the petition procedure. Pursuant to Article 127 of the Slovak Constitution, the SCC had the power to hear complaints against enforceable decisions of a number of governmental agencies, excluding the ordinary courts. Pursuant to Article 130.3, the Court could admit for a hearing petitions alleging rights violations, with no qualification as to the authority claimed to have committed the violation. Until 2001, the text of the constitution did not grant the SCC the authority to annul the contested decisions either in the case of complaints under Article 127 or in the case of petitions under Article 130.3. It is the SACC that provides some grounds for differentiation. Pursuant to Article 57 of the SACC, if the SCC finds a violation upon reviewing a constitutional complaint, it is bound to annul the contested decision. The SACC does not contain any specific regulation of the petition procedure with the exception of one saying that provisions regulating the constitutional complaints apply to the Court's adjudication of petitions.* This is, in sum, the legal state from which the SCC inferred that for it to quash decisions contested by means of a petition would be unconstitutional, as governmental authorities may proceed only on the basis of law. According to the Court, the fact that the SACC did not explicitly allow for the annulment of decisions held unconstitutional within the petition procedure meant that there was no legal basis for the SCC to do so. 'The powers of the constitutional court are enumerated in Articles 125–130 of the constitution, which powers

* An amendment to the SACC came into effect on March 20, 2002, reflecting the new constitutional regulation of concrete review, including the abolition of petition. See also discussion on pp. 199–200.

do not include the authority to annul enforceable decisions of ordinary courts. . . Should the constitutional court interfere with the ordinary courts' proceedings, it would violate the constitution.'[211] To the argument that the enumerated powers did not include the authority to annul decisions issued by administrative agencies, either, and that pursuant to the SACC petitions were to be proceeded upon and adjudicated as constitutional complaints, the Court responded:

> It is impossible analogically to annul decisions of ordinary courts... [because] the constitution divides judicial review of state administration and municipal self-government between the constitutional court and the ordinary courts... The analogous supervision by the constitutional court of ordinary adjudication would contradict the autonomous and procedurally self-contained administration of justice by the ordinary courts.[212]

Not that the SCC would be incapable of understanding the concept of analogy. There is in the SACC another reference that is conceptually of the same kind as the one regulating the petition procedure. In fact, both blank references are included in the same Article 31(a) of the SACC. So if the SACC does not hold otherwise and the nature of the matter does not exclude it, the relevant provisions of the Civil Code and the Criminal Code are to be applied in the Court's proceedings. The Court made good use of this delegation on various occasions, most importantly in order to provide free legal counsel to petitioners incapable of carrying the costs of qualified legal representation. The SCC also regularly applies a number of procedural rules set forth by the Civil Code but absent in the SACC. What lay at the core of its selective approach to the two references was the bizarre idea that analogy could not be employed in the case of the petition procedure because of some fundamental differences between administrative agencies and ordinary courts. How untenable would it be to say that both kinds of agencies issue decisions whose purpose is to regulate the parties' legal rights and duties, and that analogy applies not when circumstances are the same but when they are similar?

I do not need to remind the reader of all the cases in which the PCT or the HCC appropriated for themselves powers not explicitly anchored in the texts of their constitutions. Indeed, that the SCC's preference for literal interpretation might have been unduly vigorous becomes especially apparent when viewed in comparison to the *Kompetenz*-related interpretive approaches of other courts in the region. Neither do I have to stress that one can hardly talk of a struggle for constitutional justice if a constitutional court proves unwilling to interpret the applicable law so as to do justice to the purpose of concrete constitutional review, that is, remedy violations of constitutional rights. I chose to denote this approach of the Slovak Court as literalism but extreme lack of confidence would be a more fitting description.

Rather than being a necessary extension of the textual delineation of its jurisdiction, the SCC's restrictive interpretation of its operability in the realm of constitutional justice administration thus again reflected the context in which it came about and operated. I have already pointed out the heavy involvement of the 'judicial lobby' in the constitution-drafting process, and the translation of its preferences into the crippling of the Court's concrete-review authority.[213] When one of the Court's panels adopted a ruling indicating the possibility of a different development in the area, some of the high-ranking and highly respected members of the Supreme Court voiced their objections and were deferred to.[214] The Court's deliberate self-disfranchisement in the realm of concrete review was also heavily informed by the expectations of its commentators. Its deferential attitude to ordinary adjudication, especially if somewhat justifiable by reference to the text of the constitution, simply had more doctrinal support than contrary tendencies. Leaving the individual applicants out there in the cold was deemed less of a liability for the Court's image as a guarantor of the rule of law than would be its failure to confront through abstract review the power-hungry majority. The exigencies of the overall transitional environment required that the SCC kept its hands free for cultivating the country's political development; to handle individual applications with the same degree of care was simply too much of a mission for a relatively defensive court. After all, observing the letter of the law as faithfully as possible both supported the Court's claims of operating legitimately and fed its appeals that other government agencies act in the same way. Hence the SCC's choice of the restrictive option of two possible interpretations; hence its alleged lack of competence to supervise ordinary adjudication.

The SCC's *Kompetenz*-related self-restraint, however, extended beyond deference to ordinary adjudication. Several deficiencies of selective literalism surfaced, for instance, in the already noted holdings on parliamentarians' mandates, as the SCC, despite finding unconstitutionality, refused to strip the relevant resolutions of the National Council of their effect,[215] simply because neither the constitution nor the SACC explicitly list such resolutions as decisions that the Court may annul. Compare, again, this struggle for constitutional justice to the PCT's approach to a conceptually similar issue, that is, the resolution of the Sejm mandating the Interior Minister to provide information on links to the communist security service of a number of government officials. The Polish Tribunal's authority at the time was no more extensive than was that of the Slovak Court. On the contrary, the Tribunal did not have then, and does not have now, the power to annul individual decisions. It simply interpreted the above resolution as a normative act violating the constitution—primarily the rule-of-law requirements—stayed its effect, and held that if not modified within three months so as to conform to the constitution the resolution would become null and void.[216] Not so the Slovak Court, which pointed out that the respective constitutional and statutory rules did not list a resolution of the National Council among decisions that the SCC was bound to quash in case it found unconstitutionality.

The Court also dismissed a complaint against the certification of the mandate of the expelled deputy‘s substitute, arguing that its authority applied only if a mandate was certified for a deputy who had been elected. According to the SCC, a deputy who merely substituted another deputy is not to be deemed an elected deputy because '[t]he substitute candidates… acquire their mandates in another way than by means of an election'.[217] Pursuant to the election law, however, only candidates ranked in a specific order on the party ballot were eligible for substitution. Indeed, in a later ruling the SCC found a violation of the right to be elected in the case of a candidate whose rank on the ballot, as specified by the number of preferential votes, followed immediately after the rank of the deceased deputy.[218] In the former case, a substitute deputy was held not to have acquired the mandate by means of election, and his mandate was therefore not a mandate of an elected deputy. In the latter case, the Court held the substitute deputy to be a bearer of the right to be elected, which right has been transformed into an enforceable entitlement to a parliamentary mandate. If his right to be elected was violated by the Parliament's failure to certify his mandate, how is it possible that a different substitute candidate was not an elected deputy? If, as the SCC insisted, the number of deputies of the National Council could not be either increased or decreased above or below 150,[219] how is it possible that a deputy could 'lose' his mandate in violation of the constitution and the certification of a mandate of his substitute the Court may not review? How is it possible that a substitute candidate does not acquire his mandate by means of election and yet his right to be elected can be violated if his mandate is not certified? Is it so because the very wording of law requires so, or because the appearance of impartiality does?

The same question comes to mind in relation to the SCC‘s self-conscious refusal to intervene with the politicians' efforts to disfranchise one another in the realm of electoral competition.[220]

Pursuant to Article 63 of the SACC, the Court may, among other things, invalidate the contested electoral result, without further qualification as to the kind of elections. It concluded, however, that while in the case of national elections only the elections as a whole could be cancelled, in the case of municipal elections not only the entire elections, but also the election of a specific authority might be subject to annulment. The SCC substantiated this differentiation by pointing out the different character of the two kinds of election, proportional on the national level and majoritarian on the municipal level. It again relied mostly on literal interpretation of the applicable text, as it pointed out that the constitution did not provide *expressis verbis* for the possibility of 'annulling the electoral result achieved by an entity participating in the elections'.[221] This, however, is the very same thing that the Court would do in a number of instances with respect to municipal elections when on the basis of a different statutory rule it would substitute the improperly elected candidate with a candidate it deemed properly elected. Further, the SACC allows for invalidation of electoral results in different electoral districts, again without differentiating between national and municipal elections. The Court concluded that 'electoral regions'--the term used with respect to national elections--could not be deemed 'electoral districts'. In other words, the national elections are to be viewed 'as a single whole through which all the members of the National Council are elected'.[222] If the term 'candidate' includes a political party, and if there is only one electoral district for national elections, how come a party cannot contest the electoral result of another party achieved in national elections? If selective literalism means that one or several of the applicable provisions are contextualised, and another or several other applicable provisions are taken at their face value, then this indeed was selective literalism.

The preceding review is as selective as was the Court's literalism but it does expose the main concern: literalist interpretation can be as lacking in consistency and affected by factors other than the text as can be teleological interpretation (CCC), axiology-informed interpretation (PCT), or the development of an invisible constitution (HCC). It seems that the letter of the law, after all, might not be so reliable in eliminating from interpretation extra-textual considerations.

Rule of (text of) law. The notions that a constitutional court infers from a *Rechtsstaat* clause are a good indicator of the content of the country's constitutional and political discourse. There were disputes in Poland about the scope of freedom of speech in radio and TV broadcasting, abortions, religious instruction, lustrations, or criminal prosecution of former communist potentates. There were disputes in Hungary about restitution, retribution, the death penalty, the media, and welfare policy. There were disputes in the Czech Republic about restitution, various purgation measures, and economic protectionism. The respective constitutional courts related all these issues in one way or another to the notion of the rule of law and its a-textual essentials.

The Slovak Court used the clause, too. However, given the lack of a coherent value foundation of the regime and the availability of an extensive catalogue of human rights, the content of the *Rechtsstaat* clause as developed by the SCC is, if not vacuous, relatively meagre. The SCC did not need, and did not have many opportunities, to construct on the basis of the notion of law's rule concepts such as human dignity, inviolability of the right to life, ban or support, respectively, of retributive transitional justice, and so forth. It did need, and had many opportunities, to preserve the rule of law against statutory violations. The Slovak jurisprudential version of the *Rechtsstaat* clause thus focused on aspects that proved most in need of constitutional protection: the principle of legal certainty, the requirement that all government officials observe in their decision-making the applicable constitutional imperatives, that is, proceed and act only as allowed by law, the protection of a normative hierarchy of legal rules, and the requirement of a balance of powers between the different branches of government. In Slovakia, there were too many attempts at retroactive economic legislation, too many transgressions of their authority by the different agencies, and too many inter-branch disputes not to have dominated the content of the *Rechtsstaat* clause. Hence the Slovak Court's cry for legal certainty and other basics of a democratic government rather than for 'luxurious' accessories such as human dignity, value consensus on the part of the community, nature's right to protection, or other fancy apparel of supra-constitutional law.

In 2000, the Slovak Court issued a publication mapping the most important aspects of its jurisprudence to date. There are 17 decisions listed under the *Rechtsstaat* clause—13 of them concern the issue of legal certainty and balance of powers between branches of government. I would not want to overemphasise the impact on the Court's interpretive methodology of context at the expense of text. That issues related to the separation-of-powers aspects of Slovakia's constitutional arrangements surfaced more frequently in the SCC's employment of the *Rechtsstaat* clause was partly due to the fact that the catalogue of rights and freedoms offered by the Slovak constitution was complete; complete enough not to require any further extension at the time of the major constitutional reform in 2001. Like other courts in the region, the Slovak Court, too, used to rely on the *Rechtsstaat* clause mostly when explicit textual imperatives were lacking. It was especially with respect to the regulation of the different branches' authority that ambiguities would regularly emerge. That these ambiguities became apparent in as frequent and pervasive a manner, however, is largely due to the fact that inter-branch disputes and the utter lack of cooperation between concrete government officials were the focus of the country's transitional constitutional discourse, and not—to stress this for the very last time—specific rights-oriented issues by regulation of which, and by adjudication of which, other legislatures and constitutional courts in the region have developed their distinct characters.

In other words, the SCC's selection of interpretive techniques was as heavily affected by the exigencies of Slovakia's political development as was its opting for a particular adjudicative philosophy. The *Rechtsstaat* clause therefore had its time in the spotlight especially in the months following the infamous parliamentary session in November 1994, which put the rule of law on the list of endangered species in Slovakia. Consequently, the SCC used the rule-of-law clause against the establishment of investigative committees,[223] a statute that took away from the President the authority to appoint the Chief of Joint Staff,[224] statutes that retroactively regulated issues related to inheritance of real estate[225] or to bankruptcy proceedings,[226] the Attorney General's authority to effectively contest enforceable judgments of ordinary courts,[227] and a number of other similar acts and measures.

Even though a *Rechtsstaat* clause is a quintessential case for interpretative constructivism, the variety of tenets of non-written constitutional law that the SCC inferred from it is smaller than that developed by other courts in the region. The same can be said about the concept of proportionality. In fact, the SCC's proportionality jurisprudence is even scantier than its rule-of-law jurisprudence, and a variety of factors were again in play.

First, rights and freedoms that are by definition prone to mutual balancing have not made it to the Court often enough to force the justices into doctrinal development, a project some of them probably would not fare well at anyway. Secondly, proportionality usually requires taking account of extra-textual considerations, and thus does not go well with reverence for literal interpretation. Thirdly, reliance on the proportionality principle seems to have been unnecessary for the Court's purposes of preservation of a normative hierarchy of rules. Nonetheless, the SCC has done less than was possible and at times even less than was desirable.

Indeed, even in cases where at least hints of a mutual balancing of rights would seem necessary, the Court would guide itself solely by the law's text. In a case concerning the right to privacy, it stated:

> The government authorities are authorised to interfere with the right to protection of personal data as long as such interference could be deemed authorised under Article 19.3 of the Constitution of the Slovak Republic.... Interference is unauthorised if performed by an authority... that lacks any statutory power to interfere, if performed by an authority that does have the statutory power but interferes in a manner that the statute does not allow for, and lastly if performed by an authority that neither has the statutory power nor interferes in a manner stipulated by law.[228]

This is statutory rather than constitutional interpretation. There is no mention whatsoever of any other than the statutory criteria, and no mention of the constitutionality of a legally authorised but disproportionate or unreasonable interference. The Court hints at the need to assess material conditions when it says that 'personal data are abused if... used for any other purpose than that for which they must be used pursuant to a statute',[229] but again does so only by reference to the statutory text.

The Court's review of a provision of the act on misdemeanours according to which judicial review was available only if a sanction either exceeded a specific financial amount or imposed upon the perpetrator various restraints for a specific period of time exemplifies its tendency to avoid excursions into anything but the rule's text. The SCC found the above provision to be in violation of the right to court and the principle of equality. The relevant constitutional rule stipulates that judicial review of administrative decisions may be sought unless a statute stipulates otherwise. In the case at hand, the statute indeed stipulated otherwise. The different statutory regime for different administrative sanctions, however, did not lead the Court to assess the reasonableness of statutory limitations imposed upon the right to court. The SCC simply pointed out that the statute differentiated between different kinds of penalties, and said that this differentiation 'demonstrate[d] the provision's lack of conformity to Article 46.2 of the constitution'.[230] Similarly, inequality between the different groups of addressees of administrative sanctions was not held unreasonable but simply 'obvious and unsubstantiated in any way'.[231] There is no assessment of when statutory qualifications of constitutional rights could be deemed substantiated, and no inquiry into the legislator's duty to restrict rights only in a reasonable and necessary manner. The only signs of substantive interpretation in this and many other cases would come with the Court's recitation of the ECHR's judgments.

Indeed, the Court's reasoning usually contains a close scrutiny of the Slovak constitution's text, and a citation of ECHR case law, which includes substantive interpretation of the textual provision relevant to the case. As far as domestic law is concerned, the Court examines whether the constitution allows for statutory qualification of the affected right, and whether the respective limitation was in fact issued on the basis of a statute. In assessing whether a statutory qualification could be deemed in material conformity to the constitutionally permissible limitations, the SCC routinely refers to their interpretation by the ECHR.

The Court's understanding of the ECHR's interpretations not only as a complementary reference point, but often as the one yardstick applicable again demonstrates the combined effect on its interpretive preferences of the text and the context. First, unlike the PCT, which was unable directly to apply supra-national law in its interpretive enterprise, and could therefore rely on the ECHR's case law as merely a form of doctrinal support, the SCC was able to rely on Article 11 of the Slovak Constitution, granting international human-rights agreements normative superiority to domestic legislation.[232] Moreover, the direct applicability of international agreements in national adjudication led the petitioners to allege violations of rights thus protected in parallel to rights protected by the national constitution. The allegations of violations of international agreements thus gave the Court a good opportunity to refer to the ECHR's case law without forcing it to account for the extra-textual universe.

Secondly, unlike the CCC, which has operated in a context that tended to exaggerate the country's prominence in the integration process and which was therefore more confident in applying primarily the domestic constitutional provisions, the situation of Slovakia was very different. One of the reasons for the extensive use of all-European jurisprudence lies in the fact that in the course of the 1990s, the Court established itself as *the* authority linking Slovakia's constitutional culture to that of Western European civilisation. The reliance on the ECHR's dicta proved instrumental in preserving the axiological affinity between the Slovak constitutional order and the pan-European one. Moreover, as the process of law approximation is now at a highly developed stage and Slovakia desperately wants to improve its position within the European integration process, it makes a lot of sense to harmonise the country's constitutional jurisprudence with European 'constitutional' law as elaborated, inter alia, by the ECHR. If in a less charitable mood, however, one could also point out that substituting their own interpretive efforts by those of the ECHR lifted from the justices the burden of constructing a constitution of their own, one that would reflect their legal philosophies and their self-understanding as makers of constitutional law *sui generis*. After all, the Court used to rely on the ECHR's case law even when reviewing applications that did not allege a violation of rights granted by international instruments.[233] I have no objections against the method used by the Court, quite the contrary. It does, however, point to the SCC's lack of confidence as a constitutional interpreter.

Or was it rather the justices' tactical savvy which was on display? After all, the more extensive the Court's reliance on European law, the less exposed were its judgments to politically motivated critique. This brings us back to Ackerman's point that 'a politician considering whether to defy a particular judicial judgment... must engage in a broader analysis, taking into account economic and military benefits that may be lost if domestic political defiance leads to exclusion from the federation'.[234] The Court's reliance on the case law of the ECHR instead of meta-constitutional law of purely domestic origin made it difficult for an unhappy government official to question that interpretive methodology and, by extension, the outcomes it produced.

So did the Court's constant refusal to transcend the particularities of a given case and engage in a reasoning which would outline the essentials of its substantive jurisprudential agenda. In other words, by minimising the scope of issues to be discussed with respect to a petition the SCC would narrow not only the legal argument, but also the space for subsequent criticism of its interpretive approach. Its ruling on the establishment of investigative commissions accurately illustrates this point. The SCC said that establishing within the Parliament an investigative body would not necessarily have to amount to a violation of the balance of powers, and that in fact there were in a number of other countries parliamentary commissions with powers akin to those of law-enforcement agencies. 'The essence of such legal regulations, however, is the establishment of an investigative body of parliament on the basis of an explicit constitutional provision.'[235] The commissions therefore were held inadmissible because the text of the constitution did not foresee their establishment, not because their establishment constituted an unreasonable interference with the right to privacy or other possibly affected rights. To touch upon the rationality of the measure instead of pointing out the lack of observance of formal criteria would simply expose the Court to accusations of excessive judicial activism, that is, the kind of attack that it did not feel it could afford.

So while the HCC, for instance, would regularly strive to enrich the invisible constitution, the Slovak Court would confine its handling of the matter to specific circumstances of the case. One notes again the effect of the availability of text. Where constitutional arrangements were lacking in complexity or coherence, constitutional review was employed to substitute the law as written with supra-positive doctrinal fundamentals of higher law. The lack of text, or the lack of reverence for it, thus encouraged development of (meta)legal dogmatics. Where constitutional arrangements were conceptually definite and self-supporting, constitutional review was employed to preserve their internal consistency and normative superiority to ordinary legislation. The availability of text and reliance on it as the primary source of reference thus encouraged issue-specific legalistic analysis. The HCC, for instance, tended to give answers to questions that were not asked, apparently in order to develop a body of extra-textual principles to serve as the principal source of reference for both the law-making and the law-implementing agencies. The Slovak Court was happy concerning itself only with issues it was asked to concern itself with, and working with rules and principles that were directly available through textual references.

The SCC's lack of readiness to engage in doctrinal development, and the contrary propensity of the HCC, had some rather ironic consequences. Despite the provisionality of its transitional constitutional arrangements, no constitutional amendments were adopted in Hungary in the late 1990s, and it is safe to say that the Hungarian Court's active involvement in the construction of constitutional law is one of the major factors to be taken note of in this respect. In Slovakia, several constitutional amendments were adopted in the late 1990s, and the Slovak Court's relative unwillingness to make constitutional law played some role. The issue of a period within which the President could veto a statute offers a striking illustration: in 1997, the Court dealt with the issue within abstract review but limited itself to holding unconstitutional the specific legislative restriction.[236] Most importantly, it stopped short of saying that the 15-day period should be available from the date of the statute's delivery to the President. The constitution-maker therefore said so a few years later, and the Court now knows. Similarly, rather than establishing on its own the doctrinal foundations of constitutional review of ordinary adjudication, the SCC waited for the constitution-maker to say that a constitutional court is actually competent to invalidate decisions that it is competent to review and find unconstitutional.

There were legitimate concerns attendant on the HCC's interpretive constructivism, but its furnishing of constitutional rules unavailable through the text does not seem to have weakened either democracy or the rule of law in Hungary. Would the Slovak Court's filling of those few gaps that emerged in the country's constitutional order have weakened democracy or the rule of law in Slovakia? Or was it rather the other way around?

The difference between the two courts' interpretive methodologies extends beyond the effect of the lack/availability of text. The ways of framing an issue, as well as of phrasing its constitutional solution, for instance, illustrate the impact on a constitutional court's interpretive techniques of local legal culture rather than of factors immediately related to the text. In the *ratio decidendi* of its ruling on welfare reform,[237] the HCC referred to a specific law or its provision about 15 times, while it referred more often to its own case law. In the *ratio decidendi* of a similar ruling on investment coupons,[238] the SCC referred to a specific law or its provision virtually hundreds of times, without referring a single time to constitutional case law. Even in decisions dealing with the very same subject matter—that is, interference by the public prosecutor with ordinary courts' judgments[239]—the number of times that the SCC referred to a law's text is several times higher than the number of corresponding references by the HCC. The Hungarian Court's policy- and case law-oriented interpretation points to a tradition in which courts are allowed, even called upon, to consider factors beyond the law's text, and to rely on their own jurisprudential achievements. The Slovak Court's rule-oriented interpretation points to a tradition in which courts are expected and accustomed to approach law as a body of rules fit only for logical analysis. While the HCC does not shy away from building upon some 'phantom' rules of supra-positive constitutional law, the SCC's reasoning resembles mathematical analysis. The difference in the degree of reverence for *lex scripta* between the two courts points to immense differences in the justices' professional cognitions. These differences have not come about only by virtue of adopting, or failing to adopt, a specific legal act, but locate their origins in decades of pursuing a particular kind of legal practice.

Systemic as literal. Indeed, the SCC's adherence to the country's positivist tradition accounts for some important aspects of its interpretive approach. One can explain the fact that there is almost no constructivism detectable in its case law by pointing out the availability of text and the Court's context-informed defensive posture. That there is, however, not much of teleological interpretation, either, suggests that there were, again, other factors at play.

When the SCC expressly discusses its interpretive techniques, it usually points out literal and systemic interpretation, that is, methods locating the decisive reference sources in law as written. The following sentence neatly sums up the method:

> Deriving from the provisions of the Constitution and the [SACC] from which it does not explicitly result [sic!] that procedural eligibility for filing a petition for the protection of constitutional rights would transfer to descendents... the constitutional court concludes that the right to litigate a claim at the [SCC] expires by the litigant's death.[240]

Again, not only is it suggested that something must 'explicitly result' from the text in order to be relevant, but also there is no review of the possible lack of purpose of constitutional protection of rights of those who have deceased, and no examination of the nature of the given right. The only reference is that to the lack of explicit provisions.

The Court also displayed a complete lack of concern for anything but the text when dealing with an application for the exclusion of the rapporteur from proceedings because of his alleged bias. The defendant argued that at the oral hearing, the respective justice had posed to the petitioner questions already including the 'correct' answers, and, on the other hand, displayed hostility to the defendant, acting as if he was the petitioner's legal counsel. The SCC responded by pointing out that, pursuant to Article 28.1 of the SACC, a party might apply for the exclusion from proceedings of a biased justice at the beginning of the oral hearing at the latest.[241] Since the defendant had so applied only after the oral hearing, the application was dismissed as filed upon the expiry of the respective period. Again, since the law's text did not answer how it was possible for a litigant to allege bias before he became exposed to it, nor did the Court.

Further, the SCC, in stark contrast to the CCC, refused to extend the applicability of the proportionality doctrine to ordinary adjudication. Article 13 of the Slovak constitution sets forth criteria for permissible qualifications of constitutional rights. It stipulates that, inter alia, rights may be restricted only by statutory means, that in restricting rights their substance and meaning must be considered, and that restrictions may be effectuated only for the determined purpose. This is one of those constitutional imperatives that are perfectly fit for assessment according to the criteria of reasonableness. As far as ordinary courts are concerned, however, the matter could never get that far because, as the SCC believes, Article 13 'specifies the position and the role of statutes in imposing duties and restricting fundamental rights and freedoms, and thus applies exclusively to the legislator and not to judicial authorities'.[242] Accordingly, a petition alleging violation by ordinary courts of the principle of equal protection of property rights was held manifestly ill-founded because 'violation of this constitutional provision could occur only by the legislator's action, that is, by the adoption of laws regulating the content and the method of the protection of property rights, and not by the action of authorities implementing these laws in their decision-making'.[243]

What becomes clear here is not so much the structure of the constitution's text but rather the legacy of the country's positivist legal culture. The SCC namely continues to view ordinary adjudication as a Montesqieuan 'mouth of law', that is, as a machinery that simply is to translate the letter of the law into concrete judgments.[244] Since ordinary courts are incapable of making law, they are by definition incapable of violating the constitutional requirement that restrictions of rights must be informed by considerations of their substance and meaning.

The question arises, however, why the SCC has not struggled to erase, or at least alleviate, the positivist undercurrents of the local legal culture as much as has the CCC. First, sensitivity to *ius natura* was a much more significant element of the Czech legal revolution than was the case in Slovakia, which, after all, can be said about most aspects of the ethos accompanying the Velvet Revolution. Secondly, it is the experience that many of the Czech justices had with the communist version of positivism that seems to have informed their dislike of the law-is-law principle. A former dissident is much more likely to look for justice-through-law instead of law-despite-justice than is a former member of the communist machinery. Without belittling the seriousness and the candour of many Slovak legal practitioners' conversion from beneficiaries of the communist regime into believers in democracy, one's ability to appreciate what no legal text can offer is something that will require years of humble learning.

This brings me to the last set of questions to be addressed. How much does the personality of one or two justices matter to the country's constitutional development? Would the HCC have done all of what it has done had it not been led by Sólyom but by its current Chief Justice Németh? Most likely not. Would the CCC have struggled so vigorously to preserve the ideas of the Velvet Revolution were it staffed not by former dissidents but by former party-members? Certainly not. Would the PCT try to help out the legislature were a number of its justices not inclined to view Solidarity's agenda favourably? Probably not. But would the respective courts' case law have come out significantly differently if, for instance, CCC Chief Justice Kessler had led the Hungarian Court, the PCT's Garlicki the Slovak Court and Sólyom the Polish Tribunal, to suggest a random combination? It would not. The scope and structure of the respective Courts' jurisdiction, the politial environment they were to work in, the reactions to their operation by both the professional elite and the lay public, and other variables I have tried to account for in explaining the Visegrád constitutional jurisprudence have come to constitute a decisive part of the justices' experiential background. In other words, these circumstantial, or, if you will, exogenous factors have become the source of the constitutional judiciary's professional and social cognisance. Taking into account the various institutional designs, political circumstances, the wider socio-cultural contexts, and the legal culture-related aspects, none of the courts I have described, let alone the Slovak Court, would have produced radically different case law even if Earl Warren had been its Chief Justice. In short, 'one's gotta do what one's gotta do'.

CHAPTER 5

FOUNDING AND BEYOND

The very first paragraph of this book suggested that the Polish, Hungarian, Czech, and Slovak constitutional courts have achieved a place in their countries' constitutional politics comparable to that of the world's more advanced constitutional courts. I believe the book to have validated this claim. It was to a significant extent by virtue of the respective courts' engagement in the founding of liberal democracies in Europe's (ex)semi-periphery that the Visegrád nations may now confidently stake a claim for a more suitable place in European constitutional space.

It took only a few years for the post-communist citizenries to become accustomed to the availability of mechanisms designed to protect their autonomy and rights from excessive interference by government. The notion that a citizen is both worth, and entitled to, institutional protection against government abuse has become a constitutive element of the consciousness of the former *Homo sovieticus*. To hold a government accountable for its exercise of power and to expect that it address and redress one's justified grievances was nothing short of revolutionary, and is now nothing short of normal, for a majority of the respective populations. The kind of democracy that operates by a constitution and derives its legitimacy from observance by the government of *Rechtsstaat* imperatives appears to be the kind that large and significant enough segments of the Central European polities are willing to support. The constitutional courts' role in bringing about this state of affairs has been, and continues to be, crucial.

BIRTH

The courts themselves, however, have not come out of the blue, as if sent by heaven to redeem a *populus* for its collective failure to assert itself against the tyranny of the *ancien régime*. It was what Whitehead described as the prescriptive connotations of the region's return to Europe that played an extremely instrumental role in the emergence of constitutional review in Central and Eastern Europe. The end of history suggested by Fukuyama, in rather eschatological terms, to have legitimised liberal democracy as the ultimate solution to the civilised world's search for a sustainable utopia was the very kind of development of which Central and Eastern Europe wished to be a successful example. The logic of geographic proximity and political/ideological affinity between the region and the hegemons of constitutional development in Western Europe translated into the more specific institutional elaboration of the government-of-choice. If one adds to the equation the fact that the European Union offered its prospective members rather rigorous orientational guidelines, the revolutionaries' urge to conform to what has come to be expected of them by Europe's leading supra-national institutions seems a most natural reaction. Regional competition for a comparative advantage in the process of continent-wide economic and political integration thus affected the path of reform they have embarked upon in a relatively direct way: among other things, it contributed to the region's adherence to the concept of constitutional review.

There were other factors to encourage subscription to that idea. The informational cascades resulting from the region's relatively direct exposure to Western standards of rights protection in the wake of the Helsinki Accords have placed in the orbit of social and legal reforms in the socialist camp institutions and structures that have, when the time became ripe, facilitated the smooth transition from authoritarian regimes to systems exhibiting a high degree of similarity with those in place in the Euro-Atlantic space. Similarly, the reputational cascades deriving from the post-revolutionary elites' wish for a European image have made the concept of constitutional review an integral component of the transition mantra.

The extrication environment thus has been conducive to the incorporation by the post-communist establishments of constitutional review. As Reisman put it, however, this was a time when 'functions and not specific institutional implementations of functions' were being deliberated and selected.[1] The series of contexts that have affected the specific institutional implementations of the functions of constitutional review are too complex to warrant a clear-cut categorisation but a few themes do appear determinative of the Visegrád courts' positioning in the overall institutional designs of their polities.

The 'indigenous' element of the equation proved decisive for the shaping of constitutional adjudication and equipping it with distinct country-specific features. The centuries-long development of local legal and social consciousness, with its own traditional codes of behaviour for the different institutions, was as much a source of cognisance for agencies involved in the project of founding as was the pool of variables stemming from the immediate context of transition. In other words, those who were to design constitutional review would derive as much from the expectations that the respective polities have developed of the different instruments of government as they would from the expectations voiced by the Community of Europe.

The French model of public governance, still firmly rooted in the concept of parliamentary sovereignty, affected, for instance, the catalogue of options that the Polish elites were willing to consider as viable for their own turf. This made Poland gravitate towards a model in which the legislature was to enjoy considerable immunity from challenges to its policy-making discretion by the judiciary, and in which the role of constitutional review, as originally conceived, was to protect the legislature's will against abuse by the administration. The Hungarian institutional designers, on the other hand, worked with the legacies of the judiciary's active involvement in modernising the country and the society's *longue-durée* exposure to polycentric law-making. This has contributed to an adjudicative equipment of the Constitutional Court that in most ways was without precedence in the history of the institution and was heavily biased in favour of the constitutional judiciary's policy-making role. The Czechs were the first in the world to provide for a specialised constitutional tribunal and even though the First Republic Constitutional Court's achievements were less than impressive, the local legal academe's reverence for Kelsen has left the notion of constitutional review in the orbit of the country's legal thought even in times extremely hostile to the idea. Slovakia's lack of a history of statehood suggests the corresponding lack of autonomous elaboration of governance concepts but the country has internalised, through the multi-layered experience of a common state with the Czechs, many of their relevant traditions and subscribed to the idea of constitutional review without much pondering.

No less relevant to the specification of the constitutional courts' designs were variables relating to a country's political economy and the attendant search for transitional leaders. On the one hand, all the Central European constitutional courts were invited and expected to engage in the process of their societies' making sense of the dilemmas attendant on the founding project. Most of these dilemmas emanated from the tension between the need for incorporation and observance of human rights on one side and the need for speedy realisation of the principal tenets of political and economic transformation on the other. The underlying rationale for these expectations, however, differed between the respective countries, and the original constitutional choices as to the conceptualisation of a constitutional court's authority reflected these differences. In other words, the courts' adjudicative equipment was to some significant degree harnessed to the institutional interest of agencies authorised to draft and carry out reform.[2]

Poland, for instance, as proud as it deservedly is of its constitutional traditions, kept oscillating between the preference for a powerful executive and the wish to make its parliamentarism as inclusive as possible. This served to marginalise the Constitutional Tribunal in the constitutional reform—meagre in itself—that Poland was able to effectuate between 1989 and 1997. The PCT was therefore designed so as to operate mostly as the legislature's assistant in effectuating transition and thus made subject to control by the Sejm in the realm of posterior abstract review. Hungary's lack of a convincing 'public relations' asset in the quest for a spotlight in the region's transition, and its fascination with the West, induced the appointment of the Constitutional Court as a flagship of the country's readiness for progress. Accordingly, the post-revolutionary constitutional reform laid down firm grounds for what has become a co-leadership in the process of transition of the Parliament and the Constitutional Court. The Czech Constitutional Court was not in the immediate focus of the local constitution-makers. Moreover, the almost universal preference for as rapid and efficient a transformation as possible translated into relatively restrictive standing rules in the realm of abstract review, reflecting the lack of willingness of those who governed to expose their policy choices to constitution-based challenges from a wide variety of agents. A similar rationale accompanied constitution-making in Slovakia, where, in addition, the involvement of the judicial lobby in the drafting process contributed decisively to the crippling of the Slovak Constitutional Court's authority in the realm of incidental review. In addition, the Czech and the Slovak constitution-makers were able to draw from their neighbours' experiences with a constitutional court with an extremely powerful and with a limited competence, respectively. They were also preoccupied with those aspects of the founding that had to do with the immediate institutional and political implications of their countries' emergence as separate states. Accordingly, the Czech and the Slovak Constitutional Courts were designed so as to conform to the German/Austrian standard model of constitutional review, as if the founding was largely complete and no specific arrangements for the role of constitutional review in it had to be provided for.

In many ways, however, things went differently than expected. Even though the courts' institutional designs proved of considerable significance for their jurisprudence, less tangible variables, such as the exigencies of local political development, the justices' ideological inclinations, or *Kompetenz*-related technicalities, have affected constitutional case law in ways unforeseeable at the time when the respective courts were modelled.

CHILDHOOD

The exigencies of transition to which the emerging polities and their constitutional courts had to respond were similar across the region—history's end required that the rule of law be domesticated and the Visegrád nations founded as modern constitutional democracies. This has catapulted the courts into the centre of domestic constitutional politics. Their interpretive and adjudicative undertakings therefore reflected a uniform mission: that of carrying the polities through the transition by building the fundamentals of constitutional law and practice.

However, the degree of the courts' engagement in the reconstruction of their polities—that is, the extent to which they strove to accomplish their founding missions—varied, as did the method of this engagement, namely the adjudicative and interpretive techniques that the respective courts employed in order to complete the founding. It was both the design-bound features of constitutional review—that is, the institutional environment in general and the extent and the structure of a constitutional court's authority in particular—and the text-related variables (namely the completeness and the finality of texts available for interpretation) that have brought about different kinds of constitutional adjudication and interpretation.

Poland's transitional constitutional arrangements, for instance, left the Tribunal at a disadvantage against the Sejm, allowing for exposure to political supervision of constitutional review and often leading the Tribunal to lend the legislature a helping hand and taking account in its decision-making of a variety of extra-legal considerations reflecting the ideological essentials of the transitional agenda. Simultaneously, however, the provisionality of the constitutional framework offered the PCT the main rationale for a constructive interpretation of the underdeveloped constitutional law. One can thus trace to the interim nature of Poland's transitional reform the origins of both the Tribunal's interpretive creativity and its recurring deference to the Sejm.

Similarly, the patchwork of constitutional amendments in Hungary allowed the HCC to keep stepping beyond the constitution's text, which lacked indisputable legitimacy for the public and decisive authority for the Court. In addition, the HCC's extensive adjudicative equipment allowed it regularly to assert its counter-majoritarian features against the Parliament, engage actively in the shaping of transitional policies and elaborate a relatively autonomous theory of the change of regime, with significant consequences for the country's constitutional development. The Hungarian Court's activism thus can be attributed mostly to its extensive competence portfolio and the lack of respect that the HCC had for the patchwork of constitutional amendments.

The restrictive standing rules in the realm of abstract review in the Czech Republic have affected the operation of constitutional review by limiting the variety of challenges addressed to the CCC and thereby insulating some major tenets of transformation policies from tinkering by the constitutional judiciary. In addition, the extensive concrete-review competence that the CCC was invited to employ has divided the justices' attention between the review of statutory and sub-statutory enactments of policies on the one hand, and the review of their implementation by administrative agencies and the ordinary courts on the other. In Slovakia, the less extensive concrete-review equipment and the more generous abstract-review standing rules opened up space for the SCC to perform its counter-majoritarian commission and frustrate a number of the then governing majority's attempts to instil authoritarian features into the country's framework of public governance. In addition, the relative finality of the Czech and Slovak constitutional reforms led the respective courts to refrain from construing their own constitutions.

But neither the institutional environment nor the texts can explain several other features of constitutional adjudication in Central Europe. While only the CCC and the SCC enjoyed the ability to engage in concrete review and assess individual decisions, it was the Polish Tribunal that joined the Czech Court in asserting its authority against the ordinary courts while the Slovak Court made use of the available powers to a lesser degree than possible. Similarly, the abstract review instruments of the CCC and the PCT were subject to very different constraints, and yet these courts proved less ready than did the HCC and the SCC to halt some key legislative efforts. There also is nothing in the positioning of constitutional review within the Czech and Slovak frames of government that should suggest and validate their different approaches to the pursuit of transitional agendas through legislative and/or executive venues. Simply, the Visegrád courts are as different as they are from each other not only because they were equipped with relatively different adjudicative tools, but also because they chose different opponents.

The simple equation linking unfinished constitutional reform to judicial creativity or a nominally strong constitutional court to a pattern of confrontation between the legislature and constitutional review therefore must be enriched by an adequate account of the deeper layers of the courts' motivational horizons. It is the wider social and political context as well as the local legal traditions that shed light on the differences in both the nature and the goals of the courts' adjudicative and interpretive enterprises. The contingent political circumstances and the country-specific variations of the civil law tradition therefore belong to the pool of relevant variables as much as does institutional design or the available texts. The courts' DNA informed by traditional codes of institutional behaviour, for instance, proved as instrumental in reinforcing or undermining, respectively, their creativity and assertiveness as did the design within which the respective courts were to operate and the texts they were to work with.

The Polish Tribunal, for instance, tended to show sympathy for the fragmented political arena's attempts at completing the transition even when it was apparent that its decisions would withstand the Sejm's subsequent scrutiny. Moreover, it continued upholding legislative solutions to certain transition-related moral dilemmas even upon insulation from direct political control. The local legal tradition, rooted firmly in the concept of popular and, by extension, parliamentary sovereignty, as well as in the classical triangular theory of separation of powers, contributed significantly to the PCT's permissive attitude towards the legislature's efforts to effectuate transition. Also, the justices' preference for a particular path of social development—or, at times, rather the notion that any development based on political consensus might be better than no consensus and no progress—appear to have been as relevant to the outcome of many a case dealt with by the Tribunal as was the extent of its authority or the text it would employ to handle an issue. Indeed, the exigencies of the country's political development—tainted by the all too frequent occurrences of legislative impasse—seem to have informed in a decisive way the PCT's relative readiness to refrain from questioning the rationale of political agreement.

Similarly, the Czech Court's whole-hearted adherence to the ideology fostered by the post-revolutionary establishment, and its consequent support of the translation of this ideology into legislation, was rooted in the justices' moral and professional cognitions rather than a necessary extension of the CCC's adjudicative equipment. The society's preference for efficient policy making and its relatively firm support of Klaus' No-Third-Way transformation path dominated the transitional discourse and the justices have both derived from, and enhanced, these aspects of Czech constitutional politics. Moreover, the Court's readiness to move beyond the default presumption of rationality and legitimacy of legislature-produced policy choices when the government's agenda would deviate from concepts rooted in the original *ethos* of the revolution demonstrates that a distinct axiology, a particular vision of legal and social development, heavily informed Czech constitutional case law.

While their adjudicative equipments differed in some important ways, both the PCT and the CCC proved relatively lenient in supervising those statutory measures that were aimed at effectuating the institution of new political, economic, and social paradigms. On the other hand, they also vigorously required that the ordinary courts observe in their decision-making the emerging axiological foundations of the new regimes. Their permissiveness in scrutinising legislation—that is, a form of 'soft' abstract review—was accompanied by their assertiveness in the intra-judicial colloquy. This conceptual similarity of philosophies of judicial activism between constitutional courts equipped with rather different adjudicative tools again proves how prone to modification by factors beyond design is the impact that a court's authority has on its jurisprudence.

In Slovakia, it was the then governing majority's utter lack of consideration for constitutional imperatives that in the mid- and late 1990s induced the Slovak Constitutional Court to establish itself as a bastion of the rule of law and the country's main asset in maintaining contact with Europe's culture of constitutionalism and its axiological foundations. That abstract review was available was of course a necessary precondition for the SCC's exercise of counter-majoritarian control. But it was the overall transitional environment, in both its institutional and political dimensions, that encouraged extensive delegation to the Court of legislative and executive measures. Its occasional failures to deliver on the promise it seemed to have made when it first stood up against Mečiar suggest, however, that the justices were not completely at ease with trumping the will of the governing majority and undermining the particularities of its transitional agenda. Even less so were they at ease with developing an autonomous jurisprudential agenda. Accordingly, the SCC remained within the boundaries of strictly negative legislating even when it was at its counter-majoritarian best. It is in this respect that the domination by the classical separation-of-powers theory of the local legal discourse, and the legacy of the judiciary's insistent staying away from policy making, were of particular relevance to the SCC's adjudicative philosophy.

It is the same type of legacy, but one with radically different content, that the Hungarian Constitutional Court was able to draw upon in its counter-majoritarian enterprise, seizing relentlessly upon the local tradition of courts acting as policy-setters and as agents of social change of their own kind. The authority it was equipped with was instrumental in feeding the Court's law making stamina. However, the most it would achieve in terms of fostering the concept of prospective constitutionalism—one of its own making—would be a result of the performance of posterior abstract-review powers, which but for some details did not differ radically from the parallel competencies of the SCC or the CCC. What made the HCC different from other constitutional courts in the region was not only the extent of its authority, but also the context in which it was invited to employ it; a context dominated by the country's intense search for a comparative advantage in the region's integration race and to which the notion of the judiciary's involvement in policy-oriented review certainly was not alien. The HCC simply updated and adjusted to its own purposes the local legacy of modernizing by means of judicial decision-making the country's legal and social landscape. It did so in a manner that might have surprised many commentators, both foreign and local, but of which as many of them have approved.

Again, however, while both the SCC and the HCC tended to operate in a prohibitive mode of abstract review, they also proved to lack confidence to intervene in ordinary adjudication, and despite differences in the structure of their authority approached the realm of implementation of law in a conceptually similar way. The Hungarian Court saw no relevant overlap between its own engagement in the founding and that of the ordinary courts. The SCC understood ordinary adjudication to be an institutionally self-contained branch of power immune from interference even by a constitutional court, except for a limited range of circumstances. Given that it was with the Polish Tribunal that the Hungarian Court shared its inability to engage in concrete review, it might have come as a surprise that it was with the Slovak Court that the HCC shared its reluctance to police the ordinary courts.

What this points to, though, is what constitutes the core of my argument: the region's constitutional courts have been using their adjudicative equipment mostly to confront those government agents that they deemed capable of threatening their notions of what the founding of a constitutional democracy entailed. In other words, the targets of the courts' adjudicative and interpretive activism differed depending on where the courts anticipated the threat to their idea of a safe way between the transitional Scylla of legitimacy and the Charybdis of efficiency to come from. The courts were not only assigned a range of opponents; they also discriminated between them and, so to speak, chose to pick fights with those they felt they needed to challenge in order to see (their versions of) the transition come through as planned.

The Czech Court, for instance, proved more or less resistant to the idea of imposing its own constitution upon the Parliament, not least because it was rather happy with the legislature's transitional agenda, and focused on making sure that it was in fact implemented as fully as possible by the agencies so commissioned. It therefore took it upon itself continuously to educate the ordinary courts in the culture of modern constitutionalism and was very active in trying to ease the grip on ordinary adjudication of the local tradition of positivist formalism. Similarly, the Polish Tribunal, albeit not unequivocally deferential to the Sejm, thought it was appropriate for the legislature to outline the contours of Poland's development and necessary for the judiciary, including its constitutional division, to observe these contours in its decision-making. Indeed, the confrontation between the Polish and Czech constitutional courts on one side and the ordinary courts on the other was as significant an element of their countries' constitutional discourses as was the Hungarian Court's interaction with the Parliament or the Slovak Court's efforts to cultivate Mečiar's constitutionality-resistant parliamentary majority.

So the Slovak Court let the ordinary courts figure things out on their own and confronted those who kept undermining the country's ongoing founding as a *Rechtsstaat*, that is, the country's founding fathers themselves. Its jurisprudence is one of the more modest in the region yet the peculiarities of what the locals call Mečiarism—that is, a quasi-authoritarian regime in place between 1992 and 1998—forced it to stand up against the power-hungry clique at the steering wheel and challenge various legislative attempts at manipulating parliamentary democracy into one that would reflect the infamous Slovak specifics. The Hungarian

Court would reach beyond positive law whenever it deemed it suitable for the advancement of its jurisprudential agenda of prospective constitutionalism and proved more of an obstacle to majoritarian politics than any other court in the region. Sólyom would blame the HCC's failure to stir much water in the intra-judicial colloquy on its confinement to abstract review but incidental review was not what the Court was in need of in order to do the one thing it felt it was called to do: assert against the impurity of political bargaining its own vision of a country living proudly by constitutional dogmatics.

Therefore, as much as the logic of the respective countries' historical legal development affected both the conceptualisation of the constitutional courts' authority and their jurisprudence, it was still subject to the modifying impact of the exigencies of transitional political development. And as much as the Visegrád courts were in one way or another affected by the constitution makers' original decisions as to the scope of their operability in constitutional politics, the justices' own cognisance of their role in bringing about social change, as well as their preferences for that or another solution to transition-related moral dilemmas, left visible traces in Central Europe's constitutional case law.

Like the dichotomy of prohibitive/permissive modes of constitutional review, the dichotomy of constructivist/preservationist modes of constitutional interpretation came about as a function of a series of factors. The provisionality of foundational texts in both Poland and Hungary was instrumental in inducing these courts to step beyond the available texts and develop an elaborate jurisprudential *corpus* deriving in large part from legal theory and political philosophy rather than merely the law's letter. The Czech and the Slovak Courts had conceptually definite constitutions to work with and, in general, refrained from supplementing the text, let alone 'fixing' it.

Yet again, differences emerge between the courts' interpretive projects, indicating a context richer than simply the lack of finality and 'purity' of textual arrangements. The PCT, for instance, would act mostly as a constitutional emergency unit, offering tenets of the country's higher law that the legislature was unable to provide for. It was largely by virtue of the Tribunal's willingness to derive from the limited language of the constitution some fundamental features of a *Rechtsstaat* that the country's *Grundrechtsdogmatik* has not suffered from the political arena's failures to update the rights-protection framework as much as it could have suffered were the PCT less creative. The lack of a coherent rights catalogue, however, also induced the Tribunal to approach the constitution as a depository of values and principles, a practice which often led it to qualify rights by some rather peculiar concepts. The notion of the ethical foundations of the Mediterranean culture, for instance, or of a budgetary equilibrium as a constitutional value equal to the protection of vested rights have had at times rather adverse consequences for the quality of citizens' protection from the government. No matter how rich its equal-protection case law, the Tribunal's firm embeddedness in the country's legal and social consciousness often precluded it from swimming against the mainstream on behalf of the society's allegedly marginal segments.

The Hungarian Court would not only furnish rules unavailable through the very text of the constitutional patchwork, but would also show notable lack of respect for some of the rules that were in fact provided in writing. It established an autonomous hierarchy of rights different from that suggested by the text of the constitution, creatively manipulated the explicit delineation of its powers, and in general tended to understand constitutional *case law* as constitutional *law*, equal if not superior in terms of normative relevance to the written rules. On the other hand, it proved much less forthcoming than the PCT to the notion that rights, including social rights, could be extensively qualified by, for instance, public interest. The HCC's motivational horizon also was heavily informed by its urge to evidence the progress that the country had made—or rather, that the Court wanted it to be willing to make. This progressivist urge translated into some revolutionary jurisprudential outcomes, for example, giving future mankind the right to a healthy environment, or allowing homosexual couples to demand that the government sanction their relationships.

The Czech Court, even though—or rather because of—having imbued the constitution with a particular value content at the very outset of its operation, would reach outside the text mostly in order to preserve the *ethos* of the revolution's achievements, and identified the ordinary courts as the main target of its interpretive enterprise. The CCC would insist on observance in ordinary adjudication of the *telos* of law, vehemently dismiss positivist interpretation and require that the law-implementing agencies reflect the legislature's will as faithfully as possible. By doing so, the Court usually has tried to reinforce those elements of the transitional dossier for which it has shown a clear preference already in communicating with the legislature. Despite the positivist undercurrents of the local legal culture, the CCC has whole-heartedly subscribed to the notion of the normative significance of natural law, suggested that unwritten principles were to be deemed part of the law of the land, and in general vigorously rejected the country's tradition of positivism. The dissidents-become-justices' first-hand experience with the implications of the communist version of the *Recht-ist-Recht* principle thus accounted in a decisive way for the defining elements of the Court's interpretive philosophy.

This was an experience upon which most of the SCC's justices were unable to draw. Accordingly, the country's positivist traditions got the better of the region's newly found sensitivity to natural law even in the realm of constitutional adjudication. Indeed, the Slovak Court would approach the constitution's text with almost religious reverence and the furthest it would go was to enrich a purely grammatical understanding of a norm with hints of what it used to denote as systemic interpretation, that is, one based on the overall structure of the relevant text. So, rather than constructing value-laden tenets of constitutional law, the SCC confined its interpretive endeavours to the preservation of the supremacy of the constitutional text. The governing majority's frequent attempts to operate with no constitutional constraints whatsoever gave the SCC good reason to keep doing so. The justices' rather cautious approach to making constitutional law on their own and the need to preserve the country's place in Europe's integration orbit have also led the Court to rely heavily on, and even prefer, the interpretive efforts of the ECHR to its own autonomous jurisprudential agenda.

I have focused in this book on describing and explaining the interdependence, and the combined effect on constitutional adjudication, of variables of dramatically different nature and origin. Indeed, as with every child growing up to be a distinct personality, so, too, the upbringing of the Visegrád constitutional courts as offspring of their countries' transitions to Euro-Atlantic models of government exposed both their genetic background and the effect of the environment. In other words, both a court's DNA and the *Kinderstube* it was to be raised in were on display in Central Europe's transitional constitutional adjudication. The courts' self-understanding as agents of social and legal change, and the traditional notions embedded in local legal consciousness of the 'proper' institutional behaviour of public authorities in general, and of the judiciary in particular, account for the genetic part of the equation. And so does the equipment with which the courts were endowed at birth. The often intractable, and at times heavily personalised, peculiarities of interaction between the relevant institutions, the subtleties of political development, and the *Bildung* offered by both the public and legal academia constitute the environmental part of the equation. Without further *dilettante* attempts at cognitive psychology, a constitutional court's manoeuvring in the founding environment was quite obviously affected by the scope of its jurisdiction.

It was, however, also informed by a kind of judicial epistemics that a court would both inherit from its predecessors wearing the judicial robe and be raised to identify with by its 'au-pairs' and peers.

ADULTHOOD

When the country-specific versions of the region-specific revolution were, as Kahn puts it, 'over and substantively complete'[3] is unclear and maybe not even that important. That a country's constitutional court was certainly involved in making the revolutions over and substantively complete is clear enough, and important, too. One is inclined to wonder what the next stage for the different courts will be. It seems that for some of them, such as the Hungarian Court, the golden era of dominating almost single-handedly the local legal topography may be over, while some others, such as the Czech Court, are now basking in the spotlight of the society's devoted, and the politicians' nervous, attention. The Polish Tribunal appears fond of orientating its jurisprudence around more than the one or two clauses of which it made such extensive use in the provisional period. And the Slovak Court, recently granted full concrete-review jurisdiction, is gradually becoming accustomed to thinking of itself as a court. Important as these variations are, however, they do not yet suggest a paradigm-shift in the institution's country-specific development.

At a time when answers had to be given to questions such as when a president's term expires, under what conditions can he dissolve the legislature, how strong a guarantee is a statute of limitations for crimes left deliberately unpunished, what is the nature of property restitution, and so on, instruments such as interpretive constructivism, considerations of 'transitional specifics', an 'invisible constitution', or discrimination between pre-revolutionary and post-revolutionary law might have been a viable way of the constitutional courts' engagement in the process of founding. What is crucial for constitutional adjudication across the region is that with most of these questions settled, references in constitutional jurisprudence to the exigencies of the change of regime appear less suited for what seem to be relatively stabilised democracies. One of the imminent paradigm-shifts therefore will concern the transformation of PCT-preferred transition-specific jurisprudence into HCC-preferred normal-development jurisprudence. It is indeed the Hungarian Court that hints at gradual domestication in its jurisprudence of an 'ordinary day' approach to issues of constitutional politics.

The exigencies of the respective countries' political development may delay this paradigm-shift for a while and as much, if not more, activism as we have seen so far still may have to be required from certain courts in the region in order for 'Europe' to prevail in their domestic discourses. Moreover, the growing overlap between the making of law and its implementation, especially on the level of constitutional law, will inevitably affect Visegrád constitutional politics as much as Damaška suggests it has affected the United States,[4] and as much as Stone Sweet argues it has affected Western Europe.[5]

But the more distant the founding, the less politically and doctrinally feasible the courts' involvement in outlining political, social, and economic agendas. In short, the region will not be post-communist forever; after all, it is already pre-European more than it is anything else. And it is in fact the elimination of both the 'post' and the 'pre' part that makes up for the biggest challenge awaiting the Visegrád courts. Having more or less successfully accomplished their founding agendas, they are poised to move on and into a space that will be dominated by the exigencies of a different transition; that from a nation state to a member of an increasingly federalised supra-national structure.

In about two years from now, the Visegrád nations most likely will become full-members of the European Union, and their jurisdictions directly exposed to the *acquis communautaire*, including the *acquis jurisprudentiel*. Accompanying this process will be the need for the Central European constitutional courts to make sense of their role in the complex structure of transnational bodies of legislative, executive, and judicial pedigree. The Ackermanian 'European-Federation' constraint will thus receive a wholly new quality, and its effect will be all the more direct. The history of the colloquy between the German Constitutional Court, the Italian Constitutional Court, or the French Constitutional Council on one side and the European Court of Justice or the European Commission on the other suggests that the Visegrád constitutional judiciary, too, may be headed towards some head-butting with Brussels or Luxembourg. The lack of consensus among Europe's leading institutional architects as to the future relationship between the EU's Charter of Fundamental Rights and the ECHRFF is something that certainly will impact the Central European constitutional courts' efforts to harmonise national with various kinds of supranational and international law. As in helping to found their polities as constitutional democracies, so, too, in helping to domesticate them in the European constitutional space the role of constitutional judiciary will be of the utmost importance. One mission accomplished, another one assigned.

NOTES

NOTES TO INTRODUCTION

1 Throughout the book, Central Europe refers to the Czech Republic, Hungary, Poland, and Slovakia, unless otherwise indicated.

2 By 'legitimacy' as a component of the transitional equation I mean a specific quality of the transition constituted by the government agenda's principal correspondence to the fundamental guidelines for societal transformation as elaborated via venues commissioned for that purpose in the countries concerned. By 'efficiency' I mean a specific feature of the processes of transition constituted by both the institutional capacity and the actual ability of the government to implement the essential aspects of its transitional agenda.

3 See, for example, Brzezinski, Struggle for Constitutionalism in Poland; Brunner and Garlicki, Verfassungsgerichtsbarkeit in Polen; Sólyom and Brunner, Constitutional Judiciary in a New Democracy; Schwartz, The Struggle for Constitutional Justice; Bröstl, Kl'učka and Mazák, Constitutional Court of the Slovak Republic.

4 See Brunner, Hofmann, and Holländer, Verfassungsgerichtsbarkeit in der Tschechischen Republik.

5 The only other constitutional court in the region that I understand as belonging to the top echelon is the Constitutional Court of Slovenia. For an authoritative discussion of the Slovenian Court, see Mavčič, Slovenian Constitutional Review. For a more recent study, see Bugarič, 'Courts as Policy Makers'.

6 For a recent discussion of collective identities in Central Europe and the region's common cultural, social, and ideological conceptions, see Csáky and Mannová (eds), Kolektívne identity.

7 For more detail on both the history and the current developments of intra-Visegrád cooperation, see Lukáč, 'Visegrád Co-operation'. See also Máša, 'Visegrád se vrací na scénu'.

8 See, for example, Banac, Eastern Europe in Revolution; Grudzinska-Gross (ed.), Constitutionalism in East Central Europe; Greenberg et al. (eds), Constitutionalism and Democracy; Pridham (ed.), Building Democracy?; Linz and Stepan, Problems of Democratic Transition; Elster (ed.), The Roundtable Talks; Elster, Offe, and Preuss, Institutional Design in Post-Communist Societies; Plasser, Ulram, and Waldrauch, Democratic Consolidation in East-Central Europe; Krygier and Czarnota, The Rule of Law After Communism.

9 For an illuminating discussion of informational and reputational cascades and their effect on deliberation, see Sunstein, 'Deliberative Trouble', which provides a comprehensive list of scholarly sources on the issue as well as a range of empirical accounts. For my contextualized treatment of cascades, see the discussion in Chapter One under the heading 'Intra-Regional Pressure'.

10 For the purposes of this book, I draw on Van Hoecke and Warrington in understanding legal culture to mean both the axiological and the institutional articulation of the regulatory authority of law (government), which articulation is based on the communal understanding of what role is legitimate for law (government) to play in the community's life and is informed by the religious, philosophical, political, and geographical coordinates of the community's development. For more on the definition of legal culture, see Van Hoecke and Warrington, 'Legal Cultures and Legal Paradigms'. See also Nicholson, 'Roots and Routes'.

11 For the purposes of this book, I draw on Reitz in understanding political economy to mean a set of principles affecting the design of the public regulatory framework on the basis of the polity's conceptualization of the role of the government in the polity members' lives. For more on the 'architectural' notion of political economy to which I adhere, see Reitz, 'Political Economy as a Major Architectural Principle'.

NOTES TO CHAPTER 1
ESTABLISHING CONSTITUTIONAL REVIEW

1 Eliade, Dejiny náboženských predstáv a ideí [*A History of Religious Ideas*], 13.

2 Ibid.

3 Linz and Stepan distinguish between the different models of a non-democratic regime and describe Poland in 1989 as an authoritarian regime, Hungary as a post-totalitarian one, and Czechoslovakia as a totalitarian regime. *Problems of Democratic Transition,* 255–344.

4 Bronisław Geremek, a prominent figure in Polish academia and politics, expresses it as follows: 'The saga of Poland—particularly in the invention of Solidarity—tells of how a proud and impoverished people sought to rid themselves of an alien body introduced into their midst.' Geremek, 'Between Hope and Despair', 95.

5 The 1921 Constitution of Poland reflected the democratic standards of the time and the Poles did make use of it in their post-1989 deliberations over constitutional options. Nevertheless, it functioned for only four-and-a-half years and, according to former Vice-President of the Sejm's Constitutional Committee Wojciech Ciemniewski, even during those years 'it functioned badly'. *See Constitutionalism in East Central Europe* 12 (comment by Ciemniewski).

6 Offe, 'Cultural Aspects of Consolidation', 65.

7 Whitehead, 'East-Central Europe in Comparative Perspective', 41.

8 See, for example, the European Council's Declaration on Central and Eastern Europe adopted at the summit of the European Council in Strasbourg in December 1989, available at http://europa.eu.int/council/off/conclu/index. The Declaration stated, '[t]he current changes and the prospects for development in Europe demonstrate the attraction which the political and economic model of Community Europe holds for many countries'. The Western leaders would continue to produce similar feel-good statements, especially during political turmoil on their local podium.

9 The only notable exception to this rule was the 1994–1998 Slovak government in which two of the three parties held openly hostile attitudes towards the West. But even that government's official agenda presented accession to the European Union and NATO as its primary political objective.

10 Kundera, 'The Tragic Destiny'.

11 For a detailed discussion of the minimum definition of democracy, see Plasser, Ulram, and Waldrauch, *Democratic Consolidation in East-Central Europe,* 6–10.

12 Murphy, for instance, understands the institutional minimum of democracy to require popular election of representatives, free access of citizens to candidacy for electoral office, and freedom of political communication and association. Murphy, 'Constitutions, Constitutionalism and Democracy', 17.

13 Reisman, 'Introductory Remarks', 190.

14 The region's development copied the path of continental Europe more than it did the splendidly isolated Anglo-American one. Therefore, when discussing the Western Europe-bound constraints of transition, I tend to think in terms of continental Europe, the interaction of which with Central and Eastern Europe traditionally has been more immediate and thus more imposing than that of, for instance, the United Kingdom. For a discussion of historical impermeability between the Western and the Eastern parts of the European continent, see Wandycz, *Price of Freedom,* 3–26. For a claim that 'transatlantic cross-fertilization' is insignificant in the realm of constitutionalism, see Stone Sweet, Governing with Judges, 132.

15 I use the term 'European Communities' for the pre-1993 environment, as it was only then that the Maastricht Treaty officially instituted the European Union.

16 Ackerman, 'The Rise of World Constitutionalism', 776–777.

17 Havel, for instance, described the European Union as 'an entity that is relatively little bothered by appeals for distance, for detachment from everyday hassle, by appeals for a major civilisational self-reflection. This Europe is relatively egocentric, despite the nice words it at times produces; it is Europe for which the shirt of immediate economic interests feels closer than the coat of global philosophy.' Havel, 'Evropa jako společně sdílený osud'. Timothy Garton Ash identifies the Havelian/Gönczian political ideal as that of an 'intelligentsia democracy' and retrospectively finds Western Europe at fault for its failure to employ this ideal in expanding liberal values to the entire continent. See Garton Ash, 'Všichni trpíme Waldheimerovou nemocí'.

18 Sokolewicz, 'Constitution-building in Poland', 253.

19 Ten years later, Havel lamented as the biggest failure of post-1989 Central Europe the fact that it did not manage to convey to the West its peculiar historical experience, namely that it did not teach Europe the lesson Europe needs to learn in order to survive spiritually. See Havel, 'Address to Forum 2000'.

20 The original association agreement of Czechoslovakia was executed but never came into force due to a stringent ratification procedure and the division of the country at the end of 1992.

21 Sokolewicz, 'Constitution-building in Poland', 251.

22 Wandycz argues that history has forced Poles, Hungarians, Czechs, and Slovaks to defend and fight for freedom more frequently than many other nations, and that freedom in the region thus 'has been gained at a high price and must not be lost'. Wandycz, *Price of Freedom,* 273. Although freedom is, of course, precious to any nation, it certainly is true that the post-1989 Central European regimes were not ready to put the newly found freedom in jeopardy by tampering with their geopolitical alignment with the West. And when they did, as was the case with Slovakia's 1994–1998 government, they soon were to find themselves isolated, even ostracized, not only by the EU, but also by their neighbours.

23 I would not dare to call *Polska* a small nation, but in the absence of an ally it too has proved very vulnerable to the expansionist urges of its neighbours, and too many times and up until relatively recently (for example, in 1791–1795, 1939, 1947) to take the issue of the regional power balance lightly.

24 In Slovakia, the European-integration card proved effective even as late as 1998 when the insurgent coalition managed to overthrow the local populist leader Mečiar, largely because of his utter failure to achieve any progress on the integration front. The government which emerged from the 1998 elections also successfully relied on the theme of European integration when it managed to talk the electorate out of participating in the November 2000 referendum on whether early elections should be held.

25 Given the lack of immediate and tangible results of deference to Brussels, it is ironic that support for EU membership has not withered away among the Central European populations as much as it did in relation to the overall post-1989 political development. For detailed figures, see regularly conducted Eurobarometer polls, available at http://europa.eu.int. See also Plasser, Ulram, and Waldrauch, *Democratic Consolidation in East-Central Europe.*

26 For a detailed discussion of the concept of partial regimes, see Plasser, Ulram, and Waldrauch, *Democratic Consolidation in East-Central Europe,* 34–39.

27 Cappelletti, 'Repudiating Montesqieu?', 5.

28 See Zupančič, 'Od souboje ke smlouvě', 487.

29 As far as the European Court of Human Rights (ECHR) is concerned, there is no gainsaying the fact that it may hold a government accountable for actions performed by a constitutional court, for on the supranational level it is the national rather than the judicial nature of a constitutional court that determines its standing. See, for example, the judgment of the ECHR in 'Krčmář and Others vs. Czech Republic', available at http://www.echr.coe.int.

As far as the European Court of Justice (ECJ) is concerned, Article 234 of the European Agreement explicitly binds any national court to refer to the ECJ any issue that involves the application of European law, save for a limited range of circumstances. What is noteworthy is that the ECJ has vigorously rejected the suggestion that national constitutional courts be granted the power to control domestic applications of European law, and the German and Italian constitutional courts, for instance, have refrained from the practice. See Rubio Llorente, 'Constitutionalism'. For more on transnational judiciary, see also Slaughter who, relying on 'many observers of the ECJ, including a number of judges', argues that the fact that 'the national courts refer cases raising European law issues to the ECJ and then use its analysis of these issues to guide their disposition of the case' has increased the Court's relevance in the all-European colloquy. Slaughter, 'A Typology of Transjudicial Communication', 100. For a thorough discussion of the impact on national policies of European rights case law and its integrative quality, see Kuhnhardt, 'European Courts and Human Rights'.

30 Casper, 'European Convergence', 443.

31 Davy, 'Perceptions and Performance', 251.

32 Ibid., 263 (referring to *détente* as such).

33 The ambiguous relationship between national and international law in the Polish pre-1997 constitutional order prevented the PCT from acquiring the power to adjudicate upon conformity of national norms to international agreements. Where the superiority to national legislation of international obligations was explicitly provided for,

as was the case with the constitutions of Hungary and Czechoslovakia (and the Czech and the Slovak Republics), the respective constitutional courts were not deprived of this competence.

34 Ackerman, 'The Rise of World Constitutionalism', 776.

35 An illustrative exchange took place in 1995 between Václav Klaus, then Prime Minister of the Czech Republic and Hans van Broek, then European External Relations Commissioner. When Klaus took the liberty of heavily criticizing the Common Agricultural Policy of the EU, and suggested it be radically reformed, he was brusquely disciplined by van Broek who did not shy away from pointing out that one should always remember that 'it is the Czech Republic joining the European Union and not the European Union joining the Czech Republic'. See 'Czech Republic Update 1996', 8.

36 Schimmelfennig, 'The Double Puzzle'.

37 In the context of constitutional review, the notion of a bandwagon effect reflects a particular version of what Pridham denotes as 'transnational dynamics of system change' ('The International Dimension', 29). In other words, under a given set of circumstances institutional reform in one country serves to inspire or reinforce similar reform in another country. As far as Central and Eastern Europe is concerned, constitutional review is now in operation in Albania, Bulgaria, Croatia, Czech Republic, Federal Republic of Yugoslavia, Hungary, Macedonia, Poland, Romania, Russia, Slovakia, Slovenia, and Ukraine. There are constitutional-review chambers of supreme courts in operation in Estonia and Lithuania. There are constitutional courts in some of the former Soviet Republics in Central Asia, too.

38 Sólyom, 'On the Co-operation of Constitutional Courts'.

39 Sajó, 'Rule by Law', 472.

40 Pinder, 'The European Community and Democracy', 132.

41 Schimmelfennig argues, for instance, that it was rational for Central Europe's transition agencies to focus on the institutionalisation of values and norms because if the EU were to ignore or counter their commitments to immaterial aspects of transition, it would expose itself to the loss of credibility and legitimacy. See Schimmelfennig, 'The Double Puzzle'.

42 Batt, 'Czecho-Slovakia and Hungary', 247.

43 See Linz and Stepan, 'Problems of Democratic Transition', 76–81. Similarly, Hellmann undertook an elaborate analysis of the relation between constitutional reform and economic progress and provided data illustrating that 'postponing the adoption of new constitutions does not appear to advance the process of economic reform', and that 'the adoption of a new constitution does appear to have some positive effect on the process of economic reform' ('Constitutions and Economic Reform', 52).

44 Checkel, 'Institutional Dynamics'.

45 Schimmelfennig, 'The Double Puzzle'.

46 See, for example, Lemann, 'Annals of Marketing'.

47 Plasser, Ulram, and Waldrauch, *Democratic Consolidation in East-Central Europe*, 9.

48 Elster, 'Forces and Mechanisms in the Constitution-Making Process', 376–377.

49 In some cases, few of the framers were later to become constitutional justices. According to first-hand anecdotal evidence, their influence on the outcome of constitution making was marginal. See Sólyom, 'Interview', 71.

50 For a discussion of the slightly different situation of Poland, which provided for constitutional review during the regime's last years but did not enhance significantly its rights-protection features after the regime collapsed, see the discussion on p. 67ff.
51 Bruszt and Stark, for instance, point out that the opposition's appeals addressed to the establishment before the fall of the regime evolved from 'restrain yourself' to 'allow yourself to be restrained' 'Remaking the Political Field in Hungary', 23.
52 Páczolay describes this as a 'no consent–too much consent dynamics' 'Constitutional Transition', 569.
53 Here, the Polish lawmakers appear to have been more cautious than the Hungarian, Czech, or Slovak ones, as they retained until 1999 the competence to overrule a particular type of constitutional ruling. For more detail, see the discussion on pp. 67ff.
54 Elster, 'Constitutionalism in Eastern Europe', 456.
55 Sunstein, 'On the Expressive Function of Law', 66.
56 For a discussion of reputational utility, see Sunstein, 'Deliberative Trouble, 83.
57 This is not unheard of in the history of Central Europe, as its institutional advancement has often preceded parallel progress in the social or economic realm by several decades. See Wandycz, *Price of Freedom*, 6.
58 Schimmelfennig, 'The Double Puzzle'.

NOTES TO CHAPTER 2 DESIGNING CONSTITUTIONAL REVIEW

1 Elster, Offe, and Preuss, *Institutional Design*, 35.
2 Göncz, *Karpaty a pril'ahlý vesmír*, 25
3 The cultural heritage of the communist era includes a legacy of reliance on informal dispute resolution rather than on formalised structures of societal interaction, a tendency based on differentiating between the 'mere rules of decision—and those norms which are factually valid in the course of everyday life and independently of their reaffirmation or declaration in legal procedure' (Weber, *Economy and Society*, 72), and stemming from what Jowitt denotes as a 'dichotomic antagonism between the official and the private realms'. Jowitt, 'The Leninist Legacy', 210. Examples abound across the region. A Polish sociologist argues that Polish democracy is getting sicker and sicker by preferring negotiations in smoked-filled rooms to official policy and laws (Mokrzycki, 'Iluzórna moc l'udu'); Sajó points out the persistence in Hungary of 'the tradition that timely political compromises may be elevated into constitutional principles' (Sajó, 'The Roundtable Talks in Hungary', 92); and the 'opposition agreement' between the two major Czech parties offers an even more striking example, as the principal pre-electoral opponent of the governing party renounced its traditional role in the Parliament in exchange for political clout. For more detail on this 'Agreement on creating a stable political environment in the Czech Republic', see 'Czech Republic Update 1999', 11–12; Marada, 'Party realignment'.
4 Elster, Offe, and Preuss, *Institutional Design*, 60.
5 See Brzezinski, *Struggle for Constitutionalism in Poland*, 158.
6 Zoll, 'Interview', 77.
7 Varga, *Transition to Rule of Law*, 23, 87.

8 See Örkény and Scheppele, 'The Complexity of Legality in Hungary', 56.
9 Sajó, 'The Judiciary in Contemporary Society', 294.
10 Ibid. See also Kupper, 'Die Justizreform in Ungarn', 255.
11 Sajó, 'The Judiciary in Contemporary Society', 294.
12 Sartori, *Comparative Constitutional Engineering*, 157.
13 Oakeshott, 'The Activity of Being an Historian', 182.
14 The Constitutional Tribunal Act of 29 April 1985 (hereinafter the 'PCTA'), English translation available in Pol and Sypniewski, *Polskie Prawo*.
15 Brzezinski and Garlicki, 'Judicial Review in Post-Communist Poland', 22.
16 Brzezinski, *Struggle for Constitutionalism in Poland*, 145.
17 See, for example, Osiatynski, 'The Roundtable Talks in Poland', 24, 27.
18 Garlicki, 'Constitutional Review and Legislation'.
19 The 1952 Constitution of Poland, Article 33a.4.
20 'The Constitutional Act of 17 October 1992, on the mutual relations between the legislative and executive institutions of the Republic of Poland and on local self-government with constitutional provisions in force', *Dziennik Ustaw* (Official Gazette), No. 84, item 426 (hereinafter the 'Little Const.'), English translation available in Pol and Sypniewski, *Polskie Prawo*; Amendments to the PCTA, as listed in Pol and Sypniewski, *Polskie Prawo*, 449.
21 PCTA, Article 5.
22 PCTA, Article 3.4.
23 Brzezinski and Garlicki, 'Judicial Review in Post-Communist Poland', 59.
24 Kurczewski, 'Democracy and the Rule of Law', 215.
25 Ibid.
26 The Constitutional Tribunal of Poland, 'The National Report'.
27 Brzezinski, 'Constitutionalism Within Limits', 38.
28 For the Tribunal's creative handling of this limitation, see discussion pp. 389.
29 Frankowski, 'Lech Wałesa's Draft', 67.
30 Osiatynski, 'Perspectives', 313.
31 Ibid.
32 Ibid.
33 Czeszejko-Sochacki, 'Origins of Constitutional Review', 17.
34 Ibid., 19.
35 See, for example, Brzezinski, *Struggle for Constitutionalism in Poland*, 43–45.
36 See Cole, 'Poland's 1997 Constitution', 14.
37 Brzezinski, 'Constitutionalism and Post-Communist Polish Politics', 450.
38 For a thorough analysis of the historical development of the executive branch in Poland, see Domagala, ed., *Konstytucyjne systemy rzadow*.
39 But see Geremek who argues that, despite a widespread belief in the destructive effect on Polish statehood of *liberum veto*, it 'worked well for almost 200 years'. Geremek, 'Interview', 44.
40 Brzezinski, 'Constitutional Heritage and Renewal', 84.
41 Osiatynski, 'Perspectives', 313.
42 Czeszejko-Sochacki, 'Origins of Constitutional Review', 30.
43 Id.
44 Leszek Lech Garlicki, 'Constitutional and Administrative Courts', 1305.
45 Kurczewski, 'Democracy and the Rule of Law', 215.

46 Brzezinski, *Struggle for Constitutionalism in Poland*, 153.

47 For a thorough discussion of the notion of elite settlement, see Plasser, Ulram, and Waldrauch, *Democratic Consolidation in East-Central Europe*, 34-37 (referring mostly to works by Burton, Gunther, and Hingley).

48 According to Osiatynski, among the elements of the Round Table agreement that have survived the early years of the transition were the division of powers, the strong presidency and the Senate. See Osiatynski, 'The Roundtable talks in Poland', 21.

49 Kolarska-Bobinska, 'The Role of the State', 304.

50 Id.

51 See Geremek, 'Interview', 44.

52 See Brzezinski, 'Constitutionalism and Post-Communist Polish Politics', 446.

53 See, for example, Skapska, 'Paradigm Lost?', 161–162; Brzezinski and Garlicki, 'Judicial Review in Post-Communist Poland', 18.

54 Skapska, 'Paradigm Lost?', 158.

55 See Brzezinski, 'Constitutionalism and Post-Communist Polish Politics', 434.

56 See Plasser and Ulram, 'Measuring Political Culture', 24. The corresponding figures elsewhere in the region oscillate around 10 percent (ibid.).

57 Ibid., 238 (Table 4).

58 Reitz, 'Political Economy and Abstract Review', 83.

59 Such patterns seem deeply entrenched in Poland's social life, as eleven years into a new regime, a local commentator pointed out that 'collective reactions tend to dominate in Poland'. See Maziarski, 'Inteligent hodený napospas trhu'.

60 These included the President of the Republic, the Presidium of the Sejm/Senate, Sejm/Senate committees or a group of fifty Deputies/thirty Senators, the Tribunal of State, the Council of Ministers or the Prime Minister, the Commissioner for Citizens' Rights, President of the Supreme Chamber of Control, the First President of the Supreme Court, the President of the Supreme Administrative Court, and the Public Prosecutor-General. See PCTA, Article 22.4. In 1997, constitutional change redefined these authorities so as to substitute the Presidium of the Sejm/Senate with the Marshal of the Sejm/Senate. See Constitution of the Republic of Poland (hereinafter the '1997 Const.'), Article 191.4.

61 PCTA, Article 23.4. Due to the enactment of the 1997 Constitution, which provided for a constitutional complaint, the authorities noted above were redefined so as to include the National Council of the Judiciary, the municipal authorities, the national trade unions, the national authorities of employers' organisations and socio-vocational organisations, and churches and religious organisations. See 1997 Const., Article 191.4–5.

62 Reitz, 'Political Economy and Abstract Review', 81.

63 Patrźalek, 'Obywatel a kontrola konstytucyjnośći prawa', 12.

64 Ibid., 10.

65 Dzialocha, 'Der Rechtsstaat', 9 (emphasis added).

66 It must be said, though, that Poles do trust the new trade unions and the Catholic Church much more than do citizens elsewhere in Central Europe. For the relevant data, see Plasser, Ulram, and Waldrauch, *Democratic Consolidation in East-Central Europe*, 114. The PCT itself stressed the representative function of trade unions and acknowledged that they had an 'important public function' to perform, which function was to be deemed of constitutional relevance. See Decision of the PCT No. K 19/96, *Orzecznictwo Trybunalu Konstytucyjnego* (hereinafter the '*OTK*') 1997, Vol. 1, item 6.

67 PCTA, Article 22.4. The right to mediate citizens' complaints to the PCT belonged to each of the social organisations enumerated in Article 22.4 of the PCTA but because of the limitations attendant on the subject matter of their petitions, the ombudsman's use of the instrument was both more extensive and more relevant.

68 Brzezinski describes the early equal protection case law of the PCT as 'remarkably progressive'. See 'Constitutional Refolution', 92. For a detailed account of the PCT's pre-1997 equal protection jurisprudence, see Brzezinski and Garlicki, 'Judicial Review in Post-Communist Poland'; Garlicki, 'The Principle of Equality'.

69 'Constitutional Revolution', 94 (comment by Brzezinski).

70 Linz and Stepan (see Linz and Stepan, *Problem of Democratic Transition,* 255 and ff.), as well as Sanford (see Sanford, 'Communism's Weakest Link', 190) argue convincingly that Poland has always been the least 'sovietised' of all the former Warsaw Pact polities.

71 See, for example, Schutz,'Mad'arsko je rozčarováno'. The notion that Poland was to be given special attention within the integration agenda proved strikingly accurate at the EU summit in Nice in December 2000. The most delicate issue was the distribution of European Parliament seats among the members/prospective members. When a proposal was put on the table that Poland deemed unfavourable, most countries' delegations rushed to Poland's side, and the Polish delegation scored a great political victory without much effort on its own part.

72 Brzezinski, 'Constitutionalism and Post-Communist Polish Politics', 447.

73 For a detailed account of the situation, see 'Poland Update', 19–20.

74 Brzezinski, *Struggle for Constitutionalism in Poland*, 95.

75 In the realm of substantive policies, there were other conflict-generating issues, such as abortion, religious education in public schools, economic policy, and—above all—the problem of how to come to terms with the past. On the issue of neuralgic points of the draft of the 'real' constitution, Geremek suggested that there were only two truly problematic issues: the relationship between state and church, and the extent of presidential powers. See Geremek, 'Interview', 42.

76 See 1997 Const., Article 188.

77 1997 Const., Articles 79.4 and 188.5; 'The Act on the Constitutional Tribunal of August 1, 1997, *Dziennik Ustaw* (Official Gazette), No. 102, item 643 (hereinafter the 'PACT'), Article 47.

78 1997 Const., Article 190.4.

79 Brzezinski, *Struggle for Constitutionalism in Poland*, 91.

80 Brzezinski, 'Constitutionalism within Limits', 43. See also Zoll, 'Interview', 78; Geremek, 'Interview', 42-43.

81 Brzezinski, *Struggle for Constitutionalism in Poland*, 185.

82 There were disagreements over some elements of the PCT's authority, and the final solution reflected an imperfect compromise. First, rulings on unconstitutionality of statutes adopted prior to the coming into force of the new constitution were to be subject to the Sejm's reconsideration for two more years. Secondly, the constitutional complaint scheme stopped short of granting citizens the right to challenge individual decisions. For the scholarship's take on the issue, see, for example, Dzialocha, 'Model ustrojowy Trybunalu Konstytucyjnego', and 'Wizja Trybunalu Konstytucyjnego'; Czeszejko-Sochacki, 'Trybunal Konstytucyjny w swietle pro-

jektow konstytucji', and 'Zarys modelu polskiego Trybunalu Konstytucyjnego'; Brzezinski, 'Constitutionalism within Limits'; Garlicki, 'Trybunal Konstytucyjny w projekcie Komisji Konstytucyjnej'.

83 The Constitution of the Socialist Allied Council Republic of Hungary was adopted on 23 June 1919 by the National Assembly of Allied Councils. See Rácz, 'The Historical Basis of Hungarian Law'.

84 The monarchy was re-introduced by Statute I of 1920, and reaffirmed by Statute XLVII of 1921. The republican form of government came into being upon the promulgation of Statute I of 1946. See id., 4–5.

85 See Arato, *Civil Society*, 203.

86 See, for example, Antal, 'Historical Forerunners of the Hungarian Constitution'.

87 *Constitutionalism in East-Central Europe*, 60 (comment by Sólyom).

88 The Constitutional Court of Hungary, 'The National Report'.

89 Elster, 'On Majoritarianism and Rights', 19–20.

90 Páczolay, 'Constitutional Transition', 567.

91 It should be noted that Hungarians resisted the Josephinian reform aimed at centralisation of the law making process not only for reasons having to do with differences in their legal development but also, if not mostly, for political reasons. The Hungarian aristocracy, for instance, strongly resisted the egalitarian and anti-particularist background of the Josephinian reform as endangering its power-base.

92 Malý and Sivák, *Dějiny*, 161–162, 344.

93 Ibid., 345.

94 Ibid., 445–446.

95 Ibid., 500. In 1881, Act 59 on Civil Procedure made the decisions of the *Curia* universally binding.

96 For a detailed account of Hungarian legal development in the nineteenth century, see Zlinszky, *Wissenschaft und Gerichtsbarkeit* (providing an extensive list of additional bibliographical resources).

97 Varga, *Transition to Rule of Law*, 16.

98 According to the *lag saga* tradition, a legal professional would recite the law whenever a written code was absent. See ibid., 122.

99 As Sólyom points out, the Court would not draw from 'the language of the law itself ...but rather the meaning and the content that can be attributed to it from the consistent and unitary practice of applying the law.' See Sólyom, 'Introduction to the Decisions of the Hungarian Constitutional Court', 4.

100 Weber, *Economy and Society*, 656–657. Compare Kronman, *Max Weber*, 72–92 (analysing Weber's theory of formal legal rationality).

101 Halmai, 'Development of Civil Law', 15.

102 Decision of the HCC No. 43/1995 (VI.30.) AB, cited in Sólyom and Brunner, *Constitutional Judiciary*, 325.

103 See 'Constitutional Revolution', 96. The author of the comment, Kim Lane Scheppele, also says: 'The Constitutional Court Act was thrown together reasonably quickly. And as a result, the Act gave the court a number of powers [but] at the time no one understood exactly what an activist court would make out of these powers.' Ibid.

104 Sólyom, 'The First Year of the Constitutional Court', 5.

105 Páczolay, 'Judicial Review of the Compensation Law', 807.

106 The Constitutional Court of Hungary, 'The National Report'.

107 Sajó, 'The Roundtable Talks in Hungary', 93.
108 Andrew Arato, 'Dilemmas of Constitution Making', 681. See also Bruszt and Stark, 'Remaking the Political Field in Hungary', 41.
109 Bruszt and Stark, for instance, claim that after the EKA's establishment, the negotiations between the communist reformers and the opposition reflected the 'politics of escalating confrontation'. Ibid., 27. Moreover, the EKA members launched their campaigns for political recognition before they reached agreement with the incumbents. The conflict over the presidential elections-which exposed the frontrunner among the opposition, the Hungarian Democratic Forum (MDF), to hostile treatment by its co-insurgents, the Alliance of Free Democrats (SZDSZ) and Fidesz-exemplified the confrontational dynamics of the Round Table process.
110 Sólyom argues that as early as 'summer 1990, any traces of the former political compromise between Communists and the then Opposition at the Round-Table-Negotiations in 1989 were rubbed out of the constitution'. See *Constitutionalism in East Central Europe*, 50 (comment by Sólyom).
111 Decision of the HCC No. 11/1992 AB, cited in Sólyom and Brunner, *Constitutional Judiciary*, 214, 221.
112 Sajó, 'The Roundtable Talks in Hungary', 94. Kulcsár's story is quite telling of how far the authors of the accidental-birth legend were willing to go, for he claims that he got the idea of constitutional review while listening to one of the last lectures of Hans Kelsen at Berkeley, California. See 'Constitutional Refolution', 95.
113 Göncz, *Karpaty a pril'ahlý vesmír*, 85.
114 Sajó, 'Rights in Post-Communism', 150.
115 It was precisely the lack of such support that led to the gravest national tragedy of Hungary in modern times, the Treaty of Trianon. Even the more liberal Hungarians have a hard time coping with what their former President Göncz describes as 'the trauma of the Versailles peace with its ridicule of the principle of national self-determination, a peace that forced one-third of Hungarians to accept foreign domination.' Göncz, *Karpaty a pril'ahlý vesmír*, 185. Göncz also argues that the fact that Hungary has lost all the three wars in which it participated in the twentieth century—First World War, Second World War, and Cold War—is determinative of the contemporary identity of the country. See ibid.
116 Batt, 'The Role of the State', 178.
117 Schimmelfennig, 'The Double Puzzle'.
118 Klingsberg, 'Judicial Review', 137. Interestingly, Hungary proved to be the most innovative of all the Visegrád countries in institutional reform in general and in the area of constitutional review in particular. It could be deemed a paradox that factors conducive to imitation led Hungary to lay down foundations for a 'juridical democracy' of a kind that can hardly be seen elsewhere. But then, fascination hardly induces moderation.
119 Schutz, 'Mad'arsko: Najveselší barak'.
120 Ibid. This is how Hungarians used jokingly to refer to themselves during the socialist era.
121 Plasser, Ulram, and Waldrauch, *Democratic Consolidation in East-Central Europe*, 126.
122 See Decision of the HCC No. 23/1990 (X.16.) AB, cited in Sólyom and Brunner, *Constitutional Judiciary*, 123.

123 Such efforts are not unheard of in Hungarian history. Varga points out the role that legal professionals played in placing 'the European horizon in the legislature and government of interwar Hungary' and in elevating the 'level of modernisation through the law and its academic backing on European standards'. Varga, *Transition to Rule of Law*, 23-24.

124 Klingsberg, 'Judicial Review', 137.

125 The parallel I see here between Marshall in *Marbury vs. Madison* and Sólyom in the death penalty decision is not only in the outcome—providing for, or radically extending, the powers of the Court—but also in the method. Both justices inserted into their reasoning an argument structurally empowering their courts while actually providing the legislature-bound political establishment with what it was, explicitly or less so, asking for. They have thereby made their respective attempts somewhat less exposed to attack than they might have been had the merits of the holdings been less forthcoming as regards the establishment's immediate interests.

126 Decision of the HCC No. 23/1990 (X.16.) AB, cited in Sólyom and Brunner, *Constitutional Judiciary*, 126.

127 Ackerman, 'The Rise of World Constitutionalism', 777.

128 See *Constitutionalism in East Central Europe*, 51 (comment by Sólyom).

129 Ibid., 56 (comment by Sajó).

130 The Hungarian parliament attracted widespread criticism in early 1990 when it overruled by incorporating into the constitution a statutory provision held unconstitutional by the HCC's holding on an electoral law. By doing so, however, the parliament was neither declaring war on the Court nor establishing a pattern of defiance. Due to immense time pressure, it simply opted for administrative expediency. More importantly, it subsequently refrained from such behaviour. But most importantly for my argument, this happened before the Court put itself at the fore of the march to Europe.

131 See *Constitutionalism in East Central Europe*, 56 (comment by Sólyom).

132 Ibid. (comment by Sólyom).

133 A prominent Czech political commentator blames Havel for having contributed significantly to the dissidents' lack of readiness to take over power and deal with the communist incumbents in a competent way. See Doležal, 'Odkaz Václava Havla'. Ackerman blames Havel for having done a 'spectacularly poor job in using the materials at his disposal to constitutionalise the charisma he had earned as an anti-Communist spokesman' ('Ackerman, 'The Rise of World Constitutionalism', 784). Some local politicians blame Havel for not having called the elections for an earlier date than June 1990. See Langoš, 'Interview'.

134 The federal parliament consisted of two chambers-the House of the People (200 deputies) and the House of the Nations (150 deputies). The House of the People was elected proportionally and thus reflected the two-to-one ratio between the Czech and Slovak populations. The House of the Nations had 75 deputies elected in the Czech Republic and 75 deputies elected in the Slovak Republic. Both chambers had equal decision-making authority, and a federal statute had to pass through both of them. The quorum in the House of the Nations required that a majority of both 75-member factions be present. The constitution provided that the two factions of the House of the Nations had to vote separately in a large number of areas of federal lawmaking, and required an absolute majority for both factions. In these areas of regulation, 38 out of 150 deputies of the House of the Nations (and out of 350 total) were there-

fore able to block a legislative initiative. For constitutional amendments, a three-fifths majority was required for both factions of the House of the Nations so 31 out of 350 federal deputies were able to obstruct a constitutional amendment.

135 Havel, never tiring of symbolic acts, presented his draft of the Act on CSCC on 10 December, celebrated as the International Day of Human Rights. It was, by coincidence, also the first anniversary of the first post-revolutionary government in which the communists formed a minority.

136 Act No. 491/1991 on the organisation of the Constitutional Court of the Czech and Slovak Federal Republics and its proceedings.

137 See note 324 to Chapter 3 and accompanying text.

138 The patents, prescripts, and instructions of the ruler substituted the traditional form of resolutions of diets or intra-estate rulings. The reform of judicial administration, introduced in 1783, preserved the principle of personality (namely procedural discrimination between different categories of litigants) only for proceedings in the lower courts, and anchored formal equality of parties in any appellate proceedings. The Hungarian nobility vigorously-and for a long period of time successfully, too—resisted these and similar attempts.

139 Sládeček, 'Nástin vývoje ústavniho soudnictví', 545.

140 The section on rights was produced by a three-member parliamentary committee one member of which was the Czech Deputy Frantisek Ladislav Rieger. There were other Czech deputies actively involved in the drafting process, too. See Malý and Sivák, *Dějiny*, 366.

141 Sládeček, 'Nástin vývoje ústavniho soudnictví', 542. See also Malý and Sivák, *Dějiny*, 368–370.

142 For more details on the Imperial Court, see Brauneder and Lachmayer, *Österreichische Verfassungsgeschichte*, 154ff.

143 Act No. 3/1918 on the Supreme Administrative Court, in connection with Act No. 36/1870 on the Supreme Administrative Court and Act No. 4/1918 on the reception of the legal order of Austria.

144 Act No. 121/1920 Constitutional Charter; Act No. 162/1902 on the Constitutional Court.

145 The Court issued 65 rulings. It admitted for review two motions against a statute but did not complete either of the two proceedings. The core of its adjudication concerned the quasi-legislative acts of the Permanent Committee of the National Assembly, the so-called 'emergency measures'. However, the Court held unconstitutional an emergency measure of the Permanent Committee only in its very last ruling, issued in May 1939, that is, after the first split of Czechoslovakia. Interestingly, the Czechoslovak parliament had been as deferential to the cabinet as the Constitutional Court had been deferential to the legislature—not a single cabinet was subject to a motion of no confidence during the existence of the First Republic. See Zemko, 'História ako učitelka života'.

146 Before it ceased to exist in 1933, the average number of unconstitutionality findings was one per year, 16 in total. See Welan, 'Constitutional Review and Legislation in Austria', 79–80. Even though the Austrian court was outlived by its Czechoslovak counterpart, it left a bigger imprint on the face of Austrian law than the Czechoslovak court ever tried to. For an authoritative discussion of the interwar Constitutional Court of Austria, see Eisenmann, 'La Justice Constitutionnelle'.

147 Sládeček, 'Nástin vývoje ústavního soudnictví', 546.

148 For more detail, see Bröstl, 'Formovanie doktríny', 4.

149 Sládeček, 'Nástin vývoje ústavního soudnictví', 547–548.

150 Blahož, 'Human Rights in Poland, Hungary and Czechoslovakia', 59.

151 The so-called 'reception norm' contained in Act No. 11/1918 provided for the validity and effectiveness of the Hungarian law on the territory of Slovakia.

152 The 'gaol of nations' is a reference to the ruthless minority policies of the late Hapsburg monarchy, especially severe 'Magyarization' which took place also, but not only, on what is now Slovakian territory.

153 See Chmel, 'The Slovak Question', 67.

154 Závacká, 'Vyznam vzniku Československej republiky', 73. One notes, however—and Závacká brings out this point herself—that it took a few decades for Slovak political representation to internalise the European standard of rights protection, which was tragically neglected during and even before the era of the Slovak fascist state.

155 Barány, 'Odkaz československej štátnosti', 182.

156 According to former President of Hungary Göncz, Slovaks and Hungarians are, mentality-wise, closer to each other than to any other nation. See Mikloško, 'Moji Maďári'.

157 The leading Czech legal philosopher of those times was František Weyr, a staunch believer in the *Rheine Rechtstheorie* of Kelsen, his close friend and founder of the regionally influential Brno school of legal thought. For more detail on the Brno school, see Weinberger, 'Od Brněnské školy k neo-institucionalismu'.

158 See Antonín Procházka, 'České soudy trpí formalistickým manýrismem'.

159 See, for example, Kresák, 'Gramatika nepustí?'; Radoslav Procházka, 'Dobré a zlé správy'. For more on the ordinary courts' 'defensive formalism', see Zupančič, 'Od souboje ke smlouvě', 487.

160 The Constitution of the Czech Republic (hereinafter the 'Czech Constitution'), Article 84.4.

161 The Constitution of the Slovak Republic (hereinafter the 'Slovak Constitution'), Article. 134.2.

162 The Constitution of the Hungarian Republic (hereinafter the 'Hungarian Constitution'), Article 32/A.4.

163 Little Constitution, Article 33(a); 1997 Const., Article 194.1. The President of the Republic, however, has the right to appoint the PCT's President and Vice-President from among candidates proposed by the Plenary Session of the Tribunal. 1997 Const., Article 194.2

164 The most controversial topics included the issue of territorial administrative units, the specification of the rights catalogue as either concerning merely negative rights or including also so-called second and third generation rights, and the issue the political delicacy and divisiveness of which proved to be of the most enduring nature, that is, bicameralism. Indeed, the Senate continued to be the focal point of controversy in the realm of institutional design for years following the adoption of the constitution. The proposal to eliminate the Senate altogether—after it was provided for in the constitution but before the first senatorial elections took place—was not rejected on its merits but because the necessary constitutional amendment would require amending almost half of the constitution's provisions. The suggestions to get rid of the Senate surface in local media on regular basis to date.

165 Act No. 182/1993 on the Constitutional Court of the Czech Republic (hereinafter the 'CACC').
166 Act No. 38/1993 on the organisation of the Constitutional Court of the Slovak Republic, its proceedings and the status of its justices (hereinafter the 'SACC').
167 Reitz, 'Political Economy and Abstract Review', 79. For an excellent discussion of the effect of political economy on certain legal practices and paradigms, see Damaška, *The Faces of Justice.*
168 See Plasser and Pribersky, eds., 'Political Culture', 235.
169 I borrowed the term from Brunner. See Brunner, 'Structure and Proceedings', 96.
170 See Plasser and Pribersky, eds., 'Political Culture', 237 (Table 1).
171 See 'Slovakia Update 1996', 28–29.

NOTES TO CHAPTER 3
ADJUDICATIVE APPROACHES

1 Stone Sweet, *Governing with Judges*, 45 (providing additional sources on the issue).
2 Decision of the CCC No. Pl. US 19/98, *Sbírka nálezu a usnesení Ústavního soudu Česke republiky* (hereinafter the '*CCC Collection*'), Vol. 13, 136. Compare Brunner, 'Development of a Constitutional Judiciary', 546.
3 See Decision of the SCC No. Pl. US 14/96, *Zbierka nálezov a uznesení Ústavného súdu Slovenskej republiky* (hereinafter the '*SCC Collection*') 1996, 297–299.
4 See Decision of the PCT No. P 3/00, *OTK* 2000, Vol. 5, item 138.
5 See, for example, Decision of the PCT No. Ts 58/99, *OTK* 2000, Vol. 1, item 7. See also Decision of the PCT No. SK 28/99, *OTK* 2000, Vol. 3, item 88.
6 See Czeszejko-Sochacki, 'Interview'.
7 Kreimer presents the same argument and even similar wording. See Kreimer, 'Explaining the Dark Matter of Judicial Review', 507.
8 Hofmanski, 'Poland After Ratification of the ECHR', 49.
9 Kreimer, 'Explaining the Dark Matter of Judicial Review', 507.
10 Ackerman, *The Future of Liberal Revolution*, 107.
11 In fact, most countries in the region shared the experience, although the extent to which the ordinary courts tended to undermine the project of constitutional review varied. In general, Zupančič is right in pointing out that the resistance to constitutional review often 'comes from corners where it would be least expected. It does not come from the new legislatures and neither does it come from the executive branches of power: it comes from the rest of the judicial branch, from the ordinary courts' (Zupančič, 'Od souboje ke smlouvě', 487). Although he seems to underestimate the various ways in which both the legislature and the executive have tried to undermine the effect of constitutional adjudication on their policy-making capacity, it is true that in several countries—most notably in the Czech Republic, Poland, and Slovakia—the inter-judicial tensions have proved to be as relevant to the operation of the respective constitutional courts as their colloquies with the legislatures and/or the executive branches. Zupančič offers the parallel examples of Croatia and Slovenia.
12 One of the CCC justices summed up the above approach in a single illustrative sentence: '[I]n the realm of norm control, [the principle of judicial self-restraint] leads

to self-restraint and moderation on the part of the constitutional court in its relation to the legislator (but on the other hand, it leads to the necessity of ordinary courts' observance of legal opinions of the Constitutional Court)' (Holländer, 'Hlavní doktríny', 67).

13 Stone Sweet, *Governing with Judges*, 130–131.

14 Skapska, 'Paradigm Lost?', 153. But Michnik, who turned from a professional anticommunist into a staunch opponent of what he dubbed the 'anticommunist witchhunt', calls this idea a myth. See Michnik, 'Address to Forum 2000'.

15 Skapska, 'Paradigm Lost?', 153.

16 'Constitutional Revolution', 93 (comment by Brzezinski).

17 For a complex review of reversals by the Sejm of the Tribunal's decisions, see Garlicki, 'Das Verfassungsgericht und das Parlament'.

18 Stone Sweet, *Governing with Judges*, 90.

19 Bickel, *The Least Dangerous Branch*, 251. For a review of various modes of colloquy between a high court and a legislature, see Eskridge and Levinson, eds., *Constitutional Stupidities, Constitutional Tragedies*.

20 In this case, by statutes I mean universally binding normative acts assessed within the abstract-review procedure. For more detail, see discussion on p. 171.

21 See Garlicki, 'Chroniques: Pologne 1991', 672.

22 Decision of the PCT No. S 6/91, *OTK* 1991, 294.

23 Ibid.

24 Garlicki, 'Chroniques: Pologne 1991', 672.

25 Although the Sejm's capacity to overrule a PCT finding of unconstitutionality of a statute was preserved for another two years following the coming into force of the new constitution, it was applicable only to statutes promulgated before the enactment of the constitution. See 1997 Const., Article 293.1.

26 Pursuant to the constitution, the Tribunal is bound to apply for such an opinion only with respect to the effective date of its respective ruling. See 1997 Const., Article 190.3. The PACT, however, extends the obligation to apply for the opinion as to the consequences of the very finding of unconstitutionality. See PACT, Article 44.1.

27 For a detailed discussion of the PCT's jurisprudence in the years preceding the change of regime, see Garlicki, 'Chroniques: Pologne 1986–1989'; Oniszczuk, *Orzecznictwo*.

28 It was, for instance, before the fall of the regime that the PCT produced its seminal ruling on the issue of equal protection, a ruling to which it would confidently refer for years to come. See Decision of the PCT No. P 2/87, *OTK* 1987, 20–32. In its very first decision, the PCT ruled unconstitutional a regulation of the Council of Ministers retroactively modifying maintenance fees to be paid by tenants of state-owned apartments. See Decision of the PCT No. U 1/86, *OTK* 1986, 32–52. Soon thereafter, the Tribunal increased its visibility among, and acceptance by, the public by striking down a delegation of authority from the Council of Ministers to the Minister of Trade to reduce the number of liquor stores in a particular geographic area. See Decision of the PCT No. U 3/86, *OTK* 1986, 59–76.

29 See, for example, Frankowski, 'A Comment on Professor Garlicki's Article', 737.

30 See Decision of the PCT No. W 10/94, *OTK* 1994, Vol. 2, 236–248.

31 See Decision of the PCT No. U 6/92, *OTK* 1992, Vol. 1, 196–213.

32 See Decision of the PCT No. U 10/92, *OTK* 1993, Vol. 1, 19–36.

33 See Decision of the PCT No. K 7/90, *OTK* 1990, 42, 54–58. The Little Constitution then transformed the relevant part of the Tribunal's holding into constitutional text. See Little Const., Article 18.4 in fine. See also Decision of the PCT No. W 1/95, *OTK* 1995, Vol. 2, 237–239, 244.
34 See Decision of the PCT No. W 6/93, *OTK* 1993, Vol. 2, 495–509.
35 See Decision of the PCT No. W 1/95, *OTK* 1995, Vol. 2, 230–257.
36 See, for example, Decisions of the PCT Nos. W 10/94, *OTK* 1994, Vol. 2, 245; K 10/95, *OTK* 1995, Vol. 2, 52–71. The HCC, on the other hand, extended from posterior to preliminary review its authority to scrutinize domestic law for its conformity to international treaties. See discussion on p. 418.
37 The so-called turning points in the Tribunal's jurisprudence are not necessarily chronological. In the realm of welfare rights, retreat did follow emancipation but as far as retribution measures are concerned, the PCT continued to display deference simultaneously with creative employment of the *Rechtsstaat* and equal-protection clauses. Rather than providing a clear sequence of events, the respective paradoxes account for the central aspects of the PCT's conceptual approach to the legislature's efforts to effectuate transition.
38 Decision of the PCT No. K 7/90, *OTK* 1990, 54.
39 Decision of the PCT No. K 3/91, *OTK* 1992, Vol. 1, 23. See also Decisions of the PCT Nos. K 12/90, *OTK* 1990, 66–78; K 4/91, *OTK* 1992, Vol. 1, 40–58; K 4/92, *OTK* 1992, Vol. 2, 11–26; K 3/98, *OTK* 1998, Vol. 4, 308–371.
40 See Decision of the PCT No. K 15/93, *OTK* 1994, Vol. 1, 21–27. It should be added, however, that the PCT disallowed reduction of pension rights for those pensioners who were not directly employed by the repressive machinery. It thus proved stricter than the Czech Court, which did not find it important to insist on a differentiation between the different categories of military and security personnel. See discussion pp. 272–273.
41 The Act of 4 May 1991 on the amendment to the statute on the establishment of a main commission on the investigation of Hitlerist crimes in Poland, available at http://www.rzeczpospolita.pl.
42 Decision of the PCT No. S 6/91, *OTK* 1991, 294.
43 Calabresi, *A Common Law for the Age of Statutes*, 105.
44 Ruth Wedgwood, 'Cousin Humphrey', 248.
45 See Brzezinski, *Struggle for Constitutionalism in Poland*, 179–180.
46 Decision of the PCT No. K 14/91, *OTK* 1992, Vol. 1, 119, 128.
47 Decision of the PCT No. K 11/94, *OTK* 1995, Vol. 1, 129.
48 See Decisions of the PCT Nos. K 14/92, *OTK* 1993, Vol. 2, 319–331; K 29/95, *OTK* 1996, Vol. 1, 87–88; K 8/96, *OTK* 1996, Vol. 2, 63–65; K 7/95, *OTK* 1996, Vol. 2, 236–237; K 11/97, *OTK* 1998, 659–663.
49 See Garlicki, 'Die Verfassungsgerichtsbarkeit in Polen', 79.
50 See, for example, Decisions of the PCT Nos. K 14/91; K 15/91; P 4/92; K 9/92; K 14/92; K 8/93; K 4/94; K 12/94; P 4/95; K 5/96; K 10/97; K 10/98; K 27/98; K 4/99.
51 See, for example, Decisions of the PCT Nos. W 3/94, *OTK* 1994, Vol. 1, 245; W 10/93, *OTK* 1994, Vol. 2; K 21/95, *OTK* 1997, Vol. 1, 94; K 7/95, *OTK* 1996, Vol. 2, 231.
52 Garlicki put it plainly: '[Y]ou can always quote the principle of equality.' See Garlicki, 'Social Rights', 127.

53 Decision of the PCT No. K 21/95, *OTK* 1997, Vol. 1, 89–90. See also Decisions of the PCT Nos. K 9/95, *OTK* 1996, Vol. 1, 56–62; K 7/95, *OTK* 1996, Vol. 2, 236–238.
54 Decision of the PCT No. K 13/94, *OTK* 1995, Vol. 1, 72–74.
55 Decisions of the PCT Nos. K 21/95, *OTK* 1997, Vol. 1, 96; K 22/96, *OTK* 1997, Vols. 5–6, 568. The notion that budgetary equilibrium is to be understood as a constitutional value became an integral part of the Tribunal's case law and continues to inform it also in the post-1997 era.
56 Decision of the PCT No. K 22/96, *OTK* 1997, Vols. 5–6, 570.
57 Decision of the PCT No. K 11/97, *OTK* 1998, 662. See also Decisions of the PCT Nos. K 21/95, *OTK* 1997, Vol. 1, 96; K 22/97, *OTK* 1997, Vols. 3–4, 444.
58 Kozak, 'Rodzaje wykladni prawa', 60.
59 Dzialocha, 'Der Rechtsstaat', 13. Justice Laczkowski also hints at the strategy of discriminating between 'old law' and 'new law'. See Laczkowski, 'Constitutional Courts', 5–6. On a more specific note, Garlicki argued that the special nature of fiscal law required that individual rights be harmonized with the interests of the state. See Garlicki, 'Chroniques: Pologne 1993', 603.
60 Zieliński, 'The Rule of Law', 127.
61 See Decision of the PCT No. K 7/93, *OTK* 1993, Vol. 2, 411. The notion that systemic changes warrant the granting of very broad manoeuvrability to the legislature in pursuing its political and economic objectives became a trademark of the PCT's case law.
62 See, for example, Decisions of the PCT Nos. W 4/90, *OTK* 1991, 184; W 12/92, *OTK* 1994, Vol. 1, 134; K 24/96, *OTK* 1997, Vol. 2, 246–262; K 3/97, *OTK* 1997, Vol. 2, 272–286.
63 See, for example, Decision of the PCT No. W 9/92, *OTK* 1993, Vol. 1, 135–141.
64 Ibid.
65 Kozak, 'Rodzaje wykladni prawa', 59 (referring to Decision of the PCT No. W 9/92).
66 Ibid., 60 (referring to Decisions of the PCT Nos. W 15/92; W 5/91; W 7/91; W 5/92).
67 Decision of the PCT No. K 6/94, *OTK* 1994, Vol. 2, 95.
68 The Tribunal suggested as much when it held that it was the role of the electorate, not the PCT, to assess substantive pertinence of legislative choices. See, for example, Decisions of the PCT Nos. K 12/94, *OTK* 1995, Vol. 1, 27; K 23/95, *OTK* 1995, Vol. 2, 122; K 22/95, *OTK* 1996, Vol. 1, 120; K 10/96, *OTK* 1996, Vol. 2, 70–71.
69 See Holmes, 'Back to the Drawing Board', 22–24.
70 Decision of the PCT No. K 6/99, *OTK* 1999, Vol. 7, 834. See also Decisions of the PCT Nos. P 2/98, *OTK* 1999, Vol. 1, 18; K 3/99, *OTK* 1999, Vol. 4, 362; K 5/99, *OTK* 1999, Vol. 5, 539; K 13/99, *OTK* 1999, Vol. 7, 775.
71 Decision of the PCT No. K 2/98, *OTK* 1999, Vol. 3, 223.
72 Decision of the PCT No. K 10/97, *OTK* 1998, Vol. 3, 112. This conceptual approach can be traced back to 1993 when the PCT stated: 'it is within the authority of the law maker to adopt laws that reflect political and economic goals and to adopt such legal solutions that it believes will best serve the realization of these goals.' Decision of the PCT No. K 7/93, *OTK* 1993, Vol. 2, 410. The number of decisions in which the Tribunal relied on this or similar wording is too large for an exhaustive citation, but amongst the recent such rulings are Decisions of the PCT Nos. K 25/96, *OTK* 1997, Vols. 3–4, 337–366; K 22/97, *OTK* 1997, Vols. 3–4, item 41; K 24/97, *OTK* 1998, Vol. 2, item 13; K 24/98, *OTK* 1998, Vol. 6, 434–476; U 17/97, *OTK* 1998, Vol. 3, item 34.

73 Decision of the PCT No. K 10/99, *OTK* 1999, Vol. 7, 864. See also Decision of the PCT No. K 11/94, *OTK* 1995, Vol. 1, 134–136.
74 See Decision of the PCT No. K 1/00, *OTK* 2000, Vol. 6, item 185 (the quoted part cited in Garlicki, 'Orzecznictwo Trybunalu Konstytucyjnego w 2000 roku', 82).
75 See Decisions of the PCT Nos. K 18/98, *OTK* 1999, item 26; P 4/98, *OTK* 1999, item 29.
76 See Decision of the PCT No. K 5/99, *OTK* 1999, Vol. 5, 536.
77 See Decision of the PCT No. P 4/98, *OTK* 1999, Vol. 5, item 98.
78 See Decisions of the PCT Nos. K 7/98, *OTK* 1998, Vol. 6, 421–433; K 37/98, *OTK* 2000, Vol. 4, item 112.
79 See Decision of the PCT No. K 25/96, *OTK* 1997, Vols. 3–4, 337–366.
80 See Decision of the PCT No. K 11/99, *OTK* 1999, Vol. 6, item 116.
81 See Decision of the PCT No. P 2/99, *OTK* 1999, Vol. 5, item 103.
82 See Decision of the PCT No. K 3/98, *OTK* 1998, Vol. 4, item 52.
83 See Decisions of the PCT Nos. K 24/98, *OTK* 1998, Vol. 6, 434–476; K 39/97, *OTK* 1998, Vol. 6, 491–557.
84 Decision of the PCT No. K 3/99, *OTK* 1999, Vol. 4, item 73.
85 See Decision of the PCT No. P 3/2000, *OTK* 2000, Vol. 5, item 138.
86 Kabat provides an elaborate account of the implementation by the Supreme Administrative Court of the constitutional provisions. See Kabat, 'Przepisy konstytucyjne'.
87 See Hauser, 'Założenia reformy', 26. More than 70 percent of the petitions claimed violation by administrative authorities of the applicable procedural provisions. See Hauser, 'Założenia reformy', 25.
88 See Decisions of the PCT Nos. W 16/92, *OTK* 1993, Vol. 1, 156–165; K 21/96, *OTK* 1997, Vol. 2, 287–315.
89 During the first decade of the ombudsmen's functioning, about a quarter of a million petitions were filed with them, and currently the annual number of petitions exceeds 50,000. In the years preceding the change of regime, the claims filed with the ombudsman were classified into groups and brought to attention of the respective authorities in a quasi class action. Intervention on behalf of individual citizens is claimed to have been rare, concerning only 'exceptionally urgent matters'. See Kanski, 'Human Rights in Poland'. The pattern did not change significantly after 1989.
90 Interestingly, the availability of constitutional complaints in the post-1997 constitutional space led to a notable decrease in the number of ombudsman's petitions to the Tribunal. While there were 25 petitions filed by the ombudsman in 1997, there were only 16 such petitions filed in 1998, 15 in 1999, and 19 in 2000.
91 See Adam Zieliński, 'Osierocona skarga'.
92 The Little Constitution stated this implicitly rather than *expressis verbis*, as it read: 'Judges are independent and subordinate only to parliamentary statutes'. Little Const., Article 61. The related provision of the new Constitution provides that 'judges shall be independent and subject only to the Constitution and statutes'. 1997 Const., Article 178.4.
93 See Judgment of the PSC No. 3 CR 702/56. See also the Resolution of the Civil Law Chamber of the PSC of 12 February 1955 which held that constitutional provisions were not directly applicable unless enacted through a statute.

94 The PCT stated as much in numerous decisions in which it held that it was within the authority of any judicial body 'autonomously to assess the conformity of substatutory acts to the constitution and statutes and refuse to apply such acts if nonconformity is found'. Decision of the PCT No. U 7/96, *OTK* 1997, Vol. 1, 59. See also Decisions of the PCT Nos. W 10/95, *OTK* 1996, Vol. 1, 315–318; P 5/96, *OTK* 1996, Vol. 2, 446–450.

95 For the relevant case law, see Kabat, 'Przepisy konstytucyjne' (referring to Decisions of the Supreme Administrative Court No. IV SA 1314/91, SA/Ka 776/92, SA/Gd 1056/93, SA/Gd 1114/93, SA/Wr 1374/95).

96 Ibid. See also Council of Europe, *The Role of the Judiciary in a State Governed by Law*, 123 (contribution of the Polish participant).

97 See Judgment of the PSC No. PRZ 8/87, *Orzecznictwo Sadu Najwyszego* (hereinafter '*OSN*') 1987, Vol. 12, item 199. The PSC adhered in several other instances to the prevailing jurisprudential approach in Poland, namely the dualist theory of international law. According to the PSC, in order for any international treaty to have legal consequences within Poland it would have to be incorporated into domestic law by means of a transformation act. See Judgments of the PSC, Nos. III CZP 71/73, *OSN* 1975, Vol. 5; II CR 200/89; *OSN* 1990, Vol. 10.

98 See Judgment of the PSC of October 17, 1991, *OSN* 1991, Vols. 3–4, item 19.

99 See Decision of the PCT No. K 8/91, *OTK* 1992, Vol. 1, 84.

100 See Decision of the PCT No. K 29/95, *OTK* 1996, Vol. 1, 78–94.

101 See Szumski, 'Pre-Trial Detention and Human Rights', 253.

102 Osiatynski, 'Dualism in Constitutional Adjudication', 13. For more on Polish judiciary, see Letowska, *Courts and Tribunals*.

103 Czeszejko-Sochacki, 'O wymiarze sprawiedliwosci', 9.

104 For a thorough analysis of problems attendant on justice administration in Poland, see Instytut Wymiaru Sprawedliwosci, *Założenia zmian* (cited in Czeszejko-Sochacki, 'O wymiarze sprawiedliwosci', 10).

105 See Strážnická, 'Úloha judikatúry Európskeho súdu pre l'udské práva', 120.

106 Cholewinski, for instance, argues that 'the system of protecting human rights in the new Polish Constitution is innovative and far-reaching and can serve as a useful model for development elsewhere'. Cholewinski, 'The Protection of Human Rights', 238.

107 See, for example, Kolasiński, 'Orzecznictwo Trybunalu Konstytucyjnego', 3–13.

108 For a detailed account of the issue of re-opening judicial or administrative proceedings following a holding of unconstitutionality, see Czeszejko-Sochacki, 'Wznowienie postepowania', 14–26.

109 See Article 39 of the PCTA as amended by the Act of 9 July 2000.

110 In the realm of administrative procedure—the one procedure that is most likely to offer incidents of rights violation—this includes proceedings by the PSAC. See, for example, Decisions of the PCT, Nos. Ts 27/97, *OTK* 1998, Vol. 2, item 20; Ts 62/98, *OTK* 1998, Vol. 5, item 70; Ts 14/99, *OTK* 1999, Vol. 2, item 35; Ts 4/97, *OTK* 1999, Annex, item 2; Ts 45/99 *OTK* 2000, Vol. 2, item 70. In the realm of civil procedure, if a possibility exists to apply to a cassation instance—that is, the PSC—it must be taken before the issue may be referred to the PCT. See, for example, Decisions of the PCT Nos. Ts 53/98, Ts 43/98, Ts 45/98, Ts 124/98, Ts 165/98, Ts 51/99. For more detail and precise citations, see Garlicki, 'Orzecznictwo Trybunalu Konstytucyjnego

w 1998 roku', 105, 113; idem., 'Orzecznictwo Trybunalu Konstytucyjnego w 1999 roku', 106, 115–116.

111 Brunner also points out the inspiration offered by the Hungarian model of constitutional complaint. See Brunner, 'Entwicklung der polnischen Verfassungsgerichtsbarkeit', 51.

112 The PSAC has acquired the power to rule on the conformity to statutes of both the resolutions of municipal authorities and normative acts of local authorities of regional administration. See 1997 Const., 184.

113 For a thorough discussion of the issue, see Dzialocha, 'The Direct Application'.

114 See, for example, Spiewak, 'The Battle for a Constitution', 94.

115 See Decision of the PCT No. Uw 9/88, *OTK* 1989, item 9.

116 Decision of the PCT No. K 3/91, *OTK* 1991, Vol. 1, 26.

117 See, for example, Decisions of the PCT Nos. K 4/91, K 8/91, K 4/92, K 3/92, K 17/92; K 4/94; S 4/94; W 5/94; W 4/93; K 11/93, W 3/92, W 15/93, W 14/94; K 19/95.

118 See Decision of the PCT No. K 8/91, *OTK* 1992, Vol. 1, 81.

119 This also was the first time that the PCT invoked an international instrument, and observed that the contested act violated both Article 4 of the Constitution and Article 14 of the ICCPR. Given the lack of authority to review domestic law for its conformity to international law, it did so only within the dictum, used the international norms as persuasive rather than a binding source, and made sure that it emphasized clearly enough that it did not usurp the power deliberately omitted in the PCTA.

120 See Decision of the PCT No. K 4/92, *OTK* 1992, Vol. 2, 11–26.

121 See Decision of the PCT No. K 14/96, *OTK* 1997, Vol. 2, 125–136. This also was the first decision in which the PCT invoked the ECHRFF; again, as part of the dictum, not the holding.

122 See Decision of the PCT No. K 11/98, *OTK* 1999, Vol. 5, item 97.

123 See Decision of the PCT No. K 21/99, *OTK* 2000, Vol. 4, item 109.

124 See Decision of the PCT No. K 36/97, *OTK* 1998, Vol. 5, 401–420.

125 See Decision of the PCT No. SK 19/98, *OTK* 1999, Vol. 3, 209.

126 Decision of the PCT No. K 5/96, *OTK* 1996, Vol. 2, 24. The PCT later reaffirmed this notion on several occasions. See, for example, Decisions of the PCT Nos. K 17/93, *OTK* 1994, Vol. 1, 92; K 8/95, *OTK* 1995, Vol. 2, 29–37; W 20/94, *OTK* 1995, Vol. 2, 258–265; K 10/95, *OTK* 1995, Vol. 2, 52–71; U 3/97, *OTK* 1997, Vols. 3–4, 436; K 12/98, *OTK* 1998, Vol. 6, 540–541. For a more detailed account, see Kolasiński, 'Orzecznictwo Trybunalu Konstytucyjnego', 9.

127 Decisions of the PCT Nos. K 5/96, *OTK* 1996, Vol. 2, 22; W 4/96, *OTK* 1996, Vol. 6, 478. See also Decisions of the PCT Nos. K 8/96, *OTK* 1996, Vol. 2, 46–65; W 13/94, *OTK* 1995, Vol. 1, 238–251.

128 See Sanetra, 'W sprawie zwiazania sadow', 8–9.

129 Letowski, 'A Constitution for Everyday Use', 117.

130 Czeszejko-Sochacki, 'Zarys modelu polskiego Trybunalu Konstytucyjnego', 106.

131 See Resolution of the PSC No. I PZP 3/93, cited in Jozefowicz, 'Skutki prawne orzeczenia TK', 32.

132 See ibid.

133 See Decision of the PCT No. W 6/93, *OTK* 1993, Vol. 2, 495–509. Garlicki points out that unlike the Polish Supreme Court, the PSAC held that statutes found uncon-

stitutional by the Tribunal lose their effect immediately upon the issuance of the holding. See Garlicki, 'Orzecznictwo Trybunalu Konstytucyjnego w 1995 roku', 112.

134 See Decision of the PCT No. W 14/94, *OTK* 1995, Vol. 1, 262–276. For a detailed account, see Stelmachovski, 'Sad Najwyzszy kontra Trybunal Konstytucyjny'.

135 See Decision of the PCT No. W 19/94, *OTK* 1995, Vol. 1, 212–221.

136 See Resolution of the PSC No. I PZP 13/95, cited in Jozefowicz, 'Skutki prawne orzeczenia TK', 33.

137 See Decisions of the PCT Nos. W 9/94, *OTK* 1995, Vol. 1, 221–246; W 18/95, *OTK* 1995, Vol. 2, 266–272; W 12/95, *OTK* 1996, Vol. 1, 299–314; W 4/96, *OTK* 1996, Vol. 6, item 58.

138 For Polish scholarship's take on the issue of the PCT–PSC confrontation, see, for example, Stelmachovski, 'Sad Najwyzszy kontra Trybunal Konstytucyjny'; Letowska, 'Szkoda wykladni Trybunalu Konstytucyjnego'; Dudek, 'Sady wobec wykladni ustaw'; Sanetra, 'W sprawie zwiazania sadow'; Czeszejko-Sochacki, 'O niektorych problemach'.

139 See, for example, Decisions of the PCT Nos. K 8/95, *OTK* 1995, Vol. 2, 29–37; K 10/95, *OTK* 1995, Vol. 2, 52–71; K 11/94, *OTK* 1995, Vol. 1, 126–139; K 4/95, *OTK* 1995, Vol. 2, 72–101; K 7/98, *OTK* 1998, Vol. 6, item 96; K 39/97, *OTK* 1998, Vol. 6, 491–557; K 3/99, *OTK* 1999, Vol. 4, item 73.

140 See Jozefowicz, 'Orzeczenia interpretacyjne', 30–31.

141 See Garlicki, 'Trybunal Konstytucyjny a sadownictvo', 18–19.

142 See ibid., 18.

143 Resolution of the PSC No. III ARN 93/95, cited in Jozefowicz, 'Skutki prawne orzeczenia TK', 33.

144 Resolution of the PSC No. I PKN 90/98, available at http://www.prawozycie.infor.pl/2000/0700-1755/spis.html; Resolution of the PSC No. III SW 1/98, *OSN* 1998, No. 5, item 219.

145 Resolution of the PSAC No. II SA 1246/98, cited in *Rzeczpospolita*, 21 July 2000.

146 See Sanetra, 'Orzecznictwo sadowe', 18; idem., 'Sad Najwyzszy', 13.

147 See Rymarz, 'Problem prawa miejscowego', 6.

148 See Garlicki, 'Trybunal Konstytucyjny a sadownictvo', 20.

149 See Kolasiński, 'Orzecznictwo Trybunalu Konstytucyjnego'.

150 See, for example, Wasilewski, 'Wladza sadownicza', 18; idem., 'Pytania prawne', 3, 6–7; Maczynski, 'Bezprosriedne stosowanie Konstytucji', 3–14.

151 These obstacles include going through all available judicial instances, including that of cassation, if foreseen by law, hiring an attorney for drafting the complaint and representing the claimant at the PCT, and the hassle of going through the original proceedings again if the contested statute is indeed found unconstitutional.

152 See Decision of the PSC III RN 96/98, cited in Maniewska, 'Konstytucja Rzeczypospolitej Polskiej', 17.

153 Compare Garlicki, 'Trybunal Konstytucyjny a sadownictvo', 22; Kolasiński, 'Orzecznictwo Trybunalu Konstytucyjnego', 12.

154 See Garlicki, 'Trybunal Konstytucyjny a sadownictvo', 4.

155 That calls for a restructuring of the PCT's authority in this very area have already surfaced in Poland is telling of the disappointment with the new 'concrete' review equipment. For one such vocal suggestion, see Czeszejko-Sochacki, 'Wznowienie postepowania', 28. Compare Garlicki, 'Chroniques: Pologne 1999', 717.

156 The number applies to petitions qualified as constitutional complaints. The number of 'letters' alleging rights violations that the PCT received during the first year of the new regulation exceeded 1,000. See Semprich, 'Straźnik straźnikow'.
157 See Garlicki, 'Orzecznictwo Trybunalu Konstytucyjnego w 1998 roku', 106.
158 See Garlicki, 'Orzecznictwo Trybunalu Konstytucyjnego w 1999 roku', 108–109.
159 Ibid., 108.
160 See Semprich, 'Straźnik straźnikow'.
161 See Garlicki, 'Orzecznictwo Trybunalu Konstytucyjnego w 1999 roku', 109.
162 See Semprich, 'Straźnik straźnikow'.
163 See Decision of the PCT No. SK 21/99, *OTK* 2000, Vol. 5, item 144.
164 See Decision of the PCT No. SK 11/98, *OTK* 1999, Vol. 2, item 22.
165 See Maniewska, 'Konstytucja Rzeczypospolitej Polskiej', 3.
166 It also was expected that Imre Pozsgay, a reform communist, would be elected head of state. This, too, had an effect on the conceptualisation of presidential authority, especially as far as the EKA's agenda was concerned. See Bruszt and Stark, 'Remaking the Political Field in Hungary', 44–49.
167 Ágh, 'The Permanent "Constitutional Crisis"', 315.
168 The constitutional basis for the HCC's operation was provided for already in January 1989 but was adjusted in response to the Round Table talks in October 1989. Article 32/A of the constitution limits itself to stating that the 'Constitutional Court shall review the constitutionality of laws and perform tasks assigned to its jurisdiction by statute', and to a few provisions related to standing, office eligibility, and so on.
169 For a detailed analysis of the Court's powers, including procedural implications, see Brunner, 'Structure and proceedings', 76–89.
170 In Poland, Czech Republic and Slovakia, it is explicitly stated that the respective acts/provisions are to be reviewed for their conformity to the norms of higher legal force. The cabinet decrees, for instance, must conform not only to the constitution, but also to statutes. In Hungary, however, all legal norms, regardless of their rank in the hierarchy, are to be reviewed for their conformity to the constitution, which is thus the sole standard of review. The Court nonetheless transformed other norms into a standard of review by relying on the normative hierarchy provided for both in the constitution and in Act XI/1987 on Legislative Proceedings. For more detail, see Brunner, 'Structure and Proceedings', 76.
171 See HACC, Article 43.4.
172 One possible limitation is the President's ability to veto a statute, that is, send it back to the legislature for reconsideration. This, however, can be of significance only in the case of a narrow parliamentary majority, as the veto does not raise the threshold for re-adoption of the bill, and the same number of votes—that is, a simple majority of the quorum—is required for passing the statute.
173 See Holmes, 'Back to the Drawing Board', 22.
174 *Constitutionalism in East Central Europe*, 51 (comment by Sólyom).
175 Ibid. (comment by Sólyom).
176 Decision of the HCC No. 11/1992 AB, cited in Sólyom and Brunner, *Constitutional Judiciary*, 221.
177 Lábady, 'Address', 11.
178 The idealism/pragmatism dichotomy originates with Sólyom and is cited by Ágh. See Ágh, 'The Permanent "Constitutional Crisis"', 318.

179 When a Western European participant at an international conference suggested that a common Central European constitutional space seemed to be emerging, the Hungarian representative, Chief Justice Sólyom, vigorously disagreed: 'Hungary has long been trying to be European rather than Central European.' Sólyom also added that he observed the emergence of a common European constitutional space of which the HCC, needless to say, saw itself—and rightly so—as a full member. See Lentz, 'Das Rechtsstaatprinzip', 83.
180 *Constitutionalism in East Central Europe*, 65 (comment by Sólyom).
181 Ibid., 66.
182 Ibid.
183 Decision of the HCC No. 15/1993 (III.12.) AB, cited in *East European Case Reporter* (hereinafter the '*Case Reporter*') 3, No. 1/1996, 22.
184 Decision of the HCC No. 30/1992 (V.26.) AB, cited in Sólyom and Brunner, *Constitutional Judiciary*, 237.
185 Decision of the HCC No. 60/1994 (XII.24.) AB, cited in ibid., 312.
186 Ibid., 313.
187 Decision of the HCC No. 60/1994 (XII.24.) AB (the quoted part available in *Case Reporter* 2, No. 2/1995, 168).
188 Decision of the HCC No. 4/1993 (II.12.) AB, cited in Sólyom and Brunner, *Constitutional Judiciary*, 259.
189 Decision of the HCC No. 13/1990 AB, cited in Sólyom, 'Introduction to the Decisions of the Hungarian Constitutional Court', 17.
190 Ibid.
191 Decision of the HCC No. 32/1991 (VI.6.) AB, cited in Páczolay, 'Chroniques: Hongrie 1991', 610.
192 Sólyom, 'Interview', 74–75.
193 A similar twist can be detected in the HCC's case law on property rights. In its early years, the HCC succumbed to the prevailing political and ideological understanding of the free market economy, assisted the then establishment in fostering that understanding rather than challenged it, and even strengthened the 'overemphasized property protection' through its own jurisprudence. See Sólyom, 'Anmerkungen', 220. But over time, the HCC liberated itself from mainstream diction and came up with an autonomous concept of property rights, different not only from the one fostered by political rhetoric, but also from that espoused by the ordinary courts.
194 Sólyom, 'Introduction to the Decisions of the Hungarian Constitutional Court', 39.
195 In Zétényi, the notion of specific transitional justice was rejected by nine votes to none. Interestingly, the transitional-specifics argument tended to be rejected either unanimously or by overwhelming majorities.
196 See, for example, Decision of the HCC No. 55/1995 (IX.15.) AB, cited in Páczolay, 'Chroniques: Hongrie 1995', 809.
197 See Seitzer, 'Experimental Constitutionalism', 50.
198 Klingsberg, 'Contextualizing the Calculus of Consent', 332.
199 Ibid.
200 Ackerman, *The Future of Liberal Revolution*, 110.
201 Klingsberg, 'Safeguarding the Transition', 45.
202 Klingsberg, 'Contextualizing the Calculus of Consent', 325.

203 Decision of the HCC No. 15/1993 (III.12.) AB, cited in Sólyom and Brunner, *Constitutional Judiciary*, 22.
204 Ibid.
205 For more detail, see discussion on pp. 417–419.
206 See Decision of the HCC No. 46/2000 AB, cited in *Bulletin of Constitutional Case Law* 3/2000, 501–502.
207 Decision of the HCC No. 23/1990 (X.16.) AB, cited in Sólyom and Brunner, *Constitutional Judiciary*, 126.
208 Decision of the HCC No. 64/1991 (XII.17.) AB, cited in ibid., 182.
209 Decision of the HCC No. 37/1992 (VI.10.) AB, cited in ibid., 242.
210 Decision of the HCC No. 4/1993 (II.12.) AB, cited in ibid., 253 (referring to Decision of the HCC No. 64/1991 AB).
211 Ibid., 254.
212 Ibid., 261.
213 Decision of the HCC No. 64/1991 (XII.17.) AB, cited in Sólyom and Brunner, *Constitutional Judiciary*, 183.
214 Decision of the HCC No. 43/1995 (VI.30.) AB, cited in ibid., 331. The Court relied on the very same duty also in the ultra-progressive decision on environmental protection. See Decision of the HCC No. 28/1994 (V.20.) AB, cited in ibid., 301.
215 Decision of the HCC No. 43/1995 (VI.30.) AB, cited in ibid., 331.
216 Ibid.
217 Decision of the HCC No. 60/1994 (XII.24.) AB, cited in ibid., 180.
218 Decision of the HCC No. 37/1992 (VI.10.) AB, cited in ibid., 241.
219 Ibid., 244.
220 Decision of the HCC No. 1270/B/1997, cited in *Bulletin of Constitutional Case Law* 2/2000, 305.
221 Decision of the HCC No. 37/1992 (VI.10.) AB, cited in Sólyom and Brunner, *Constitutional Judiciary*, 245.
222 Decision of the HCC No. 21/1996 AB, cited in ibid., 337.
223 Decision of the HCC No. 28/1994 (V.20.) AB, cited in ibid., 302.
224 Ibid., 301 (referring to Decision No. 996/G/1990 AB).
225 Therein lies the reason for the Court's refusal to invalidate the media decree despite finding unconstitutionality—the HCC simply preferred unconstitutional regulation to no regulation. This preference for a lesser evil, however, resulted in the legislature's failure to remedy the situation for the next five years. A similarly unfortunate development followed the resolution of some other cases, too. See discussion pp. 249-250.
226 Stone Sweet, *Governing with Judges*, 61–91. For a discussion of the increasing overlap between a constitution and a judge-made constitutional law with regard to US constitutional development, see Damaška, 'Reflection on American Constitutionalism', 432–436.
227 A substantial turnover of justices occurred in 1998–1999, and none of the justices who served on the 'first' Court remained on the bench. For more detail on the turnover, see Scheppele, 'The New Hungarian Constitutional Court', 81–87.
228 See Decision of the HCC No. 14/1999 AB, cited in *Bulletin of Constitutional Case Law* 2/1999, 69–70.
229 See Decision of the HCC No. 2/2001 AB, cited in *Bulletin of Constitutional Case Law* 1/2001, 63–64.

230 Decision of the HCC No. 14/2000 AB, cited in *Bulletin of Constitutional Case Law* 2/2000, 303–304.
231 For more detail on the early case law, see discussion pp. 430ff.
232 See Scheppele, 'The New Hungarian Constitutional Court', 82.
233 Sólyom, 'The First Year', 5.
234 Ibid.
235 *Constitutionalism in East Central Europe*, 50 (comment by Sólyom).
236 Galligan, 'Procedural Rights in Administrative Contexts', 26.
237 Ibid.
238 Sólyom, 'The First Year', 9.
239 The Court would hold public sessions twice a week but from what Sólyom has to say about the matter it appears that the justices were reluctant to embrace the practice and remained unconvinced that public sessions were of much meaning to the Court's deliberation. See Sólyom, 'Anmerkungen', 555, 565.
240 See Brunner, 'Structure and Proceedings', 91–92. See also Majoros, 'Zur Entwicklung der Verfassungsgerichtsbarkeit', 123.
241 Sólyom, 'The First Year', 5.
242 Sólyom, 'Introduction to the Decisions of the Hungarian Constitutional Court', 23.
243 See Páczolay, 'Chroniques: Hungary 1991', 602–603.
244 See Brunner, 'Structure and Proceedings', 91.
245 This claim, however, is somewhat at odds with Sólyom's suggestion that there were no underlying assumptions about the Court's role. See note 104 to Chapter 2 and accompanying text.
246 See 'Podiumsdiskussion', 559–560 (comment by Zoll).
247 The President, having at his disposal both the constitutional veto—that is, standing to petition the Court for pre-enactment review—and political veto (ability to send a bill back for re-consideration to the Parliament), preferred to use the former rather than the latter in the early years of the transition, but following the 1994 elections refrained from the practice and learned to rely almost exclusively on the political veto.
248 Advisory opinion is a term used to denote the Court's abstract interpretation of constitutional provisions under Article 4/G of the HACC. It is, however, more than an advice, as it is binding *erga omnes*.
249 Decision of the HCC No. 31/1990 (XII.18.) AB, cited in Halmai, 'Chroniques: Hongrie 1990', 751.
250 The only other attempt to make use of the preliminary review standing occurred in 1996 when the Court accepted a petition of the Parliament's standing committee. See Brunner, 'Structure and Proceedings', 78–79, 98 (n. 24).
251 See Act I of 1998 amending the HACC.
252 Decision of the PCT No. K 6/94, *OTK* 1994, Vol. 2, 95.
253 Sólyom, 'The Hungarian Constitutional Court and Social Change', 237.
254 Ibid.
255 Schanda, 'Rechtsstaatlichkeit in Ungarn', 223.
256 The Constitutional Court of Hungary, 'The National Report'.
257 Sólyom, 'To the Tenth Anniversary of Constitutional Review', 28.
258 See Decision of the HCC No. 31/1990 (XII.18.) AB, cited in Halmai, 'Chroniques: Hongrie 1990', 751.
259 Decision of the HCC No. 36/1992 (VI.10.), available at http://www.mkab.hu.

260 Decision of the HCC No. 21/1996 AB, cited in Sólyom and Brunner, *Constitutional Judiciary*, 335.
261 See Decision of the HCC No. 17/1993 AB, cited in *Case Reporter* 1, No. 2/1994, 238. The Parliament eventually adopted the law, three years after the initial deadline had passed.
262 Decision of the HCC No. 12/1999 AB, cited in *Bulletin of Constitutional Case Law* 3/1999, 387–388. See also 'Hungary Update 1999', 22.
263 See Decision of the HCC No. 48/1998 (XI.23) AB, cited in *Bulletin of Constitutional Case Law* 3/1998, 421–423. See also 'Hungary Update 1998', 17–18.
264 Bard, 'Access to Legal Aid'.
265 Sajó, 'Rights in Post-Communism', 153. See also Kupper who offers detailed information on Hungary's justice administration reform and its effect on the efficiency of the ordinary courts' organization and operation. Kupper, 'Justizreform in Ungarn'.
266 See Decision of the HCC No. 32/1990 (XII.) AB. The HCC further reiterated its position in Decision No. 39/1997 AB, cited in Sólyom and Brunner, *Constitutional Judiciary*, 364–370.
267 See Brunner, 'Structure and Proceedings', 85.
268 See 'Constitutional Refolution', 111.
269 In its own draft amendment to the HACC, however, the HCC proposed that it acquire the authority to review so-called judicial instructions, that is, abstract-interpretation decisions of the Supreme Court with universally binding effect for all ordinary courts. See Brunner, 'Structure and Proceedings', 77.
270 See, for example, Decision of the HCC No. 57/1991 (XI.8.) AB, cited in Sólyom and Brunner, *Constitutional Judiciary*, 171–177.
271 See Sólyom, 'Zum Geleit zu den Entscheidungen', 65–68.
272 See, for example, Decisions of the HCC Nos. 36/1994 (VI.24) AB, cited in *Case Reporter* 3, No. 2/1996, 148–162; 21/1996 AB, cited in Sólyom and Brunner, *Constitutional Judiciary*, 337.
273 Sólyom, 'Introduction to the Decisions of the Hungarian Constitutional Court', 13.
274 See Decision of the HCC No. 17/1994 (III.29.) AB, cited in *Bulletin of Constitutional Case Law* 1/1994, 30. The Court also pointed out that any external intervention in the courts' activities was a much more serious threat than the possibility of excess on the part of the judiciary itself.
275 Schwartz, referring to his conversation with Páczolay and an unpublished manuscript by Halmai, puts the number at around 20 per year. See Schwartz, 'Struggle for Constitutional Justice', 81.
276 See Brunner, 'Structure and Proceedings', 82.
277 See Mavi, 'Limitations of and Derogations from Human Rights', 108–109.
278 See Brunner, 'Structure and Proceedings', 85, 100 (n. 59) (referring to public communications by justices Sólyom, Halmai, Lábady, and others).
279 The Constitution provides that a statute can grant the Supreme Administrative Court—which, however, has not yet been established—the authority to review substatutory norms and to resolve competence disputes between regional administration and municipal authorities.
280 The turn-out at senatorial elections tends to be very low and feeds the recurrent appeals for a thorough reform of both the Senate's positioning within the legislative

process, and its composition. It is not uncommon to come across appeals from political or media personalities to completely eliminate the Senate as an institution. The record low 20-percent turn-out at the 2000 senatorial elections offered these voices new ammunition.

281 The most obvious failure of the Senate to establish itself as a meaningful barrier against pure majoritarianism concerned the infamous electoral reform, which was drafted by the two major parties and established unduly harsh electoral thresholds requiring, for instance, a coalition of four parties to receive 20 percent of the votes in order to enter the Parliament's lower chamber. It is only since a clear victory of the right-wing/centrist opposition in the 2000 senatorial elections that the Senate has become a serious obstacle to the governing majority's legislative projects. The most significant display of its attempts at political emancipation concerned a veto of a major constitutional bill in 2001.

282 See Malenovský, 'Treaties in the Czech Republic', 218.

283 Decision of the CCC No. Pl. US 13/94, *CCC Collection*, Vol. 2, item 56.

284 Examples include the ILO Treaty No. 122 on employment policy (Decision of the CCC No. Pl. US 36/93, *CCC Collection*, Vol. 1, 175–187) or ILO Treaties No. 17 and No. 42 governing the indemnification of employment-related injuries and sicknesses. See Decision of the CCC No. Pl. US 31/94, *CCC Collection*, Vol. 3, 175–188.

285 In one restitution-related decision, the Court, referring to the UN Human Rights Committee's interpretation, pointed out that the ban on discrimination set forth by Article 26 of the ICCPR was not applicable only to rights expressly included in the ICCPR but was an autonomously enforceable right. See Decision of the CCC No. Pl. US 45/97, *CCC Collection*, Vol. 10, 280–281. In a different restitution-related decision, however, the Court based its validation of legislative differentiation partly on the fact that the very same Article 26 of the ICCPR did not include nationality as one of the discriminating criteria. See Decision of the CCC No. Pl. US 33/96, *CCC Collection*, Vol. 8, 163–174. For detailed analysis of the applicability in Czech constitutional system of international law, see Hofmann, *Volkerrecht.*

286 In the case of pensioners' mandatory contributions, the CCC interpreted restrictively the ban on discrimination set forth by both the ICCPR and the ICESR. See Decision of the CCC No. Pl. US 12/94, *CCC Collection*, Vol. 3, 123–134. Similarly, the Court interpreted narrowly the obligation of the Czech Republic, arising from Article 13.4 of the ICCESR, gradually to institute free higher education, as it allowed for elimination of free higher education even in the case it was previously provided for. See Decision of the CCC No. Pl. US 27/95, *CCC Collection*, Vol. 4, 293–300. It also failed thoroughly to deal with the Convention of the Rights of a Child when it upheld a statutory rule allowing the Security and Intelligence Service to gather data on natural persons without any restrictions as to the age of the affected persons. See Decision of the CCC No. Pl. US 34/95, *CCC Collection*, Vol. 5, 233–240.

287 It is also considerably higher than are the voting requirements applicable in the concrete-review procedure. A three-member panel, deciding by a simple majority, is competent to hear and dispose of a constitutional complaint—two votes thus are enough to find a violation of a constitutional right by a decision of a public authority.

288 With the extension of the number of justices from 10 to 13, effective from 1 January 2002, the required majority changed from 6 out of 10 to 7 out of 13.

289 The competence of the PCT's plenary session in the realm of abstract review is con-

fined to hearing the president's motion for preliminary review. See PACT, Article 25.

290 A motion for the invalidation of a statute also can be filed in conjunction with a constitutional complaint, as long as there is a causal link between the statute and the violation of a constitutional right by the contested administrative or judicial ruling.

291 See PCTA, Article 22; 1997 Const., Article 191.

292 The immediate source of this comment is a conversation with Justice Pavel Holländer at a conference in Levoča, Slovak Republic, on 28 October 2000. But the fact that the left-wing opposition had no good reason to rely on the Court's backing is obvious to any student of Czech constitutional politics.

293 See Decision of the CCC No. Pl. US 19/93, *CCC Collection*, Vol. 1, 1–16.

294 Ibid., 5.

295 See Decision of the PCT No. S 6/91, *OTK* 1991.

296 See Decision of the PCT No. K 15/93, *OTK* 1994, Vol. 1, 21–27.

297 Decision of the CCC No. Pl. US 9/95, *CCC Collection*, Vol. 5, 135.

298 Ibid., 131.

299 Ibid., 133.

300 See Decision of the CCC No. Pl. US 36/93, *CCC Collection*, Vol. 1, 175–187.

301 Cepl and Gillis, 'Making Amends After Communism', 119.

302 Decision of the CCC No. Pl. US 3/94, *CCC Collection*, Vol. 1, 279–291. In a later decision, the Court invalidated the very same requirement anchored in a statute dealing with a different kind of indemnification. See Decision of the CCC No. Pl. US 8/95, *CCC Collection*, Vol. 4, 279–292. Two Slovak petitioners challenged the very same restriction at the ECHR, which, however, found no violation of the Convention. See note 415 to Chapter 3.

303 Decision of the CCC No. Pl. US 33/96, *CCC Collection*, Vol. 8, 163–174.

304 Decision of the CCC No. Pl. US 46/95, *CCC Collection*, Vol. 6, 485–492.

305 Decision of the CCC No. Pl. US 45/97, *CCC Collection*, Vol. 10, 277–283.

306 Decision of the CCC No. Pl. US 15/99, *CCC Collection*, Vol. 17, item 38.

307 Decision of the CCC No. Pl. US 16/94, *CCC Collection*, Vol. 2, 227–232.

308 Decision of the CCC No. Pl. US 47/95, *CCC Collection*, Vol. 5, 209–213.

309 Decision of the CCC No. Pl. US 16/93, *CCC Collection*, Vol. 1, 189, 194.

310 Decision of the CCC No. Pl. US 15/93, *CCC Collection*, Vol. 1, 24.

311 Ibid.

312 Ibid.

313 Decision of the CCC No. Pl. US 24/98, *CCC Collection*, Vol. 15, 211–219.

314 Decision of the CCC No. Pl. US 1/98, *CCC Collection*, Vol. 12, 71–79. A previous decision on a similar issue invalidated a scheme based on which those who satisfied the eligibility criteria only after the statutory periods had expired were entitled to financial compensation only. Decision of the CCC No. Pl. US 24/96, *CCC Collection*, Vol. 6, 133. In this case, as in several others, the dissenters prevailed within a relatively short period of time.

315 Decision of the CCC No. Pl. US 17/99, *CCC Collection*, Vol. 16, 267–276.

316 Decision of the CCC No. Pl. US 25/98, *CCC Collection*, Vol. 13, 274.

317 Compare, for instance, Decisions of the CCC Nos. Pl. US 21/96 (infra note 321) and Pl. US 24/96 (supra note 314) to Decisions of the CCC Nos. Pl. US 24/98 (supra note 313), PL. US 1/98 (supra note 314) and Pl. US 17/99 (supra note 315). In gen-

eral, the Court would find false retroactivity acceptable if serving the availability of indemnification, but unacceptable if unduly restricting the access to indemnification. See also notes 401–403 to Chapter 3 and accompanying text.

318 Decision of the CCC No. Pl. US 12/94, *CCC Collection*, Vol. 3, 126.

319 Ibid.

320 See Decision of the PCT No. K 9/2000, *OTK* 2000, Vol. 8, item 294.

321 Decision of the CCC No. Pl. US 21/96, *CCC Collection*, Vol. 7, 96.

322 Decision of the CCC No. Pl. US 17/96, *CCC Collection*, Vol. 7, 315. This doctrinal position was not immaterial to the case law. Even though the Court found any statutory qualification of the right to free elementary and secondary education to be in violation of the constitution as well as certain international agreements (Decision of the CCC No. Pl. US 35/93, *CCC Collection*, Vol. 1, 51–54), it later rejected a claim that the right to free education entailed governmental subsidies fully covering the cost of course materials and basic schooling equipment in the realm of elementary and secondary education (Decision of the CCC No. Pl. US 25/94, *CCC Collection*, Vol. 3, 233–239). The right to free education also was found inapplicable to education above secondary level, which finding allowed the CCC to uphold a statute eliminating free education at higher vocational schools. See Decision of the CCC No. Pl. US 27/95, *CCC Collection*, Vol. 4, 293–300.

323 See, for example, Decisions of the CCC Nos. Pl. US 4/95, *CCC Collection*, Vol. 3, at 209–226; Pl. US 5/95, *CCC Collection*, Vol. 4, 218; Pl. US 40/97, *CCC Collection*, Vol. 12, 35; Pl. US 46/97, *CCC Collection*, Vol. 12, 378.

324 See, for example, Decisions of the CCC. Nos. Pl. US 16/93, *CCC Collection*, Vol. 1, 205–206; Pl. US 36/96, *CCC Collection*, Vol. 1, 179; Pl. US 5/95, *CCC Collection*, Vol. 4, 218; Pl. US 9/95, *CCC Collection*, Vol. 5, 137.

325 Decision of the CCC No. Pl. US 4/95, *CCC Collection*, Vol. 3, 209.

326 Ibid.

327 Ibid., 217.

328 Decision of the CCC No. Pl. US 13/94, *CCC Collection*, Vol. 2, item 56.

329 Decision of the CCC No. Pl. US 37/93, *CCC Collection*, Vol. 1, 61–76.

330 Decision of the CCC No. Pl. US 3/2000, *CCC Collection*, Vol. 18, item 33.

331 See Decision of the PCT No. P 4/96, *OTK* 1997, Vol. 1, 27–44.

332 Decision of the CCC No. Pl. US 9/2000, available at http://www.concourt.cz.

333 See Decisions of the CCC Nos. Pl. US 9/94, *CCC Collection*, Vol. 2, 7–25; Pl. US 22/94, *CCC Collection*, Vol. 2, 267–271; Pl. US 5/95, *CCC Collection*, Vol. 4, 205–223.

334 Decision of the CCC No. Pl. US 25/97, *CCC Collection*, Vol. 11, 25–41.

335 Decision of the CCC No. Pl. US 27/97, *CCC Collection*, Vol. 11, 67–75.

336 Decision of the CCC No. Pl. US 29/98, *CCC Collection*, Vol. 14, 195–202.

337 Decision of the CCC No. Pl. US 5/94, *CCC Collection*, Vol. 2, 155–163.

338 Decision of the CCC No. Pl. US 2/97, *CCC Collection*, Vol. 8, 325–351.

339 Decision of the CCC No. Pl. US 4/94, *CCC Collection*, Vol. 2, 57–74.

340 Decision of the CCC No. Pl. US 43/93, *CCC Collection*, Vol. 1, 113–121.

341 For more detail, see note 3 to Chapter 2.

342 Decision of the CCC No. Pl. US 42/2000, available at http://www.concourt.cz.

343 Decision of the CCC No. Pl. US 53/2000, available at http://www.concourt.cz.

344 See Decision of the CCC No. Pl. US 16/99, available at http://www.concourt.cz.

345 The Court, however, failed to display the same sensitivity when reviewing the citizenship law, which made it impossible for a vast number of members of the Roma ethnic minority to become nationals of the Czech Republic because of the requirement of a clean criminal record. For a detailed analysis of the effect on Roma of the citizenship law, see Šiklová and Miklušáková, 'Denying Citizenship to the Czech Roma', 58.

346 The Court has held so for the first time in 1995 (see Decision of the CCC No. Pl. US 48/95, *CCC Collection*, Vol. 5, 171–175) and then relied on this technique in a number of other cases.

347 Decision of the CCC No. Pl. US 2/97, *CCC Collection*, Vol. 8, item 91.

348 See, for example, Decision of the CCC No. IV. US 246/96, *CCC Collection*, Vol. 6, 455–459.

349 Decision of the CCC No. Pl. US 25/97, *CCC Collection*, Vol. 11, 34.

350 Decision of the CCC No. Pl. US 18/96, *CCC Collection*, Vol. 6, 109–114.

351 Decision of the CCC No. Pl. US 30/95, *CCC Collection*, Vol. 5, 17–23. The CCC's lack of confidence in the courts' ability to fully take into account the parties' rightful interests extended to administrative authorities. Acting on a constitutional complaint, and taking into account some recent decisions of the ECHR against Slovakia (see, for example, 'Lauko vs. Slovakia', available at http://www.ehcr.coe.int), the CCC annulled the provision of the Civil Procedure Code which prevented judicial review of financial penalties imposed for minor misdemeanours. Decision of the CCC No. Pl. US 28/98, *CCC Collection*, Vol. 16, item 161. It also struck down an administrative law provision which excluded certain decisions of the Ministry of Environment from the general application of the Administrative Procedure Act because of its non-conformity with the constitutional right to judicial protection. Decision of the CCC No. Pl. US 14/96, *CCC Collection*, Vol. 6, 323–328.

352 The Supreme Court raised this objection as early as the first year of the CCC's operation. See Decision of the CCC No. I. US 131/93, *CCC Collection*, Vol. 1, 135.

353 Decision of the CCC No. III. US 83/96, *CCC Collection*, Vol. 6, 123–144.

354 Decision of the CCC No. IV. US 81/95, *CCC Collection*, Vol. 4, 48.

355 Decisions of the CCC Nos. I. US 184/96, *CCC Collection*, Vol. 7, 209–217, IV. US 82/97, *CCC Collection*, Vol. 8, 409–415; I. US 322/96, *CCC Collection*, Vol. 9, 161–168; I. US 400/97, *CCC Collection*, Vol. 10, 189–193.

356 Decision of the CCC No. I. US 184/96, *CCC Collection*, Vol. 7, 216.

357 Decision of the CCC No. III. US 425/97, *CCC Collection*, Vol. 10, 285–288.

358 See, for example, Mikule and Sládeček, 'O závaznosti rozhodnutí Ústavního soudu'. For a contrary opinion, see Antonín Procházka, 'Závaznost rozhodnutí Ústavního soudu'. Compare Holländer, 'Role Ústavního soudu'; Gillis, 'Vztah mezi Ústavním soudem a systémem obecných soudu'.

359 See Decision of the CCC No. IV. US 418/97, *CCC Collection*, Vol. 10, 119–124.

360 See Decision of the CCC No. III. US 206/98, *CCC Collection*, Vol. 11, 235.

361 Decision of the CCC No. III. US 61/94, *CCC Collection*, Vol. 3, 54.

362 Decisions of the CCC Nos. IV. US 23/93, *CCC Collection*, Vol. 1, 221; II. US 101/95, *CCC Collection*, Vol. 4, 267; I. US 487/97, *CCC Collection*, Vol. 10, 361.

363 Ibid., 361–362.

364 See Decision of the CCC No. II. US 81/95, *CCC Collection*, Vol. 6, 575–578.

365 See Decision of the CCC No. I. US 2/93, *CCC Collection*, Vol. 1, 277.
366 Ibid.
367 Decision of the CCC No. I. US 425/97, *CCC Collection*, Vol. 13, 309.
368 Decision of the CCC No. II. US 127/96, *CCC Collection*, Vol. 7, 21–26.
369 Decision of the CCC No. I. US 2/93, *CCC Collection*, Vol. 1, 278.
370 See, for example, Decisions of the CCC Nos. III. US 84/94, *CCC Collection*, Vol. 3, 257–260; III. US 166/95, *CCC Collection*, Vol. 4, 255–258; III. US 271/96, *CCC Collection*, Vol. 7, 153–158; III. US 51/96, *CCC Collection*, Vol. 8, 69–92; III. US 94/97, *CCC Collection*, Vol. 8, 287–290; III. US 224/98, *CCC Collection*, Vol. 15, 17–24.
371 Decision of the CCC No. IV. US 418/97, *CCC Collection*, Vol. 10, 119–124.
372 Decision of the CCC No. III. US 224/98, *CCC Collection*, Vol. 15, 17–24. In a related ruling, the Court flavoured its finding of arbitrary interpretation by ordinary courts with a reference to Joseph Heller's *Catch 22*. See Decision of the CCC No. III. US 150/99, *CCC Collection*, Vol. 17, item 9.
373 Decision of the CCC No. II. US 517/99, *CCC Collection*, Vol. 17, item 32.
374 Decisions of the CCC Nos. II. US 101/95, *CCC Collection*, Vol. 4, 269; II. US 127/96, *CCC Collection*, Vol. 7, 25 (emphasis added).
375 Decision of the CCC No. III. US 464/99, *CCC Collection*, Vol. 18, item 56.
376 Decision of the CCC No. III. US 61/94, *CCC Collection*, Vol. 3, item 10. The lack of a court's attention to all available evidence was found to constitute a violation of procedural rights in a vast number of cases. See, for example, Decisions of the CCC Nos. I. US 30/94, *CCC Collection*, Vol. 3, 189–194; IV. US 69/97, *CCC Collection*, Vol. 11, 187–192; III. US 87/99, *CCC Collection*, Vol. 15, 31–37.
377 See, for example, Decisions of the CCC Nos. I. US 2/93, *CCC Collection*, Vol. 1, 277 and ff.; II. US 81/95, *CCC Collection*, Vol. 6, 575–578.
378 Decision of the CCC No. III. US 275/96, *CCC Collection*, Vol. 6, 293–300.
379 Decision of the CCC No. II. US 156/95, *CCC Collection*, Vol. 5, 63–67.
380 Decision of the CCC No. III. US 23/93, *CCC Collection*, Vol. 1, 41–46.
381 Houbová, 'Dílči úvahy', 71.
382 Compare, for instance, Decisions of the CCC Nos. I. US 425/97, I. US 484/97, I. US 4/93, I. US 108/93, II. US 81/95, II. US 101/95, and II. US 127/96 to Decisions of the CCC Nos. III. US 61/94, III. US 84/94, III 123/97, III. US 224/98, III 505/98, III 68/99, III. US 269/99, IV. US 25/98, IV. US 36/98, IV. US 418/97. In criminal cases, however, both the first and the second panel seem to require a higher standard than in civil cases. See, for example, Decisions of the CCC Nos. II. US 441/99, *CCC Collection*, Vol. 17, item 48; II. US 301/98, *CCC Collection*, Vol. 14, 325–328; II. US 406/97, *CCC Collection*, Vol. 12, 267–272; I. US 394/97, *CCC Collection*, Vol. 10, 179–187; II. US 271/97, *CCC Collection*, Vol. 11, 199–204.
383 This much has been suggested by several justices of the Slovak Court with extensive knowledge of the CCC's working methods and environment (conversation with Justices Babjak, Mészáros and Šváby, Košice, 6 April 2001).
384 See Schwartz, 'Struggle for Constitutional Justice', 82 (referring to Sólyom's unpublished manuscript).
385 See Halmai, 'Constitutional Court', 243–244 (referring to the German Constitutional Court).
386 Decisions of the CCC Nos. III. US 142/98, *CCC Collection*, Vol. 11, 131–137; II. US 254/98, *CCC Collection*, Vol. 17, item 3.

387 Decisions of the CCC Nos. II. US 108/93, *CCC Collection*, Vol. 3, 305–307; IV. US 155/99, *CCC Collection*, Vol. 15, 255–257; IV. US 406/99, *CCC Collection*, Vol. 17, item 11; IV. US 484/99, *CCC Collection*, Vol. 17, item 37; IV. US 100/99, *CCC Collection*, Vol. 18, item 53.
388 Decisions of the CCC Nos. III. US 127/96, *CCC Collection*, Vol. 5, 525; IV. US 28/97, *CCC Collection*, Vol. 9, 81; III. US 269/99, *CCC Collection*, Vol. 17, item 33.
389 Decision of the CCC No. IV. US 508/98, *CCC Collection*, Vol. 13, 353, 357.
390 Decision of the CCC No. III. US 84/94, *CCC Collection*, Vol. 3, 260.
391 Decision of the CCC No. III. US 269/99, *CCC Collection*, Vol. 17, item 33 (referring to a long line of decisions in which numerous elements were set forth by the Court as falling within the subject matter of concrete review).
392 See, for example, Decisions of the CCC Nos. IV. US 246/96, *CCC Collection*, Vol. 6, 455–459; III. US 337/97, *CCC Collection*, Vol. 9, 269–278; III. US 240/97, *CCC Collection*, Vol. 10, 293–300; III. US 308/97, *CCC Collection*, Vol. 11, 119–123; IV. US 264/98, *CCC Collection*, Vol. 11, 261–263; II. US 151/97, *CCC Collection*, Vol. 12, 53–56; IV. US 370/98, *CCC Collection*, Vol. 12, 257–260.
393 Decision of the CCC No. III. US 149/97, *CCC Collection*, Vol. 9, 319–325.
394 Decisions of the CCC Nos. II. US 98/95, *CCC Collection*, Vol. 5, 359–361; III. US 83/96, *CCC Collection*, Vol. 6, 123–144.
395 Decisions of the CCC Nos. III. US 86/98, *CCC Collection*, Vol. 11, 225–230; III. US 162/98, *CCC Collection*, Vol. 12, 235–238.
396 The cases in which such decisions were invalidated are too numerous to be cited. A few relatively recent rulings containing references to the Court's previous decisions on the issue include Decisions of the CCC Nos. III. US 123/97, *CCC Collection*, Vol. 8, 291–295; IV. US 418/97, *CCC Collection*, Vol. 10, 119–124; I. US 394/97, *CCC Collection*, Vol. 10, 179–187; III. US 398/97, *CCC Collection*, Vol. 11, 125–130; I. US 271/97, *CCC Collection*, Vol. 11, 199–204; II. US 301/98, *CCC Collection*, Vol. 14, 325–328; III. US 505/98, *CCC Collection*, Vol. 15, 25–30.
397 Decision of the CCC No. II. US 347/96, *CCC Collection*, Vol. 9, 349–355.
398 Decisions of the CCC Nos. III. US 84/98, *CCC Collection*, Vol. 10, 163–168; I. US 152/97, *CCC Collection*, Vol. 12, 199–206; IV. US 427/98, *CCC Collection*, Vol. 13, 147–150; II. US 178/98, *CCC Collection*, Vol. 14, 27–32; II. US 242/97, *CCC Collection*, Vol. 16, 3–8.
399 Decision of the CCC No. III. US 287/96, *CCC Collection*, Vol. 6, 119–126.
400 See, for example, Decisions of the CCC Nos. III. US 398/97, *CCC Collection*, Vol. 11, 125–130; I. US 394/97, *CCC Collection*, Vol. 10, 179–187; II. US 441/99, *CCC Collection*, Vol. 17, item 48.
401 The Court took the opposite path on the issue of anonymous witnesses. It first invalidated within abstract review a statutory rule providing for anonymous witnesses. See Decision of the CCC No. Pl. US 4/94, *CCC Collection*, Vol. 2, 57–74. A few years later, however, when handling a constitutional complaint, the CCC upheld the decision of the criminal court preventing the defendant from confronting his witnesses, for other necessary precautions were taken to protect the defendant's due process rights, such as the possibility of his counsel to interrogate the witnesses without being able to see them. See Decision of the CCC No. III. US 210/98, *CCC Collection*, Vol. 13, 241–245.

402 Decision of the CCC No. Pl. US 33/96, *CCC Collection*, Vol. 8, 163–174.

403 The CCC held on various occasions that so-called 'false retroactivity' was generally acceptable, as it merely subjected existing legal relations to a new rule. That that was more or less what happened in this case did not prevent the Court from holding for the petitioner.

404 Decision of the CCC No. IV. US 136/97, *CCC Collection*, Vol. 9, 438.

405 Whenever I speak of annulment of a statute, it is *de facto* annulment only. If the SCC finds a statute to be in violation of the Constitution, it suspends its effect, and unless modified within six months by the legislator, the norm becomes void.

406 Stone Sweet, *Governing With Judges*, 130–131.

407 The only other authority more successful in terms of the ratio of applications to favourable rulings was the President (Kováč) whom the Court has found to be right in six out of his seven abstract-review petitions. The number of his applications, however, was several times lower than the number of applications filed by the attorney general (46). These numbers apply to the Court's first term (March 1993-February 2000) but have not changed significantly during the second term, except for the fact that the new president Schuster is yet to file an application with the SCC. For more detail on the statistics, see Kresák (ed.), *Rozhodovacia Činnost.*

408 More specifically, the Slovak specifics were meant to warrant, for instance, a third way between free market economy and state interventionism, a more cautious attitude towards integration in the EU and especially NATO, and relations with Russia more intense than the rest of the region was willing to pursue. In practice, this prevented Slovakia from becoming a member of NATO and a member of the pool of first-round applicants to the EU, allowed for a pursuit by Russia of its political and economic interests in Slovakia, contributed to the 'Balkanisation' of the local political culture, and had adverse consequences for the morale of the population in general.

409 See Decision of the SCC No. Pl. US 9/93, *SCC Collection* 1993–94, 65–70. Within concrete review, the Court refused to hear two of the three individual petitions concerning in one way or another the issue of lustration requirements. See Decisions of the SCC Nos. II. US 9/93, *SCC Collection* 1993–94, 28–29; I. US 1/96, *SCC Collection* 1996, 335–338. In the third case, it found that the right of the petitioner to have his claim adjudicated without undue delay was violated by the Regional Court, without, however, dealing substantively with the lustration issue. See Decision of the SCC No. II. US 64/99, *SCC Collection* 1999, 315–318. All that the SCC ever had to say about lustration was that 'to stipulate conditions for performance of a particular office [could] not be deemed discrimination in employment or profession' because it was within the legislature's powers to restrict access to security-related public offices (see Decision of the SCC No. II. US 9/93, *SCC Collection* 1993–94, 29), and that 'lustrations [were] not a standard legal relation', as their purpose was 'rapidly to come to terms with the past and purge public life'. See Decision of the SCC No. II. US 64/99, *SCC Collection* 1999, 317–318.

410 See Korecký, 'Talárokracie'.

411 See Decision of the SCC No. Pl. US 23/98, *SCC Collection* 1999, 462–470.

412 Ibid., 467.

413 A few petitions against restitution-related legislation were filed earlier but these were challenging some very specific arrangements, without questioning either the underlying rationale of the policy or its scope.

414 See Decision of the SCC No. I. US 20/94, *SCC Collection* 1993–94, 152–166.
415 The ECHR upheld the rule in a restitution-related case brought against Slovakia. See 'Brežný and Brežný v. Slovakia', available at http://www.echr.coe.int.
416 See Decision of the SCC No. I. US 23/94, *SCC Collection* 1993–94, 175–176.
417 See Decision of the SCC No. I. US 59/97, *SCC Collection* 1998, 268–278.
418 The Court was given two opportunities in 2001 to improve its restitution record but decided against accepting the invitation and upheld both of the contested regulations. See Decisions of the SCC Nos. Pl. US 3/00, Pl. US 17/00, available at http://www.concourt.sk.
419 The petitioner argued that the DU did not meet the legal criteria for running in the elections since it allegedly falsified some of the citizens' signatures on its electoral application. See Decision of the SCC No. Pl. US 16/94, *SCC Collection* 1993–94, 228–235.
420 The petitioner argued that the MDS and public TV violated electoral rules by broadcasting before and during the elections reports and messages that were aimed against the MDS's electoral competitors. See Decision of the SCC No. Pl. US 17/94, *SCC Collection* 1993–94, 236–247.
421 See Decision of the SCC No. II. US 804/00, available at http://www.concourt.sk.
422 See Decision of the SCC No. I. US 7/96, *SCC Collection* 1996, 220–233.
423 Only four of these abstract-interpretation petitions were filed directly by Kováč, however.
424 See Decision of the SCC No. I. US 58/94, *SCC Collection* 1995, 159–160.
425 See Decision of the SCC No. II. US 65/97, *SCC Collection* 1997, 425–440.
426 See Decision of the SCC No. Pl. US 4/97, *SCC Collection* 1998, 29–46. Interestingly, the SCC took more than 13 months to issue a ruling on this matter of extreme legal and political significance, while the busier Czech Court handled a similar claim within about 10 weeks. See Decision of the CCC No. Pl. US 33/97, *CCC Collection*, Vol. 9, item 163.
427 See Decision of the SCC No. Pl. US 32/95, *SCC Collection* 1996, 188–199.
428 See Decision of the SCC No. Pl. US 41/95, *SCC Collection* 1996, 292–296.
429 See Decision of the SCC No. Pl. US 42/95, *SCC Collection* 1996, 79–93.
430 See Decision of the SCC No. Pl. US 43/95, *SCC Collection* 1996, 123–155.
431 See Decision of the SCC No. Pl. US 17/96, *SCC Collection* 1998, 47–87.
432 See Decision of the SCC No. Pl. US 16/95, *SCC Collection* 1995, 38–51.
433 See Decision of the SCC No. Pl. US 1/96, *SCC Collection* 1996, 199–219.
434 See Decision of the SCC No. Pl. US 38/95, *SCC Collection* 1996, 59–68.
435 See Decision of the SCC No. Pl. US 19/98, *SCC Collection* 1998, 173–199.
436 See Decision of the SCC No. Pl. US 15/98, *SCC Collection* 1999, 27–75.
437 Although the circumstances were obviously different, the Slovak Court's functioning in the transitional environment resembles in some ways the early jurisprudence of the US Supreme Court, which, as Damaška points out, 'until about 1870 . . . dealt mostly with the framework of political institutions'. Damaška, 'Reflection on American Constitutionalism', 432. Similarly, the pre-1870 judicial review in the United States was prohibitory, and focused on correcting *ultra vires* measures rather than on shaping legislative policies. See ibid., 433.
438 See Decisions of the SCC Nos. Pl. US 21/2000, *SCC Collection* 2000, 32–39; Pl. US 3/01, available at http://www.concourt.sk.

439 Šimko, 'Interview'.
440 For more detail, see Radoslav Procházka et al., 'Právny štát, legislatíva a aplikácia práva'.
441 See discussion pp. 134–136.
442 See Drgonec, 'Interview'.
443 For a comparative discussion of the Court's working methods, see Radoslav Procházka, 'Metódy práce Ústavneho súdu I–III'.
444 The 2001 constitutional amendment acknowledged the problem, and the Court may now suspend the effect of a contested regulation if its further application could endanger fundamental rights and freedoms, if it could result in serious economic harm, or if it could produce other irreparable consequences. See Slovak Const., Article 125.2.
445 Decision of the SCC No. Pl. US 33/95, *SCC Collection* 1995, 123–142.
446 Ibid., 137.
447 Interestingly enough, the ruling on the municipal elections act is as lengthy and complicated as is the ruling on the national elections act, and yet it took the Court only two months to issue it. For more on the SCC's different approach to municipal electoral matters, see discussion pp. 360–361.
448 Stone Sweet, *Governing with Judges*, 200.
449 The Court is bound to disregard this limitation if it finds the relevance of the complaint significantly to exceed the applicant's personal interest. See SACC, Article 53.2.
450 The 2001 constitutional amendment, however, abolished the petition procedure and restructured the provisions regulating constitutional complaints so as to include decisions of ordinary courts as subject matter of concrete constitutional review. The new rules became effective on 1 January 2002. See Slovak Const., Article 127.
451 For a thorough discussion of similar, but not identical, problems relating to the relevant rules of procedure in the Czech Republic, see Kratochvíl, 'K procesnímu postupu'.
452 The ECHR has so held, for instance, in I.S. vs. Slovakia, available at http://www.echr.coe.int. But while the ECHR would 'only' decline to deem Slovak constitutional review an effective venue for the purposes of the ECHRFF, the then Chief Justice of the SCC put it more plainly, calling its own Court an 'impotent body, which cannot do anything.' See 'Čičova rozlúčka'.
453 For a detailed examination of the Court's interpretation of its concrete-review competence, see discussion pp. 467–469.
454 For recent displays of this attitude, see, for example, Decisions of the SCC Nos. II. US 27/98, *SCC Collection* 1998, item 29; II. US 4/99, *SCC Collection* 1999, item 24.
455 Decision of the SCC No. I. US 79/93 (on file with the SCC).
456 See Decision of the SCC No. I. US 59/94, *SCC Collection* 1993–94, 264–265.
457 See Decision of the SCC No. I. US 26/93, *SCC Collection* 1993–94, 36.
458 See Decision of the SCC No. I. US 138/93, *SCC Collection* 1993–94, 168.
459 Decision of the SCC No. II. US 1/95, *SCC Collection* 1995, 269.
460 Decision of the SCC No. I. US 75/97, *SCC Collection* 1997, 562. The number of cases in which the SCC has relied on this or a similar formulation is too great to warrant citations but the ones to which the SCC tends to refer include Decisions of the SCC Nos. I. US 40/95, *SCC Collection* 1995, 310–311; II. US 21/96, *SCC Collection*

1996, 357–359; I. US 36/96, *SCC Collection* 1996, 366–370; I. US 6/97, *SCC Collection* 1997, 506–510; I. US 36/97, *SCC Collection* 1997, 533–538; I. US 55/98, *SCC Collection* 1998, 497–499; I. US 4/00, available at http://www.concourt.sk.

461 For more on the context, see discussion pp. 470–471.

462 See Decision of the SCC No. I. US 20/97, *SCC Collection* 1997, 142.

463 Slovakia is half the size of the Czech Republic in terms of both area and population. Until late 2001, there were 10 judgments issued by the ECHR against Slovakia and five issued against the Czech Republic.

464 See Decision of the SCC No. II. US 110/95, *SCC Collection* 1995, 314.

465 Ibid., 312–314.

466 Decision of the SCC No. I. US 62/97, *SCC Collection* 1997, 546.

467 See Decision of the SCC No. I. US 53/96, *SCC Collection* 1996, 377–381.

468 Decision of the SCC No. I. US 38/97 (on file with the SCC).

469 Decision of the SCC No. I. US 6/97, *SCC Collection* 1997, 510. Unless, however, it decides to say, as it in fact did, 'any action by the court or other agency which is in violation of the applicable statute is also in violation of the constitutional right to judicial or other legal protection'. See Decision of the SCC No. I. US 26/94, *SCC Collection* 1993–94, 50. For a comprehensive discussion of the extent of the SCC's competence in relation to ordinary adjudication, see Drgonec, 'Vzt'ah všeobecného a ústavného súdnictva v Slovenskej republike.

470 In 1998, for instance, 10 of the 16 petition-related holdings concerned unreasonable delays in civil proceedings, in 1999, 14 out of 30, and in 2000, 13 out of 23.

471 See Decisions of the SCC Nos. II. US 62/99, *SCC Collection* 1999, 587–590; II. US 14/00, available at http://www.concourt.sk.

472 See Decision of the SCC No. II. US 813/00, available at http://www.concourt.sk.

473 See Decisions of the SCC Nos. Pl. US 17/95, *SCC Collection* 1995, 21–24; Pl. US 18/99 *SCC Collection* 1999, 173–182; Pl. US 50/99, *SCC Collection* 2000, 101–115.

474 See Decision of the SCC No. Pl. US 16/99, *SCC Collection* 1999, 167–170.

475 See Decisions of the SCC Nos. Pl. US 29/94, *SCC Collection* 1995, 15–17; Pl. US 7/95, *SCC Collection* 1995, 18–20; Pl. US 10/99 *SCC Collection* 1999, 171–172; Pl. US 1/00, *SCC Collection* 2000, 116–126.

476 See Decision of the SCC No. I. US 33/95, *SCC Collection* 1995, 82–104.

477 See Decision of the SCC No. I. US 8/97, *SCC Collection* 1997, 183–199.

478 See Decision of the SCC No. I. US 9/97, *SCC Collection* 1997, 474–479.

479 See Decision of the SCC No. II. US 48/97, *SCC Collection* 1998, 279–299.

480 See Decision of the SCC No. I. US 60/97, *SCC Collection* 1998, 318–336. The SCC has held to the same effect in two other factually and legally related petitions. See Decisions of the SCC Nos. I. US 76/97, *SCC Collection* 1998, 337–349; II. US 37/98, *SCC Collection* 1999, 200–207.

481 After the elections, the new Prime Minister Dzurinda cancelled both amnesties, but the Court stated within an abstract-interpretation ruling that it was not possible under the Constitution to either change the original amnesty or annul it altogether. See Decision of the SCC No. I. US 30/99, *SCC Collection* 1999, item 59.

482 These are the words that the Chief Justice has used to justify his assignment of the case to a particular rapporteur. For more on the controversy surrounding the assignment of the case, see 'Radio Free Europe Daily Report', 9 November 1999, available at http://www.rferl.org/bd/sl/slovak/sl-ascii/archiv/991109.html.

483 See Drgonec et al., 'Výpočet nesprávnych stanovísk'.
484 See note 455 to Chapter 3 and accompanying text.
485 See Decision of the SCC No. II. US 4/99, *SCC Collection* 1999, 297–298.
486 Decision of the SCC No. II. US 47/97, *SCC Collection* 1997, 319.
487 See Decision of the SCC No. II. US 60/99, *SCC Collection* 1999, 612–615.
488 See Decision of the SCC No. I. US 13/00, available at http://www.concourt.sk.
489 See Decision of the SCC No. III. US 6/00, *SCC Collection*, 205–217.
490 See Decision of the SCC No. II. US 811/00, available at http://www.concourt.sk.
491 See Decision of the SCC No. I. US 1/01, available at http://www.concourt.sk.
492 Ibid.
493 Ibid.
494 See Decision of the SCC No. II. US 804/00, available at http://www.concourt.sk.

NOTES TO CHAPTER 4 INTERPRETIVE TECHNIQUES

1 Kahn, *The Reign of Law*, 66.
2 Sajó, 'Rights: More or Less', 261.
3 See *Constitutionalism in East Central Europe*, 50 (comment by Sólyom).
4 For a seminal discussion of moments of constitutive self-definition, see Ackerman, *We the People*, 122, 196.
5 That the Slovaks were psychologically more inclined to accept the separation was a function of their lesser identification with both the unitary state of pre-communist Czechoslovakia and the post-1968 federation. The Czechs, on the other hand, kept the old federal flag, claimed continuity with the First Republic, and saw Mečiar rather than Klaus to be the founder of their somewhat unwanted new state.
6 A number of local commentators contested the legitimacy of the split, as well as of the new constitution. See Valko, 'On the Constitution', 315; Radoslav Procházka, 'čakanie na reinkarnáciu'. Compare *Constitutionalism in East Central Europe*, 113–116 (comment by Bútora). However, given the West's rapid acceptance of the separation, and the emergence of a vast array of legal and political problems within the newly founded constitutional orders, the issue of the legitimacy of the founding act itself orbited on the periphery of local public discourse. Moreover, both constitutions were adopted by relatively wide margins, and in countries where constitution making is often based on purely numerical considerations—having or not having enough votes—this is what counted.
7 Constitutional Court of the Czech Republic, 'The National Report'.
8 Constitutional Court of the Slovak Republic, 'The National Report'.
9 Constitutional Tribunal of Poland, 'The National Report'.
10 Constitutional Court of Hungary, 'The National Report'.
11 Dzialocha, 'Der Rechtsstaat', 9.
12 See Varga, *Transition to the Rule of Law*, 126.
13 See, for example, Decisions of the PCT Nos. P 2/87, *OTK* 1987, 30; Uw 3/87, *OTK* 1988, item 14; U 8/90, *OTK* 1991, 134–141; K 8/91, *OTK* 1992, Vol. 1, 76–84; K 15/93, *OTK* 1994, Vol. 1, 21–27.

14 See, for example, Decisions of the PCT Nos. K 5/94, *OTK* 1995, Vol. 1, 36–47; K 10/95, *OTK* 1995, Vol. 2, 52–71; K 4/95, *OTK* 1995, Vol. 2, 72–101; K 17/95, *OTK* 1995, Vol. 2, 173–189. For a thorough account of the PCT's case law relating to the domestic applicability of international law, see Oniszczuk, 'Umowy miedzynarodowe'.
15 See Decision of the PCT No. U 6/92, *OTK* 1992, Vol. 1, 201.
16 See Decisions of the PCT Nos. K 11/93, *OTK* 1993, Vol. 2, 350–367; K 3/98, *OTK* 1998, Vol. 4, item 52.
17 See Decision of the PCT No. K 6/94, *OTK* 1994, Vol. 2, 95.
18 See Decision of the PCT No. W 19/95, *OTK* 1996, Vol. 1, 283–298.
19 See Decisions of the PCT Nos. U 14/92, *OTK* 1992, Vol. 2, 57–74; K 5/93, *OTK* 1993, Vol. 2, 376–392. For post-provisionality jurisprudence on the same subject matter, see Decisions of the PCT Nos. K 25/97, *OTK* 1997, Vols. 3–4, 316–335; K 3/98, *OTK* 1998, Vol. 4, item 52; K 24/98, *OTK* 1998, Vol. 6, 434–476.
20 See Decision of the PCT No. W 10/94, *OTK* 1994, Vol. 2., 236–248.
21 See Decision of the PCT No. W 1/95, *OTK* 1995, Vol. 2., 230–257.
22 See Decisions of the PCT Nos. W 2/95, *OTK* 1995, Vol. 1, item 22; K 6/94, *OTK* 1994, Vol. 2, 83–99.
23 Brzezinski, *Struggle for Constitutionalism*, 174.
24 Schlink's dichotomy builds on Alexy's differentiation between fundamental rights as subjective rights and as objective norms. See Alexy, 'Grundrechte', 49; idem., *Theorie der Grundrechte*, 485. Schlink characterises the 'fundamental rights as subjective rights' as 'entitlements of the individual subject to be respected by the state in his individual freedoms, to participate as an individual in the practice of state power, or to be considered in the distribution of positions, means and opportunities'. On the other hand, 'fundamental rights as objective principles' are 'maxims according to which social relationships, as well as the relationship between state and society, are to be ordered'. Schlink, 'German Constitutional Culture', 722.
25 Ibid. See also Damaška, *Faces of Justice*, 83–84.
26 Kommers, 'German Constitutionalism', 851.
27 See Decisions of the PCT Nos. K 6/90, *OTK* 1991, 15–26; K 4/91, *OTK* 1992, Vol. 1, 40–58; U 6/92, *OTK* 1992, Vol. 1, 196–213; K 17/93, *OTK* 1994, Vol. 1, 84–96; W 3/93, *OTK* 1994, Vol. 1, 154–164.
28 Decision of the PCT No. K 12/90, *OTK* 1990, 66–78.
29 Ibid.
30 Decision of the PCT No. K 4/91, *OTK* 1992, Vol. 1, 40–58.
31 Decision of the PCT No. P 6/92, *OTK* 1993, Vol. 1, 89.
32 Decision of the PCT No. K 3/97, *OTK* 1997, Vol. 2, 272–286.
33 Decision of the PCT No. W 3/93, *OTK* 1994, Vol. 1, 162.
34 Ibid., 158.
35 Ibid. (referring to Article 36(b).4 of the Polish Constitution).
36 Ibid. Some support for this position may be found in the opinion of the ECHR according to which '[w]hoever exercises the rights and freedoms enshrined in the free speech guarantees undertakes duties and responsibilities. Among them—in the context of religious opinions and beliefs—may legitimately be included an obligation to avoid as far as possible expressions that are gratuitously offensive to others and

thus an infringement of their rights, and which therefore do not contribute to any form of public debate capable of furthering progress in human affairs'. 'Otto-Preminger Institute vs. Austria', cited in Kommers, 'The Constitutionalism of Mary Ann Glendon', 1344.

37 Decision of the PCT No. W 3/93, *OTK* 1994, Vol. 1, 163.

38 Ibid., 159.

39 Decision of the PCT No. K 17/93, *OTK* 1994, Vol. 1, 90.

40 Ibid., 91.

41 Ibid.

42 Decision of the PCT No. K 11/90, *OTK* 1991, 34.

43 See ibid., 39–40. See also Decision of the PCT No. U 12/92, *OTK* 1993, Vol. 1, 111–112.

44 Ibid., 115–116.

45 See Decision of the PCT No. K 26/96, *OTK* 1997, Vol. 2, 173–245.

46 Ibid., 184.

47 Ibid., 185.

48 Ibid., 187.

49 Ibid., 196–197. I feel the urge to state for the record that even though I find the PCT's interpretation cumbersome, I fully adhere to the outcome of this case.

50 A less strict version of this concept can also be found in German constitutional case law, as according to the GCC 'the image of a man in the Basic Law is not that of an isolated, sovereign individual; rather, the Basic Law has decided in favour of a relationship between the individual and the community in the sense of a person's dependence on and commitment to the community, without infringing upon a person's individual value.' See Kommers, 'Constitutional Jurisprudence', 305.

51 The 1921 Constitution had six articles on civic duties for 19 articles on rights. The duties included loyalty and allegiance to the state, respect for, and observance of, the constitution, military service, other services for the benefit of the state, performance of public duties, and a duty to raise children as righteous citizens. Under the 1935 constitution, the state's task was to make sure that individual efforts are made within a framework of harmonious cooperation for the benefit of the common good. The government was to organise public life, and political rights and liberties were to be balanced for the benefit of the common good. No action could contradict the state's objectives, and everyone was to profess Polish statehood as a value. The 1952 constitution, in addition to a separate section on citizens' duties, also expressly limited some of the most important personal freedoms. It stated, 'the setting up of, and participation in, associations the aims of which are directed against the political system or against the legal order of the Polish People's Republic are forbidden' (1952 Const., Article 72). Further, it was a criminal act to 'abuse freedom of conscience and religion for the purpose of undermining the interests of the Polish People's Republic' (1952 Const., Article 70).

52 Osiatynski, 'Perspectives', 317–318.

53 Los, 'Property Rights', 54. For illustrations of the effect on Poland's post-revolutionary legislative discourse of this philosophy, see Los, 'In the Shadow of Totalitarian Law', 303–315.

54 Kowalski, *Solidarnošč*, 140 (cited in Los, 'Property Rights', 55).

55 Kowalski, *Solidarnošč*, 141.
56 Glendon, *The Rights Talk*, 14.
57 See Holmes, 'Back to the Drawing Board', 23–24.
58 The rights themselves, however, were not to be taken as prima facie equal. The Tribunal held, for instance, that the principle of proportionality served 'to protect all rights and freedoms and thus the criteria of "excess" must be relativised, among other things by taking into account the nature of the different rights and freedoms' (Decision of the PCT No. K 11/94, *OTK* 1995, Vol. 1, 132).
59 See Garlicki, 'Chroniques: Pologne 1990–1997'.
60 See discussion pp. 127ff.
61 Kramer, 'Social Protection Policies', 53.
62 Ackerman, however, points out that even in the United States there is now 'no substitute for an engaged national politics and activist government'. Ackerman, *We the People*, 318. He also understands *Brown* and *Griswold*, for instance, to have validated the New Deal vision of an activist government. See ibid., 149–159.
63 Schlink, 'German Constitutional Culture', 722. For an excellent discussion of the American experience, see Damaška, 'Reflection on American Constitutionalism'.
64 Kedzia, 'The Implementation of Social and Economic Rights', 239.
65 Kramer, 'Social Protection Policies', 47.
66 See, for example, Sunstein, 'Against Positive Rights'; Posner, 'The Costs of Enforcing Legal Rights'.
67 Garlicki, 'Orzecznictwo Trybunalu Konstytucyjnego w 1997 roku', 54.
68 Decision of the PCT No. U 17/97, *OTK* 1998, Vol. 3, 185. See also Decision of the PCT No. K 36/98, *OTK* 1999, Vol. 3, item 40.
69 See, for example, Decisions of the PCT Nos. SK 11/98, *OTK* 1999, Vol. 2, item 22; K 5/98, *OTK* 1999, Vol. 3, item 39; P 4/98, *OTK* 1999, Vol. 5, item 98; K 6/98, *OTK* 1999, Vol. 6, item 117.
70 Decision of the PCT No. K 2/98, *OTK* 1999, Vol. 3, 222.
71 Decision of the PCT No. P 4/98, *OTK* 1999, Vol. 5, 518.
72 Decision of the PCT No. K 28/97, *OTK* 1998, Vol. 4, 291.
73 Decision of the PCT No. U 5/97, *OTK* 1998, Vol. 4, 203.
74 Ibid. The above decision is also the first instance in which the Tribunal combined the novel substantive provisions on rights with its newly acquired authority to scrutinise domestic law for its conformity to international agreements. For more examples of the same approach, see Decisions of the PCT Nos. K 40/97, *OTK* 1998, Vol. 2, 53–71; K 38/97, *OTK* 1998, Vol.3, 131–150.
75 Garlicki, 'Orzecznictwo Trybunalu Konstytucyjnego w 1999 roku', 126–131.
76 Decision of the PCT No. P 4/98, *OTK* 1999, Vol. 5, 516.
77 Ibid., 518. See also Decision of the PCT No. K 13/98, *OTK* 1999, Vol. 4, 374.
78 See *Constitutionalism in East Central Europe*, 50 (comment by Sólyom).
79 See Decision of the HCC No. 23/1990 (X.16.) AB, cited in Sólyom and Brunner, *Constitutional Judiciary*, 123 and ff.
80 The Court, however, justified its rigor in refusing to sacrifice legal certainty on the altar of material justice by arguing that substantive justice could be attained without violating the applicable constraints, especially the principle of legal certainty. See Decision of the HCC No. 9/1992 (I.30.) AB, cited in ibid., 226.
81 See, for example, Decisions of the HCC Nos. 11/1992 AB, cited in ibid., 214; 30/1992

(V. 26.) AB, cited in ibid., 229. See also Decision of the HCC No. 42/1993 (VI.30) AB, cited in *Case Reporter* 1, No. 2/1994, 240.

82 See Decision of the HCC No. 4/1993 (II.12.) AB, cited in Sólyom and Brunner, *Constitutional Judiciary*, 246.

83 See Decision of the HCC No. 53/1993 AB, cited in *Case Reporter* 1, No. 2/1994, 241. Here again, as in *Capital Punishment*, the Court strengthened its power base through a ruling with the substantive elements of which the legislature would not want to argue. Being aware of the preference of both the political arena and the society at large for an acceptable solution to the issue of past injustices, and the criticism *Zétényi* aroused, the Court proved itself willing to let certain retroactive measures pass the muster of constitutionality. It has so hinted in a couple of earlier decisions (see Decisions of the HCC Nos. 41/1993 AB; 42/1993 AB) but of most relevance to the issue was its holding that it was compatible with the Hungarian constitution retroactively to punish crimes qualifiable as crimes against humanity.

84 See Decision of the HCC No. 4/1997 AB, cited in Sólyom and Brunner, *Constitutional Judiciary*, 356–363.

85 Decision of the HCC No. 64/1991 (XII.17.) AB, cited in ibid., 182.

86 *Constitutionalism in East Central Europe*, 52 (comment by Sólyom).

87 See Hungarian Const., Article 8.4.

88 These include the freedom of movement and residence, protection of personal data, freedom of belief and religion, freedom of press and free access to information of public interest, the right of association and of assembly, right to citizenship, right of asylum, rights of national and ethnic minorities, and the right to strike. See Hungarian Const., Articles 58.3; 59.2; 60.4; 61.4; 62.2; 63.3; 65.2; 68.5; 69.4; 70(C).3

89 Decision of the HCC No. 4/1993 (II.12.) AB, cited in Sólyom and Brunner, *Constitutional Judiciary*, 258.

90 See Varga, *Transition to Rule of Law*, 16.

91 Ibid., 26.

92 Ibid.

93 Sólyom, 'The Hungarian Constitutional Court and Social Change', 237.

94 The HCC proved less willing than the PCT to borrow or to learn from other authorities in various areas of adjudication. Unlike the PCT, which took advantage of a complex case law of the Supreme Court in the realm of personality rights, the HCC refused to do the same and instead elaborated its own doctrine of personality rights based predominantly on the concept of human dignity. Similarly, the HCC presented its concept of novation as different from the one espoused by the Civil Code, and argued that the constitutional application of property rights should be different from the civil law's approach.

95 Mauro Cappelletti argues, '[r]ealistically speaking, the law in Italy is to a large extent what the scholar says it is'. See Cappelletti, *The Italian Legal System*, 243. This comment can be applied to most civil law countries. See also Calabresi, *Common Law for the Age of Statutes*, 251, n. 4, 6.

96 See *Constitutionalism in East Central Europe*, 52 (comment by Sólyom).

97 See discussion pp. 92ff. See also Halmai, who notes the nineteenth- and twentieth-century Hungarian courts' tendency to rely heavily on local legal theory. Halmai, 'Development of Civil Law'.

98 Varga, *Transition to Rule of Law*, 23.

99 See Brunner, 'Structure and Proceedings', 73.
100 Decision of the HCC No. 8/1990 (IV.23.) AB, cited in Sólyom and Brunner, *Constitutional Judiciary*, 107.
101 Ibid.
102 Decision of the HCC No. 64/1991 (XII.17.) AB , cited in ibid., 186.
103 See Decision of the HCC No. 75/1995 AB, cited in Dupré, 'The Right to Human Dignity', 72.
104 Decision of the HCC No. 23/1990 (X.16.) AB, cited in Sólyom and Brunner, *Constitutional Judiciary*, 126.
105 Decision of the HCC No. 9/1992 (I.30.) AB, cited in ibid., 200.
106 Decision of the HCC No. 1/1994 (I.7.) AB, cited in *Bulletin of Constitutional Case Law* 1/1994, 28.
107 Decision of the HCC No. 22/1992 (IV.10.) AB, available at http://www.mkab.hu.
108 Decision of the HCC No. 57/1991 (XI.8.) AB, cited in Sólyom and Brunner, *Constitutional Judiciary*, 171.
109 Decision of the HCC No. 35/1995 AB, cited in Sólyom, 'Justice At Work', 1733.
110 Decision of the HCC No. 14/1995 (III.13.) AB, cited in Sólyom and Brunner, *Constitutional Judiciary*, 316.
111 Decision of the HCC No. 46/1991 AB, cited in Dupré, 'The Right to Human Dignity', 76.
112 Decision of the HCC No. 27/1990 AB, cited in ibid., 76.
113 Decision of the HCC No. 39/1997 AB, cited in Sólyom and Brunner, *Constitutional Judiciary*, 366.
114 See Decision of the HCC No. 36/2000 AB, cited in *Bulletin on Constitutional Case Law* 3/2000, 496–497.
115 Decision of the HCC No. 30/1992 (V.26.) AB, cited in Sólyom and Brunner, *Constitutional Judiciary*, 232.
116 Ibid., 233.
117 Ibid., 235.
118 See Decision of the HCC No. 36/1994 (VI.24) AB, cited in *Case Reporter* 3, No. 2/1996, 148–162.
119 Decision of the HCC No. 37/1992 (VI.10.) AB, cited in Sólyom and Brunner, *Constitutional Judiciary*, 242.
120 Sólyom, 'The First Year', 19.
121 Decision of the HCC No. 37/1992 (VI.10.) AB, cited in Sólyom and Brunner, *Constitutional Judiciary*, 241.
122 Decision of the HCC No. 64/1991 (XII.17.) AB (the quoted part available in *Case Reporter* 1, No. 1/1994, 10).
123 Decision of the HCC No. 20/1990 (X.4.) AB, cited in Halmai, 'Chroniques: Hongrie 1990'.
124 See, for example, Decisions of the HCC Nos. 64/1991 (XII.17.) AB, cited in Sólyom and Brunner, *Constitutional Judiciary*, 178; 11/1992 AB, cited in ibid., 214.
125 Decision of the HCC No. 30/1992 (V.26.) AB, cited in ibid., 235 (emphasis added).
126 See Sólyom, 'Introduction to the Decision of the Hungarian Constitutional Court', 5.
127 Decision of the HCC No. 60/1994 (XII.24.) AB, cited in Sólyom and Brunner, *Constitutional Judiciary*, 173. Compare Decision of the HCC No. 64/1993 AB, cited in ibid., 284–291.

128 Decision of the HCC No. 30/1992 (V.26.) AB, cited in ibid., 235.
129 Ibid., 236. See also Decision of the HCC No. 36/1994 (VI.24) AB, cited in ibid., 152.
130 See Decision of the HCC No. 14/2000 AB, cited in *Bulletin of Constitutional Case Law* 2/2000, 303–304.
131 Decision of the HCC No. 23/1990 (X.16.) AB, cited in Sólyom and Brunner, *Constitutional Judiciary*, 127.
132 The unambiguous preference for using the ECHR decisions as referential standards in its dicta is just another indication of the HCC's taking seriously the political aspects of its Europeanisation mission in addition to the legalistic ones (for example, the direct applicability on the national level of the ECHRFF). For an analysis of the similar approach of the Slovak Court, see discussion infra pp. 482ff.
133 Sólyom, 'The First Year', 5. See also *Constitutionalism in East Central Europe*, 65 (comment by Sólyom). But see Pogány who points out flaws in the Court's analysis of international law, and the justices' 'insufficient familiarity . . . with international law principles', Pogány, 'The Restitution', 228.
134 *Constitutionalism in East Central Europe*, 61.
135 See Decision of the HCC No. 20/1990 (X.4.) AB, cited in Halmai, 'Chroniques: Hongrie 1990'.
136 Decision of the HCC No. 29/1994 (V.20.) AB, cited in *Bulletin of Constitutional Case Law* 2/1994, 129.
137 See Decision of the HCC No. 32/1992 AB, cited in *Case Reporter* 2, No. 1/1995, 1–7.
138 Decision of the HCC No. 34/1994 (VI.24.) AB, cited in *Bulletin of Constitutional Case Law* 2/1994, 128–129.
139 Decision of the HCC No. 37/1992 (VI.10.) AB, cited in Sólyom and Brunner, *Constitutional Judiciary*, 243.
140 See Mórvay, 'Nepoučitel'ní?'. See also Decision of the HCC No. 22/1999 AB, cited in *Bulletin of Constitutional Case Law* 3/1999, 390–391.
141 Decision of the HCC No. 14/1995 (III.13.) AB, cited in Sólyom and Brunner, *Constitutional Judiciary*, 318.
142 Decision of the HCC No. 28/1994 (V.20.) AB, cited in ibid., 302.
143 Ibid.
144 Ibid., 303.
145 Ibid.
146 Ibid.
147 *Constitutionalism in East Central Europe*, 51 (comment by Sólyom).
148 Ibid., 61 (comment by Sólyom).
149 Decision of the CCC No. Pl. US 19/93, *CCC Collection*, Vol. 1, 14.
150 Decision of the CCC No. Pl. US 14/94, *CCC Collection*, Vol. 3, 76.
151 Ibid., 79–85.
152 Ibid., 84–85.
153 Ibid., 89.
154 Ibid., 73, 96–97.
155 Decision of the CCC No. IV. US 98/97, *CCC Collection*, Vol. 8, 309–311.
156 Ibid., 309.
157 Decision of the CCC No. II. US 66/98, *CCC Collection*, Vol. 13, 129.
158 Ibid.
159 Decision of the CCC No. Pl. US 15/93, *CCC Collection*, Vol. 1, 25.

160 Decision of the CCC No. Pl. US 33/97, *CCC Collection*, Vol. 9, 406.
161 Ibid., 407.
162 Decision of the CCC No. Pl. US 13/99, *CCC Collection*, Vol. 15, 195. Interestingly, the very cornerstone to which the Court referred proved weaker than one would expect of a basic cement-block of society. Only a few months later the majority shifted, and the CCC upheld the statutory elimination of bonus salaries for a number of government agents, including judges, as it found the contested law to be a proportionate restriction imposed for a legitimate aim. See Decision of the CCC No. 16/2000, available at http://www.concourt.cz.
163 Decision of the CCC No. IV. US 98/97, *CCC Collection*, Vol. 8, 310.
164 See Holländer, 'Hlavní doktríny', 63 (referring to Decision of the CCC No. IV. US 35/97, *CCC Collection* Vol. 7, 275–278.
165 Decision of the CCC No. Pl. US 33/97, *CCC Collection*, Vol. 9, 407.
166 Decision of the CCC No. Pl. US 19/98, *CCC Collection*, Vol. 13, 138.
167 Ibid., 273.
168 See, for example, Decisions of the CCC Nos. IV. US 275/96, *CCC Collection*, Vol. 6, 252; III. US 276/96, *CCC Collection*, Vol. 6, 280.
169 Decision of the CCC No. II. US 276/96, *CCC Collection*, Vol. 6, 271, 274.
170 Decisions of the CCC Nos. IV. US 275/96, *CCC Collection*, Vol. 6, 252; III. US 276/96, *CCC Collection*, Vol. 6, 280.
171 Decision of the CCC No. IV. US 275/96, *CCC Collection*, Vol. 6, 252–253.
172 Decision of the CCC No. II. US 276/96, *CCC Collection*, Vol. 6, 272.
173 Decision of the CCC No. III. US 127/96, *CCC Collection*, Vol. 5, 519, 525.
174 Decisions of the CCC Nos. II. US 108/93, *CCC Collection*, Vol. 3, 305–307; IV. US 28/97, *CCC Collection*, Vol. 9, 77–82; IV. US 484/99, *CCC Collection*, Vol. 17, item 37.
175 Decision of the CCC No. III. US 84/98, *CCC Collection*, Vol. 10, 167.
176 I purposefully say 'almost', for the CCC adjudicated in excess of a petition on a few occasions. The most prominent of these cases concerned the eligibility criterion of permanent residence in the realm of indemnification policies. The Court invalidated not only the criterion, but in excess of the petition annulled the related temporal provisions, which, if left in the statute, would preclude indemnification despite the striking down of the permanent-residence requirement. See Decision of the CCC No. Pl. US 3/94, *CCC Collection*, Vol. 1, 279–291.
177 See Decision of the CCC No. Pl. US 16/94, *CCC Collection*, Vol. 2, 227, 229.
178 See ibid., 231.
179 See Decision of the CCC No. Pl. US 6/95, available at http://www.concourt.cz.
180 See Decision of the CCC No. Pl. US 1/95, *CCC Collection*, Vol. 3, 241–247.
181 See Decision of the CCC No. Pl. US 29/98, *CCC Collection*, Vol. 14, 195–202.
182 See Decision of the CCC No. Pl. US 30/95, *CCC Collection*, Vol. 5, 23.
183 See ibid., 25.
184 See, for example, Decisions of the HCC Nos. 10/1990 (IV.27.) AB; 24/1990 (XI.8.) AB. The Chief Justice justified this technique of shaping the law by labelling it as 'practicable'. Sólyom, 'The First Year', 8.
185 Decision of the CCC No. Pl. US 21/96, *CCC Collection*, Vol. 7, 97.
186 See, for example, Decisions of the CCC Nos. II. US 22/94, *CCC Collection*, Vol. 4, 67–72; III. US 39/95, *CCC Collection*, Vol. 4, 101–107; II. US 83/96, *CCC Collection*,

Vol. 8, 399–403; IV. US 318/96, *CCC Collection*, Vol. 8, 353–355; III. US 337/97, *CCC Collection*, Vol. 9, 269–278; IV. US 508/98, *CCC Collection*, Vol. 13, 353–358.

187 Decision of the CCC No. Pl. US.-st.-5/97, *CCC Collection*, Vol. 9, 346.

188 Decision of the CCC No. III. US 127/96, *CCC Collection*, Vol. 5, 523.

189 Decision of the CCC No. III. US 224/98, *CCC Collection*, Vol. 15, 23.

190 Decision of the CCC No. Pl. US 33/97, *CCC Collection*, Vol. 9, 407.

191 Decision of the CCC No. Pl. US-st.-1/96, *CCC Collection*, Vol. 9, 476.

192 The Czech regulation at the time distinguished between attorneys at law ('*advokáti*'), who were eligible to represent clients also in criminal proceedings, and corporate lawyers ('*komerční právníci*') whose practice is largely confined to commercial law. The two groups even had separate bar chambers. This system is still in place in Slovakia.

193 Decision of the CCC No. I. US 89/94, *CCC Collection*, Vol. 2, item 20.

194 Decision of the CCC No. III. US 244/95, available at http://www.concourt.cz.

195 Decision of the CCC No. Pl. US 23/96, *CCC Collection*, Vol. 8, 29.

196 See note 207 to Chapter 3 and accompanying text.

197 Decisions of the CCC Nos. Pl. US 4/94, *CCC Collection*, Vol. 2, 61; Pl. US 15/96, *CCC Collection*, Vol. 6, 221; Pl. US 16/98, *CCC Collection*, Vol. 13, 179, 186.

198 See, for example, Decision of the CCC No. Pl. US 16/98, *CCC Collection*, Vol. 13, 179–180.

199 Decision of the CCC No. Pl. US 4/94, *CCC Collection*, Vol. 2, 57–74.

200 Decisions of the CCC Nos. II. US 357/96, *CCC Collection*, Vol. 9, 355–360; I. US 156/99, *CCC Collection*, Vol. 17, item 19.

201 See Decision of the CCC No. Pl. US 16/98, *CCC Collection*, Vol. 13, 179–194.

202 Decision of the CCC No. IV. US 311/97, *CCC Collection*, Vol. 13, 329.

203 Decision of the CCC No. Pl. US 4/94, *CCC Collection*, Vol. 2, 57–74.

204 Decision of the CCC No. III. US 210/98, *CCC Collection*, Vol. 13, 241, 244.

205 Decision of the CCC No. III. US 127/96, *CCC Collection*, Vol. 5, 524.

206 Decision of the CCC No. II. US 357/96, *CCC Collection*, Vol. 9, 360.

207 Decision of the CCC No. I. US 156/99, *CCC Collection*, vol. 17, item 19.

208 Ibid.

209 Přibáň, 'Ústavní soud posílil svou autoritu'. Compare Navara, 'Paragrafy nejsou vše'.

210 See, for example, Neměček, 'I soudce je politik'.

211 Decision of the SCC No. II. US 120/95, *SCC Collection* 1995, 316–317.

212 Decision of the SCC No. II. US 1/95, *SCC Collection* 1995, 268.

213 See discussion pp. 135–136.

214 See discussion pp. 354.

215 See Decisions of the SCC Nos. I. US 9/97, *SCC Collection* 1997, 474–479; II. US 48/97, *SCC Collection* 1998, 279–299.

216 See note 31 to Chapter 3 and accompanying text.

217 Decision of the SCC No. I. US 9/97, *SCC Collection* 1997, 478.

218 See Decision of the SCC No. II. US 48/97, *SCC Collection* 1998, 279–299.

219 See Decision of the SCC No. Pl. US 17/94, *SCC Collection* 1993–94, 245.

220 True, the SCC found voting rights violated in a number of instances. See, for example, Decisions of the SCC Nos. Pl. US 29/94; Pl. US 7/95; Pl. US 17/95; II. US 48/97; Pl. US 50/99; Pl. US 16/99; 10/99; Pl. US 18/99; Pl. US 1/00. But these were hardly difficult cases, and many of the aspects that did prove polemical were simply not

decided because of the SCC's failure to muster the requisite majority for a finding of either conformity or non-conformity. See, for example, Decisions of the SCC Nos. Pl. US 15/98, *SCC Collection* 1999, 27–75; Pl. US 19/98, *SCC Collection* 1998, 173–199.

221 Decision of the SCC No. Pl. US 17/94, *SCC Collection* 1993–94, 243.

222 Ibid., 244.

223 See Decision of the SCC No. Pl. US 29/95, *SCC Collection* 1995, 68–81.

224 See Decision of the SCC No. Pl. US 32/95, *SCC Collection* 1996, 188–199.

225 See Decision of the SCC No. Pl. US 36/95, *SCC Collection* 1996, 39–59.

226 See Decisions of the SCC Nos. Pl. US 11/96, *SCC Collection* 1998, 88–110; Pl. US 33/98, *SCC Collection* 1999, 114–134.

227 See Decision of the SCC No. Pl. US 43/95, *SCC Collection* 1996, 123–155.

228 Decision of the SCC No. I. US 33/95, *SCC Collection* 1995, 88.

229 Ibid., 89.

230 Decision of the SCC No. Pl. US 12/97, *SCC Collection* 1998, 165.

231 Ibid., 167.

232 For more detail on the statutory regulation of the domestic applicability of the ECHR decisions, see Kl'učka, 'Vplyv rozhodovacej činnosti'.

233 See, for example, Decisions of the SCC Nos. II. US 94/95, *SCC Collection* 1995, 104–122; Pl. US 29/95, *SCC Collection* 1995, 68–81; Pl. US 7/96, *SCC Collection* 1997, item 2; II. US 58/97, *SCC Collection* 1998, 350–358.

234 Ackerman, 'The Rise of World Constitutionalism', 777.

235 Decision of the SCC No. Pl. US 29/95, *SCC Collection* 1995, 78.

236 See Decision of the SCC No. Pl. US 4/97, *SCC Collection* 1998, 29–46.

237 See Decision of the HCC No. 43/1995 (VI.30.) AB, cited in Sólyom and Brunner, *Constitutional Judiciary*, 325 and ff.

238 See Decision of the SCC No. Pl. US 43/95, *SCC Collection* 1996, 123–155.

239 See Decision of the HCC No. 9/1992 (I.30.) AB, cited in Sólyom and Brunner, *Constitutional Judiciary*, 200 and ff.; Decision of the SCC No. Pl. US 43/95, *SCC Collection* 1996, 123–155.

240 Decision of the SCC No. I.US 92/93, *SCC Collection* 1993–94, 38.

241 See Decision of the SCC No. I. US 13/00 (on file with the SCC).

242 Decision of the SCC No. I. US 32/98, cited in Kl'učka and Fet'kova, eds., *Právne vety*, 32.

243 Decision of the SCC No. II. US 27/00 (on file with the SCC).

244 A recent ruling, however, suggests the possibility of an impending shift in the Court's consciousness, as it found an ordinary court to have acted in violation of the constitution despite observance of the text of the relevant law. The court's fidelity to text was found to have constituted a breach of the duty to concern itself with the implications of such fidelity, which finding resembles the core of the Czech Court's concrete-review jurisprudence. For more detail, see Decision of the SCC No. I. US 59/00, available at http://www.concourt.sk.

NOTES TO CHAPTER 5
FOUNDING AND BEYOND

1 Reisman, 'Introductory Remarks', 190.
2 Compare Elster, 'Forces and Mechanisms in the Constitution-Making Process'.
3 Kahn, *Reign of Law*, 66.
4 See Damaška, 'Reflection on American Constitutionalism', 432–436.
5 See Stone Sweet, *Governing with Judges*, 61–91.

BIBLIOGRAPHY

Ackerman, Bruce. *The Future of Liberal Revolution*. New Haven, Conn.: Yale University Press, 1991.

—. *We The People: Foundations*. Cambridge, Mass.: Harvard University Press, 1991.

—. 'The Rise of World Constitutionalism'. *Virginia Law Review* 83 (1997): 771–797.

Ágh, Attila. 'The Permanent "Constitutional Crisis" in the Democratic Transition: The Case of Hungary'. In *Constitutional Policy and Change in Europe*, edited by Joachim Jens Hesse and Nevil Johnson. New York: Oxford University Press, 1995.

Alexy, Robert. *Theorie der Grundrechte* [A theory of fundamental rights]. Baden Baden: Nomos Verlagsgesellschaft, 1985.

—. 'Grundrechte als subjektive Rechte und als objektive Normen' [Fundamental rights as subjective rights and as objective norms]. *Staat* 29 (1990): 49–68.

Antal, Adam. 'Historical Forerunners of the Hungarian Constitution'. In Adam Antal and Hans-Georg Heinrich, *Society, Politics, and Constitutions*. Wien: Böhlau, 1987.

Arato, Andrew. 'Dilemmas of Constitution Making'. *Cardozo Law Review* 14 (1993): 661–690.

—. *Civil Society, Constitution, and Legitimacy*. Lanham, Mar.: Rowman & Littlefield Publishers, 2000.

Banac, Ivo, ed. *Eastern Europe in Revolution*. Ithaca, N.Y.: Cornell University Press, 1992.

Barány, Eduard. 'Odkaz československej štátnosti pre Slovensko' [The legacy of Czechoslovak statehood for Slovakia]. *Acta Universitatis Carolinae: Iuridica* 1–2 (1999): 81–84.

Bard, Károly. 'Access to Legal Aid for Indigent Criminal Defendants in Central and Eastern Europe, Country Report: Hungary'. *Parker School Journal of East European Law* 5 (1998): 151–171.

Batt, Judy. 'International Dimension of Democratisation in Czecho-Slovakia and Hungary'. In *Building Democracy? The International Dimension of Democratisation in Eastern Europe*, edited by Geoffrey Pridham. New York: St. Martin's Press, 1994.

Bickel, Alexander. *The Least Dangerous Branch: The Supreme Court At the Bar of Politics*. New Haven, Conn.: Yale University Press, 1986.

Blahož, Josef. 'Human Rights in Poland, Hungary and Czechoslovakia'. In *Human Rights in the New Europe: Problems and Progress*, edited by David Forsythe. Lincoln, Neb.: University of Nebraska Press, 1994.

Brauneder, Wilhelm, and Friedrich Lachmayer, *Österreichische Verfassungsgeschichte* [Constitutional history of Austria]. Wien: Mainz, 1987.

Bröstl, Alexander. 'Formovanie doktríny Ústavného súdu Slovenskej republiky' [Forming the doctrine of the Constitutional Court of the Slovak Republic]. *Ústavnosť a politika* 3, No. 1 (2001): 3–26.

Bröstl, Alexander, Ján Kl'učka, and Ján Mazák. *The Constitutional Court of the Slovak Republic: Organization, Process, Doctrine.* Košice: Constitutional Court of the Slovak Republic, 2001.

Brunner, Georg. 'Structure and Proceedings of Hungarian Constitutional Judiciary'. In László Sólyom and Georg Brunner. *Constitutional Judiciary in a New Democracy.* Ann Arbor, Mich.: University of Michigan Press, 2000.

——. 'Entwicklung der polnischen Verfassungsgerichtsbarkeit in rechtsvergleichender Sicht' [The development of Polish constitutional adjudication in a comparative perspective]. In Georg Brunner and Leszek Lech Garlicki. *Verfassungsgerichtsbarkeit in Polen: Analysen und Entscheidungssammlung: 1986–1997* (Constitutional adjudication in Poland: analyses and a collection of decisions: 1986–1997]. Baden Baden: Nomos Verlagsgesellschaft, 1999.

——. 'Development of a Constitutional Judiciary in Eastern Europe'. *Review of Central and Eastern European Law* 18, No. 6 (1992): 535–553.

Brunner, Georg, and Leszek Lech Garlicki. *Verfassungsgerichtsbarkeit in Polen: Analysen und Entscheidungssammlung: 1986–1997* [Constitutional adjudication in Poland: analyses and a collection of decisions: 1986–1997]. Baden Baden: Nomos Verlagsgesellschaft, 1999.

Brunner, Georg, Mahulena Hofmann, and Pavel Holländer. *Verfassungsgerichtsbarkeit in der Tschechischen Republik. Analysen und Sammlung ausgewählter Entscheidungen des Tschechischen Verfassungsgerichts* [Constitutional adjudication in the Czech Republic. Analyses and selection of selected decisions of the Czech Constitutional Court]. Baden-Baden: Nomos Verlagsgesellschaft, 2001.

Bruszt, László, and David Stark. 'Remaking the Political Field in Hungary: From the Politics of Confrontation to the Politics of Competition'. In *Eastern Europe in Revolution*, edited by Ivo Banac. Ithaca, N.Y.: Cornell University Press, 1992.

Brzezinski, Mark. 'Constitutional Heritage and Renewal: The Case of Poland'. *Virginia Law Review* 77 (1997): 49–112.

——. 'Constitutionalism within Limits'. *Eastern European Constitutional Review* 2, No. 2 (1993): 38–43.

——. 'Constitutionalism and Polish Post-Communist Politics'. *Loyola Los Angeles Comparative and International Law Journal* 20 (1998): 433–453.

——. *Struggle for Constitutionalism in Poland.* New York: St. Martin's Press, 1999.

Brzezinski, Mark, and Leszek Garlicki. 'Judicial Review in Post-Communist Poland: The Emergence of a Rechtsstaat?'. *Stanford Journal of International Law* 31 (1995): 13–59.

Bugarič, Bojan. 'Courts As Policy Makers: Lessons From Transition'. *Harvard International Law Journal* 42 (2001): 247–288.

Calabresi, Guido. *A Common Law For the Age of Statutes.* Cambridge, Mass.: Harvard University Press, 1982.

Cappelletti, Mauro. *The Italian Legal System: An Introduction* (1965). Stanford, Cal.: Stanford University Press, 1967.

—. 'Repudiating Montesqieu? The Expansion and Legitimacy of "Constitutional Justice"'. *Catholic University Law Review* 35 (1985): 1–32.

Casper, Gerhard. 'European Convergence'. *University of Chicago Law Review* 58 (1991): 441–446.

Checkel, Jeffrey. 'Institutional Dynamics in Collapsing Empires: Domestic Structural Change in the USSR, Post-Soviet Russia and Independent Ukraine'. *Arena Working Papers*, available at http://www.sv.uio.no/arena/publications/wp99_2.htm.

Cepl, Vojtěch, and Mark Gillis. 'Making Amends After Communism'. *Journal of Democracy* 7, No. 4 (1996): 119–124.

Chmel, Rudolf. 'The Slovak Question in the 20th century'. In *Skepticism and Hope*, edited by Miroslav Kollár. Bratislava: Kalligram, 1999.

Cholewinski, Ryszard. 'The Protection of Human Rights in the New Polish Constitution'. *Fordham International Law Journal* 22 (2000): 236–291.

—. 'Čičova rozlúčka' [Čič's farewell]. *Pravda* (Bratislava) (20 January 2000).

Cole, Daniel H. 'Poland's 1997 Constitution in Its Historical Context'. *St. Louis-Warsaw Transatlantic Law Journal* 1998: 1–44.

Constitutional Court of the Czech Republic, The. 'National Report to the 11th Conference of European Constitutional Courts'. Available at http://www.mkab.hu/conference/okh/lengyhe.

—. *Sbírka nálezua rozhodnutí Ústavního soudu České republiky* [The collection of findings and resolutions of the Constitutional Court of the Czech Republic], vol. 1–16. Praha: C. H. Beck, 1994–2001.

Constitutional Court of Hungary, The. 'National Report to the 11th Conference of European Constitutional Courts'. Available at http://www.mkab.hu/conference/okhe/lengyhe.

Constitutional Court of the Slovak Republic, The. 'National Report to the 11th Conference of European Constitutional Courts'. Available at http://www.mkab.hu/conference/okhe/lengyhe.

—. *Zjednocovanie a vývoj judikatúry ústavných súdov* [Harmonisation and development of constitutional jurisprudence]. Košice: Ústavný súd Slovenskej republiky, 2001.

—. *Zbierka nálezov a uznesení Ústavného súdu Slovenskej republiky 1993-2000* [Collection of findings and resolutions of the Constitutional Court of the Slovak republic 1993–2000]. Košice: Ústavny súd Slovenskej republiky, 1995–2001.

—. 'Constitutional "Resolution" in the Excommunist World: the Rule of Law. Symposium. 26 September 1996'. *American University Journal of International Law and Policy* 12 (1997): 45–143.

Constitutional Tribunal of Poland, The. 'National Report to the 11th Conference of European Constitutional Courts'. Available at http://www.mkab.hu/conference/okhe/lengyhe.

—. *Constitutionalism in East Central Europe: Discussions in Warsaw, Budapest, Prague, Bratislava. Proceedings*, edited by Irena Grudzinska-Gross. Bratislava: Czecho-Slovak Committee of the European Cultural Foundation, 1994.

Council of Europe. *The Role of the Judiciary in a State Governed by Law. Round Table Talks of Ministers of Justice of Countries of Central and Eastern Europe: Warsaw 1995*. Strasbourg: Council of Europe Publications, 1996.

—. *Judicial Systems in a Period of Transition.* Strasbourg: Council of Europe Publications, 1997.

Csáky, Móritz, and Elena Mannová, eds. *Kolektívne identity v strednej Európe v období moderny* [Collective identities in Central Europe in the modern era]. Bratislava: Academic Electronic Press, 1999.

—. 'Czech Republic Update'. *East European Constitutional Review* 5, No. 1 (1996): 7–9.

—. 'Czech Republic Update'. *East European Constitutional Review* 8, Nos. 1–2 (1999): 10–12.

Czeszejko-Sochacki, Zdislaw. 'Trybunal Konstytucyjny w swietle projektow konstytucji RP' [The Constitutional Tribunal in light of the drafts of the Polish Constitution]. *Panstwo i Prawo* 588 (1995): 5–31.

—. 'O niektorych problemach powszechnie obowiazajucej wykladni ustaw ustalanej przez Trybunal Konstytucyjny' [On selected issues of the universally binding interpretation of statutes as set forth by the Constitutional Tribunal]. In *Konstytucja i gwarancje jej przestrzegania* [The Constitution and the guarantees of its observance]. Warszawa: Wydawnictwo Sejmowe, 1996.

—. 'Origins of Constitutional Review in Poland'. *St.Louis–Warsaw Transatlantic Law Journal* (1996): 15–32.

—. 'Zarys modelu polskiego Trybunalu Konstytucyjnego' [A sketch of the model of the Polish Constitutional Tribunal]. In *Prawo i kontrola jego zgodnosci z Konstytucja* [Law and the review of its conformity to the Constitution], edited by Eugeniusz Zwierchowski. Warszawa: Wydawnictwo Sejmowe, 1997.

—. 'O wymiarze sprawiedliwosci w swietle Konstytucji, miedzynarodowych standardow i praktyki' [On justice administration in light of the Constitution, international standards and practice]. *Panstwo i Prawo* 643 (1999): 3–11.

—. 'Obywatel obala zle prawo—Interview' [A citizen eliminates improper law]. Interview by Jolanta Kroner. *Rzeczpospolita* (Warsaw) (5 May 1999).

—. 'Wznowienie postepowanie jako skutek posredni orzeczenia Trybunalu Konstytucyjnego' [Re-opening of the proceedings as an auxiliary effect of a ruling of the Constitutional Tribunal]. *Panstwo i Prawo* 648 (2000): 14–28.

Damaška, Mirjan. *The Faces of Justice and State Authority: A Comparative Approach to the Legal Process.* New Haven, Conn.: Yale University Press, 1986.

—. 'Reflection on American Constitutionalism'. *American Journal of Comparative Law (Supplement)* 38 (1990): 421–443.

Davy, Richard. 'Perceptions and Performance: An Evaluation.' In *European Détente: A Reappraisal*, edited by Richard Davy. London: Royal Institute of International Affairs: Sage Publications, 1992.

Davy, Richard, ed. *European Détente: A Reappraisal.* London: Royal Institute of International Affairs: Sage Publications, 1992.

—. 'Podiumsdiskussion: Die Bedeutung der Westeuropäischen Verfassungsrechtsprechung in Mittel- und Osteuropa' [Panel discussion: The relevance to Central and Eastern Europe of Western European constitutional jurisprudence]. In *Grundfragen der Verfassungsgerichtsbarkeit in Mittel- und Osteuropa* [Fundamental issues of Central and Eastern European constitutional adjudication], edited by Jochen Frowein and Thilo Marauhn. Berlin; New York: Springer, 1998.

Doležal, Bohumil. 'Odkaz Václava Havla nebude nicotný' [The legacy of Vaclav Havel will not be worthless]. *Lidové noviny* (Prague) (17 January 2000).

Domagala, Michal, ed. *Konstytucyjne systemy rzadow I mozliwosci adaptacji do warunkow polskich* [Constitutional forms of government and the possibilities of adapting them to Poland]. Warsawa: Wydawnictwo Sejmove, 1997.

Drgonec, Ján. 'Vzťah všeobecného a ústavného súdnictva v Slovenskej republike' [The relation between ordinary adjudication and constitutional adjudication in the Slovak Republic]. *Časopis pro právní vědu a praxi* 1 (1999): 46–52.

—–. 'Ján Drgonec – právnik alebo recesista?-- Interview' (Ján Drgonec—a lawyer or a joker?]. Interview by Dáša Matejčíková. *Sme* (Bratislava) (5 March 2001).

Drgonec, Ján et al. 'Výpočet nesprávnych stanovísk a právnych záverov I. senátu Ústavného súdu' [The list of incorrect positions and legal conclusions of the Panel I. of the Constitutional Court]. *Sme* (Bratislava) (29 December 1999).

Dudek, Daniel. 'Sady wobec wykladni ustaw ustalanej przez Trybunal Kostytucyjny' [The courts on statutory interpretation as established by the Constitutional Tribunal]. *Przeglad Sadowy* 2 (1997): 70–90.

Dupré, Catherine. 'The Right to Human Dignity in Hungarian Constitutional Case Law'. *Science and Technique of Democracy* 26 (1998): 68–79.

Dzialocha, Kazimirz. 'Model ustrojowy Trybunalu Konstytucyjnego de lege ferenda' [The organisational model of the Constitutional Tribunal de lege ferenda]. *Panstwo i Prawo* 564 (1993): 3–12.

—–. 'Der Rechtsstaat unter den Bedingungen einer grundlegenden Umformung des rechtssystems dargestellt am Beispiel Polen' [The Rechtsstaat under the conditions of a fundamental transformation of the legal order: the case of Poland]. *Osteuroparecht* 39 (1993): 1–21.

—–. 'Wizja Trybunalu Konstytucyjnego w projektach Konstytucji RP' [The vision of the Constitutional Tribunal in the drafts of the Polish Constitution]. *Acta Universitatis Wratislaviensis* 1745 (1995).

—–. 'The Direct Application of the Constitution of the Republic of Poland'. In *Kontinuität und Neubeginn. Staat und Recht in Europa zu Beginn des 21. Jahrhunderts* [Continuity and new beginning. State and law in Europe at the beginning of the 21st century], edited by Mahulena Hofmann and Herbert Kupper. Baden-Baden: Nomos Verlagsgesellschaft, 2001.

Eisenmann, Charles. *La Justice Constitutionnelle de la Haute Court Constitutionnelle d'Autriche* [Constitutional justice of the High Constitutional Court of Austria]. Paris: La Librairie générale de droit et de jurisprudence, 1928.

Eliade, Mircea. *Dejiny náboženských predstáv a ideí* [The history of religious ideas]. Bratislava: Agora, 1995.

Elster, Jon, ed. *The Roundtable Talks and the Breakdown of Communism.* Chicago: University of Chicago Press, 1996.

—–. 'Forces and Mechanisms in the Constitution-Making Process'. *Duke Law Journal* 45 (1995): 364–396.

Elster, Jon, Claus Offe, and Ulrich Preuss. *Institutional Design in Post-Communist Societies: Rebuilding the Ship at Sea.* Cambridge, UK–New York: Cambridge University Press, 1998.

Eskridge, William N., Jr., and Sanford Levinson, eds. *Constitutional Stupidities, Constitutional Tragedies.* New York: New York University Press, 1998.

Forsythe, David, ed. *Human Rights in the New Europe: Problems and Progress.* Lincoln, Neb.: University of Nebraska Press, 1994.

Frankowski, Stanislav. 'Lech Wałesa's Draft of the Charter of Rights and Freedoms: An Overview'. *St. Louis-Warsaw Transatlantic Law Journal* 1996: 65–72.

—. 'A Comment on Professor Garlicki's Article "Constitutional Development in Poland": The Lyrics Sound Familiar but are They Really Playing our Song?'. *St. Louis University Law Journal* 32 (1988): 737

Frowein, Jochen, and Thilo Marauhn, eds. *Grundfragen der Verfassungsgerichtsbarkeit in Mittel- und Osteuropa* [Fundamental issues of Central and Eastern European constitutional adjudication]. Berlin; New York: Springer, 1998.

Galligan, Dennis. 'Procedural Rights in Administrative Contexts'. In *Western Rights? Post-Communist Application,* edited by András Sajó. The Hague, Boston: Kluwer Law International, 1996.

Garlicki, Leszek. 'Constitutional and Administrative Courts as Custodians of State Constitutions-the Experience of East European Countries'. *Tulane Law Review* 61 (1987): 1285–1306.

—. 'Constitutional Review and Legislation–The Polish Constitutional Tribunal'. In *Constitutional Review And Legislation: An International Comparison*, edited by Christine Landfried. Baden Baden: Nomos Verlagsgesellschaft, 1988.

—. 'Chroniques: Pologne' [Chronicles: Poland]. In *Annuaire International de Justice Constitutionelle* 6–15 (1990–1999).

—. 'Social Rights in the Judicature of the Constitutional Court in Poland'. In *Constitutional Court in Poland in a Period of System Transformation.* Warszawa: Trybunal Konstytucyjny, 1993.

—. 'Trybunal Konstytucyjny w projekcie Komisji Konstytucyjnej Zgromadzenia Narodowego' [The Constitutional Tribunal in the draft by the Constitutional Committee of the National Assembly]. *Panstwo i Prawo* 600 (1996): 3–19.

—. 'Orzecznictwo Trybunalu Konstytucyjnego w 1995 roku' (Jurisprudence of the Constitutional Tribunal in 1995), *Przeglad sadowy* 7–8 (1996): 110–138.

—. 'Orzecznictwo Trybunalu Konstytucyjnego w 1997 roku' [Jurisprudence of the Constitutional Tribunal in 1997]. *Przeglad sadowy* 6 (1998): 35–58.

—. 'Verfassungsgerichtsbarkeit in Polen' [Constitutional adjudication in Poland]. In Georg Brunner and Leszek Lech Garlicki. *Verfassungsgerichtsbarkeit in Polen: Analysen und Entscheidungssammlung: 1986–1997.* Baden Baden: Nomos Verlagsgesellschaft, 1999.

—. 'Trybunal Konstytucyjny a sadownictvo' [The Constitutional Tribunal and the judiciary]. *Przeglad Sadowy* 1 (1998): 3–21.

—. 'Orzecznictwo Trybunalu Konstytucyjnego w 1998 roku' [Jurisprudence of the Constitutional Tribunal in 1998). *Przeglad Sadowy* 6 (1999): 104–128.

—. 'The Principle of Equality and the Prohibition of Discrimination in the Jurisprudence of the Constitutional Tribunal of Poland'. *St.Louis-Warsaw Transatlantic Law Journal* 1999: 1–16.–

—. 'Orzecznictwo Trybunalu Konstytucyjnego w 1999 roku' [Jurisprudence of the Constitutional Tribunal in 1999]. *Przeglad Sadowy* 7–8 (2000): 106–132.

—. 'Orzecznictwo Trybunalu Konstytucyjnego w 2000 roku' [Jurisprudence of the Constitutional Tribunal in 2000]. *Przeglad Sadowy* 9 (2001): 77–106.

—. 'Das Verfassungsgericht und das Parlament. Die Zurückweisung von Entscheidungen des polnischen Verfassungsgerichtshofs durch den Sejm' [The Constitutional Tribunal and the Parliament. Reversals by the Sejm of decisions of the Polish Constitutional

Tribunal]. In *Kontinuität und Neubeginn. Staat und Recht in Europa zu Beginn des 21. Jahrhunderts* [Continuity and new beginning. State and law in Europe at the beginning of the 21st century], edited by Mahulena Hofmann and Herbert Kupper. Baden-Baden: Nomos Verlagsgesellschaft, 2001.

Garton Ash, Timothy. 'Všichni trpíme Waldheimerovou nemocí' [We all suffer from the Waldheimer disease]. *Lidové noviny* (Prague) (14 October 1999).

Geremek, Bronislaw. 'Between Hope and Despair'. In *Eastern Europe-Central Europe-Europe*, edited by Stephen Graubard. Boulder, Col.: Westview Press, 1991.

—. 'Bronislaw Geremek on Constitution-making in Poland-Interview'. Interview by Viktor Osiatynski. *East European Constitutional Review* 4, No. 1 (1995): 42–45.

Gessner, Volkmar et al., eds. *European Legal Cultures*. Aldershot, Hants–Brookfield, Vt.: Dartmouth Publications, 1996.

Gillis, Mark. 'Vztah mezi Ústavním soudem a systémem obecných soudů' [The relation between the Constitutional Court and the ordinary adjudication system]. In *Ústava České republiky po pěti letech* [The Constitution of the Czech Republic after five years], edited by Vojtěch Šimíček. Brno: Masarykova univerzita, 1998.

Glendon, Mary Ann. *The Rights Talk: The Impoverishment of Political Discourse*. New York: Maxwell Macmillan, 1991.

Göncz, Árpád. *Karpaty a priľahlý vesmír* [The Carpathian Mountains and the surrounding universe]. Bratislava: Kalligram, 1999.

Graubard, Stephen, ed. *Eastern Europe-Central Europe-Europe*. Boulder, Col.: Westview Press, 1991.

Greenberg, Douglas et al., eds. *Constitutionalism and Democracy: Transitions in the Contemporary World*. New York: Oxford University Press, 1993.

Grudzinska-Gross, Irena, ed. *Constitutionalism and Politics: International Symposium, 11–14 November 1993: Proceedings*. Bratislava: Slovak Committee of the European Cultural Foundation, 1993.

Halmai, Gábor. 'Chroniques: Hongrie' [Chronicles: Hungary]. In *Annuaire International de Justice Constitutionnelle* 6 (1990).

—. 'Constitutional Court'. In *Lawful Revolution in Hungary 1989–1994*, edited by Béla Király. Boulder, Col.: Social Sciences Monographs, 1995.

—. 'Development of Civil Law'. In *Introduction to Hungarian law*, edited by Attila Harmathy. The Hague; Boston: Kluwer Law International, 1998.

Halmai, Gábor, ed. *The Constitution Found? The First Nine Years of Hungarian Constitutional Review on Fundamental Rights*. Budapest: Indok, 2000.

Harmathy, Attila, ed. *Introduction to Hungarian Law*. The Hague; Boston: Kluwer Law International, 1998.

Hauser, Roman. 'Założenia reformy sadownictwa administracyjnego' [Foundations of the administrative judiciary reform]. *Panstwo i Prawo* 646 (1999): 21–33.

Havel, Václav. 'Evropa jako společně sdílený osud' [Europe as a shared destiny]. *Lidové noviny* (Prague) (16 May 1996).

—. 'Address to the 1999 conference of Forum 2000', available at http://www.forum2000.cz.

Hellman, Joel. 'Constitutions and Economic Reform in Postcommunist Transitions'. *East European Constitutional Review* 5, No. 1 (1996): 46–56.

Hesse, Joachim Jens and Nevil Johnson, eds. *Constitutional Policy and Change in Europe*. New York: Oxford University Press, 1995.

Hofmanski, Piotr. 'Poland after Ratification of the ECHR'. *Helsinki Monitor* 6 (1995): 45–55.

Hoffman, Rainer, et al., eds. *Rechtsstaatlichkeit in Europa* [Rule of law in Europe]. Heidelberg: C. F. Muller, 1996.

Hofmann, Mahulena. 'Volkerrecht in der Rechtsprechung des tschechischen Verfassungsgerichts' [International law in the jurisprudence of the Czech Constitutional Court]. In Georg Brunner, Mahulena Hofmann and Pavel Holländer, *Verfassungsgerichtsbarkeit in der Tschechischen Republik. Analysen und Sammlung ausgewählter Entscheidungen des Tschechischen Verfassungsgerichts* [Constitutional adjudication in the Czech Republic. Analyses and selection of selected decisions of the Czech Constitutional Court]. Baden-Baden: Nomos Verlagsgesellschaft, 2001.

Hofmann, Mahulena and Herbert Kupper, eds., *Kontinuität und Neubeginn. Staat und Recht in Europa zu Beginn des 21. Jahrhunderts* [Continuity and new beginning. State and law in Europe at the beginning of the 21st century]. Baden-Baden: Nomos Verlagsgesellschaft, 2001.

Holländer, Pavel. 'Role Ústavního soudu při uplatňování Ústavy v judikatuře obecných soudů' [The role of the Constitutional Court in the implementation of constitutional law in ordinary adjudication]. In *Ústava České republiky po pěti letech* [The Constitution of the Czech Republic after five years], edited by Vojtěch Šimíček. Brno: Masarykova univerzita, 1998.

——. 'Hlavní doktríny Ústavního soudu České republiky' [The main doctrines of the Constitutional Court of the Czech Republic]. In *Zjednocovanie a vývoj judikatúry ústavnych súdov* [Harmonisation and development of constitutional jurisprudence]. Košice: Ústavný súd Slovenskej republiky, 2001.

Holmes, Stephen. 'Back to the Drawing Board'. *East European Constitutional Review* 2, No. 1 (1993): 21–25.

Houbová, Dagmar. 'Dílčí úvahy o argumentaci při rozhodování Ústavního soudu České republiky' [Some considerations on the argumentation of the Constitutional Court of the Czech Republic in its decision-making]. In *Zjednocovanie a vývoj judikatýry ústavnych súdov*. Košice: Ústavný súd Slovenskej republiky, 2001.

——. 'Hungary Update'. *East European Constitutional Review* 7, No. 2 (1998): 17–19.

——. 'Hungary Update'. *East European Constitutional Review* 8, No. 4 (1999): 21–23.

Instytut Wymiaru Sprawedliwosci. *Założenia zmian w ustawie z dnia 20 czerwca 1985 r. – Prawo o ustroju sadow powszechnych oraz projekt nowelizacji*. Warsaw: Instutyt Wymiaru Sprawedliwosci, 1998.

Jarebørg, Nils, ed. *Towards Universal Law: Trends in National, European and International Lawmaking*. Uppsala: Iustus Forlag, 1995.

Jozefowicz, Adam. 'Skutki prawne orzeczenia TK o nezgodnośći aktu normatyvnego z Konstytucja' [Legal effects of a decision of the Constitutional Tribunal on the lack of conformity to the Constitution of a normative act]. *Panstwo i Prawo* 587 (1995): 25–36.

——. 'Orzeczenia interpretacyjne Trybunalu Konstytucyjnego' [The interpretive sentences of the Constitutional Tribunal]. *Panstwo i Prawo* 645 (1999): 28–34.

Jowitt, Kenneth. 'The Leninist Legacy.' In *Eastern Europe in Revolution*, edited by Ivo Banac. Ithaca, N.Y.: Cornell University Press, 1992.

Kabat, Andrzej. 'Przepisy konstytucyjne w praktyce orzeczniczej Naczelnego Sadu Administracyjnego' [Constitutional provisions in the decision-making of the Supreme

Administrative Court]. In *Studia nad prawem konstytucyjnym*. Wroclaw: Wydawnictwo Uniwersytetu Wroclawskiego, 1997.

Kahn, Paul W. *The Reign of Law: Marbury v. Madison and the construction of America*. New Haven, Conn.: Yale University Press, 1997.

Kanski, Leslaw. 'Human Rights in Poland From a Historical and Comparative Perspective'. In *Human Rights and Constitutionalism: America, Poland and France*, edited by Kenneth W. Thompson and Rett R. Ludwikowski. Lanham, Md.: University of America Press, 1991.

Kapstein, Ethan B. and Michael Mandelbaum, eds. *Sustaining the Transition: The Social Safety Net in Postcommunist Europe*. New York: Council on Foreign Relations, 1997.

Kedzia, Zdislaw. 'The Implementation of Social and Economic Rights in Central and Eastern European Countries'. In *Die Durchsetzung Wirtschaftlicher und Sozialer Grundrechte: Eine rechtsvergleichende Bestandsaufnahme* [The implementation of economic and social rights: a comparative review], edited by Franz Matscher. Kehl am Rein–Arlington, Va.: N.P. Engel, 1991.

Kenney, Sally J. et al. (eds.) *Constitutional Dialogues in Comparative Perspective*. New York: St. Martin's Press, 1999.

Király, Béla, ed. *Lawful Revolution in Hungary 1989–1994*. Boulder, Col.: Social Sciences Monographs, 1995.

Klingsberg, Ethan. 'Judicial Review and Hungary's Transition from Communism to Democracy: The Constitutional Court, the Continuity of Laws, and the Redefinition of Property Rights'. *Brigham Young University Law Review* 1992: 41–144.

—. 'Safeguarding the Transition'. *East European Constitutional Review* 2, No. 2 (1993): 44–47.

—. 'Contextualizing the Calculus of Consent: Judicial Review of Legislative Wealth Transfers in a Transition to Democracy and Beyond'. *Cornell International Law Journal* 27 (1994): 303–342.

Kl'učka, Ján,'Vplyv rozhodovacej činnosti Európskeho súdu pre ľudské práva na právny poriadok a judikatúru súdnych orgánov Slovenskej republiky' [The effect on the legal system and judicial decision-making in the Slovak Republic of the case law of the European Court of Human Rights]. *Ústavnosť a politika* 2, No. 4 (2000): 59–65.

—. and Gabriela Fet'ková, eds. *Právne vety z rozhodovacej činnosti Ústavneho súdu 1993-2000* [Legal sentences from the decision making of the Constitutional Court 1993–2000]. Košice: Ústavný súd Slovenskej republiky, 2000.

Kolarska-Bobinska, Lena. 'The Role of the State: Contradictions in the Transition to Democracy'. In *Constitutionalism and Democracy: Transitions in the Contemporary World*, edited by Douglas Greenberg et al. New York: Oxford University Press, 1993.

Kolasiński, Krzystof. 'Orzecznictwo Trybunalu Konstytucyjnego a orzecznictwo sadowe' [Jurisprudence of the Constitutional Tribunal and jurisprudence of the ordinary courts]. *Panstwo i Prawo* 628 (1998): 3–13.

Kollár, Miroslav, ed. *Skepticism and Hope*. Bratislava: Kalligram, 1999.

Kollár, Miroslav and Grigorij Mesežnikov, eds. *Slovensko 2001. Súhrnná správa o stave spoločnosti* [Slovakia 2001. A global report on the state of society]. Bratislava: Inštitút pre verejné otázky, 2001.

Kommers, Donald. 'German Constitutionalism: A Prolegomenon'. *Emory Law Journal* 40 (1991): 837–873.

——. *The Constitutional Jurisprudence of the Federal Republic of Germany*. Durham, N.C.: Duke University Press, 1997.

——. 'The Constitutionalism of Mary Ann Glendon'. *Notre Dame Law Review* 73 (1998): 1333–1353.

Korecký, Miroslav. 'Talárokracie' [A gownocracy]. *Lidové noviny* (Prague) (4 December 2000).

Kowalski, Sergiusz. *Solidarność Polska. Studium z socjologii myslenia potocznego* [Polish Solidarity. A study of the sociology of common thinking]. Warszawa: University of Warsaw, 1988.

Kozak, Artur. 'Rodzaje wykladni prawa w uchwalach Trybunalu Konstytucyjnego' [The types of interpretation of law in the resolutions of the Constitutional Tribunal]. *Prawo* 262 (1997): 51–68.

Kramer, Mark. 'Social Protection Policies and Safety Nets in East-Central Europe: Dilemmas of the Post-Communist Transition'. In *Sustaining the Transition: The Social Safety Net in Postcommunist Europe*, edited by Ethan B. Kapstein and Michael Mandelbaum eds. New York: Council on Foreign Relations, 1997.

Kratochvíl, Vladimír. 'K procesnímu postupu obecného soudu po zrušení jeho rozhodnutí v trestní věci nálezem Ústavního soudu České republiky' [On the proceedings of an ordinary court after the annulment of its decision in a penal matter through a finding of the Constitutional Court of the Czech Republic]. *Časopis pro právní vědu a praxi* 3 (1996): 388–410.

Kreimer, Seth F. 'Explaining the Dark Matter of Judicial Review: A Constitutional Census of the 1990s'. *William and Mary Bill of Rights Journal* 5 (1997): 427–526.

Kresák, Peter. 'Gramatika nepustí' [The grammar won't let go]. *Domino fórum* (Bratislava) (17 July 1999).

——., ed. *Rozhodovacia činnosť Ústavného súdu Slovenskej republiky 1993–1997*. [The decision-making of the Constitutional Court of the Slovak Republic 1993–1997]. Bratislava: Kalligram, 1999.

Kronman, Anthony. *Max Weber*. London: E. Arnold, 1983.

Krygier, Martin, and Adam Czarnota, eds. *The Rule of Law After Communism: Problems and Prospects in East-Central Europe*. Aldershot, Hants.--Brookfield, Vt.: Ashgate, 1999.

Kundera, Milan. 'The Tragic Destiny'. *New York Review of Books* (16 April 1984).

Kuhnhardt, Ludgar. 'European Courts and Human Rights.' In *Constitutionalism and Democracy: Transitions in the Contemporary World*, edited by Douglas Greenberg et al. New York: Oxford University Press, 1993.

Kupper, Herbert. 'Die Justizreform in Ungarn' [The reform of the judiciary in Hungary]. *Osteuroparecht* 44 (1998): 255–271.

Kurczewski, Jacek. 'Democracy and the Rule of Law: Poland after 1989'. In *Constitutionalism and Politics: International Symposium*, edited by Irena Grudzinska-Gross. Bratislava: Slovak Committee of the European Cultural Foundation, 1993.

Lábady, Tamás. 'Address'. In *Judicial Systems in a Period of Transition*. Strasbourg: Council of Europe Publications, 1997.

Laczkowski, Wojciech. 'Constitutional Courts in a Period of State System Transformation'. In *Constitutional Court in Poland in a Period of System Transformation*. Warszawa: Trybunal Konstytucyjny, 1993.

Langoš, Ján. 'Založením SDKU sa Dzurinda oslabil—Interview' [By founding SDKÚ, Dzurinda has weakened himself]. Interview by Štefan Hríb. *Domino Fórum* (Bratislava) (15 November 2000).

Lemann, Nicholas. 'Annals of Marketing: The Word Lab'. *New Yorker* (16 and 23 October 2000).

Lentz, Dominik. 'Das Rechtsstaatprinzip in der Verfassungsrechtsprechung mittel- und osteuropäischer Staaten (Diskussionbericht)' [The principle of the rule of law in the jurisprudence of the Central and Eastern European countries (Discussion report)]. In *Grundfragen der Verfassungsgerichtsbarkeit in Mittel- und Osteuropa* [Fundamental issues of Central and Eastern European constitutional adjudication], edited by Jochen Frowein and Thilo Marauhn. Berlin; New York: Springer 1998.

Letowska, Ewa. 'Courts and Tribunals under the Constitution of Poland'. *St. Louis-Warsaw Transatlantic Law Journal* 1997: 69–90.

——. 'Szkoda wykladni Trybunalu Konstytucyjnego' [The interpretation of the Constitutional Tribunal in vain]. *Rzeczpospolita* (8 January 1997).

Letowski, Janusz. 'A Constitution for Everyday Use.' In *Constitutionalism and Politics: International Symposium November 11–14, 1993: Proceedings*, edited by Irena Grudzinska-Gross. Bratislava: Slovak Committee of the European Cultural Foundation, 1993.

Linz, Juan, and Alfred Stepan. *Problems of Democratic Transition and Consolidation.* Baltimore, Mar.: Johns Hopkins University Press, 1996.

Los, Maria. 'Property Rights, Market and Historical Justice'. *International Journal of Sociology and Law* 22 (1994): 39–58.

——. 'In the Shadow of Totalitarian Law: Law-Making in Post-Communist Poland'. In *Totalitarian and Post-Totalitarian Law*, edited by Adam Podgorecki and Vittorio Olgiatti. Aldershot, Hants.–Brookfield, Vt.: Ashgate, 1996.

Lukáč, Pavol. 'Visegrád Co-operation—Ideas, Developments and Prospects'. *Slovak Foreign Policy Affairs* 2, No. 1 (2001): 6–23.

Maczynski, Andrzej. 'Bezprosriedne stosowanie Konstytucji przez sady' [The direct application of the constitution by the judiciary]. *Panstwo i Prawo* 654 (2000): 3–14.

Majoros, Ferenc. 'Zur Entwicklung der Verfassungsgerichtsbarkeit in Ungarn' [On the development of constitutional adjudication in Hungary]. *Osteuroparecht* 39 (1993): 106–131.

Malenovský, Jiří. 'Treaties in the Czech Republic: Unresolved Division of Labor Between Parliament and the Constitutional Court'. In *Constitutional Reform And International Law in Central And Eastern Europe*, edited by Rein Mullerson et al. The Hague, Boston: Kluwer Law International, 1998.

Malý, Karel, and Florián Sivák. *Dějiny státu a práva na území Československa do roku 1918* [The history of state and law on the territory of Czechoslovakia before 1918]. Prague: H&H, 1993.

Maniewska, Eliza. 'Konstytucja Rzeczypospolitej Polskiej v orzecznictwie Sadu Najwyzszego' [The Constitution of the Republic of Poland in the decision-making of the Supreme Court]. *Przeglad Sadowy* 4 (2000): 3–18.

Marada, Radim. 'Party realignment, cloakroom politics and civic culture'. *East European Constitutional Review* 7, No. 4 (1998): 51–58.

Máša, Pavel. 'Visegrád se vrací na scénu' [Visegrád is back on scene]. *Lidové noviny* (Prague) (15 April 2000).

Matscher, Franz, ed. *Die Durchsetzung Wirtschaftlicher und Sozialer Grundrechte: Eine rechtsvergleichende Bestandsaufnahme* [The implementation of economic and social rights: a comparative review]. Kehl am Rein–Arlington, Va.: N. P. Engel, 1991.

Mavčič, Arne. *Slovenian Constitutional Review: Its Position in the World and Its Role in the Transition to a New System.* Ljubljana: Nova revija, 1995.

Mavi, Viktor. 'Limitations of and Derogations from Human Rights in International Human Rights Instruments'. *Acta Juridica Hungarica* 38, No. 3–4 (1997): 107–114.

Maziarski, Wojciech. 'Inteligent hodený napospas trhu' [An intellectual at the mercy of a free market]. *Sme* (Bratislava) (24 November 2000).

Michnik, Adam. 'Address to the 1999 Conference of Forum 2000', available at http://www.forum2000.cz.

Mikloško, František. 'Moji Maďári' [My Hungarians]. *Domino fórum* (Bratislava) (29 August 2001).

Mikule, Vladimír, and Vladimír Sládeček. 'O závaznosti rozhodnutí Ústavního soudu' [On the binding effect of the decisions of the Constitutional Court]. *Bulletin advokacie* 8 (1995): 35–51.

Mokrzycki, Edmund. 'Iluzórna moc ľudu' [The illusionary power of the people]. *Sme* (Bratislava) (8 January 2000).

Mórvay, Peter. 'Nepoučiteľní?' [Unable to learn?]. *Domino fórum* (Bratislava) (3 March 2000).

Müllerson, Rein et al., eds. *Constitutional Reform And International Law in Central And Eastern Europe.* The Hague, Boston: Kluwer Law International, 1998.

Murphy, Walter. 'Constitutions, Constitutionalism and Democracy'. In *Constitutionalism and Democracy: Transitions in the Contemporary World*, edited by Douglas Greenberg et al. New York: Oxford University Press, 1993.

Navara, Luděk. 'Paragrafy nejsou vše, budou si soudci říkat čím dál častěji' [Black-letter law isn't everything, the judges will be telling themselves more and more often]. *Mladá fronta* (Prague) (3 March 2000).

Neměček, Tomáš. 'I soudce je politik' [Even a judge is a politician]. *Respekt* (Prague) (29 January 2001).

Nicholson, Pip. '"Roots and Routes"—Comparative Law in a Postmodern World'. Available at http://www.unimelb.edu.au/alc/assets/roots and routes.

Oakeshott, Michael. 'The Activity of Being an Historian'. In Michael Oakeshott, *Rationalism in Politics and Other Essays.* Indianapolis, Ind.: Liberty Press, 1991.

Offe, Claus. 'Cultural Aspects of Consolidation: A Note on the Peculiarities of Post-communist Transformations'. *East European Constitutional Review* 6, No. 4 (1997): 64–68.

Oniszczuk, Jerzy. *Orzecznictwo Trybunalu Konstytucyjnego w latach 1986–1993: Wybrane zagadnienia, vols. 1–2* [Jurisprudence of the Constitutional Tribunal in 1986–1993: selected cases]. Warszawa: Wydawnictwo Sejmowe, 1993–1994.

——. 'Umowy miedzynarodowe w orzecznictwie Trybunalu Konstytucyjnego' [International agreements in the jurisprudence of the Constitutional Tribunal]. *Panstwo i Prawo* 593 (1995): 14–26.

Örkény, Antal, and Kim Lane Scheppele. 'The Complexity of Legality in Hungary'. In *The Rule of Law after Communism*, edited by Martin Krygier and Adam Czarnota. Brookfield, Vt.: Ashgate, 1999.

Osiatynski, Wiktor. 'Perspectives on the Current Constitutional Situation in Poland'. In *Constitutionalism and Democracy: Transitions in the Contemporary World*, edited by Douglas Greenberg et al. New York: Oxford University Press, 1993.

—. 'Dualism in Constitutional Adjudication'. In *Constitutional Courts in Central And Eastern Europe in the Period of Transformation: Papers of The International Conference, Warsaw, 9-11 September 1994*, edited by Andrzej Rzeplinski. Warsaw: Helsinki Foundation for Human Rights, 1995.

—. 'The Roundtable Talks in Poland'. In *The Roundtable Talks and The Breakdown of Communism*, edited by Jon Elster. Chicago: University of Chicago Press, 1996.

Páczolay, Péter. 'Judicial Review of the Compensation Law in Hungary'. *Michigan Law Review* 13 (1992): 887.

—. 'Constitutional Transition and Legal Continuity'. *Connecticut Journal of International Law* 8 (1993): 559–574.

—. 'Chroniques: Hongrie' [Chronicles: Hungary]. In *Annuaire International de Justice Constitutionelle* 7—9, 11 (1991–1993, 1995).

Patrźalek, Aleksander. 'Obywatel a kontrola konstytucyjnośći prawa w Polsce de lege lata'. [The citizen and constitutional review in Poland de lege lata]. *Prawo* 239 (1995): 1–21.

Pinder, John. 'The European Community and Democracy in Central and Eastern Europe'. In *Building Democracy? The International Dimension of Democratisation in Eastern Europe*, edited by Geoffrey Pridham. New York: St. Martin's Press, 1994.

Plasser, Fritz, and Peter Ulram. 'Measuring Political Culture in East Central Europe: Political Trust and System Support'. In *Political Culture in East Central Europe*, edited by Fritz Plasser and Andreas Pribersky. Aldershot, Hants.–Brookfield, Vt.: Ashgate, 1996.

Plasser, Fritz, and Andreas Pribersky, eds. *Political Culture in East Central Europe*. Aldershot, Hants.–Brookfield, Vt.: Ashgate, 1996.

Plasser, Fritz, Peter A. Ulram, and Harald Waldrauch. *Democratic Consolidation in East-Central Europe*. New York: St. Martin's Press, 1998.

Podgorecki, Adam and Vittorio Olgiatti, eds. *Totalitarian and Post-Totalitarian Law*. Aldershot, Hants.–Brookfield, Vt.: Ashgate, 1996.

Pogány, István. 'The Restitution of Former Jewish-Owned Property and Related Schemes of Compensation'. *European Public Law* 4, No. 2 (1998): 211–231.

Pol, Albert, and Wojciech Odrowaz Sypniewski, eds. *Polskie Prawo Konstytucyjne/Polish Constitutional Law*. Warszawa: Wydawnictwo Sejmove, 1996.

—. 'Poland Update'. *East European Constitutional Review* 4, No. 2 (1995): 18–21.

Posner, Richard. 'The Costs of Enforcing Legal Rights'. *East European Constitutional Review* 4, No. 3 (1995): 71–83.

Přibaň, Jiří. 'Ústavní soud posílil svou autoritu' [The Constitutional Court has strengthened its authority]. *Lidové noviny* (Prague).

Přibáň, Jiří, and James Young. *The Rule of Law in Central Europe*. Aldershot, Hants.–Brookfield, Vt.: Ashgate, 1999.

Pridham, Geoffrey. 'The International Dimension of Democratisation: Theory, Practice and Inter-Regional Comparisons'. In *Building Democracy? The International Dimension of Democratisation in Eastern Europe*. New York: St. Martin's Press, 1994.

Pridham, Geoffrey, ed. *Building Democracy? The International Dimension of Democratisation in Eastern Europe*. New York: St. Martin's Press, 1994.

Procházka, Antonín. 'Závaznost rozhodnutí Ústavního soudu' [The binding effect of the decisions of the Constitutional Court]. *Bulletin advokacie* 8 (1995): 32–34.

—. 'České soudy trpí formalistickým manýrismem' [The Czech judiciary suffers from formalist maneerism]. *Lidové noviny* (Prague) (18 August 1999).

Procházka, Radoslav. 'Metódy práce Ústavného súdu v komparatívnej perspektíve I' [The working methods of the Constitutional Court in a comparative perspective I]. *Justična revue* 50, No. 12 (1998): 20–28.

—. 'Metódy práce Ústavného súdu v komparatívnej perspektíve II' [The working methods of the Constitutional Court in a comparative perspective II]. *Justičná revue* 51, No. 2 (1999): 1–10

—. Metódy práce Ústavného súdu v komparatívnej perspektíve III' [The working methods of the Constitutional Court in a comparative perspective III]. *Justičná revue* 51, No. 3 (1999): 12–20.

—. 'Čakanie na reinkarnáciu' [Waiting for reincarnation], *Sme* (Bratislava) (4 September 1999).

Procházka, Radoslav et al. 'Právny štat, legislatíva a aplikácia práva' [Rule of law, legislation, and implementation of law]. In *Slovensko 2001. Súhrnna správa o stave spoločnosti* [Slovakia 2001. A global report on the state of society], edited by Miroslav Kollár and Grigorij Mesežnikov. Bratislava: Inštitút pre verejné otázky, 2001.

Rácz, Attila. 'The Historical Basis of Hungarian Law'. In *Introduction to Hungarian Law*. The Hague–Boston: Kluwer Law International, 1998.

Reitz, John. 'Political Economy and Abstract Review in Germany, France and the United States'. In *Constitutional Dialogues in Comparative Perspective*, edited by Sally J. Kenney et al. New York: St. Martin's Press, 1999.

—. 'Political Economy as a Major Architectural Principle of Public Law'. *Tulane Law Review* 75 (2001): 1121–1158.

Reisman, Michael W. 'Introductory Remarks, Symposium: Constitutionalism in the Post-Cold War Era'. *Yale Journal of International Law* 19 (1994): 189–192.

Rubio Llorente, Francisco. 'Constitutionalism in the "Integrated" States of Europe'. *The Jean Monnet Working Papers*, available at http://www.jeanmonnetprogram.org/papers/98/98-5.html.

Rymarz, Ferdynand. 'Problem prawa miejscowego jako przedmiot skargi konstytucyjnej' [The issue of local law as a subject matter of a constitutional complaint]. *Przeglad sadowy* 5 (1999): 3–9.

Rzeplinski, Andrzej, ed. *Constitutional Courts in Central And Eastern Europe in The Period of Transformation: Papers of The International Conference, Warsaw, 9-11 September 1994*. Warszawa: Helsinki Foundation for Human Rights, 1995.

Sajó, András. 'The Judiciary in Contemporary Society: Hungary'. *Case Western Reserve Journal of International Law* 25 (1993): 293–301.

—. 'Rights: More or Less: Judicial Review in Hungary'. In *Constitutionalism And Politics: International Symposium, 11-14 November 1993: Proceedings*, edited by Irena Grudzinska-Gross. Bratislava: Slovak Committee of the European Cultural Foundation, 1993.

—. 'Rule by Law in East Central Europe'. In *European Legal Cultures*, edited by Volkmar Gessner. Aldershot, Hants–Brookfield, Vt.: Dartmouth Publications, 1996.

—. 'The Roundtable Talks in Hungary'. In *Roundtable Talks and The Breakdown of Communism*, edited by Jon Elster. Chicago: University of Chicago Press, 1996.

——. 'Rights in Post-Communism'. In *Western Rights? Post-Communist Application*, edited by András Sajó. The Hague, Boston: Kluwer Law International, 1996.

Sajó, András, and Vera Losonci. 'Rule by Law in East-Central Europe: Is The Emperor's New Suit a Straightjacket?'. In *Constitutionalism and Democracy: Transition in Contemporary World*, edited by Douglas Greenberg et al. New York: St. Martin's Press, 1993.

Sanetra, Walerian. 'Orzecznictwo sadowe wobec obwieszczen Prezesa Trybunalu Konstytucyjnego o niezgodnośći aktov ustawowych z Konstytucja' [The ordinary jurisprudence on the issue of notices by the president of the Constitutional Tribunal on constitutional non-conformity of statutes]. *Przeglad sadowy* 4 (1995): 3–18.

——. 'W sprawie zwiazania sadow powszechnie obowiazajuaca wykladnia ustaw' [On the effect on courts of the universally binding interpretation of statutes]. *Przeglad sadowy* 9 (1996): 3–18.

——. 'Sad Najwyzszy w systemie wymiaru sprawiedliwosci' [The Supreme Court in the justice administration system]. *Przeglad sadowy* 7–8 (1999): 3–15.

Sanford, George. 'Communism's Weakest Link-Democratic Capitalism's Greatest Challenge: Poland'. In *Building Democracy? The International Dimension of Democratisation in Eastern Europe*, edited by Geoffrey Pridham. New York: St. Martin's Press, 1994.

Sartori, Giovanni. *Comparative Constitutional Engineering: An Inquiry into Structures, Incentives, and Outcomes*. New York: New York University Press, 1994.

Schanda, Balázs. 'Rechtsstaatlichkeit in Ungarn' [Rule of law in Hungary]. In *Rechtsstaatlichkeit in Europa*, edited by Rainer Hoffman et al. Heidelberg: C.F. Muller, 1996.

Scheppele, Kim Lane. 'The New Hungarian Constitutional Court'. *East European Constitutional Review* 8, No. 4 (1999): 81–87.

Schimmelfennig, Frank. 'The Double Puzzle of EU Enlargement', *Arena Working Papers*, available at http://www.sv.uio.no/arena/publications/ wp99_15.

Schlink, Bernhard. 'German Constitutional Culture in Transition'. *Cardozo Law Review* 14 (1993): 711–736.

Schutz, Peter. 'Maďarsko: Najveselší barak v lágri' [Hungary: the happiest barracks in the camp]. *Domino fórum* (Bratislava) (11 November 1999).

——. 'Maďarsko je rozčarováno z výsledku summitu EU' [Hungary is disenchanted by the outcomes of the EU summit]. *Lidové noviny* (Prague) (14 December 1999).

Schwartz, Herman. *The Struggle for Constitutional Justice in Post-Communist Europe*. Chicago: University of Chicago Press, 2000.

Seitzer, Jeffrey. 'Experimental Constitutionalism: A Comparative Analysis of the Institutional Bases of Rights Enforcement in Post-Communist Hungary'. In *Constitutional Dialogues in Comparative Perspective*, edited by Sally J. Kenney et al. New York: St. Martin's Press, 1999.

Semprich, Źaneta. 'Straźnik straźnikow' [The guardian of guardians]. *Rzeczpospolita* (Warsaw) (14 April 1998).

Šiklová, Jiřina, and Marta Miklušáková. 'Denying Citizenship to the Czech Roma'. *East European Constitutional Review* 7, No. 2 (1998): 58–64.

Šimíček, Vojtěch ed. *Ústava České republiky po pěti letech* [The Constitution of the Czech Republic after five years]. Brno: Masarykova univerzita, 1998.

Šimko, Ivan. 'Interview'. Noviny Slovenskej televízie [Slovak Television Evening News] (6 September 2001).

Skapska, Grazyna. 'Paradigm Lost? The Constitutional Process in Poland and the Hope of a Grassroots Constitutionalism'. In *Rule of Law After Communism*, edited by Martin Krygier and Adam Czarnota. Aldershot, Hants.–Brookfield, Vt.: Ashgate, 1999.

Sládeček, Vladimír. 'Nástin vývoje ústavního soudnictví na území Československa (a Čéské republiky)' [Sketching the development of constitutional adjudication on the territory of Czechoslovakia and the Czech Republic]. *Právní rozhledy* 11 (1998): 544–553.

Slaughter, Anne-Marie. 'A Typology of Transjudicial Communication.' *University or Richmond Law Review* 29 (1994): 99–137.

—. 'Slovakia Update'. *East European Constitutional Review* 5, No. 2 (1996): 27–30.

Sokolewicz, Wojciech. 'The Relevance of Western Models for Constitution-building in Poland'. In *Constitutional Policy and Change in Europe*, edited by Joachim Jens Hesse and Nevil Johnson. New York: Oxford University Press, 1995.

Sólyom, László. 'On the Co-operation of Constitutional Courts: Introduction to the 10th Conference of European Constitutional Courts'. Available at http://www.mkab.hu/conference/introduction.

—. 'The First Year of the Constitutional Court'. *Acta Juridica Hungarica* 33, No. 1–2 (1991): 5–22.

—. 'The Hungarian Constitutional Court and Social Change'. *Yale Journal of International Law* 19 (1994): 223–238.

—. 'Zum Geleit zu den Entscheidungen des Verfassungsgerichts der Republik Ungarn' [Introduction to the decisions of the Constitutional Court of the Republic of Hungary]. In László Sólyom and Georg Brunner, *Verfassungsgerichtsbarkeit in Ungarn: Analysen und Entscheidungssammlung 1990–1993* [Constitutional adjudication in Hungary: Analyses and a collection of decisions 1990–1993]. Baden Baden: Nomos Verlagsgesellschaft, 1995.

—. 'Interview'. Interview by András Mink. *East European Constitutional Review* 6, No. 4 (1997): 71–73.

—. 'Justice At Work: Opinion of Justice Sólyom'. *Cardozo Law Review* 18 (1997): 1725–1743.

—. 'Anmerkungen zur Rezeption auf dem Gebiet der wirtschaftlichen und sozialen Rechte aus ungarischer Sicht' [Observations from the Hungarian point of view on the reception in the real of economic and social rights]. In *Grundfragen der Verfassungsgerichtsbarkeit in Mittel- un Osteuropa* [Fundamental issues of Central and Eastern European constitutional adjudication], edited by Jochen Frowein and Thilo Marauhn. Berlin–New York: Springer 1998.

—. 'Introduction to the Decisions of the Hungarian Constitutional Court'. In László Sólyom and Georg Brunner. *Constitutional Judiciary in a New Democracy*. Ann Arbor, Mich.: University of Michigan Press, 2000.

—. 'To the Tenth Anniversary of Constitutional Review.' In *The Constitution Found? The First Nine Years of Hungarian Constitutional Review on Fundamental Rights*, edited by Gábor Halmai. Budapest: Indok, 2000.

Sólyom, László, and Georg Brunner. *Verfassungsgerichtsbarkeit in Ungarn: Analysen und Entscheidungssammlung 1990–1993*. Baden Baden: Nomos Verlagsgesellschaft, 1995.

——. *Constitutional Judiciary in a New Democracy*. Ann Arbor, Mich.: University of Michigan Press, 2000.

Spiewak, Pawel. 'The Battle for a Constitution'. *East European Constitutional Review* 6, No. 4 (1997): 92–95.

Stelmachovski, Andrzej. 'Sad Najwyzszy kontra Trybunal Konstytucyjny – czyli spor o wykladnie' [The Supreme Court v. the Constitutional Tribunal-a dispute over interpretation]. *Przeglad sadowy* 2 (1996): 3–12.

Stone Sweet, Alec. *Governing With Judges*. New York: Oxford University Press, 2000.

Strážnická, Viera. 'Úloha judikatúry Európskeho súdu pre l'udské práva v zjednocovaní a vývoji judikatury ústavnyh súdov' [The role of the jurisprudence of the European Court of Human Rights in the process of harmonisation and development of constitutional jurisprudence]. In *Zjednocovanie a vývoj judikatúry ústavných súdov*. Košice: Ústavny súd Slovenskej republiky, 2001.

Sunstein, Cass. 'Against Positive Rights'. *Eastern European Constitutional Review* 2, No. 1 (1993): 35–37.

——. 'Deliberative Trouble'. *Yale Law Journal* 110 (2000): 71–119.

——. 'On the Expressive Function of Law'. *Eastern European Constitutional Review* 5, No. 4 (1996): 66–72.

Szumski, Jerzy. 'Pre-Trial Detention and Human Rights in Poland: Basic Problems'. In *Protection of Human Rights in Poland and The European Communities*, edited by Leszek Leszczynski. Den Bosch: Book World Publications, 1997.

Valko, Ernest. 'On the Constitution of the Slovak Republic'. In *Constitutionalism and Politics: International Symposium 11–14 November 1993: Proceedings,* edited by Irena Grudzinska-Gross. Bratislava: Slovak Committee of the European Cultural Foundation, 1993.

Van Hoecke, Mark, and Mark Warrington. 'Legal Cultures and Legal Paradigms: Towards a New Model for Comparative Law'. *International and Comparative Law Quarterly* 47, No. 3 (1998): 495–536.

Varga, Csaba. *Transition to the Rule of Law: On The Democratic Transformation in Hungary*. Budapest: Institute for Legal Studies of the Hungarian Academy of Sciences, 1995.

Wandycz, Piotr. *Price of Freedom: A History of East Central Europe from the Middle Ages to the Present.* London; New York: Routledge, 1992.

Wasilewski, Andrzej. 'Wladza sadownicza w Konstytucji Rzeczypospolitej Polskiej' [The judicial power in the Constitution of the Republic of Poland]. *Panstwo i Prawo* 629 (1998): 3–20.

——. 'Pytania prawne do Trybunalu Konstytucyjnego' [Interlocutory appeals to the Constitutional Tribunal]. *Przeglad sadowy* 5 (2000): 3–11.

Weber, Max. *Economy and Society: An Outline of Interpretive Sociology,* vol. II, edited by Gunther Roth and Claus Wittich. Berkeley, Cal.: University of California Press, 1978.

Wedgwood, Ruth. 'Cousin Humphrey'. *Constitutional Commentary* 14 (1997): 247–269.

Weinberger, Ota. 'Od Brněnské školy k neo-institucionalismu [From the Brno school to neo-institutionalism]. *Časopis pro právní vědu a praxi* 4 (1999): 307–316.

Welan, Manfried. 'Constitutional Review and Legislation in Austria'. In *Constitutional Review and Legislation,* edited by Christine Landfried. Baden Baden: Nomos Verlagsgesellschaft, 1988.

Whitehead, Laurence. 'East-Central Europe in Comparative Perspective'. In *Building*

Democracy? The International Dimension of Democratisation in Eastern Europe, edited by Geoffrey Pridham. New York: St. Martin's Press, 1994.

Závacká, Katarina. 'Význam vzniku Československej republiky pre uplatňovanie občianskych práv a slobôd na Slovensku' [The role of the founding of the Czechoslovak Republic in the implementation of civic rights and freedoms in Slovakia]. *Acta Universitatis Carolinae: Iuridica* 1–2 (1999): 73–78.

Zemko, Milan. *História ako učitelka života* [History as magistra vitae], *Domino fórum* (Bratislava) (1 December 1999).

Zieliňski, Adam. 'Osierocena skarga'. *Rzeczpospolita* (3 August 1998).

Zieliňski, Tadeusz. 'The Rule of Law in the Transition Process from Totalitarianism to Democracy'. In *Towards Universal Law: Trends in National, European and International Lawmaking,* edited by Nils Jarebørg. Uppsala: Iustus Forlag, 1995.

Zliňsky, János. *Wissenschaft und Gerichtsbarkeit: Quellen und Literatur der Privatrechtsgeschichte Ungarns im 19. Jahrhundert* [Society and judiciary: sources and bibliography on the history of private law in 19th century Hungary]. Frankfurt am Main: V. Klostermann, 1997.

Zoll, Andrej. 'Interview with Professor Andrzej Zoll, Chief Justice of the Polish Constitutional Tribunal', interview by Irena Grudzinska-Gross. *East European Constitutional Review* 6, No. 4 (1997): 76–79.

Zupančič, Boštjan. 'Od souboje ke smlouvč aneb co vlastně ustavuje ústava'. *Pravnik* 137, No. 6 (1996): 476–510.

TABLES

Table 1. Polish Constitutional Tribunal.
Overall profile 1986–12/2001

Abstract review of statutes	Abstract review of sub-statutory acts	Abstract interpretations	Interlocutory appeals	Constitutional complaints
302	146	101	68	73

Source: http://www.trybunal.gov.pl.

Table 2. Polish Constitutional Tribunal.
Constitutional complaints 1997–12/2000

Actions filed	Meritorious examinations	Findings issued	Whole or partial unconstitutionality
2 511	48	21	8

Source: http://www.trybunal.gov.pl.

Table 3. Hungarian Constitutional Court.
Overall profile 1990–02/2002

Actions total	Actio popularis	Interlocutory appeals
17 150	12 706	238

Source: Hungarian Constitutional Court.

Table 4. Hungarian Constitutional Court.
Abstract review of statutes 1990–02/2002

Actions filed	Whole or partial unconstitutionality
638	102

Source: Hungarian Constitutional Court.

Table 5. Czech Constitutional Court.
Overall profile 1993–12/2001

	Petitions total	Findings issued
Abstract review	369	203
Concrete review	16 184	989

Source: Czech Constitutional Court; http://www.concourt.cz.

Table 6. Slovak Constitutional Court.
Abstract review of statutes 1993–02/2002

	Findings issued	Whole or partial unconstitutionality
03/1993-01/2000	52	31
02/2000-02/2002	10	4

Source: Slovak Constitutional Court; http://www.concourt.sk.

Table 7. Slovak Constitutional Court.
Concrete constitutional review 1993–12/2001

	Actions filed	Findings issued	Whole or partial violation
Constitutional complaints	364	10	8
Petitions	2 022	167	148

Source: Slovak Constitutional Court; http://www.concourt.sk.

INDEX

For Product Safety Concerns and Information please contact our EU representative GPSR@taylorandfrancis.com Taylor & Francis Verlag GmbH, Kaufingerstraße 24, 80331 München, Germany

Batch number: 10725793

Printed by Printforce, the Netherlands